The Parameters of Urban Fiscal Policy

THE PARAMETERS OF URBAN FISCAL POLICY

Socioeconomic Change and Political Culture in San Francisco, 1860–1906

Terrence J. McDonald

University of California Press / *Berkeley Los Angeles London*

University of California Press
Berkeley and Los Angeles, California

University of California Press, Ltd.
London, England

Copyright © 1986 by The Regents of the University of California

Library of Congress Cataloging-in-Publication Data

McDonald, Terrence J.
   The parameters of urban fiscal policy.

   Bibliography: p.
   Includes index.
   1. Fiscal policy—California—San Francisco—History.   2. Finance, Public—
California—San Francisco—History.   3. San Francisco (Calif.)—Politics and
government.   4. San Francisco (Calif.)—Economic conditions.
5. San Francisco (Calif.)—Social conditions.   I. Title.
HJ9205.S3M34   1986   336.794'61   85–28815
ISBN 0–520–05494–6 (alk. paper)

Printed in the United States of America

1   2   3   4   5   6   7   8   9

For the McDonalds:
John Joseph
Grace Janann
Timothy Patrick
Maureen Sheila
Sheila Elizabeth
and now, Mary Ann

Contents

Preface

This is not the book I intended to write when I began to work on it some time ago, and therein lies a story worth sharing briefly with the reader. Like many of my fellow historians trained in the 1970s, I set out to be a social historian. Our feelings were summarized by two essays in a now famous 1971 issue of *Daedalus* on "Historical Studies Today." In one of the essays, Eric Hobsbawm reviewed the "florescence" of social history in such areas as demography, urban studies, the study of classes, and social protest, and concluded that it was "a good time to be a social historian." In the other, on whether politics was still the backbone of history, Jacques Le Goff noted that the "old" political history was not only dead but "a corpse that has to be made to lie down." We agreed and arranged our studies both to avoid the rotting corpse of political history and to pursue the cutting edge in social history.[1]

Not satisfied with merely avoiding political history, I itched to prove that in the face of large-scale social change it was not only epiphenomenal but hardly worth mentioning. As my interests began to coalesce around urban history, I decided to try to demonstrate that the focus of urban political history on bosses and reformers, political parties and electoral struggles as the determinants of the size and shape of the urban public sector was fundamentally misguided.

My belief that political influences on the public sector would be minimal next to social changes such as urbanization and industrialization was supported by work both outside and inside of history. Sociologists, political scientists, and economists had investigated the contemporary determinants of public expenditure extensively. These analyses argued that variables measuring what political sociologist Robert Alford has called structural factors (e.g., an area's economic base and social composition) were best able to explain the variation in expenditure among governmental units such as cities or states. Moreover, when these var-

iables were controlled for statistically, electoral political variables explained little or none of the variation, leading one political scientist to
conclude that "we can no longer assume a priori that such facets of . . .
political structures as competitiveness, partisanship, turnout, or apportionment have any relationship to patterns of public policy."[2]

Although historians had not done much systematic work in this area,
their theories of the development of the urban public sector shared
other social scientists' assumption that the municipal public sector was
a dependent variable but differed as to the independent variables influencing it. As I explain in more detail in chapter 1, some historians
maintained the traditional theory that political struggle between bosses
and reformers was the primary influence on the urban public sector,
with bosses expanding municipal government and reformers trying to
contract or at least streamline it. But others argued that the public
sector was shaped primarily by demands generated by socioeconomic
change, regardless of politics. When I began my work, the latter argument, made most forcefully by those writing within the framework of
a social analysis of urban politics, was in the ascendant.

Taking as my motto the declaration of Joseph Schumpeter that "the
budget is the skeleton of the state stripped of all misleading ideologies,"
I set out in my dissertation to determine the relative ability of measures
of socioeconomic development and political culture to explain statistically the development of municipal government—as measured by municipal expenditure—in San Francisco from 1860, when regular fiscal
records became available, until the earthquake and fire in 1906. It was
in these years that the city became urbanized and industrialized at the
most rapid rate. It was also during this period that the city experienced
political regimes that have become archetypes in the literature of urban
history and political science, including those of an interlocking commercial elite, machine politicians, and self-conscious progressive reformers. Thus the city provided an interesting arena in which to test
the theories just mentioned, and I expected that the results would suggest that the role of politics had been overestimated.[3]

I was wrong. This work indicated that social change was a necessary
but insufficient explanation for the development of the public sector in
San Francisco; the patterns in expenditure could not be explained without reference to politics. Moreover, these results required that I become
more of a political historian in order to explain them. In the years since
this early work I have immersed myself in the old institutional and

political history of the city, while broadening my analysis of fiscal policy to include taxation, assessed valuation, and revenue.

The book at hand, then, has changed from an analysis of the growth of municipal government to an explanation of the influences on urban fiscal policy more broadly conceived. It argues not that politics was irrelevant, but that political factors of all sorts had a crucial impact on fiscal policy in San Francisco in ways both predictable and surprising. This analysis demonstrates, among other things, that socioeconomic development drove up the supply of revenue, but not the demand for expenditure; that aspects of political culture had a statistically significant effect on fiscal policy even in the presence of variables measuring socioeconomic change; and that political ethos, in the sense of bosses versus reformers, was less important than aspects of electoral political strategy and fiscal political culture which bound all politicians equally.

San Francisco politicians kept the local public sector from being merely an artifact of socioeconomic structural change because they responded not to externally generated demands for services, but to an internally generated fiscal political culture composed of habit, timidity, ideological conviction, and political savvy. During most of the nineteenth century, the heart of this culture was a commitment to low taxation and thus low expenditure. Politicians did not campaign by promising benefits from an expanding public sector; on the contrary, they condemned such expansion and promised to prevent it. In practice, however, once these men became policymakers they allowed incremental growth in municipal expenditure in response to demands from within local government—namely, from their political colleagues, who sought more money for their departments. And even this marginal growth was regulated by political strategy. Typically, increases in assessed valuation, the tax rate, and thus expenditure occurred only during nonelection years. Moreover, under the so-called Dollar Limit pledge, when political competition was most intense, municipal taxation and expenditure decreased to historic lows.

This no-growth basis for urban fiscal politics was challenged in the 1890s by a pro-growth coalition led by self-conscious progressive reformers. By exaggerating the defects of the old fiscal political system, mobilizing outside groups to demand increased expenditure from municipal government, and promising benefits for all from an expanded public sector under their control, the reformers reorganized the basis of fiscal politics in the city. The reform coalition, which included businessmen, labor, and neighborhood improvement groups, succeeded in passing a reform city charter in 1898 and bonds for municipal improvements in 1899. The key to the success of these campaigns was the reform leaders' ability to direct the members of the reform coalition to the public sector for the solution of their problems. This break with the past was a political strategy, not a socioeconomic necessity. The achievement of reform was the introduction and legitimation of this new role of the public sector in municipal politics and policymaking.

Thus the public sector in San Francisco was the result both of socioeconomic development, which generated the taxable wealth available to the city's government, and of the institutional and ideological boundaries on the acceptable use of that wealth, which were worked out in the city by charter, custom, and political competition. The parameters of urban fiscal policy in this analysis refer, therefore, both to quantitative measures of the average impact of these variables on fiscal policy and to the effect of institutional and political boundaries on that policy at any one time. This understanding of the public sector may seem to be mere common sense, and perhaps it is. But such common sense has been in short supply in a field preoccupied with the exploits of bosses and reformers on the one hand, and with the determining influence of the "logic of socioeconomic development" on the other.

The challenge to urban political history—and one that it has too often failed to meet—has been to combine successfully the viewpoint and techniques of both the "old" political history and the "new" social history. The kernel of the former was an all-important recognition both of the centrality of politics in nineteenth-century public life and of the necessity for studying the institutions and men involved in politics. Alas, surrounding this kernel was a gigantic husk of endless detail, special pleading, and ignorance of the impact on political action of the structures of politics and social change. The new social history has excelled at examining the relationship between structure and action in many areas of life by means of the application of quantitative methods. On the whole, however, it has failed to extend its vision to include the political, primarily because of its adoption of theoretical models that exclude the realm of politics.

Because this book focuses on fiscal policy, which is in a sense a nexus between urban politics and urban society, it draws from both of these traditions. My argument that municipal politics was a more independent variable than some have thought moves in the direction of the old political history, and indeed, portions of the book resemble that history very much. To make this argument, however, I borrow the new social history's concern with structure and use quantitative methods in an attempt to measure the amount of autonomy from social and political structures that was available to policymakers.

The quantitative means by which this argument is made are at times difficult to grasp. In what follows, I have attempted to be as clear as possible about the variety of techniques I used to analyze both quantitative and nonquantitative data. Some of the finer points of quantitative method are discussed in the appendixes. Nonetheless, I hope the reader will examine graphs and tables and consider the results of multiple regression equations. Those who hold that such material clutters the text or impedes the narrative are simply mistaken. Without the presence of these types of evidence in the text, the historian is a sort of Wizard of Oz, a Kansas con man creating pyrotechnic effects from behind a curtain.

This incorrect perception frequently goes hand in hand with another—namely, that the appropriate dividing line among historians is between those who use quantitative methods and those who do not. In fact, the meaningful division is between historians who are theoretically and methodologically self-conscious and those who are not. In an important analysis of the relationship between history and theory, the late David Potter argued that the historian cannot escape theory. The choice, he wrote, is not between a factual and a theoretical approach, but between "on the one hand, theoretical assumptions which have been recognized and, so far as possible, made rational and explicit and, on the other, unrecognized, half-hidden assumptions which remain unordered and chaotic." As with theory, I would argue, so with method: historians can escape neither of these elements of analysis, and ignore them at their peril. Indeed, the depoliticized world of urban history today is the result of historians' failure either to examine carefully or to test explicitly the reigning theoretical propositions in the field.[4]

Acknowledgments

It was Flaubert who wrote that "the pen is a heavy oar," and generations of historians have demonstrated that it takes many hands to pull it through the water. A work of history appears not only because of the determination of the author but also because of the generosity of individuals and institutions who have helped along the way. I have received more than my share of such help, and it is my pleasure to acknowledge those who provided it.

My interest in history was first sparked by the teaching and research of Athan G. Theoharis of Marquette University. It was his suggestion that I consider graduate training in history and his encouragement that helped me through it. This book began during that training, as a dissertation at Stanford University influenced by the teaching of David B. Tyack and guided by a committee that included Barton J. Bernstein, Carl N. Degler, and John H. Mollenkopf, all of whom encouraged its completion and gave me useful guidance for its revision. Without knowing it, Samuel P. Hays has been one of my most important teachers, as my debt herein to his stimulating work makes clear. Whether or not he would choose to admit paternity, he is truly the father of a whole generation of urban historians.

Colleagues at the institutions at which I have taught since graduate school—Marquette University, San Francisco State University, the California Institute of Technology, and the University of Michigan—have been unfailingly helpful. At Marquette, Robert Hay was a supportive chairman, while Athan Theoharis, F. Paul Prucha, and William Rooney were generous colleagues. At San Francisco State, Eldon Modisette was kind enough to hire me in the first place, and Robert Cherny and William Issel, experts on San Francisco history themselves, encouraged my work. At Caltech, J. Morgan Kousser gave me much useful advice on this project and other work. He also introduced me to other members of the Division of Humanities and Social Sciences who were similarly helpful, including Bruce Cain, Lance Davis, John Ferejohn, Daniel Kevles, and especially Forrest Nelson. At Michigan, Robert F. Berkhofer, Jr., Jerome Clubb, Geoff Eley, Bradford Perkins, Louise Tilly, Charles Tilly, and Maris Vinovskis made useful comments on various versions of this manuscript. I am also grateful to Professor Vinovskis for his advice and support all along the way. My colleagues in the Program in American Institutions at Michigan, and especially its director, John E. Jackson, provided both encouragement and intellectual stimulation.

Colleagues outside of my departments who helped me by reading earlier papers and the final version of the manuscript included M. Craig Brown of the State University of New York at Albany, Roger Lotchin of the University of North Carolina at Chapel Hill, Richard L. McCormick of Rutgers University, John Modell of Carnegie-Mellon University, and Jon Teaford of Purdue University. Professors Brown, Sally K. Ward of the University of New Hampshire, and Colin Loftin of the University of Maryland gave me useful methodological advice. Special thanks must go to Eric Monkkonen of the University of California, Los Angeles, who has read every word I have written since 1978 and helped me in innumerable other ways as well.

I have received financial aid for this work in its various incarnations from Stanford University, the Giles Whiting Foundation, the Institute for Humane Studies, the National Endowment for the Humanities Summer Stipend Program, the Henry Huntington Library, the research fund of the Division of Humanities and Social Sciences at Caltech, and the Rackham Faculty Research Fund at the University of Michigan. A term off from teaching provided by the Department of History at the University of Michigan greatly facilitated the completion of the manuscript.

I was fortunate to have the help of several research assistants, including Lisa Salter, Martin Burke, Kevin Boyle, Stephen Grossbart, Mark Greene, and especially Rebecca Reed, whose help was indispensable. My research was also facilitated by librarians at the Bancroft Library, the California Historical Society, the California State Library, the Henry Huntington Library, and the University of Michigan Library.

The friends who provided intellectual and moral support included Geoff Eley, Cynthia Herrup, Judith Bennett, Rob Griswold, Bert Faerstein, and Nick Dirks. My editor at the University of California Press, Stanley Holwitz, saw promise in this book when it was little more than a set of hopeful plans, and I am grateful to him for his help in making those plans a reality. Victoria Scott provided a very careful copyediting of the manuscript.

My wife, Mary Ann, was busy with her own professional life and thus had little to do with the manuscript in any traditional sense. But she buoyed me up many times when I thought I would drown very near the shore.

T. J. McD.

Ann Arbor, Michigan
September 1985

1

The Problems of Politics and Public Policy in the History of the American City

Samuel P. Hays was only partially correct when he wrote in 1974 that the prevailing pattern of writing about the history of American urban politics was a reform framework in which "cities grew, they gave rise to problems, and reform forces arose to cope with those problems."[1] In fact, this was also the nonreform or "boss" framework in which cities grew, gave rise to problems, and political entrepreneurs arose who were willing to cope with these problems for a fee; so, also, was it the non-political framework in which cities grew, gave rise to problems, and municipal governments, regardless of bosses or reformers, struggled to cope with them.

Anyone who has examined recent writings on the history of urban politics will recognize this fill-in-the-blank framework, which is both pervasive and frustrating. It has been used to explain a wide variety of urban political movements and regimes, but it has actually explained none of them. Given its lack of specificity, this is not surprising. Which problems stimulated which forces? Why did similar patterns of growth and types of problems give rise to different political forces? What were the substantive differences between the attempts of reformers, bosses, and others to cope with urban problems?

The problem with urban political history has not been, as Hays has argued, the lack of a conceptual framework,[2] but the existence of an all-purpose one. A "manifest and latent" functionalism in various guises has been used to explain the rise and persistence of both bosses and reformers, as well as the growth and development of the American urban public sector in general. Over the years, in fact, two potentially contradictory variants of this framework have developed and coexisted in the historical literature, one explaining the overall development of the urban public sector, the other, the special cases of bosses and reformers.

According to the first view, politics or the exercise of power played a minimal role in the development of urban government and the formulation of government policy. Instead, socioeconomic structural factors (e.g., a city's economic base, social structure, population size and composition) were primary. Changes in these factors (population growth, industrialization, etc.) created problems that generated demands for various goods and services from the public sector; urban government grew, and its functions multiplied, in response to these demands. In their influential history of the American city, for example, Charles N. Glaab and A. Theodore Brown noted that these developments produced an increasing number of tasks to be fulfilled and needs for community action.[3] Municipal governments grew and became more important "by necessity"; they "spent more money in order to satisfy growing needs," and there was no way to avoid the increasing range and scale of government activity, regardless of whether bosses or reformers were in control.[4]

A tradition of analysis in opposition to this one runs through the works of Oscar Handlin, Richard Hofstadter, and Hays himself. As different as they may have been in other respects, these authors shared both a focus on the ethos or culture of political actors and the position that there were substantive differences between the fiscal politics of machine and reform politicians. According to Handlin, the bosses marched beneath the banner, "I never saw a man in my life who made economy his watchword who was not defeated before the people," while in Hofstadter's interpretation, the reformers were obsessed with efficiency, economy, and businesslike management. In Hays's well-known view, the reformers were a coalition of businessmen, professionals, and members of the urban upper class who attempted to stifle the grass-roots democracy of the ward system to "advance their own conceptions of desirable public policy."[5] In these interpretations, too, social changes generated problems or needs, but the political system responded selectively, rewarding political clients such as immigrants, small businessmen, or members of the urban elite who were willing to trade political support for satisfaction of their social needs.

Despite their differences in emphasis, these variants of the "problem" framework bear the marks of functionalist analysis. First, and most obviously, they share the assumption that social institutions—in this case urban government and urban political regimes—persist and develop because they fulfill certain functions, either for urban society as a whole or for diverse subgroups of that society. Indeed, looming behind the works of Handlin, Hofstadter, and Hays is the more theoretical work of sociologist Robert Merton on manifest and latent functions. Second, they share what Alvin Gouldner has called the "elementary domain assumption" of functionalism—namely, that "everything influences everything else."[6] Therefore, they provide no clues about which variables are more and which are less important to their arguments. The growth of the local public sector may have been influenced by the onrush of industrialization, needy immigrants, elitist reformers, or some combination thereof, but the effects of these influences are not untangled.

The problem with a functionalist framework is not that it is necessarily wrong, but that its assumptions (e.g., that functions are fulfilled) are frequently unexamined, and that its framework (i.e., that some variables influence some other variables) is unclear. Thus this prevailing framework of urban political history is best considered as a set of educated guesses, or perhaps as some preliminary hypotheses. It does not, as Hays contended, constitute a "rejection of the city," but a lack of information about it, especially about urban politics. Furthermore, urban historians are by no means alone in their lack of information about the polity. As Morton Keller has recently noted for the national case, the polity has received very little attention of the sort "lavished on the nation's social and economic systems."[7]

To note that there has been a dearth of good urban political history is to repeat a truism, however, for as Eric Lampard has noted, good political history of American cities is "precisely what is lacking."[8] More interesting and important are the reasons for this lack. These reasons appear to be the pattern of historical development in the field, the impact (somewhat ironically) of the work of Hays himself, and a general confusion among historians of two important political questions: "Who governs?" and "How are public resources authoritatively allocated?."[9]

URBAN HISTORY BECOMES SOCIAL HISTORY

In the beginning, of course, there were no urban historians, just social historians who happened to write about cities—a fact that was to prove fateful for the later development of the history of urban politics. In its early years, the 1920s and 1930s, American social history was, as E. J. Hobsbawm has suggested, something of a "residual category," that portion of history left out of the established branches of the discipline. The social history of an Arthur M. Schlesinger, Sr., or of a Dixon Ryan Fox arose, as Hays has pointed out, in a profession dominated by the fields of constitutional, political, and diplomatic history. This social history was defined not so much by what it was as by what it was not. Early investigations in social history were of topics that did not fit into the other, dominant categories; social history grew rapidly not by developing a positive theory of its task, but by ambitiously staking its claim to undeveloped professional territory.[10]

Urban history was claimed by social history with little regard for its framework or focus. In Schlesinger's work, which is generally considered to be the modern beginnings of the field, the definition of urban history was not explicit; rather, it seemed to include anything that happened in a city. In spite of its shortcomings, this "activity context" definition of urban history dominated the field for twenty years after Schlesinger's seminal 1940 essay on "The City in American History." Since there was already an established field of political history, urban history focused more and more on those "activities" outside of this field. Although political history was exclusively national, urban history became almost exclusively social—history "with the politics left out," to use G. M. Trevelyan's phrase. Thus urban political history as urban history slipped, so to speak, through the definitional cracks of the historical profession.[11]

Until the early 1960s, therefore, much of the political history done by urban historians appeared in works of marginal concern to the historical profession, such as those of urban "biographers" or specialists in urban "local color." The urban biographers adopted the method of individual biography in order to reveal the unique "personalities" of their cities. The result was usually a massive and unwieldy narrative characterized both by local boosterism and an unwillingness to go beyond the event to a consideration of urban social or political change. This sort of idiosyncratic local focus was magnified by the historians of local color, who specialized in the prostitutes and politicians, crimes and corruption of the big cities. Numerous studies of "boss" politics were written within the "debonair scoundrel" approach of this type of urban history.[12]

At the same time, much of the urban political history of great professional interest was produced almost as an aside by historians attempting to explain other phenomena. In fact, the archetypes of post–World War II American urban political history were created in this period in Handlin's *The Uprooted*, an examination of the effect on immigrants of their "arduous transplantation," and Hofstadter's *The Age of Reform*, an analysis of the "reform tradition" in America. From these books emerged the portraits of the free-spending, grass-roots, machine politicians who defended an expanded public sector, and of the fiscally conservative, upper-class reformers who attempted to shrink it.

Relying primarily on the bosses' descriptions of themselves, Handlin suggested that they were the crucial link in the immigrants' political acculturation. The boss was the "feudal noble transplanted from the manor to the ward"; he was "above the law" and therefore capable of "doing better justice than the law." The boss had usually arisen from among the immigrants and "remained one with them," championing the little man against the big and seeing to the ward and neighborhood issues that affected the immigrants' day-to-day existence. At the center of his attractiveness to the immigrant was the possibility of a job, and it was here that the boss's fiscal position was crucial. According to Handlin, the boss understood—as the reformers did not—that the people he represented did not want government to be a business. Indeed, a "progressive" administration often was one that "laid off men to balance the budget," and to the immigrants, the abstract principle of a balanced budget was not worth the suffering it entailed. Thus a robust public sector was an important link between the boss and his constituents, and because he understood this, "ultimately he was always the victor."[13]

This rather appalling political obtuseness on the part of the reformers was the result of their cultural background, according to Hofstadter. Unlike the easygoing and pragmatic boss, who understood the immigrant's desire for concrete personal gains from political participation, the reformers viewed urban politics as an arena "for the realization of moral principles of broad application." Therefore, the reformers "prodded the immigrant toward the study of American ways," "reproached the immigrant for having no interest in broad principles," and stood for ideas that were "altogether bizarre" to the immigrant, such as good government and fiscal conservatism. Because the reformers threatened to "lop needed jobs off the payroll," their attacks on the bosses drove the immigrants closer to their allegedly corrupt benefactors. Meanwhile, the reformers' insulation from "the most exploited sector of the population" reduced the "social range and radical drive" of the urban reform program.[14]

Although these portraits of bosses and reformers raised fascinating questions, their immediate impact on urban history was limited, both because they were ancillary to their authors' main tasks and because of the increasingly apolitical definition of the field itself. As a major restatement of the image of the bosses popularized by Lincoln Steffens and by the bosses themselves, Handlin's portrayal became the received wisdom in urban political history. What controversy his book did provoke came in the field of immigration (later "ethnic") history, and concerned whether or not Handlin minimized the strength and resilience of immigrant culture. Hofstadter's book set off a storm of controversy, although, with the exception of the work of J. Joseph Huthmacher, little of that controversy dealt directly with Hofstadter's conception of urban politics.[15]

Meanwhile, the field of urban history continued to be defined more carefully and more explicitly as the analysis of social and economic structure. In one of the first of these efforts, in 1961, Eric Lampard suggested two approaches to urban history: "the study of urbanization as a social process," and the "comparative study of communities in a framework of human ecology." The first would be concerned, he wrote, with the phenomenon of population concentration and the resulting increase in the number and size of cities; the second, with "the changing structure and organization of communities" in terms of the interrelationships among environment, technology, and organization. While not specifically excluding the analysis of urban politics, Lampard noted that his frameworks were offered to provide a "more certain and systematic foundation for the writing of American social history."[16]

Summarizing a decade's concern for this systematic urban history exactly ten years later, Stephan Thernstrom defined the "new" urban history as "the attempt to understand how and why the complex of changes suggested by the concept 'urbanization' reshaped society." For Thernstrom, too, urban history stood squarely in the area of social history and included research in topics such as urban population fluidity, class and ethnic differentials in opportunity, and social and spatial mobility. In the new urban history, as in the old, politics was of little concern.[17]

In the most influential recent restatement of this "ecological" position,

Theodore Hershberg wrote in 1981 that the focus of urban history must be on "urban as process," which he defined as "the dynamic modeling of the interrelationships among environment, behavior, and group experience." For Hershberg, the foci of urban historical research were three: the changing urban environment over time, the social experiences correlated with different aspects of urban settings, and the mechanisms through which environmental and social change were effected. Although Hershberg's framework did not specifically exclude the analysis of politics, it was no error of omission that not a single essay on political history was included in the collection "toward an interdisciplinary history of the city," which emerged from the Philadelphia Social History Project under his editorship.[18]

These essays did not denounce urban political history, of course, nor did they need to do so, because many of the products of that field were self-incriminating evidence of its bankruptcy. Motivated by concern with event rather than political process, restricted by a narrow definition of the political, and peopled with jousting "debonair scoundrels" and "men of the better sort," much of the literature in urban political history fit David Potter's apt description of the "old" political history as a "grab bag of isolated events, strung together chronologically, garnished with personalities and spiced with anecdotes."[19]

In contrast, work within the ecological framework covered such topics as the urban "opportunity structure," demographic patterns among urban dwellers, and the location of urban economic activities. This work offered exciting examples of systematic, replicable analyses of the fundamental processes of urban development. The surge of urban historians into these areas was stimulated both by repeated exhortations by proponents of the ecological approach and by the high level of "payoff" of studies touching on fundamental issues in American historiography, such as mobility and opportunity. It was not surprising, then, that urban political history remained in the backwater. The new work set into motion a law of uneven development, according to which urban social history flourished under this new stimulation while urban political history essentially languished in the old framework.

THE SOCIAL ANALYSIS OF POLITICS MINIMIZES THE POLITICAL

The most influential response to both the political and the social urban historians came in a series of essays by Hays, who attempted to reconcile the analysis of socioeconomic structural and political cultural factors by proposing a framework for the linkage of social and political history both within the city and beyond it. Hays demanded the abandonment of professional and intellectual boundaries between social and political history. In their place he proposed a "social analysis of history" distinguished not by concern for a particular subject matter, but by its focus on the "structure and processes of every type of public human relationship." In specifying this framework for the history of politics, he, too, suggested a concentration on structure, but defined it as "the pattern of human relationships in the political system" and stressed the process of change in those relationships.[20]

To accomplish this type of political history, Hays argued that political institutions should be analyzed not in terms of the formal statements they produced, the "succession of outcomes of political decisions," or the issues apparently at stake in political struggle, but on the basis of "the types of human interrelationships inherent in those institutions." This required analysis of the behavior of individuals in political situations, as revealed through demographic and electoral statistics. It also required examination of the relationships in those situations, in order to discover what Robert Swierenga has called the "structural patterns among various societal groups—socio-economic, ethno-cultural, local and cosmopolitan." But in attempting to shift the focus of the field toward neglected political phenomena, such as relationships in the political system, Hays excluded traditional objects of interest, such as formal political institutions and the policies they produced.[21]

Hays's seminal essay, "The Politics of Reform in Municipal Government in the Progressive Era," demonstrated both the strengths and the weaknesses of his approach. Since its publication in 1964, the thesis of this essay—the so-called Hays thesis—has become so well known that it is almost unnecessary to summarize it here. Through analysis of the class bases of municipal reform in the progressive period, Hays contended that municipal progressivism was an attempt by upper-class, advanced professional and large business groups to "take formal political power" from previously dominant middle- and lower-class groups, so that the former might "advance their own conceptions of desirable public policy." Aside from the intrinsic interest of its thesis, Hays's essay was important because it returned questions of class interests and political power to the agenda of urban political history. Hays implied that urban reform was not the inevitable result of accumulating socioeconomic structural change in the sense of the "problem" framework, but a struggle for power over the political control of urban development.[22]

There were problems with Hays's essay, however, which stemmed from his exclusive reliance on "relationships in the political system" as his central explanatory variable. Having rejected the analysis of formal political institutions or the "succession of outcomes of political decisions," Hays attempted to deduce the nature of pre-reformed and reformed urban political regimes on the basis of their typical political relationships—in this case, the decisionmaking system and the political coalition characteristic of each. The pre-reform coalition was working class and ethnic, he contended, and its structure was the ward system, which was decentralized and local. Therefore, "ward leaders spoke for their constituencies," and there was a "direct reciprocal flow of power between wards and the center of city affairs," which allowed "wide latitude for the expression of grass roots impulses and their involvement in the political process." The reform system, in contrast, was supported by an upper-class and professional coalition, and its structure was city-wide and centralized. In this system, according to Hays, "decisions arose from expert analysis" and "flowed from fewer and smaller centers outward to the rest of the society." Political power was "centralized in the hands of a relatively small segment of the population."[23]

This focus on decisionmaking systems and electoral coalitions highlighted the relevance of broadly conceived class interests in the struggle for urban political power. But it did not and could not determine what the victors in this struggle did with the power (or, for that matter, what the losers had done with it before). Hays hinted that the competing decisionmaking systems produced different kinds of government policy. Under the ward system, therefore, councilmen were "peculiarly receptive" to the concerns of their middle- and lower-class constituents. They spoke for them, protected their cultural practices, and rolled logs in council to get things done for their districts. The reform movement, however, "objected to the structure of government which enabled local and particularistic interests to dominate" and constituted an attempt to take formal power so that reformers might "advance their own conception of desirable public policy." But because he eschewed the analysis of the "succession of outcomes of political decisions," Hays ignored the only evidence that could confirm these policy differences.[24]

Moreover, this focus left important questions unanswered. If the ward system operated as Hays described it, why did the electorate vote to abolish it in city after city? Conversely, if progressivism was an upper-class and thus presumably minority movement, how did it succeed at the polls? What role did competing conceptions—and actual delivery-of public policy play in the struggle between the two decision-making systems? The focus on "relationships in the political system" answered the question of who governed. It left unanswered the equally important question of how public resources were authoritatively allocated. Given his framework, Hays had no idea of the actual impact of the incumbencies of the competing systems, no method of explaining their rise, persistence, or decline. He had brilliantly described a sea change in the class basis of American urban politics, but he had not explained it.

Nonetheless, by rejecting what he called the moralistic emphasis on episode and ideology, Hays set in motion a revolution in urban political history. In a recent collection of essays on the history of municipal progressivism, for example, the editors note that, in part because of the influence of Hays's work, "within the last decade, the world of bosses, reformers, and moralism has all but been displaced by concern with the impact of industrialization on society." Although this development seems to be universally welcomed by historians, lurking behind it is a retreat from a political explanation of the development of the public sector and a movement toward a structural functionalist explanation.[25]

In their textbook, A History of Urban America, for example, Charles N. Glaab and A. Theodore Brown escape moralism by arguing that "urban communities should be regarded as partly organic (rather than as mere collections of individuals) such that at stages in their growth they develop needs." Ultimately, it was the satisfaction of these organic needs that necessitated increasing expenditure and this is why, they argue, there was "no way to avoid" the increasing range and scale of governmental activity, "regardless of bosses and reformers." In his recent analysis of the development of municipal expenditure in Baltimore, The Origin and Resolution of an Urban Crisis, Alan Anderson endorses a structural functionalist position even more straightforwardly, arguing that to "depersonalize the conflict" between bosses and reformers, he will focus instead on a "new" question: "What were the functional imperatives of the urban system and how were they related to the structural adaptation [of municipal government]?"[26]

The trajectory of Hays's more recent work has also been in a more functionalist direction. In his 1974 essay, "The Changing Political Structure of the City in Industrial America," there is a perceptible shift away from the "analysis of the structure and distribution of power and influence" for which he called in his 1964 essay. In the more recent work, Hays argues that urban development should be considered to be a "constant tension between forces making for decentralization and forces making for centralization in human relations and institutions, between centrifugal and centripetal tendencies, between social differentiation and social integration," and that the urban political order should be viewed as being "shaped and reshaped" according to the "inner dynamic of the changing economic and social order." This more recent framework substitutes conflict between metaphysical entities (integrative forces, decentralizing tendencies, etc.) for real political struggle. In his 1964 essay, Hays considered structure and process to be objects; in this more recent essay, they have been reified into actors themselves.[27]

The link between Hays's earlier and later work is the asserted primacy of the social over the political. In the 1974 essay, this has blossomed into the argument that urban political regimes rise and fall according to their "fit" with socioeconomic change; political structure, in other words, follows social function. This attempt to explain political change without reference to the consequences of political action has been characteristic of all the literature in the "response to industrialism" framework. For this reason, despite manifestos to the contrary, the conflict between bosses and reformers has not been depersonalized or displaced so much as ignored.

RETURNING TO POLITICS VIA THE ANALYSIS OF FISCAL POLICY

Because of a lack of theoretical clarity, the analytical stew of urban political history has thickened, and this makes it even harder to distinguish the ingredients from one another. Bosses and reformers, organic needs and latent functions now compete for explanatory preeminence, but most analyses make only mechanical and reductionist links between socioeconomic change and political culture, urban political action and public policy. The current framework for analysis of the development of the urban public sector is something like a gas: it expands to fill any intellectual volume, but obscures the issues nonetheless.

Because of the significance of urban government in the development of the public sector in America and the influence of our conception of urban political history on our evaluation of contemporary urban politics, the problems created by this obscurity are far from academic. At stake is not just the resolution of a debate about how best to write urban political history but our understanding of the institution most central to public life in pre–New Deal America, not to mention the legacy of that institution for the solution of contemporary urban problems.

Historians are only beginning to accept the point, made most explicitly by Ballard Campbell, that the focus of American political historians on national government and national fiscal issues such as the tariff fundamentally misunderstands the role of the public sector until about 1930. Until then, state and local governments were *the* government for most Americans. This was especially true in the area of fiscal affairs. Throughout the nineteenth century, state and local governments accounted for about 60 percent of all government spending in the United States, and when this expenditure was broken down for the first time in 1902, it was revealed that local governments alone accounted for 50 percent of the total. This remained the case throughout the first thirty years of this century. It was not until about 1940 that the majority of government expenditure shifted in favor of the federal government. Until 1930, too, local nonschool employees outnumbered federal government employees during all years except those of World War I. Moreover, as Anderson has pointed out, between 1899 and 1930, municipal projects accounted for about 10 percent of net national capital formation, while municipal employment generated about 6.4 percent of all wages and salaries—a larger share of national income than that generated by mining or nonmunicipal construction, two-thirds of that generated by agriculture, and one-third of that produced by all manufacturing industries.[28]

In addition, nineteenth-century citizens were regularly taxed only by state and local government, were called to the polls for local elections more often than for national ones, and depended entirely on local government for streets, sewers, education, and policing. It is probably no exaggeration to argue that the most regular connection that citizens had with government in the nineteenth century was the receipt of the annual bill for state and local taxes. Thus it is not surprising that municipal politics was filled with passionate debates over the proper size, role, and cost of local government.

Urban political history written within the "functional" framework, whether it emphasizes the role of socioeconomic forces or that of political culture, deemphasizes this debate by portraying the development of local government as a process that was automatic, rather conflict-free, and perhaps even wholly beneficent. The need for an analysis of the role of power, conflict, and ideology in this process is completely obviated if the growth of local government was inevitable, regardless of who controlled it. Ironically, the "political" version of this story is hardly more political. In that analysis, as we have seen, all-powerful bosses with fists of iron and hearts of gold rejected ideology for prag-matic action: helping the poor, assimilating the immigrants, and mobi-lizing the electorate. They were faced by reformers whose hearts were in the right place but whose political sense was minimal. The challenges of the reformers were politically ineffectual, but they probably did curb the most outrageous excesses of corruption and fiscal profligacy. In this framework, "the system" clearly worked.

In contrast, the urban political system today seems not to work at all. Power seems fragmented, treasuries empty; demands are high and the ability to respond to them low; and as crisis piles upon crisis, no one's needs seem to be adequately met. It is not surprising that some yearn nostalgically for the old party system, the powerful boss, and a return to the days when city government still "got things done." But did cities ever really get things done better than they do today? What if nineteenth-century urban politics was every bit as fractured and con-tentious as it is today, and urban policymaking similarly paralyzed, even dysfunctional? Because it assumes what it should explain, the functional framework has never really addressed these questions. The failure to do so has produced the most troublesome contemporary result of its pre-dominance. In proposing that municipal government was almost ideally functional in the past, this framework has produced a historical standard of comparison against which contemporary urban government inevit-ably fails. It fails because we compare the facts about its contemporary performance with an image of performance in the past; historians writ-ing within the functional framework, however, have not always checked their historical image against the historical facts.

As we have seen, one reason why historians have not done so has been theoretical. By failing to examine their initial assumptions or care-fully trace the course of their causal links, they have seldom specified their theories in a way that could be easily tested. A second problem has been methodological. By means of collective biographies of political actors and the aggregation and analysis of individual political preferences, Hays and others could approximate the structure and class bases of politics and identify eras of important change over time. In contrast, the analysis of the "succession of outcomes of political decisions" seemed to require a return to the anecdotal stew of the old political history.

While Hays was proposing his framework for the history of urban politics, however, economists and political scientists were developing methods appropriate for analyzing variation in per capita municipal expenditure within and among cities, in an attempt to develop what Roy Bahl has called a "positive theory of public expenditure." As in voting studies where election returns were "proxy" variables (aggregated substitutes for individual preferences), expenditure data stood in proxy for indications of policy. These studies assumed that expenditures for various purposes gave a rough indication of a governmental unit's choices of certain policies, or at least of the priority given to certain activities, as measured by expenditure on them.[29]

Beginning with the work of Harvey Brazer in 1959, scholars conducted a large number of these studies at the level of urban government. Most of them were cross-sectional analyses of the determinants of municipal expenditure. The authors of these studies collected data on the public expenditures and socioeconomic structure of a large number of cities at one point in time. They then utilized multiple regression—a technique that can calculate the statistical impact of a group of independent variables (e.g., community socioeconomic characteristics) on a dependent variable (e.g., per capita public expenditure)—to determine which variables explained the variation from city to city.[30]

Overall, the results of these studies seemed to confirm the primacy of socioeconomic structural factors in the explanation of municipal expenditure patterns. In fact, a 1974 survey of these studies noted that economic resources—private wealth and intergovernmental aid—accounted for as much as 90 percent of the variation in expenditure among cities in some of the studies. Meanwhile, when statistical controls for these variables were applied, electoral political variables such as voter turnout or party competition "were rarely significant or powerful predictors of the level of spending."[31]

Historians have not completely ignored this work. In their 1980 book, *Dimensions in Urban History: Historical and Social Science Perspectives on Middle-Size Cities*, J. Rogers Hollingsworth and Ellen Jane Hollingsworth essentially replicated a modern "determinants" analysis on midsized cities in 1900. And in his 1977 book, *The Origins and Resolution of an Urban Crisis: Baltimore, 1890–1930,* Anderson applied modern urban economic theory to the development of municipal expenditure in that city. The findings of both these studies dovetail with the results of studies of modern cities. On the basis of their statistical analysis of 154 midsized cities in 1900, the Hollingsworths conclude that "per capita wealth" best explains the variation in expenditure among these cities, and that variables measuring political participation, party competition, or the type of election system "have virtually no [statistical] influence on any of the major kinds of municipal spending." Anderson, who excludes the search for the effects of "political or ideological" values from his analysis, argues that the changing cost of land as an input to the production of municipal services is the most important factor in the rise and fall of municipal expenditure in Baltimore.[32]

The similarity between these findings and those of other analysts of modern cities occurs because the authors share methodological and intellectual predispositions. For example, by adopting a technique of cross-sectional analysis of many cities at one point in time, the Hollingsworths are prevented from discovering a pattern of historical development in the relationships among the variables they study. They are therefore interested in history but unable to include time as a variable in their analysis, other than by implicit comparison with contemporary studies. Anderson, in contrast, is interested in change over time (although not in the statistical analysis of that change), but is barred from analyzing the influence of political factors because he conceives of the development of municipal expenditure as a production function into which only the classic economic factors of production can enter (e.g., land, labor, and capital). Furthermore, in both these studies fiscal policy is a measure, not a process. Thus these authors use municipal expenditure to measure the development of municipal government without carefully considering the essentially political process by which fiscal variables are calibrated to produce enough revenue to support a given level of expenditure, and hence of government activity.

These studies are methodological advances over those that merely speculate about the development of fiscal policy without attempting to measure it or the influences on it. Yet their authors acknowledge the need for a broader approach. Anderson notes that "political activity should not be excluded from an analysis of urban development" but included "in a broader model of urban evolution which also gives proper consideration to technological and economic factors." Similarly, the Hollingsworths concede that "there is no one-to-one relationship between changes in the social and economic structure and changes in the political structures of cities," and argue that it is "imperative to explain the linkages by which socioeconomic variables get translated into public policy via the political system."[33]

This study is an attempt to move in this broader direction. It builds upon the interest in the development of the urban public sector expressed in earlier, nonquantitative works, but it attempts to avoid the sort of latent theorizing that has led to functionalist "explanations" of this process. Rather, this study tests hypotheses drawn from more clearly articulated theory. Like the more recent quantitative works, it uses fiscal data as a measure of the development of the local public sector and employs statistical techniques to analyze these data. Unlike these works, however, it also considers the process by which fiscal policy is produced, the interrelationships among the products of fiscal policy, and a wide variety of socioeconomic and political influences on that policy. Finally, it strives to understand the interaction of these variables within the possibilities and limitations of a nineteenth-century institutional and ideological context radically different from our own.

This investigation begins in the next chapter, with a look at that institutional context. Although central to a proper understanding of the development of municipal government, the set of legal and customary practices by which an idea for policy became a fully funded part of the municipal budget has been ignored by historians. We begin with this institutional framework, considering first the city's charter-mandated budgetary process and its relationship to the state legislature, and then the trends in and institutional effects on the annual levels of assessed valuation, tax rate, revenue, and expenditure.

In chapters 3 and 4, we turn to more careful summaries and tests of the explanations for the development of the urban public sector proposed by historians. Chapter 3 focuses on those explanations that give primacy to socioeconomic factors, comparing them with San Francisco's socioeconomic development and then statistically determining the ability of measures of socioeconomic development to explain the products of the fiscal process. In chapter 4, we consider those explanations that emphasize the effects of political culture, in particular the backgrounds of local officials. We reconstruct the local political history of the city in search of differences in the composition of municipal officials in different periods; then we statistically determine the ability of those differences to explain fiscal policy, both alone and in combination with the socioeconomic variables measured in chapter 3.

Chapters 5, 6, and 7 reconstruct the city's fiscal political culture in the periods 1856–1882, 1882–1896, and 1897–1906. The focus of each of these chapters is on the ideological and political environment in which fiscal policymaking took place. Thus each chapter explains the ideas about the proper role and size of the public sector expressed by partisan editorialists, candidates for office, and municipal officials themselves, and then analyzes the most interesting examples of fiscal policymaking in each period. Because we are considering the politics of fiscal policymaking, these expositions are accompanied by analyses of the structure of political participation, party strength, and partisan political control in each period. Chapter 8 combines and summarizes the analyses of quantitative and nonquantitative materials in the preceding chapters, in an attempt to reconcile theory and practice in the case of San Francisco. Chapter 9 considers the implications of these results for the history and theory of urban fiscal policymaking in general.

Taken together, I hope that these chapters demonstrate at least five major points.

First, that the institutional context within which fiscal policy was made in San Francisco was stable and relatively autonomous from the influence of the state legislature.

Second, neither socioeconomic change nor political ethos alone explains the pattern in fiscal policy or even operates in the way that most historians—and historically oriented sociologists and political scientists—have suggested. Measures of socioeconomic development had little or no direct statistical effect on municipal expenditure, but they did have a powerful positive effect on assessed valuation. Thus it appears that this development was not a disaster but a potential bonanza for the public sector. Yet political culture, at least as measured by the occupational and ethnic backgrounds of officials, explained little of the variation in fiscal policy, in part because the socioeconomic and ethnic composition of officials was, on the whole, remarkably similar over time. Moreover, during the one period when backgrounds were distinctively different from the average, the fiscal policy the officials produced was the opposite of that predicted by historians; expenditure and the tax rate were lowest when the shares of foreign-born and Irish officials were the highest.

Third, controlling for the effect of socioeconomic development, fiscal behavior was shaped more by constraints shared by all policymakers than by different sets of political ethos shared by some. The most important of these constraints were the institutional framework within which fiscal policy was made, the ideology defining acceptable fiscal policy, and the pressure of political competition, which necessitated a politically strategic fiscal policy.

Fourth, these constraints resulted in fiscal political roles for bosses and reformers in San Francisco which were the opposite of those supposed both by generations of local historians and by more general interpretations of the history of urban fiscal policy. Because of both the intensity of political competition during their era of power and their own acceptance of a no-growth position on the public sector, machine politicians in San Francisco did not campaign for the expansion of the public sector or use it to aid the needy, hire immigrants, or mobilize new groups into the electorate. But because of both a broader conception of the public sector and changed conditions of political competition in the era of their emergence, reformers did campaign for an expanded public sector, promise services to the neighborhoods, and public-sector-financed jobs for workingmen, and thereby mobilized new groups into the electorate. Thus it was elitist reformers, not their more plebian machine-politics predecessors, who introduced pragmatic interest-group politics into the city.

Fifth, these results, recent similar arguments by other historians, and the intellectual origins of functional theory suggest that it is time to move away from the functional framework of urban political history and toward a framework that accepts urban politics as it was, not as we wish it was. Such an alternative framework must be grounded in a thorough understanding of the institutional context within which local government developed. It is to that context in San Francisco that we turn in the next chapter.

2

The Institutional Context and Overall Trends

On July 1, 1856, the Hawes Act to consolidate the governments of the city and county of San Francisco went into effect, repealing all previous charters of the city of San Francisco, declaring that the territorial boundaries of the city and county of San Francisco were coterminous, and establishing a government that would continue, in that consolidated form, through the twentieth century. About two and one-half months short of exactly fifty years later, however, an earthquake of twenty-eight seconds, followed by fires lasting three days, utterly destroyed the most important physical symbols of that government, including the city hall, hall of records, hall of justice, and all the records they contained.[1]

Within a few days of the holocaust, the city government was back to business as usual, albeit in temporary quarters and at reduced levels of operation. Although the damage to the city government's physical plant was immense—more than seventy-five fire and police stations, schools, libraries, and their contents were destroyed—and the cost of replacement staggering, the government's day-to-day operations snapped back quickly. This was possible in great part because, in the years between the establishment of the consolidated government and its moment of crisis, the city had established patterns for the collection of revenue and allocation of expenditure which took it through those first years after the crisis.[2]

Between 1860, when annual financial reports first became available, and 1906, when earthquake damage required an anomalous period of extra expenditure, the sources of the city's revenue were fixed; regular patterns in the allocation of expenditure developed; and the size and role of the local public sector in normal times—and thus the level of expenditure—was determined after strenuous political debate. It was in these years, in other words, that important patterns in the relationship among social change, urban politics, and fiscal policy were established. The investigation of this broader relationship begins with narrower examinations of the city's charter-mandated fiscal machinery, the relationship between the city and the state legislature, and trends in and relationships among the components of taxation, valuation, revenue, and expenditure during these years.

THE CHARTER FRAMEWORK FOR FISCAL POLICYMAKING

The Consolidation Act or charter of 1856, as the Hawes Act was called, was a strong council–weak mayor charter that created a twelve-member, elected board of supervisors that was, among other things, to "levy and collect taxes" and to provide for the "prompt payment of all demands upon the treasury." To facilitate these tasks, the charter also specified the sources of the city's revenue, the process of the allocation of this revenue into the city's various expenditure funds, and the means by which the contents of these funds were to be disbursed. Because this charter was in effect (with amendments) from July 1856 until January 1900, the essential framework of these important tasks of municipal government remained unchanged throughout this period. Indeed, most of this framework carried over into the "reform" charter of 1900 as well.[3]

The charter defined the city's revenue as the taxes on real and personal property, all "fines, penalties, forfeitures," the income from the licensing of occupations and businesses, fees from government services such as the recording of deeds and the preparation of legal documents, and certain small portions of a state-mandated poll tax of $2, which was to be paid annually by all males between the ages of twenty-one and sixty-five, but which had no effect on one's eligibility to vote. In addition to these local revenue sources, the city received some subsidies from the state, the most important of which was the state's contribution to the operation of local schools.[4]

Given the vagaries of the income from fines, fees, and licenses, the city relied most heavily on revenue from the taxes on real and personal property. By state law, the "actual cash value" of this property was to be determined by the local assessor, and the tax rate per $100 of this assessed valuation was to be set by the board of supervisors. To prevent exorbitant taxation, the 1856 charter limited the rate for general purposes to $1.25 and that for school purposes to $0.35 per $100 of assessed valuation. In 1859 the maximum for general purposes was raised to $2.25, where it remained for the rest of the century, while that for schools remained at $0.35. However, the rates rarely were set at these maximum levels.[5]

In addition to the supervisors, the charter mandated the election of a variety of city and county officers, among whom were the most important executive officers of the city. These included the mayor (who was called the president of the board of supervisors until 1866), county clerk, chief of police, sheriff, coroner, recorder, treasurer, auditor, tax collector, assessor, surveyor, superintendent of public streets, district attorney, and harbormaster. The most important in the fiscal process were the assessor and the auditor: the former because he determined the revenue base for the city, the latter because he was, in effect, the chief financial officer of the city, required not only to keep track of the city's financial condition during the current year but also to cooperate with the board in determining revenue and expenditure for the coming year.[6]

The process of financing the activities of the coming fiscal year began in February, when the charter required that the department heads present reports of their activities to the supervisors, "embracing all their operations and expenditures during the preceding year and recommending such improvements in them as they deem necessary." At this point the executive officers functioned as lobbyists for their departments before the board. At the same time the auditor received from the assessor an estimate of the assessed valuation of real and personal property for the coming year. After reconciling the requests for new expenditure with the probable amount of revenue—usually by reducing the requests of the department heads—the auditor passed his estimates of revenue, expenditure, and the tax rate on to the finance committee of the board of supervisors. The committee then held hearings on the estimates, at which department heads and the public had a chance to discuss them. On the basis of the auditor's report and these hearings, the finance committee prepared a set of estimates that it proposed to the full board. The full board also discussed these estimates publicly and then voted on a revenue ordinance setting the rate of taxation for the next fiscal year, which was passed on to the mayor for his signature or veto. Until 1874 the rate was to be set by the first of May, after that by June 30. Throughout this period the fiscal year began on July 1.[7]

In the process of setting the tax rate, the supervisors also set the allocations of revenue among the various budgetary funds. This occurred because the charter required the apportionment of tax revenues into various expenditure funds. Thus the tax rate that was approved by the board was a single overall rate subdivided into rates for each of the various funds. In the 1856 charter there were two of these: the School Fund, from which expenses for the local schools were met, and the General Fund, which financed what some scholars have called the "common services," such as administration, police, fire, health, and social welfare. Besides being the original funds, these two received the largest shares of the city's annual total local expenditure throughout this period, the General Fund averaging 46 percent of the total, the School Fund 18 percent.[8]

Over time, the number of funds—and thus the subcategories of the tax rate—multiplied along with the city's activities. In the first rate analyzed for this study, for example, that for fiscal year 1859/60, the rate was divided among five funds, the General Fund, School Fund, Corporation Debt Fund, Street Light Fund, and a special Judgment Fund. In fiscal year 1890/91 there were fifteen subdivisions of the tax rate, including seven funds for operating expenses, four sinking funds for the repayment of bonds, and four interest accounts for the payment of interest on those bonds.[9]

Once the money was allocated, demands on the treasury were met after having passed through three checkpoints. According to the charter, an item of expenditure (e.g., a salary warrant, a bill for services, a purchase of goods) was first to be presented to the auditor, who determined whether the expenditure was to be "allowed," and if so, from what fund or category. Allowed demands were met only if approved by a majority of the board and signed by the mayor. Given these procedures, the amounts expended in most areas of city government were at the discretion of the supervisors. Within the various funds, expenditure was based on, but by no means restricted by, the estimates provided by the departments, as revised and approved by the board when the tax rate was set.[10]

Before 1900 these estimates lacked both the specificity and the force of law to be binding on either the supervisors or the executive officers.

Thus both groups could change their minds between the setting of the rates and the actual expenditure of the money. The estimates prescribed totals for various activities, not "line items" for every purpose. Therefore, although estimates usually segregated expenditure by activity categories and, for salary and "running expenses" within categories, it was not unusual for money to be switched from one activity to another or even from one fund to another. Moreover, there was no legal requirement for a balanced budget. Indeed, it was not until an 1893 state supreme court decision that the supervisors were required to appropriate enough money within the same fiscal year to pay all the expenditures included in the estimates. Prior to that decision, it was not uncommon for the board to use the inevitable lag between the auditing of an expense and its approval to delay payment of some current expenditures into the next fiscal year. This prevented "deficiencies" in the current year but postponed the solution of some problems into the next. Despite these loose institutional procedures, the city showed a cash surplus at the end of every fiscal year in this period, ranging from $26,000 to $6 million, and averaging about $1 million.

The reform charter of 1900 finally required a line-item balanced budget, and prior to that, there had been one major attempt to rationalize this process somewhat. This was a bill called the One-Twelfth Act, passed by the state legislature of 1877/78. Introduced by former mayor and then State Senator Frank McCoppin, the bill turned these estimates into more formal appropriations and then prohibited city officers from expending any more than one-twelfth of their appropriations per month. No officer was ever prosecuted under this law, although some surely violated it, but it did place a powerful moral and, more important, political sanction on this type of behavior. In fact, the only real sanction for overspending was political. An unbalanced budget or an overspent account was a political liability but never a legal one.[11]

In the end, therefore, regardless of legislative or budgetary safeguards, the responsibility for the city's fiscal policy rested with the supervisors. Like most municipal decision-making bodies established in the first half of the nineteenth century, the San Francisco supervisors combined executive and legislative functions in a list of responsibilities that must at times have overwhelmed some of these part-time officials. The supervisors were empowered by charter to pass ordinances, levy taxes, appropriate money, let contracts, and serve as a board of equalization for tax assessments, as well as to control the activities and audit the books of all city departments. In addition, each supervisor was required individually to inspect the activities of government in his own ward. San Franciscans were fully aware of the power of the board, and editorialists outdid themselves in calling for careful selection of supervisors at every municipal election. The *Examiner* noted in 1870, for example, that "the Board of Supervisors can exercise more power than all the other officers. They are invested with greater trusts and responsibilities."[12]

In many areas of city government, the power of the supervisors was nearly absolute (e.g., in the setting of tax rates and assessments); in others, the discretion of the supervisors was limited to an acceptable range set by the state legislature. This at times supervisory, at times intervening position of the state legislature raises a question of great importance to a study such as this—namely, whether there was enough fiscal independence on the part of local government to justify an analysis of local fiscal politics. The answer of many authors writing on the subject of legislative interference would be no. In fact, a recent analysis of San Francisco politics in this period has argued that the city's "dependence upon state action and authority required and encouraged the intervention of an increasingly anti-urban government at Sacramento in San Francisco affairs," and that this interference "rendered municipal government confusing, chaotic, and frequently ineffective." A closer look, however, suggests that this was not the case.[13]

THE CITY'S FISCAL AUTONOMY FROM THE STATE

When San Francisco's reform charter, passed by the citizens in 1898, was approved by the state legislature in 1899, local newspapers trumpeted: "Home Rule at Last." Indeed, home rule or freedom from the interference of the state legislature had been an issue—although by no means the most important issue—in the campaign within the city for ratification of the charter. It had also been an issue in the four attempts for a new, reformed charter mounted in 1880, 1883, 1887, and 1896, all of which had been defeated by the city's electorate.[14]

Historians of the city have adduced a number of reasons for the failure of the earlier attempts, including clouding of the "real" issues by class or ethnic antagonism, fear of centralized mayoral authority, the opposition of the regular parties, and objections to specific provisions in the proposed charters. Taken together, these explanations imply something further, which these authors have not emphasized: the home rule issue alone was not important enough to the city for political actors to choose to resolve it at the cost of some other important interests. If legislative interference was a problem of the dimensions we have been led to believe, it is striking that San Franciscans rejected every attempt to remedy this problem proposed between 1880 and 1896.[15]

The lack of salience of the home rule issue after 1880 could be explained by the "home rule features" of the state constitution of 1879. The new constitution contained three clauses tending to support municipal home rule. The first was the freeholders' clause, which for the first time specified how localities of a certain size could give themselves home rule charters subject to the ultimate approval of the legislature. It was under this new constitutional authority that the San Francisco charters were proposed. The second constitutional provision was that prohibiting so-called special legislation. Intended to block the passage of bills benefiting private corporations or individuals, this provision was also interpreted to mean that legislation for particular cities or other areas was prohibited. This did not prevent special legislation, although it did change its form and make its objects more limited. Under this provision, legislation affecting San Francisco had to be applicable to a "class" of cities (e.g., those of a certain size). For most of this period San Francisco was the only city in its class, but because of this definition, the legislation could not be too special. The final home rule provision of the new constitution declared that the regulation of water supplies and utility rates was an affair for local authority, and this extended the authority of the supervisors. While these provisions neither brought home rule to San Francisco nor delivered it entirely from legislative interference, they did, as San Francisco historian John Young has written, bring "something like" local self-government to the city. This may have been a reason for the lack of importance of the home rule issue after 1880.[16]

This, I contend, is only part of the answer, however, and not necessarily the most important part. The striking thing about home rule as a political issue is that from 1860 to 1898 it was not important in elections outside of the charter elections themselves. Even during the heyday of the so-called interference, between 1860 and 1879, the issue of interference was raised less frequently than was the exhortation to the electorate to choose state legislators who would do a good job of advancing the city's interests at Sacramento. There were two good rea-

sons for the apparent lack of fear of the legislature on the part of San
Franciscans even during the years 1860–1879: the preponderant influence of the city in the politics of the state and the state legislature, and
the system of mutual accommodation which localities within the legislature had developed.

As R. Hal Williams has argued in his study of California politics in
this period, San Francisco dominated the state politically for forty years
after the Gold Rush. In 1880, as he points out, San Francisco's population of 234,000 accounted for 27 percent of the state's total population
and one-fourth of its voters. On the basis of numbers alone, therefore,
"the city's political delegations enjoyed a preponderant position in conventions, elections, and the legislature." That San Franciscans were
aware of this was indicated frequently in the city's newspapers during
these years. As the *Bulletin* editorialized in 1873, "there is not a county
in the state which has not some pet project of its own. To them our
small army of senators and representatives . . . constitute a power which
is to be conciliated and not outraged."[17]

The editor of the *Bulletin* understood the system of local logrolling
in the state legislature—a system that has only recently come to the
attention of urban historians through the work of urban legal historian
Jon C. Teaford. Considering city-state relationships in several states, including California, Teaford concluded that "nineteenth-century legislatures, for the most part, did not make policy or fashion the legal
structure of municipal government . . . more often [they] simply responded to the demands of localities in accord with the cues given by
the local [legislative] delegation." In California, the legislative practice
was to refer all local measures to the delegation representing the affected locality. According to Teaford, "San Francisco's delegation to the
California house and senate was a well-organized body with almost complete control over local bills." Although referred to in the legislature as
"special" committees, the San Francisco delegations in each branch enjoyed the privileges of a standing committee, including a salaried clerk.
Moreover, the recommendations of the delegation carried weight. In
the session of 1873/74, which Teaford has analyzed in detail, the city's
house and senate delegations made 117 recommendations, and the bodies accepted 112 of them.[18]

This pattern is evident throughout the period from 1856 to 1879,
the years during which most historians have contended that legislative

interference was at its height. A good first example of this pattern was the passage of the charter of the city itself, which was lambasted by politicians and later historians alike for placing the city under the thrall of the state legislature. The charter prohibited the city from contracting debt and enumerated the powers of the board of supervisors specifically, so that any changes in or extensions of those powers had to be granted by the legislature. The prohibition of debt was hardly meddlesome, however, since it was patterned after a similar prohibition on the legislature itself in the state constitution of 1849. More important, as Roger Lotchin has pointed out, "these stipulations did not come from state meddling, for local citizens drafted charters and the financial restrictions were popular with the home constituency." It should be added that the Consolidation Act was introduced by a state senator from San Francisco, and that it was supported by two resolutions of what was then called the Common Council of San Francisco.[19]

It is true, of course, that there was no "implied powers" clause in the charter. The charter specifically stated that "the powers of the Board of Supervisors are those granted in this Act, and they are prohibited from exercising any others." This prohibition required the city to obtain enabling acts from the state legislature for activities ranging from the opening of streets to the expansion of the police force. For this very reason, however, using the sheer volume of legislative enactments as a measure of interference is incorrect. Many of these acts were trivial, and it was the volume of these small items which made the local deference system an efficient one for part-time, overworked legislators who, as Teaford suggests, were "confronted by eight or nine hundred bills during a sixty day session [and] did not make law so much as enact it."[20]

Some of the actions of the legislature were important, though. Among those in this category were acts considered to be supplements to the Consolidation Act because they permanently redefined or expanded the powers enumerated there. By 1876, when the supplements up to that point were collected and published, there were ninety such acts. It was possible to trace most of them back to the legislative branch in which they originated to determine the sponsor of each bill, the committee to which it was referred, the recommendation of the committee, and the vote of that house. The inadequacy of indexing in the early legislative records made it difficult to find all the information for each of the bills, but enough could be traced to determine clear patterns. Since

these acts were passed during the period of the greatest legislative interference in the city's affairs (i.e., 1856–1879), they provide an ex-
cellent test case of the city's relationship with the state in these years.[21]

Overall, Teaford's suggestions are confirmed by the histories of these
supplemental acts; the San Francisco delegations kept almost exclusively
to themselves the introduction and committee consideration of bills
affecting the city. Of the ninety supplemental acts, it was possible to
determine the sponsors of eighty-one. Every one was introduced by a
member of the San Francisco delegation. The vast majority of these bills
was also referred to the San Francisco delegation sitting as a committee.
I was able to determine the committee referrals of seventy-one (78
percent) of the ninety supplements. Fifty-seven were referred to the
San Francisco delegation; six of the bills were passed upon introduction,
without referral to any committee; and only eight were referred to other
committees. Seven of these eight, those dealing with the creation or
expansion of judicial districts and court personnel in the city, were
referred to the judiciary committee.

The reports of the delegation were usually quite brief, and the legislature made quick work of the voting as well. In 1876, for example,
the city's assembly delegation reported typically on a bill to allow the
city to use the labor of convicts held in the city's house of correction:

Mr. Speaker: The San Francisco delegation, to whom was referred . . . Assembly
Bill 463—An Act to Utilize the Prison Labor and Govern the House of Corrections of the City and County of San Francisco—report the same back with
amendments and recommend its passage as amended.

The reports of the various committees of the legislature usually took
most of the morning. That afternoon, then, the bill's sponsor moved
that the bill be brought before the house:

On motion of Mr. Clarken, the House took up Assembly Bill No. 463 reported
by the San Francisco delegation this day. The rules were suspended, the bill
considered engrossed, read a third time, passed.[22]

As the rather quick and unanimous passage suggests, the legislature
rarely troubled itself too much over San Francisco measures. Of these
ninety bills, a vote was recorded on only six (7 percent). On four of
these occasions, the delegation itself was split and the legislative body

followed the recommendation of the majority of the delegation. On the other two occasions, the delegation had recommended passage and the house agreed, although a division was demanded nonetheless.

Apparently because of the power of the city's legislative delegations, the fiscal relationship between the city and the state was also a reasonable one. Superficial analysts of the city-state relationship have tended to confuse quantity of legislative actions with the quality, nature, or impact of those actions. But an analysis of the contents of these bills reveals that thirty-five (37 percent) of the supplementary acts had no fiscal impact; instead, they dealt with election procedures, health regulations, rules for the operation of certain city offices, and so on.

Among the fifty-five remaining acts that did have fiscal impact, an important distinction must be made between those that required fiscal change and those that allowed it. The former were those that mandated the creation of a position and set its salary—for example, a bill creating a new district court and its attendants, or a new municipal office or clerk for such an office. Of the ninety supplements, only fourteen (15 percent) required fiscal change in this manner. Almost three times as numerous were the forty-one acts (44 percent) that allowed fiscal impact—that is, that permitted but did not require expenditure. Among these were acts permitting the city to contract a certain amount of bonded indebtedness and to appoint additional police officers or firemen. These acts can be distinguished from others by language setting maximum numbers of officers or maximum salaries while allowing the city to determine what it would do within that range. The function of these bills, then, was to set the parameters of municipal fiscal behavior but not to determine it absolutely.[23]

The flexibility of these acts permitted municipal leaders to follow their own fiscal lights to a degree, to respond to changing municipal conditions, and to develop their own political reputations for fiscal policy. If a mayor or supervisor wanted to demonstrate his fiscal conservatism, it was possible to do so by comparing his behavior with the legislative boundaries. In 1864, for example, the supervisors' finance committee, led by then Supervisor Frank McCoppin, justified its estimates of expenditure for the coming year in exactly these terms. Speaking for the committee members, McCoppin reported that they had "consulted economy to the last degree" and "had by no means gone to the extent of the appropriation authorized by the last session of the legislature." For example, the committee thought that an increase of ten members of the police department, instead of fifty, as authorized, was sufficient for the next year, and perhaps for two years.[24]

This analysis leaves open, of course, the important question of the origin of the initiative for these bills. The answer will probably never be known, even for a majority of these bills, because of lack of information. The city's legislative delegations left no written records of their deliberations, and their reports to the legislature were quite brief and only rarely suggested the origins of a bill. The city's supervisors also left no written records.

Legislative records and newspaper reports do suggest, however, that there were at least three paths to legislative enactment. The first, and most important, was through the board of supervisors, which organized a Committee on Amendments (to the Consolidation Act) to work with the legislative delegations when the legislature was in session. By far the largest number of bills relating to the city originated here, simply because the city charter required that many of the board's routine acts be confirmed by the legislature. For example, each time a street was opened in the city or its grade changed, a bill confirming this action of the supervisors was submitted to the legislature. Between 1856 and 1879, there were 177 of these bills, which were introduced in batches and passed routinely. Matters of higher policy and fiscal impact also originated with the board. For example, bills expanding the police force, upgrading the city's fire department, settling the thorny issue of the disposition of the city's so-called outside lands, and allowing municipal indebtedness for the improvements in the city's almshouse, hospital, and parks originated as ordinances and/or resolutions before the board of supervisors, and these bills had by far the greatest fiscal impact in this period. In fact, among the supplements to the Consolidation Act, the only source of bills mentioned in any of the records is the board.[25]

On the basis both of number and impact, then, the board of supervisors was probably the source of most bills affecting the city. Moreover, it was usually the board that first created the "effect" on the city (e.g., opened the street, proposed the ordinance, decided to repair the hospital), and the legislature that merely confirmed that effect. However, the legislative delegations themselves could also be a source of bills proposed independently of the board. As Teaford has suggested, the sheer volume of the bills delegation members were expected to present prohibited them from originating much legislation, and it is probably more accurate to consider the delegations as sources for amendments rather than original bills. Among the fifty-four supplements known to have been referred to the delegations, for example, six (11 percent) were offered with the delegation amendments and seven (12 percent) were actually substitutes proposed by the delegations.

Finally, citizens and others aware of the power of the legislative delegations were free to beat their own paths to Sacramento to importune legislators to act on their behalf. I cannot determine how widespread this practice was. Ironically, the only mention of it that I have discovered refers not to everyday citizens but to municipal officials themselves dunning state legislators for special legislation for their departments. In his 1876 inaugural address, San Francisco Mayor Andrew Jackson Bryant felt it necessary to condemn those "heads of departments of the city government and sometimes even their subordinates" who "ignore the board of supervisors and make direct application to the legislature in furtherance of schemes not designed for the public good so much as to increase their own profit, power, and patronage." He did not, however, specify the number or magnitude of such schemes.[26]

Bryant's statement is significant not only for what it reveals about the abuse of the system for producing municipal legislation but also because it defines what the system itself was. The board of supervisors was looked upon as the appropriate conduit of municipal action to the state legislature. At the time of Bryant's inaugural, in any case, the troublesome practice was on the way out, if for no other reason than that the new state constitution of three years later outlawed such special legislation and thus expanded the city's region of autonomy from the state government. Although the contours of this region were not fully mapped out until the reform charter of 1898, the issue of legislative interference was not politically salient after 1879.

Contemporary politicians, and especially the reformers of the 1890s, had their reasons for magnifying the "evil" of legislative interference, and many historians afterward have accepted these arguments uncritically. Underestimating the power of the San Francisco delegation, failing to understand the system of local accommodation within the legislature, and confusing quantity of legislation with quality of legislation, they have misrepresented the fiscal relationship between the city and the state, and thus minimized the fiscal autonomy of San Francisco officeholders. Although the legislature set the boundaries for some of the city's fiscal behavior, the flexibility within those bounds was large enough to allow local officeholders a great degree of fiscal autonomy, and thus the ability to follow their own fiscal lights and be judged accordingly by the electorate. Local officials, after all, set the tax rate and collected and allocated the money. Moreover, given the situation of the San Francisco delegation at the capital, it was possible—perhaps even easy—for legislative boundaries to be adjusted, and the preponderance of the evidence suggests that these adjustments were usually made in response to locally initiated requests. This being the case, we turn to an examination of the patterns in local revenue and expenditure.

PATTERNS IN MUNICIPAL FISCAL POLICY, 1860–1906

Volumes of annual fiscal reports originated in the reports that the auditor and other city department heads were required to present to the board of supervisors on the first Monday in February of each year. The Consolidation Act further required that the board "make up and publish an abstract from these reports and other sources of the operations, expenditures, and conditions of all departments of government." Apparently for the first time in fiscal year 1859/60, the board ordered that the reports be bound and published annually as the *Municipal Reports* for the fiscal year of the city and county of San Francisco. The result was an annual statistical compendium of the expenditures and activities of all departments of government from fiscal year 1859/60 through fiscal year 1917/18.[27]

Whatever their worth to contemporaries, these volumes are of inestimable value for historians. In the first place, the fire that followed the San Francisco earthquake destroyed the city hall and the hall of records, along with their contents. Sets of the *Municipal Reports* located elsewhere were the only remaining record of the city's governmental activities before 1906. More important from the standpoint of fiscal history, between 1860 and 1900, the major categories of revenue and expenditure and governmental activities reported in the volumes changed only slightly, and because of their consistency we can reconstitute most of the categories after 1900. The result is that the volumes provide the information for annual series of taxation, revenue, and expenditure for the entire period under consideration. This is the kind of information that, in the words of E. S. Griffith, the dean of American municipal history, "furnishes the best mirror of the extent and character of functional growth."[28]

Using these records, we can answer a seemingly simple question: How did the government of San Francisco get and spend its money in the years from 1860 to 1906? To do this, I review the overall trends in and composition of the city's assessed valuation, tax rate, revenue raised, and expenditure appropriated, along with the major legal and institutional changes affecting these components of fiscal policy. I examine overall trends by means of graphs and calculated rates of growth, and more concrete details of these trends by looking at "snapshots" of the amounts and composition of various categories during the fiscal years 1859/60, 1879/80, 1897/98, and 1904/05. There is nothing significant about these years other than the time between them, 1860 being the first and 1905 the last full year analyzed for the study, and 1880 and 1898 being about twenty years apart. I selected 1898 rather than 1900 because it was the last full year under the old charter; 1905, of course, was under the new charter. The price index underlying this analysis is discussed in appendix A.

In this chapter and those that follow, I focus exclusively on local sources of revenue and appropriations of expenditure. Transfer payments to and from the state are excluded (e.g., payment to the state of state taxes collected in the city, or payment from the state to subsidize local education). San Franciscans controlled neither the amount nor the disposition of transfer payments, so these transfers did not figure into local fiscal political debate. My focus, like theirs, is on funds raised and spent in the city itself, and I begin with the components of local revenue.

As my earlier discussion of the charter revealed, the local revenue available to the city came from three major sources: taxation on the assessed value of real and personal property, licenses from a large number of occupations in the city, and fees for services provided by the government. However, the revenue was composed overwhelmingly of the taxes on local real and personal property. Overall, this revenue accounted for 84 percent of the total, while that from licenses amounted to 10 percent and that from fees totaled 5 percent. As table 1 shows, the importance of tax revenue increased over time, while the contributions of the other two categories decreased, both in terms of their share of the total and their per capita value. On an annual basis, the real value of tax revenue grew about 2.7 percent, the fee revenue about

TABLE 1

COMPOSITION AND PER CAPITA VALUE OF LOCAL REVENUE

Category	1860	1880	1898	1905	Overall mean
Share of tax revenue	81.4%	83.4%	86.1%	88.6%	84.0%
Per capita value	$13.40	$10.29	$12.48	$14.00	$12.70
Share of license revenue	12.7%	10.9%	10.4%	8.0%	10.5%
Per capita value	$2.09	$1.34	$1.51	$1.36	$1.52
Share of fee revenue	5.6%	5.7%	3.4%	3.4%	5.6%
Per capita value	$0.97	$0.70	$0.50	$0.54	$0.87

2.7 percent, and the license revenue about 0.44 percent. On a per capita basis, all showed a slight annual decrease on average. The tax revenue was a function of the tax base and the tax rate. Thus we can begin our analysis of revenue with a look at them.[29]

Throughout the period 1860–1905, the tax base of the city of San Francisco consisted of all the real and personal property there. Although the details of these categories were changed from time to time, their fundamental definitions remained the same: real property referred to ownership of land and the improvements thereon; personal property included everything else subject to ownership. Throughout this period, the county assessor was instructed by law to assess these objects of ownership at their "full cash value," dividing the valuations into those for real estate and improvements and for personal property. Before 1872 the assessor or one of his deputies was required to visit each taxpayer to assess the property. After that year, when a revision of the state's political code resulted in a new revenue law, each taxpayer was required to file a sworn statement of his holdings—but not their value—with the assessor by a certain date each year. The assessor then figured the assessed valuation and the taxes due. For most of this period San Francisco assessors produced an assessment ranging from 60 to 75 percent of "true" cash value for all property.[30]

Somewhat surprisingly, complete tax evasion or failure to cooperate with the assessor was rare. In 1896 the city's assessor reported that of about forty thousand taxpayers, usually less than a thousand failed to cooperate formally—that is to say, failed to file a statement of their

TABLE 2
COMPOSITION AND PER CAPITA VALUE OF ASSESSED VALUATION

Category	1860	1880	1898	1905	Overall mean
Share of real estate and improvements	70.2%	67.5%	79.9%	75.6%	70.3%
Per capita value	$442.34	$578.34	$832.75	$944.40	$728.85
Share of personal property	29.8%	23.5%	20.1%	24.4%	29.7%
Per capita value	$188.09	$177.42	$208.96	$304.52	$326.06

taxable property. There were two reasons for this high degree of co-operation. First, those who failed to cooperate with the assessor were subject to a penalty assessment procedure in which the assessor would figure their valuation and then raise it ten times as a punishment. Second, the taxpayer himself answered the assessor's questions or filled out the form, so the amount of evasion within the formal cooperation was undoubtedly massive. In San Francisco it was definitely true, as C. K. Yearley has written of many other cities, that citizens boasted of what they had accumulated until tax time came around, when "destructive waves of loss, indebtedness, and impoverishment swept even the smallest bastions of capital. Pillars of the community collapsed, capital disappeared or changed form." This was confirmed locally by University of California political economist Carl Plehn, who noted in 1897 that the consciences of the state's taxpayers had not yet reached the point where it was considered a sin to lie to the assessor.[31]

Such actual evasion within formal cooperation was blatant in the case of personal property. As table 2 indicates, personal property averaged only about 30 percent of the total assessed valuation, and that share actually declined over time. Moreover, the assessed value of personal property grew at a rate of about 1.3 percent per year, while that of real estate and improvements grew at about 3.8 percent a year. On a per capita basis, the former declined an average of 1.8 percent annually, while the latter grew at an average rate of 0.6 percent. Now, one could say that because of the urbanization process itself the value of real estate would increase rapidly, but so too would items charged on the personal property list, such as "gold dust or bullion on hand or on deposit," "goods, wares, merchandise," and "fixtures of saloons, stores, offices and other business places." The evasion in the case of personal property was not just that of a workingman hiding a watch or a piano, but of bankers, merchants, and small businessmen evading on a massive scale. This evasion occurred because, for the assessor, the proper valuation of personal property presented both technical and political problems. Technically, it was difficult to challenge a merchant's valuation of his holdings. Politically, it was difficult for the assessor to remain in office if he alienated large portions of the business community.[32]

Fortunately for the public sector in California, the valuation of real property was not so difficult. The Political Code of 1872 required the county recorder to provide the assessor with information on the title to all property in the county annually, and this information made it virtually impossible to escape taxation on real property and improvements. Moreover, in a rapidly growing city like San Francisco, where there was frequent turnover in real estate, it was relatively easy to calculate the valuation of property by comparing it with similar parcels recently sold. This did not mean, of course, that the property was always assessed at what would have been full cash value, but the city did have one of the most accurate valuations in the state. The census of 1890, for example, noted that the city's assessed valuation of real property was 75 percent of "real" value. This put San Francisco ahead of all other California cities except Eureka, which was only a fraction of its size. Nonetheless, the assessed value of real estate and improvements was by no means an automatic reflection of changing real estate values. We can see this by measuring the correlation between the assessed valuation of property and the average value of real estate sales annually. This was a relatively weak 0.33. That between the change in each of these variables was an even weaker 0.23.[33]

The result of these assessment procedures was the total assessed valuation of the city, which is displayed in thousands of real dollars in figure 1 and in its per capita values in figure 2. Between 1860 and 1906 the total grew at an annual rate of 4.78 percent, from about $35 million to about $474 million, while its per capita value doubled from $630 in 1860 to $1,249 in 1906. The rate of growth in the assessed valuation was greater than that of the population, which, in increasing from about 56,000 in 1860 to about 380,000 in 1906, grew at an average rate of 3.5 percent per year. The most important and, in the case of the per capita values, most dramatic moments of change in the valuation oc-

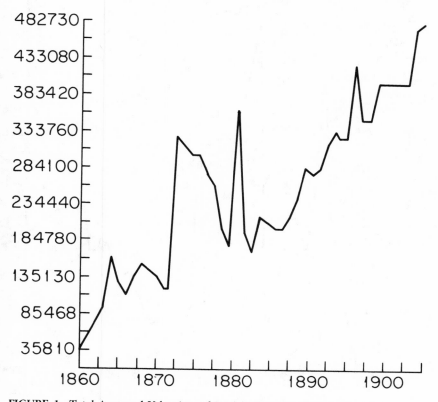

FIGURE 1. Total Assessed Valuation of Real and Personal Property in San Francisco (thousands of real dollars)

curred in fiscal years 1873/74, 1880/81, and 1896/97, and in each year the dramatic increase in the valuation can be explained by reference to change in the definition or enforcement of revenue laws.

The first great jump occurred as a result of the code of 1872, which required a statement of taxable property from each taxpayer, provided stiff penalty assessments for those who failed to cooperate with the assessor, set up the system for recording property transactions for purposes of taxation, and for the first time permitted the assessment of bank accounts and mortgages against the banks holding them. As a result of this law, the state's total valuation of real property increased 140 percent over the previous year, while that of personal property increased 155 percent. In San Francisco the increases were 137 percent and 273 percent, respectively, the latter because the mortgages and

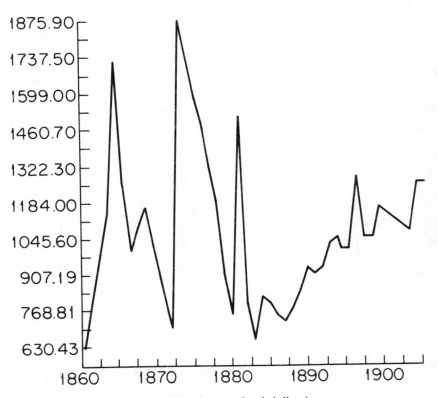

FIGURE 2.   Per Capita Assessed Valuation (real dollars)

bank accounts were included on the personal property list. Complaints by local banks led the board of supervisors, sitting as a board of equalization, to strike the mortgages off the taxable list, and a later court decision upheld this action, thus rapidly reducing the increase in the personal property assessment in the next few years. But the changed procedures for valuation of real estate remained, bolstering the contribution of real estate to the total assessed valuation throughout the period.[34]

The second jump in fiscal year 1880/81 was also the result of legal change, this time the new constitution of 1879 and the amendments to the political code in 1880 and 1881 which enforced it. The major change brought about by these acts was the establishment of a state board of equalization, which was to ensure the proper and equal assessment among the counties of the state, both by instructing the county assessors in proper assessment procedures and by raising the valuations of those counties that did not seem to be assessing close enough to the full cash value. For fiscal year 1880/81 the board again instructed local assessors to assess against the banks all the money, gold dust, and bullion on hand. This the San Francisco assessor did, increasing the county's personal property assessment by about 500 percent for that one year. But the banks' refusal to pay on the assessment, followed by legal action against it, stymied this procedure for the next year and, in fact, until 1896.[35]

Again, the impact of the taxation of bank assets on the city's valuation was ephemeral, but the overall change in the revenue law was not, for the influence of the state board of equalization continued to be felt— and feared—in San Francisco. Between 1880 and 1904 the state board raised the assessor's valuation of the city nine times, in amounts ranging from 8 to 30 percent. Luckily, because of a loophole in the revenue law, the first four of these increases—for 1882, 1885, 1886, 1892— applied only to the city's state tax payments, and thus did not affect a citizen's city-county tax bill. Beginning in 1894, however, the increases applied to all assessments, and the city's officials were forced to travel to Sacramento to plead for a reprieve each time such an increase was threatened. Their pleas were to no avail in 1895, 1897, and 1904. When such an increase occurred, the board simply announced the percentage by which the city's entire valuation had to be raised, and the assessor was required to change each taxpayer's assessment accordingly.[36]

The last major jump on the graph, that for 1896/97, was in part the result of this system, for in that year the state board of equalization ordered a 20 percent increase in the total valuation. In addition, a new procedure for the assessment of banks raised the city's personal property assessment role by 45 percent. The local commercial banks had developed several techniques of tax evasion, including the actual hiding of assets or their temporary transfer out of state or into tax-exempt bonds. In 1896, however, the state board of banking commissioners, which inspected and regulated the state's banks semiannually, was required to file one of its reports on the banks' holdings on March first of each year, so that this report could aid county assessors. Because banks had to make a careful and complete report of their holdings to the commission, they were trapped into making the same report to county assessors. As a result of this action, the assessment of money and solvent credits statewide increased 74 percent; in San Francisco, the contribution of personal property to the total assessed valuation increased about 10 percent on average for the years of 1896 to 1906.[37]

As these changes suggest, the development of the city's tax base was by no means a smooth or uninterrupted process. Nonetheless, the base did grow over time—at a rate faster than that of population—and there were strong institutional supports for that growth. That it did not grow more or faster was primarily the result of political factors, including the willingness of the assessor to produce and the supervisors to approve a valuation that was systematically below full cash value, and the power of local banks and businesses to evade and resist the proper valuation of their holdings. Between the revenue base and the production of revenue stood another highly political factor, the tax rate itself.

As will be seen in greater detail in later chapters, a low tax rate was the "Moses and the Prophets" of politicians in San Francisco for most of the nineteenth century, and the party that did not condemn governmental "extravagance" and pledge to lower the rate even further was rare indeed. It was partly for this reason that, although the Consolidation Act permitted the total tax rate to rise to $2.25, the rate hit that maximum in current dollars only in the first three fiscal years of this period. As figure 3 reveals, soon after that a plunge began that averaged −2.3 percent per year. The rate was highest before the political code of 1872, mostly because of the insecurity of the city's tax base and because the assessment roll was not completed before the tax rate had to be set. When these problems were remedied by the acts, the rate began to "seek its own level," which was declared by the political parties during the 1880s to be the 1 percent level, or a rate of $1 per $100 of assessed valuation for real and personal property. As table 3 indicates, this rate was reached regularly during the 1880s and 1890s.[38]

Generally, change in the tax rate and in the assessed valuation were

TABLE 3
TAX RATE PER $100 OF ASSESSED VALUATION IN CURRENT AND REAL DOLLARS

	1860	1880	1898	1905	Overall mean
Current dollars	$2.25	$1.37	$1.00	$1.12	$1.37
Real dollars	$2.25	$1.11	$1.19	$1.05	$1.48

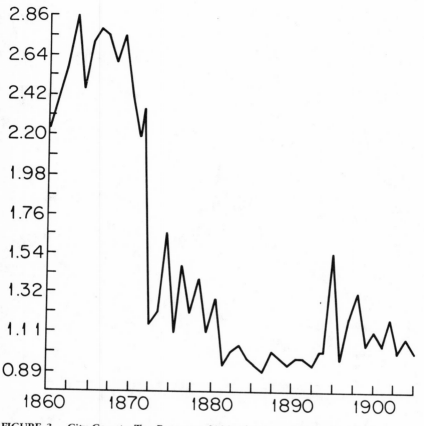

FIGURE 3. City-County Tax Rate per $100 of Assessed Valuation (real dollars)

inversely related; when the valuation went up, the tax rate went down. Thus the correlation between the two overall was a strongly negative −0.74, and the correlation between the changes in the two from year to year was −0.24. As the persistent nudging by the state board of equalization suggests, the city's political leaders preferred both a low tax rate and a low assessed valuation, but they settled for the former.

In combination, then, the assessed valuation and the tax rate produced the local tax revenue, which, together with the fees and licenses, constituted the total local revenue displayed in thousands of real dollars in figure 4 and in its per capita values in figure 5. The total revenue

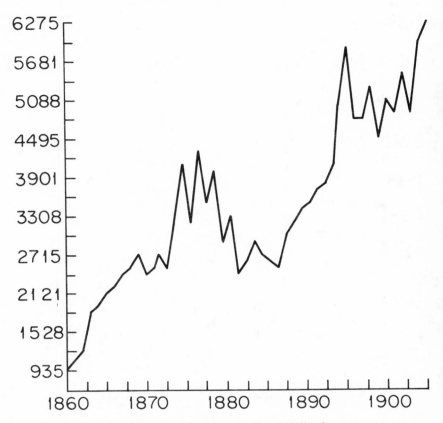

FIGURE 4. Total Local Revenue (thousands of real dollars)

increased at an average annual rate of about 2.5 percent, growing from $935,000 in 1860 to about $6 million in 1905. The overall growth was, of course, generated by the increase in the value of the city's tax base. Because the vast majority of local revenue was tax revenue, which was a simple function of the assessed valuation and the tax rate, by looking at changes in the base we have already seen most of the systemic reasons for the short-term fluctuations and the overall trend in total local revenue.

It is important to note the effect of the city's declining tax rate on its revenue-producing ability, however. As we have seen, while the total valuation grew at an average annual rate of 4.78 percent, the tax revenue grew only at 2.7 percent, and the total revenue by only 2.5 percent. The city's declining tax rate almost halved its revenue-producing

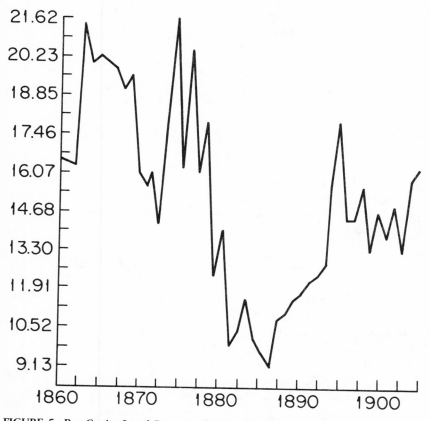

FIGURE 5. Per Capita Local Revenue (real dollars)

ability, dropping the rate of growth in the city's revenue below that of the rate of growth in population. Therefore, per capita local revenue declined at a rate of 0.8 percent per year on average and there were occasional sharp declines in per capita revenue, as shown in table 4 and figure 5. Of particular importance here is the real trough in the tax rate and in local revenue between about 1880 and 1896. Deficits were prevented, however, by the large balance of cash on hand carried by the city, which was not included in the series of revenue raised. These annual balances ranged from $26,000 to about $6 million and averaged about $1 million. For example, the city began the fiscal years in table 4 with balances of $46,000 for 1860, $1.4 million for 1880, $1.5 million for 1898, and $1.8 million for 1905.

The most important point is that, in general, there were no disabling

TABLE 4

TOTAL AND PER CAPITA LOCAL REVENUE

	1860	1880	1898	1905	Overall mean
Total (1000s)	$935.00	$2885.00	$4841.00	$6004.00	$3481.00
Per capita	16.46	12.33	14.49	15.80	15.07

shocks to the city's revenue system produced by political factors beyond its control. The state legislature provided stability in the definitions of the tax base, sanctions for refusal to cooperate with the assessor, an effective system for the valuation of real property and improvements, and a series of laws that broadened, rather than narrowed, the city's revenue base. The state did this not out of love for the city but because its revenues, too, were dependent on a stable taxation system. Of course, the personal property of the rich and powerful escaped the assessor for the most part, as did that of the poor and powerless (although they had a great deal less of it). This evasion was less a defect in the legal structure than in the political will of both state and local officials. In theory, it was always possible to find more taxable assets, raise assessments and the tax rate, and thus produce more revenue, but in political reality this was more difficult.

Although expenditure need not always be closely related to revenue, in nineteenth-century San Francisco it was, and thus the patterns in total and per capita expenditure recapitulated those we have already seen in revenue. Figure 6 displays total local expenditure in thousands of real dollars, while figure 7 displays the expenditure in per capita terms. Total local expenditure includes all operating and debt service expenditures of the city, which were financed by its own funds and which therefore resulted from the city's own fiscal policies. As figures 6 and 7 show, the total local expenditure grew over time at an annual rate of about 2.1 percent, while the per capita amount declined overall at an average rate of −1.19 percent per year. Per capita expenditure not only fell behind the growth in population but also seemed to contain two separate trends, that during the period before 1880 and that after that year (see table 5).

The components of the local expenditure included eight funds for operating or current expenditures and four for debt service. Table 6

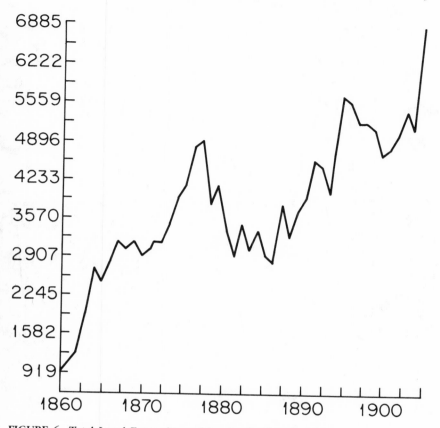

FIGURE 6. Total Local Expenditure (thousands of real dollars)

shows the shares of total operating and debt service expenditure over time, and table 7 shows the shares of total expenditure going to each of the component categories. Over the entire period, operating expenditure averaged about 80 percent of the total, although it was not until the 1880s that this share was reached regularly.

The first thing noticeable in table 7 is the changing number of expenditure categories over time; thus a brief consideration of the purpose and extent of these categories will be helpful at this point. In 1860 the city had four funds for operating expenditure—the General Fund, School Fund, School Building Fund, and Street Lighting Fund. The first of these financed police, fire, social welfare, administration, and maintenance expenses; the second, the salary and operating expenses of the school system; the third, the expenses of constructing schoolhouses

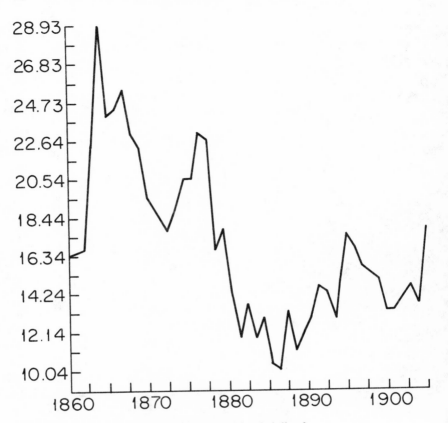

FIGURE 7. Per Capita Local Expenditure (real dollars)

TABLE 5
TOTAL AND PER CAPITA LOCAL EXPENDITURE

	1860	1880	1898	1905	Overall mean
Total (1000s)	$919.29	$4147.30	$5202.60	$5130.00	$3810.00
Per capita	16.18	17.73	15.58	13.53	16.84

TABLE 6
SHARES OF OPERATING AND DEBT SERVICE EXPENDITURE

Category	1860	1880	1898	1905	Overall mean
Share of operating expenditure	54%	67%	94%	99%	81%
Share of debt service expenditure	46%	33%	6%	0.06%	19%

TABLE 7
SHARES OF FUNDS COMPRISING TOTAL LOCAL EXPENDITURE

Expenditure	1860	1880	1898	1905	Overall mean
Operating expenditure					
General Fund	36%	38%	51%	60%	46%
School Fund	11	13	22	21	18
Street Fund	0	6	9	8	6
Street Light Fund	4	5	5	5	5
Park Improvement Fund	0	0.98	3	5	2
City Hall Fund	0	3	1	0	2
School Building Fund	3	0.64	1	0	1
Library Fund	0	0	0.95	1	0.4
Debt service expenditure					
All sinking funds	6	24	4	0.61	11
All interest accounts	5	6	1	0	3
Corporate Debt Fund	34	0	0	0	3
Railroad bonds	0	2	0	0	2

(which were built by contractors, not city labor); and the fourth, the lamps, fuel, and labor to light the streets.[39]

Street work and park improvement were originally financed through the General Fund but were split off into their own funds in 1865 and 1867, respectively. The Street Department Fund financed the building of curbs, sewers, and sidewalks and the repair and cleaning of streets.

Throughout the nineteenth century, the cost of grading and building streets was assessed directly to the adjacent property owners. The Park Fund was used primarily for the construction of the city's famous Golden Gate Park, but also for other park work. The City Hall Fund financed the construction of a building to replace the original city hall damaged in an earthquake in 1866. The building of the hall was a current expenditure because most of it was financed on a pay-as-you-go basis from year to year, and thus took from 1873 to 1899 to complete. Finally, the Library Fund originated in response to a state law establishing libraries around the state in 1880. All of these funds continued from the year of their establishment until the old charter was replaced in 1900. The city hall, of course, was completed by the end of the century, and its fund disappeared then. Under the reform charter, which went into effect in 1900, the Street and Street Light funds were combined with the General Fund again, but I have removed them here to complete the series.[40]

In the case of debt service expenditure, there was a sinking fund and an interest account for each bond issue, the former to receive specified annual sums to retire the bonds at their maturation, the latter to pay the annual interest on the bonds. Most of the bonds issued by the city in these years were for twenty to twenty-five years at 6 to 7 percent interest. Because sinking fund and interest accounts went for the same purposes for different bond issues, I have combined them into the two general sinking fund and interest account categories shown in table 7. In addition to these categories, which extended throughout the period, there were two short-term debt service expenditure funds, the Corporate Debt Fund and the Fund for Railroad Bonds. The first was established in 1851 and continued in 1856 to fund the debt of the city's pre–Consolidation Act period. The city paid into this fund until 1871. The second was for interest and principal on bonds to purchase stock in the Central Pacific Railway during the transcontinental railroad speculative fever of the 1860s. The city paid into this fund from 1864 through 1895.[41]

Three major points are suggested by the data in table 7. The first and perhaps the most important is the relatively sharp decline in the share of the city's expenditure going for debt service. Although the share of debt service was high in 1860—about 45 percent of total expenditure—by 1880 it had dropped to about 32 percent, by 1898 it took just 5 percent of the city's expenditure, and by 1905 the city was almost

TABLE 8

MAJOR SHARES OF GENERAL FUND EXPENDITURE

	1860	1880	1898	1905	Overall mean
Police and fire	27%	36%	46%	48%	39%
Executive and legislative	25	22	16	missing	19[a]
Social welfare	14	11	8	7	12
Election expenses	0	5	1	4	3

[a] For 1860–1899 only.

"free and clear." Unlike many American cities that staggered through the nineteenth century under enormous debt service expenditures, San Francisco's expenditures for this purpose were more than manageable.

A second important point is that the money freed by the retirement of the debt was not returned to the taxpayers but was reinvested in other city activities, by increasing either the number of those activities or the shares of total expenditure going to preexisting ones. Throughout this period, total real expenditure grew regularly, as, on the whole, the shares of the major activities did. Related to this is the third pattern, which is the significant stability of the shares of the major categories of expenditure throughout these years. The General Fund and school and street expenses took the lion's share of both operating and total expenditure; together, in fact, they accounted for almost 70 percent of the latter overall. Because these funds were so important, it is helpful to take a brief look at their composition, too.

As the fund for the general purpose of running the city, the General Fund financed everything from the mayor's salary to the fees paid for the removal of dead dogs from the streets. On average, however, more than 70 percent of the total fund and 84 percent of the salary expenditures on the fund went for the four groups of expenditure activities listed in table 8: (1) the salary and nonsalary operating expenses of the police and fire departments; (2) the salaries of local-government legislative and executive officials, their deputies and clerks; (3) salary and nonsalary expenses of the city's social welfare activities, including its almshouse, hospital, industrial (reform) school, and health department; and (4) the expenses of conducting local, state, and national elections.

The remaining 30 percent of the fund was composed of ad hoc or poorly segregated expenditures, which were difficult to follow over time.[42]

The importance of the General Fund in the city's political economy stemmed both from its share of the total local expenditure and from the share of the fund itself that met salary expenses. On average, 45 percent of the city's total expenditure and 55 percent of its operating expenditures went to the General Fund, while an average of 62 percent of the fund was dedicated to the payment of salaries. For good reason, then, the fund was frequently the focus of debate about the city's fiscal situation. It was also an important part of the ongoing political struggle over and commentary on patronage.

The other major funds also devoted significant portions of their funds to salary expenditures. The School Fund received 17 percent of the total local expenditure, 83 percent of which paid the salaries of teachers, janitors, and school census marshals. The street department expended about 48 percent of its resources on salaries for laborers hired by the city, and another 35 percent for contracts let for street work. About 47 percent of the Park Improvement Fund went for salaries, too. Taken together, in fact, the salary expenditures of the General, School, Street, and Park funds averaged about 65 percent of all the city's operating expenditures. The only exception to this pattern among the major funds was the Street Light Fund, the overwhelming majority of which went for gas and lamps to keep the streets lighted. In 1880, for example, 96 percent of the fund was spent for this purpose.

Like local revenue, then, local expenditure grew over time, although not as quickly as population. However, the meaning of growth in expenditure was significantly different from that of growth in revenue. Throughout this period, a dollar of revenue essentially meant a dollar of revenue, whereas the meaning of a dollar of expenditure changed radically over time. In 1860 the latter meant $0.54 for operating expenditure and $0.46 for debt service, but by 1898 those shares had shifted significantly, as had some of the shares of the components of these categories, and the shares within those components that went toward salary and nonsalary expenses.

In describing these aspects of change and stability in the city's valuation, tax rate, revenue, and expenditure, we have cleared the way for an explanation of them, by establishing that the institutional environment within which municipal fiscal policy was made was relatively autonomous, well-defined, and stable. We have also identified moments of significant institutional change affecting fiscal policy, so that we will not mistakenly attribute these changes to other factors. Having done this, we can now attempt to explain fiscal policy by means of local socio-economic or political cultural influences. In the next chapter we leave the relative stability of the city's legal and institutional history for the history of its socioeconomic development, which changed much more rapidly.

3

Testing the Socioeconomic Structural Theory

American urban historians have suggested a number of complementary explanations for developments in the scope and scale of urban government, such as those described in chapter 2. These explanations generally agree that the growth of municipal functions and expenditures was propelled by developments in what I have called socioeconomic structural factors, such as a city's economic base, social and economic composition, and demographic characteristics. The socioeconomic structural theory proposes that increasing population or economic development generated demands for increasing government administration or services, and that government functions multiplied and expenditures increased in response to these implicit or explicit demands. Accordingly, as Glaab and Brown have summarized it, urban governments "spent more money in order to satisfy growing needs."[1]

Such a theory can be distinguished analytically from what I have called the political cultural theory not only in its emphasis on socioeconomic structural factors but also by (1) its representation of urban government as primarily a dependent rather than independent variable (i.e., something influenced by the urban environment, rather than vice versa); (2) its conceptualization of the relationship between urban services and the urban environment as a "market" or supply-and-demand relationship; and (3) its general rejection of political explanations for the expansion of municipal government. Thus in a recent example of this sort of analysis, Alan Anderson argues that "whatever the nature of the decisionmaking process, it is secondary to technical and economic considerations."[2]

However, the distinction here is primarily for analytical purposes because, as noted earlier, the socioeconomic structural and political cultural theories have coexisted in the historical literature, frequently in the same works, although sometimes in different sections of them. The former theory has generally been used to explain the overall development of the urban public sector; the latter, the special cases of bosses and reformers. Moreover, few historians argue that there was no mediation of structural change by political institutions. But many do argue that socioeconomic structural change usually overwhelmed political actors and institutions, so that the balance between socioeconomic and political factors as causes of the development of municipal government was tipped decidedly in favor of socioeconomic change.

An analytical distinction between the two theories is necessary to determine more accurately the relative explanatory power of each. To this end, we first extract the general outlines of the socioeconomic structural theory from several works that have presented it in detail; then use the theory as a guide to factors in the socioeconomic history of San Francisco which might have influenced municipal expenditure there; and finally derive hypotheses from the theory which can be tested statistically with the San Francisco data.

ELEMENTS OF THE THEORY

The pervasiveness of the socioeconomic structural theory is suggested in table 9, which lists the variables presumed to have influenced the growth of municipal expenditure in representative works of three generations of urban history. From Griffith's classic two-volume study of the history of municipal government through Still's analysis of Milwaukee in the city biography genre, from the textbooks by Glaab and Brown, Miller, and Chudacoff to the most recent economic analysis of this issue by Anderson, the lists of variables have differed in size and completeness, but the overall theory has remained the same. In all these works, expenditure has been presumed to increase primarily in response to two factors: (1) the demands for municipal services resulting from the negative externalities of the processes of population growth, industrialization, and the physical expansion of the city; and (2) the choice of an urban population enjoying increasing per capita income to spend some of that income on improved municipal services.[3]

The most straightforward presentation of the theory behind the variables listed in table 9 appears in Anderson's analysis of the growth of

TABLE 9
VARIABLES IN THE HYPOTHESES

Authors	Variables in the hypotheses
Griffith (1927)	Population growth Improved economic status of the individual Social consciousness
Still (1948)	Developments in science Increased wealth Population growth and its attendant problems
Glaab & Brown (1967)	Accelerating urbanization Rapid industrialization Physical expansion of the city Commercial growth Industrial growth
Miller (1973)	Rapid population growth Expanded scale of urban life Increasing size and heterogeneity of urban electorate Social, economic, political, demographic change
Chudacoff (1975)	Increasing population Accelerating industrialization Commercial expansion Technological change Immigration Rise of tenement neighborhoods Myriad new households Myriad new businesses
Anderson (1977)	Population growth Increasing per capita income

expenditure in Baltimore. According to Anderson, nineteenth-century American cities walked a tightrope between the positive and negative aspects of the agglomeration economies they produced. On the positive side, increasing density of population and economic activities were the basis of the comparative advantage that fueled the growth of cities. On the negative side, the congestion, pollution, and illness produced by the same densities threatened to make the cities unlivable, thus undermining their economic viability. Local government was called on to internalize these negative externalities, both by dealing with the social problems caused by increasing population and economic activity and by providing services such as education and policing, which the private sector would not provide. Thus the rise in municipal outlays came about because of the growing demand that something be done about conditions in the city: "the incidence of demand is a rather simple proposition ... more people needed more services, and higher incomes will go, in part, for more municipal services."[4]

The explanations behind most of the other lists in table 9 are variations on this theme. In Griffith's analysis, population growth created a more complex urban society that needed more necessities from urban government. Prosperity, which he defined as improvement in the economic status of the individual, resulted in a demand for improved and more numerous services from city government. For Still, the expansion of municipal administration was a trend that "developments in science and increased wealth encouraged and the growth of population and its attendant problems made inevitable." In A History of Urban America, Glaab and Brown suggested simply that city growth produced an "increasing number of tasks which had to be fulfilled," so that there was "no way to avoid the increasing range and scale of governmental activity." Miller, too, argued that municipalities "found it impossible to keep up with the expanding needs" for services generated by the unexpectedly rapid growth of urban populations, while Chudacoff noted that similar factors "strained existing services and created an urgent need for more."[5]

Others echo this familiar theme. In his 1970 analysis of the breakdown of municipal finance in the late nineteenth century, C. K. Yearley argued that "demands for greater profits, comfort, and convenience prodded public expenditures upward," and that "pressures of population alone required expensive social engineering." The editors of a recent collection of essays on municipal progressivism have also noted that "the coalescence of industrialization, urbanization, and immigration telescoped urban development far beyond the existing capabilities of most city dwellers and their institutions," prompting "proliferating demands for urban services." Maury Klein and Harvey Kantor described the industrial city as "a sea of interests and ambitions, needs and demands, whose waves lapped incessantly at city hall." Alexander Callow attributed the rise of the political boss in part to the fact that "growth triggered a demand for an array of new services providing both necessities

and amenities of city living." In contrast, Hays suggested that these trans-
formations led to urban progressivism because as population density
increased, the "intensity of claim and counter-claim in [political] decisionmaking also increased," and the progressives set out to "limit the
variety of such claims."[6]

As mentioned in chapter 1, there is a great tendency toward reifi-
cation within this framework. While it may be safe to conceive of demands playing some role in determining the gross level of expenditure,
it is surely stretching the point to argue that growth or demands also
brought about major political changes. Growth and demands did not
vote, hold office, or prepare budgets. More important, a theory that
explains everthing—changes in expenditure, bosses, reformers, and so
on—ultimately explains nothing.

This surrender of analysis to reified needs and demands is a problem
not only of theoretical lassitude but also of empirical specification. To
propose that urban government expenditure is a function of change in
the urban environment, both sides of this relationship must be properly
specified, and urban historians have rarely specified the combination of
variables driving growth in governmental expenditure. As already suggested, this has been a problem both of leaving some important (perhaps political) variables out of the relationship and of defining the
variables that are included. Population growth, for example, can be
specified in any number of ways—as total population, rate of population
growth, population density, and so forth. Similarly, industrialization has
a number of specific meanings, such as value of product, value added
by manufacture, and capitalization per plant. The factors suggested by
historians are umbrella terms covering a host of processes. Some are
directly related to the growth of expenditure; but others are related
only in the sense that in nineteeth-century America, every aspect of the
urban environment was growing and changing, and thus seemed to be
related to growth.

This is clear when we consider the variables listed in table 9. First,
although the lists of environmental variables have changed somewhat
over time, the variables have retained their overall level of generality.
Taken together, these variables have been used to explain almost every
development in the nineteenth-century American urban environment.
Second, the list reveals a good deal of overlap. For example, population
growth and concentration, increasing prosperity and industrialization
appear in one form or another in each list, suggesting that beneath the

different names of the variables there are only a few fundamental processes at work.

Fortunately, in postulating a relationship between the growth of urban government expenditure and the joint additive effects of a combination of environmental variables, these historians have suggested a theory of development of urban fiscal policy from which a hypothesis can be drawn. This hypothesis can be tested by means of multiple regression analysis, a statistical technique explained in some detail in appendix B. For such a test to be valid, however, the general hypothesis must be compared with the actual history of the case study. This means it must be adjusted to the reality and specificity of San Francisco's socioeconomic structural development.

In the next section, we review those factors in the city's development which ought to have a significant effect on the development of municipal fiscal policy, according to the socioeconomic structural theory. Specifically, we consider the growth, composition, and density of the city's population; the city's changing physical size; trends in its development as a commercial center; patterns of development in manufacturing; and the economic well-being of its citizens, as revealed by wages paid and the city's developing opportunity structure. Most of this section is based on previous studies of the city's socioeconomic history, along with census data. In addition, we examine time-series of socioeconomic data collected for this study which have not been analyzed before. Some of this information is used for the statistical testing of the socioeconomic structural theory in the last section of this chapter, and some of it is reviewed here to provide necessary background for later chapters of this book.

The review that follows does not prove that San Francisco was similar to or representative of other American cities during the last half of the nineteenth century. Such proof would require complicated cross-sectional statistical analysis beyond the scope of this inquiry. But our review does demonstrate that the city's socioeconomic development was not remarkably atypical in any obvious way. More important for our purposes, it also shows that the city experienced aspects of that development identical to those which the socioeconomic structural theory suggests should influence the growth of municipal government. For example, San Francisco's population grew rapidly, was ethnically diverse, and spread rapidly through the city's area, while its economy, balanced between commercial and industrial activities, expanded steadily and produced an opportunity structure quite similar to those of other cities of comparable size. Because San Francisco's development fits the framework of the socioeconomic structural theory, it can be tested in the last section of this chapter. This test reveals that measures of this development neither explain the growth of city government very well nor explain it in the way the theory proposes.

SAN FRANCISCO'S SOCIOECONOMIC DEVELOPMENT

It is said that the first Mexican governor of California reported to his government that the area was "too good for convicts, but not exactly a desirable place for decent people." Obviously, this was the impression neither of those who flocked to San Francisco in response to the Gold Rush of 1848 nor of those who saw the various opportunities provided thereafter by a growing commercial-industrial city, building San Francisco into the nation's ninth largest, leading West Coast port and eighth most valuable manufacturing center by 1900. Throughout the latter half of the nineteenth century, San Francisco was one of the largest and fastest-growing cities in the United States. Its population, displayed in table 10, grew at an average rate of about 55 percent per decade from 1860 to 1900. In 1860, it ranked thirteenth in population among all American cities, and at the end of each subsequent decade until 1900, it remained in the top ten. Assuming that population increased at an annual rate of one-tenth the rate between decades, San Francisco experienced the steady upward growth shown in figure 8.[7]

Throughout these years, San Francisco had one of the most foreign-born populations of all American cities. The city's population was one-half foreign-born in 1860 and 1870, and it had the highest foreign-born proportion of any of the nation's fifty largest cities in those years, as

TABLE 10

CENSUS STATISTICS OF POPULATION AND PERCENT FOREIGN-BORN
SAN FRANCISCO RESIDENTS BY DECADE

	1860	1870	1880	1890	1900
Total population	56,802	149,473	233,959	298,997	342,782
Percent foreign-born	50%	49%	44%	42%	34%

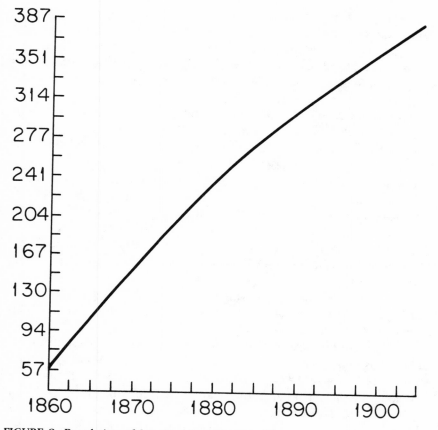

FIGURE 8. Population of San Francisco (thousands)

well as in 1880. Moreover, the drop in the share of foreign-born to about one-third of the population by 1900 was not a good measure of the decline of ethnicity in the city, because in 1900 an additional 50 percent of the population was composed of persons one or both of whose parents had been born abroad. By this measure San Francisco was the most ethnic of the largest cities of America in 1900.[8]

The largest foreign-born groups were the Chinese, the Irish, and the Germans. In addition, there were significant numbers of those born in England, Wales, Scotland, Scandinavia, and Italy. Because the Chinese were socially isolated and politically impotent, the city seemed to be dominated socially and politically by four groups: native-born Americans; Irish; Germans; and those from England, Wales, and Scotland. With the exception of the Chinese, most of the city's foreign-born did not come directly from their country of birth, but from eastern cities. For example, Robert Burchell found that only 5 percent of the Irish in San Francisco in 1852 had come directly from Ireland, and he argued that there is little evidence for an increase in this proportion from then until 1880.[9]

Because of a combination of legal and physical obstacles, the population spread rather slowly through the 47.5 square miles granted by the charter of 1856. The legal obstacles were a series of land claims to the area of the city, most of which dated from the Mexican period. Because of these claims and the litigation surrounding them, legal titles to real estate within the 1851 city limits—the Bay on the east and north, Divisadero on the west, and 22nd and Napa on the south—were not established until 1868, and titles to the area outside of that to the south and west were not confirmed until ten years later. The physical obstacles included large sand hills on what is now Market Street, which were not cleared until 1862, and stronger hills of earth and stone (e.g., Telegraph Hill, Nob Hill, Russian Hill), which were conquered by means of the cable car after its invention in 1873, and by the extension of the cable car lines to the north and west by 1880.[10]

Accounts of the spread of population through the city agree that until the 1870s most people were located within the central portions of the 1851 city limits, in districts separated by Market Street and called the 50 and 100 *vara* areas, after the Spanish yards in which they had been surveyed. The Potrero District, to the southeast of these, was the next most populous area, in part because of the manufacturing and shipbuilding there. During the 1870s the population began the movement southward and westward which would continue throughout this period. Cable car lines going up the hills allowed settlement of the western edge of the 50 vara area by 1873. By 1875 a car line ran from the 50 and 100 vara areas into the Western Addition, the district at the original city's western edge, between Divisadero and Van Ness streets. In 1880 a second line was extended into that area, and observers noted that Divisadero Street was becoming built up by 1883. In the 1870s and 1880s the Mission District, which ran southward from the 100 vara area west of the Potrero, began to fill in, and during the 1890s the Outside Lands, the area west of Divisadero to the Pacific Ocean, began to be settled.[11]

These accounts are confirmed by records of real estate sales, which indicate that the shares of sales in the 50 and 100 vara and Potrero areas were higher than average between 1860 and 1875, higher than average in the Mission and Western Addition between 1875 and 1887, and in the Outside Lands after 1887. Taken together, contemporary accounts and real estate records suggest that these years demarcate three major periods in the population's spread across the peninsula, and thus in the density of the total population. Thus although the city's legal boundaries, established in the charter of 1856, never changed, the spread and density of population within those boundaries did shift.[12]

The influx of population from elsewhere was stimulated primarily by economic opportunity in a variety of enterprises built upon the two foundation stones of the city's economy—commerce and industry. The two developed unevenly, however, with commerce dominating until about 1880 and inhibiting the growth of the city's manufacturing sector. Because the two sectors were not closely linked until later in the century, we consider them separately here.

As Peter Decker has written, San Francisco never really existed as a village, "but immediately adopted a metropolitan economy with specialized, full-time merchants." These businessmen extended their trading networks as far east as the Rockies, up and down the Pacific Coast, and ultimately west to Hawaii, China, and, of course, around the Horn to the eastern cities until the arrival of the transcontinental railroad in 1869. From the city's origins until the late nineteenth century, there were no appreciable commercial rivals on the West Coast.[13]

The city's commercial dominance was based both on its natural advantages—a deep-water harbor with inland access via the Sacramento River—and on its good fortune as the commercial gateway to the California Gold Rush in 1848. At the outset the city's trade was tied primarily to the mining industry, and thus involved exchanging gold and silver for mining equipment and the necessities of life, almost none of which were produced locally. As the state's agricultural sector began to develop in 1860s and 1870s, unprocessed agricultural products such as wheat became an important part of the trade, and when, after 1880, the processing of agricultural goods became an important industry in the city, these joined the list of exports. By 1880 the city had capitalized on its initial advantages and become the only full-service commercial center on the West Coast.[14]

An important part of the city's commercial sector was a well-developed array of financial institutions. Because the merchants needed fi-

TABLE 11

CENSUS STATISTICS OF SHARE OF OCCUPATIONS IN
TRADE AND TRANSPORTATION ACTIVITIES BY DECADE

	1860	1870	1880	1890	1900
Share of occupations in trade and transportation	25%	28%	28%	28%	33%

nancing and residents needed mortgages and deposit services, banks sprang up quickly in the city, with five commercial banks opening between 1849 and 1852 and the first savings banks incorporated in 1857 and 1859. In part because of this early start, San Francisco remained the leading banking area in the state. It was not until 1884, for example, that there was a single incorporated savings bank in California outside of San Francisco, where there were nine savings banks holding $36 million in assets and nine commercial banks holding $39 million in assets. By 1900 the nine savings banks in the city held $129 million in assets and there were eighteen commercial banks holding a total of $74 million.[15]

The significance of these activities in the city's overall economy is indicated by the share of total occupations in the trade and transportation sector during these years (see table 11). The share of trade and transportation occupations grew from one-fourth to one-third of the total during these years and was one of the fastest-growing segments of the occupational structure. The number of persons employed in this sector increased at an average rate of 47 percent per decade, jumping 71 percent between 1870 and 1880, 37 percent the next decade, and 33 percent between 1890 and 1900.[16]

In addition to this indicator of the growth of the commercial sector, contemporaries watched closely three annual measures of the health of local commerce: (1) the total value of imports and exports at the port of San Francisco, (2) the number of real estate sales, and (3) the value of bank clearings (see figs. 9, 10, and 11). The port statistics and bank clearings are given in real dollars.

Because shippers were required to register their cargoes with the U.S. Customs House, records of business at the port began to be kept in 1848. Figure 9 displays the total imports and exports there from 1860 to 1906. This is not, of course, a measure of the exports produced by San Francisco or of imports consumed in the city, because much of the

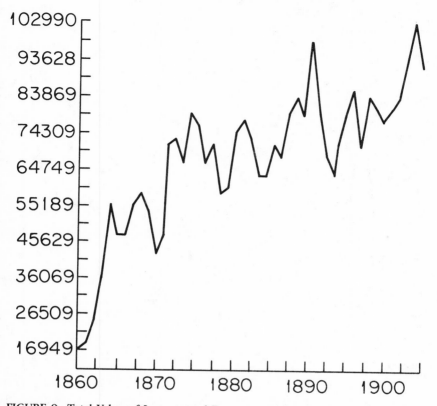

FIGURE 9. Total Value of Imports and Exports at the Port (thousands of real dollars)

total volume was the result of transshipment. Rather, figure 9 is an indication of the activity of the port, and thus of an important part of the city's commercial sector. The trend suggests that the volume of activity at the port grew significantly over time, although that growth was by no means stable. Significant downturns are evident in the late 1860s, late 1870s, and mid-1890s.[17]

In 1867, the San Francisco *Real Estate Circular* began publishing monthly summaries of the real estate transactions in the city, including the number and value of sales both citywide and within the districts of the city referred to earlier. These reports were watched closely and discussed in detail in local newspapers because it was believed, as Young has written, that "the effects of bad business very promptly exhibited themselves in the dullness of the real estate market." In fact, in these

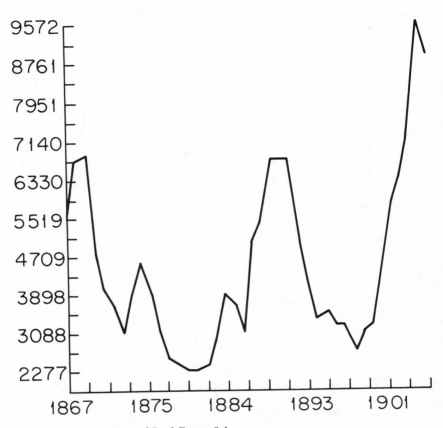

FIGURE 10. Numbers of Real Estate Sales

data we see for the first time the full-scale boom-and-bust cycle characteristic of the nineteenth-century American economy, with significant
downward movement in the late 1860s, late 1870s, and early 1890s.[18]

The city's bankers organized the San Francisco Clearing House Association in 1876 so that representatives of member banks could meet
daily to exchange drafts drawn on one another and thus relieve themselves of the burden of hauling gold bullion through the streets. Along
with the real estate reports, the monthly and annual reports of the
association were thought to be an important guide to local financial
conditions, but in fact they were not. Because of the widespread use
of gold coin instead of bank drafts, the clearings underestimated the
trends in commercial activity (see fig. 11). Moreover, because San Francisco was a regional banking center, the clearings represented not only

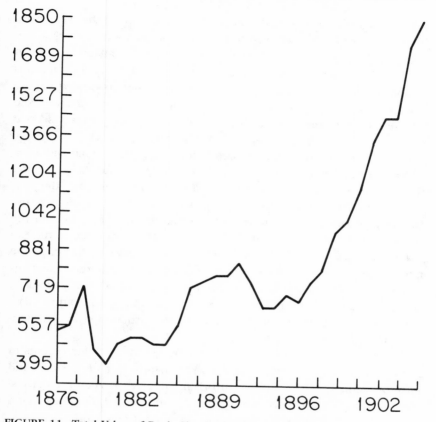

FIGURE 11. Total Value of Bank Clearings (thousands of real dollars)

activity in the city but the city's role as a regional finance center as well. Thus the cycles in the clearings imitate those in real estate sales and port business but lack the volatility of those series.[19]

Taken together, these indexes suggest that the activities of San Francisco's commercial sector grew significantly over time, but that this pattern of overall growth was punctuated by significant downturns in the late 1860s and 1870s as well as the early 1890s. To determine whether this was characteristic of the local economy as a whole, we turn to the industrial sector of the economy.

In 1860, San Francisco ranked ninth among American cities in the value of manufactured product—quite an accomplishment for a city in which only about 2.6 percent of the population was engaged in manufacturing, mostly in workshops and small factories. Unfortunately, this

ranking was spurious, because more than 52 percent of the city's manufactured "product" came from the refining of gold, a process that employed only fifteen workers in the entire city and that added only about
10 percent to the already enormous value of the gold itself. When this
"manufacturing" was subtracted from the city's total, its rank was more
precise. With about 56,000 inhabitants in 1860, San Francisco ranked
fifteenth among American cities in population but only twenty-second
in terms of its real (i.e., non-gold) manufactured product.[20]

Although the prosperity produced in San Francisco by gold and, later,
silver was real enough, production of the precious metals did inhibit
the development of manufacturing self-sufficiency, and thus the self-
sustaining economic development characteristic of a diversified manufacturing economy. This was true, in the first place, because neither the
Gold Rush of 1848 nor the silver bonanza of 1859 occurred in the San
Francisco area, but rather a significant distance east of the city. The
mining industry conducted its financial and commercial dealings
through San Francisco, since almost all manufactured and processed
goods needed for mining and miners had to be imported from the East
Coast. But it was some time before there was production in San Francisco for use in the industry.[21]

In the meantime, the mining industry pulled the vital ingredients of
manufacturing—labor, capital, entrepreneurship—out of the city and
into the mining digs. It was not surprising, then, that when the census-
takers looked for manufactures in San Francisco in 1860, they found
only 229 such establishments employing only 1,564 workers. Nevertheless, by 1880 the city had experienced what urban geographer Robert Elgie has called a "broadly based, urban centered [manufacturing]
expansion," which resulted in the city's rank of ninth among American
cities in the number of workers employed in manufacturing and in the
value of manufactures in 1880.[22]

Changes in mining itself, the growing size of the city, development
of an agricultural sector in the state's economy, and the effects of the
Civil War combined both to create a demand for manufactured goods
and to lower the costs of developing manufacturing in San Francisco.
Already by the late 1850s, mining was beginning to shift from the relatively labor-intensive placer type to the more captial-intensive quartz
and hydraulic types. This created a demand for specialized manufactured goods and, by raising the capital cost of entry into mining, limited
the number of miners who could afford to mine. Many would-be miners

TABLE 12

CENSUS STATISTICS OF INDUSTRIAL PRODUCTION BY DECADE

	1860	1870	1880	1890	1900
Number of works	229	1223	2971	4059	4002
Workers employed	1,564	12,377	28,442	48,446	46,019
Value of product (1000s of real dollars)	$19,598	$43,001	$63,272	$124,430	$131,750

thus were forced to return to San Francisco where, along with thousands of other migrants, they increased the supply of labor and the demand for food in the city. This demand encouraged both the growth of an agricultural sector in the state's economy and the development of agricultural processing activities in the city. The disruption of shipping lanes by the Civil War reduced the supply of eastern manufactured goods and encouraged their replacement by locally manufactured products. Moreover, the wartime inflation in the East made the greenback-proof environment of San Francisco attractive to both local and outside investors, thus increasing the supply of capital for manufacturing.[23]

The effects of these changes were apparent in the census figures for 1870. Compared with 1860, the total product of San Francisco factories had more than doubled, manufacturing capital had increased almost 1,000 percent, and manufacturing employment was up almost 700 percent. This made San Francisco the tenth largest employer of industrial labor among cities in the United States. As table 12 shows, between 1870 and 1880 the statistics of industrial production again increased, with the number of manufacturing works and men employed more than doubling and the value of manufactures increasing by 47 percent in real dollars. Between 1890 and 1900, however, this growth faltered.[24]

The type of industry developing in these years reflected the city's geographical isolation and its commercial activities because it was, as Elgie has written, geared almost completely to the service of regional and local markets. In 1880 the leading industries were slaughtering and meat packing, sugar refining, boots and shoes, foundries, machinery, men's clothing, and tobacco and cigars. Next in importance were printing, liquor, distilling, carpentry, and flour milling. As the industrial sector developed over the next twenty years, it diversified somewhat but continued to center on consumer rather than producer goods, and the average size of plant remained small. Until 1900, the most productive industries were in food and light consumer items such as slaughtering and packing, sugar refining, bread baking, and flour, coffee, and spice milling. By then the city ranked eighth among U.S. cities in the value of manufactured product, although the share of workers in industrial occupations was smaller than it had been in 1870.[25]

We can take a closer look at the overall trends in manufacturing development by turning to the annual records kept by the county assessor. Beginning in 1866, the assessor was required to return to the state surveyor general an annual statement of the manufacturing activity in the county, based on the assessment forms filled out by manufacturers for county tax purposes. The statement did not include all manufacturing firms in the city, but only those large enough to have assets (buildings, machinery, etc.) owned by a "corporation, association, or company." Throughout this period, the number of firms on the assessor's records was substantially smaller than that discovered by the census-takers, but the average size of those firms was substantially larger; the average number of men per plant was twenty-six on the assessor's list and ten according to the census. Figures 12, 13, and 14 display the number of these larger works, the total number of workers employed there, and the value of products manufactured by these larger firms in thousands of real dollars from 1866 through 1905.[26]

The overall trends in these annual data are similar to those in the census data for the first two decades in question, suggesting fast growth in all three categories until 1880, a slowdown during the first half of that decade, and a recovery in the latter half. But a significant plunge in the annual indicators during the 1890s reveals that the apparent stability in the census figures between 1890 and 1900 masks a sharp decline in production. Among the firms on the assessor's list, the number of manufacturing works fell off by 33 percent from 1891 through 1895, the number of men employed dropped 35 percent from 1891 to 1897, and the value of output dropped 50 percent in real dollars from 1890 to 1897.

The assumption that we can extrapolate from trends in economic activities to the economic condition of a city's inhabitants is, of course, an important part of our interest in such trends. In this sort of analysis, we use real estate sales, port business, industrial production, and so on as proxies for better measures of the effect of economic change on individuals. Two measures superior to these proxies are the average

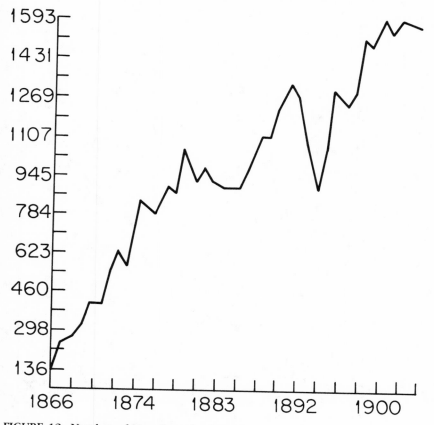

FIGURE 12. Number of Manufacturing Works

wage in manufacturing and the city's developing opportunity structure, so we conclude our analysis of economic activity by turning to them.

Many studies note that from 1860 to 1900, wages paid in San Francisco were among the highest in any city in the nation. Peter Decker has written that between 1860 and 1880, wage rates in California remained about 40 percent higher than they were in the mid-Atlantic states, and Jules Tygiel has observed that in both 1880 and 1890, San Francisco ranked first among the nation's leading industrial centers in the average wages paid to employees in manufacturing. By 1900 the city ranked third, behind Boston and New York.[27]

As both of these authors have noted, however, it is not clear that many San Francisco workers were comparing their wages with those

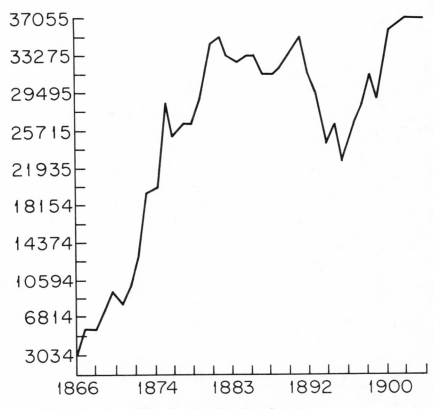

FIGURE 13. Number of Men Employed in Manufacturing

paid to workers in other cities. It is more likely that they considered their lot in terms of their own wage history. A glimpse of this is provided in table 13, where the average wage in manufacturing for the census years is given in both current and real dollars. This figure is derived by dividing the total cost of labor in manufacturing by the number of workers in manufacturing; thus it blurs important distinctions among skill levels, gender, and, in San Francisco, white and Chinese workers. It is important to remember that many employed workers earned less than this and that many other workers were employed only part of the year or were entirely unemployed.[28]

Table 13 does suggest, however, that even whites who were working full time would have been less than enthusiastic about the trend in their wages. The most striking change is the drop of almost half of the dollar value and 40 percent of the purchasing power of the average wage

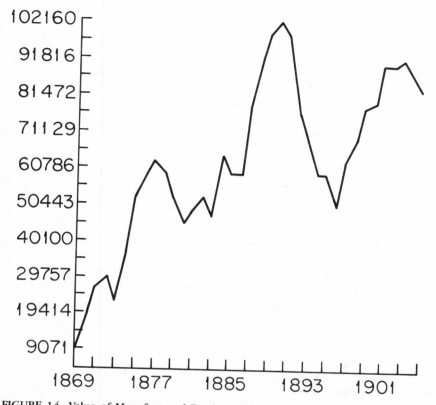

FIGURE 14. Value of Manufactured Products (thousands of real dollars)

between 1860 and 1870. A worker who had been through this decade would have had good reason to bemoan his fate. Yet very few men in San Francisco worked in manufacturing during the halcyon days of the early 1860s. Only about 1,500 persons were employed in manufacturing when wages were that high, compared with 12,377 so employed in 1870, when the wage rate had plummeted. Many of the latter, as noted earlier, had arrived in the city after 1869, when the transcontinental railroad was completed. Decker's mobility study revealed that in 1880, seven out of ten workers in the city had arrived there after 1870, and that less than 8 percent had been there since 1860. Moreover, between 1870 and 1880, despite the depression of the late 1870s, the number of plants and workers—measured by both the census and the city assessor—more than doubled. Therefore, more than 75 percent of the manufacturing jobs existing in 1900 had been created after 1870.[29]

TABLE 13

CENSUS STATISTICS OF AVERAGE WAGE IN MANUFACTURING IN
REAL AND CURRENT DOLLARS

	1860	1870	1880	1890	1900
Current dollars	$1088.92	$584.83	$524.87	$639.46	$478.87
Real dollars	$1088.92	$672.23	$426.70	$582.80	$573.50

In the long run, the change in the average wage between 1870 and 1900 evened itself out in real terms, dropping 36 percent by 1880, increasing by 36 percent by 1890, and dropping a mere 1.5 percent during the next decade. In current dollars, however, this stability was not as apparent; the average dropped 10 percent during the first decade, increased 21 percent during the 1880s, and then dropped 25 percent during the 1890s. How that was interpreted at the time would have depended on a number of factors, including one's previous employment, income, and awareness of the state of one's purchasing power. Another influential factor might have been one's position in the city's opportunity structure.

Because of the recent upsurge of interest in the history of urban opportunity structures, San Francisco has been the subject of several studies dealing with the persistence of its residents, the shape of the city's occupational structure, and the opportunities for its residents to advance in that structure. The most important conclusion of these studies is that San Francisco's experience in these areas was not different from that of other cities in any important way. Peter Decker has noted, for example, that although San Francisco was a "new and dynamic city," between 1850 and 1880 its residents "experienced no occupational gains which surpassed the career opportunities of populations in the eastern cities." For the period 1880 to 1900, Jules Tygiel has argued similarly that "the city's social structure was strikingly similar to those of other areas."[30]

Because of this similarity, the specific findings about the city can be summarized briefly. Throughout the nineteenth century, the rate of persistence in San Francisco hovered around 50 percent per decade—that is to say, about half of the residents of the city turned over every decade. Moreover, from 1850 to 1880, at least, the higher an individual's occupational status, the more likely he was to stay in the city. Within the occupational structure itself, the most important change was what Stephen Erie has called its "whitening." Between 1870 and 1900, the white-collar level of the occupational structure grew almost 36 percent, increasing from 25.9 to 35.2 percent of the total. At the same time, the share of skilled occupations remained almost stable, while that of semi-skilled jobs dropped about 3 percent. The unskilled level decreased the most during these years, from 16.4 percent of the total in 1870 to 8.1 percent in 1900, a drop of 50 percent.[31]

Occupational mobility within blue-collar and white-collar callings was available to San Francisco workers, and mobility between blue- and white-collar occupations was widely available to their children. In both cases, however, mobility was conditioned by ethnic background. In San Francisco, as elsewhere, native-born persons were more likely to be found in skilled and white-collar positions, and if not there already, were more likely than the foreign-born to experience mobility into those positions. In 1880, for example, three-fifths of the city's high white-collar positions were occupied by the native-born, while 75 percent of the semiskilled and unskilled positions were held by immigrants. In 1900, 80 percent of the blue-collar workers in the city were either immigrants or their children.[32]

Occupational attainment was further conditioned by one's ethnicity within the foreign-born group. Germans and Englishmen often rose higher and faster than did the Irish. Throughout this period, the Irish were disproportionately represented at the bottom of the occupational scale, representing two-thirds of the day laborers in 1880 and 52 percent in 1900. As Tygiel has noted, however, ethnic differences were partially eradicated in the second generation, as the sons of the foreign-born had experiences similar to those of the native-born at every level of the occupational structure except high white-collar jobs. By the turn of the century, then, "a white man's national heritage had become a less reliable predictor of occupational achievement than it had been twenty years earlier."[33]

Table 14 displays all the occupations in the city categorized according to census bureau classifications. These figures confirm the earlier accounts by underlining the significance of occupations in trade and transportation and in manufacturing. On average, these categories accounted for almost two-thirds of the occupations in the city, and with the exception of the 1890s, their development was quite balanced. The difference in that decade was significant, for while the number of workers

TABLE 14
CENSUS STATISTICS OF SHARES OF ALL OCCUPATIONS IN THE CITY BY DECADE

	1860	1870	1880	1890	1900
Trade and transportation	missing	25.6%	28.8%	28.1%	33.7%
Professional service	missing	3.6%	5.1%	5.7%	6.9%
Personal service	missing	37.5%	19.2%	30.5%	26.2%
Agriculture	missing	1.4%	1.8%	.81%	1.4%
Manufacturing	missing	32.2%	35.8%	34.7%	31.6%

in trade and transportation increased 33 percent, manufacturing workers increased a mere 1.2 percent.

This suggests that in addition to the balance in the city's economy, its diversity permitted one sector of the economy to compensate for another during hard times. There is further evidence of this in the economic indicators during the two periods that contemporaries and later historians agree were the worst for the city's economy—those around 1875–1879 and 1893–1897. As our indicators measure it, the first period was less serious than the second, and during it, the area of the economy that suffered most was the commercial sector, while the manufacturing sector seemed almost to sail through it. Measuring from pre-depression peak to mid-depression trough, business at the port dropped 26 percent between 1875 and 1879, while real estate sales dropped 48 percent between 1875 and 1880. In the manufacturing sector, however, the assessor's data reveal that in the plants included, the number of works declined only 11 percent from 1880 to 1881, the number of men employed declined 6 percent from 1877 to 1880, and the value of manufactured products declined 27 percent in real dollars between 1877 and 1880. Thus the depression in the industrial sector was of both shorter duration and less magnitude than that in the commercial sector. Because the decade from 1870 to 1880 was the "takeoff" period in the city's industrial development, the momentum of development may have carried the larger concerns through the depression relatively unscathed.

During the 1890s, in contrast, the city's economy was much more thoroughly integrated into the national economy, and the effects of the decline were more severe across the board. This time, business at the port suffered the least, dropping about 38 percent over the four-year period from 1891 to 1895, and then beginning to recover in response to the gold rush in the Klondike and the Spanish-American War. Real estate sales dropped 68 percent between 1891 and 1897, but manufacturing suffered still more, with the number of works declining 33 percent between 1892 and 1895, the number of men employed dropping 35 percent between 1891 and 1897, and the value of output dropping 50 percent in real dollars from 1890 to 1897.[34]

It may seem academic (or like splitting hairs) to compare a 38 percent drop in business at the port over four years with a 50 percent drop in the value of manufactures over a seven-year period. However, this sort of comparison is critical for a correct understanding of the effect of the city's rather balanced, diversified economy both on its economic prospects as a whole and on its political response to those prospects. In his *Preface to Urban Economics*, Wilbur Thompson has proposed that the ideal urban economy might be one in which the periodic economic cycles and long waves of economic growth in various economic activities complement one another, with the peaks in one sector occurring during the troughs in another. The evidence here suggests that the variety of major economic activities in San Francisco may have approximated this situation, in that activities in one major sector may have mitigated the effects of collapse in another. During the 1870s, when the commercial sector stumbled, the industrial sector, which was in its "takeoff" period, powered through. Similarly, although less dramatically, during the 1890s, when the collapse in the manufacturing sector was sharper and of longer duration, the shallower depression and quicker recovery of business at the port may have helped mitigate the overall effects of the depression on the city.[35]

If economic balance and diversity is one theme in the city's socioeconomic development, this account suggests that normality is another. In spite of generations of writing on San Francisco's "peculiarity," we have seen nothing to suggest that San Francisco was an American urban rara avis. The resemblance of San Francisco's opportunity structure to that of other cities is surface evidence of these deeper similarities. Its steady population growth and large population kept it in the top rank of American cities. Although it was one of the most ethnic of American cities, this did not make it especially different from other major cities. In 1880, for example, when San Francisco led the nation with 44.5 percent of its population being foreign-born, more than 35 percent of the populations of six of the other most populous cities were foreign-born, and five others had more than 30 percent foreign populations.

These distributions are similar for 1890, too. On the basis of ethnic composition and occupational structure, Stephen Erie has argued that San Francisco was quite similar to New York and Chicago in this period. The rapid development of its manufacturing sector put it on a path of development similar to those of other leading manufacturing cities, and the development of the city's industrial economy out of its commercial sector resembles the economic development of Baltimore as outlined by Alan Anderson. It is the unexceptional nature of San Francisco's socioeconomic development which now permits us to test the effect of that development on the growth of the city's government.[36]

TESTING THE HYPOTHESIS

When the socioeconomic structural theory is specified as a hypothesis, the primary proposition appears to be that municipal expenditure increases along with rising population, increasing commercial development, industrialization, the geographical expansion of the city, and increasing per capita income. The first step in testing this hypothesis is to specify these processes and select the variables that measure them in the city of San Francisco. As we saw in the previous section, there are a number of measurements of these processes available to us. Thus we will select the variables for use in the statistical tests on the basis of three criteria: first, and most important, their centrality to the socioeconomic structural theory; second, the number of extant real annual observations available for each variable; and third, statistical relationships among the variables which may influence the results of the tests.[37]

Because commercial and industrial variables clearly illustrate these selection criteria, we begin with them. As already mentioned, the city's economy was built upon commerce and industry, and contemporaries recorded business at the port, real estate sales, and the statistics of industry to measure these activities annually. These types of variables are central to the theory, and all are available as real annual observations—as opposed, for example, to annual series created by means of interpolation between census or other periodic but not annual observations. The value of imports and exports at the port is available annually from 1860 through 1906, while industry and real estate statistics are available from 1867 through 1905.

The effect of commercial development is rather straightforwardly measured by business at the port and real estate sales. In contrast, the effect of industrial development is twofold in the socioeconomic structural hypothesis, because it includes both its expansion and the increasing density of industrial activities. We can take the value of manufactures from the assessor's data as a measure of the expansion of industrial activity (in those years when the processing of precious metals was no longer a significant industry), but we must use the industrial statistics to construct a measure of increasing density. To do so, I have divided the number of manufacturing plants reported annually by the assessor by the acreage in those four districts of the city in which the vast majority of manufacturing plants was located (i.e., the 50 and 100 vara areas and the Potrero and Mission districts). This, then, measures the density of industrial activity.[38]

In the case of the economic variables, we are fortunate to have available several annual series. No such series exist for the population and income variables, both of which are available only decennially. As previously noted, income effects are to some extent proxied by the other economic variables, because per capita income was probably associated with the changes in commerce and industry. The absence of this variable, therefore, does not cripple the analysis. The complete absence of an estimate of population would be serious, however, so in this case we again employ the series estimated by interpolation (see fig. 8).

Over time, this population moved southward and westward out of the boundaries of the old city, but such geographical expansion was not incremental. In San Francisco and elsewhere, as urban geographers and historians have now made abundantly clear, the city expanded not by slow accretion of territory but by the sudden addition of large tracts of land made available by the extension of transportation facilities. In San Francisco, Young has written, "the conveniences for getting about were provided by the railroad companies in advance of active requirement, but the rapid growth of the sections traversed by their lines soon converted what at first was an accommodation to comparatively few patrons into a necessity."[39]

In the previous section, we used records of real estate sales and contemporary and historical accounts to identify three major periods in the city's geographical expansion within its charter boundaries. From 1860 to 1875, the size of the settled areas of the city was 3,852 acres (i. e., the acreage of the 50 and 100 vara areas and the Potrero District). With the expansion of transportation facilities to the Mission and Western

Addition areas after 1875, the city's size jumped to 8,595 acres. Finally, with the opening of the Outside Lands in 1887, the city reached a size of 11,699 acres. According to the socioeconomic structural theory, it was the attempt to expand urban services to these newly added areas which strained city budgets. Moreover, this expansion was not gradual but abrupt. Graphed over time, the size of the city would look like three plateaus of increasing height.[40]

Rather than attempting to represent this process of geographical expansion across some continuous range of values, we use dichotomous dummy variables to represent each of these three stages. A dummy variable is constrained to only two values, in this case 0 and 1. The value is 1 when the effect of the variable is present and 0 when it is not. This means that three dummy variables must be created, one for each of the periods of the city's development. The first will be 1 from 1860 through 1875 and zero thereafter; the second, 1 from 1876 through 1887 and zero otherwise; the third, 1 from 1888 through 1906 and zero otherwise. When placed in the regression equation, these variables allow us to compare the differing effects on expenditure of each of these stages of growth.[41]

Our formulation of the socioeconomic structural theory hypothesizes that municipal expenditure will vary in response to changes in total population, business at the port, the density of manufacturing works, the number of real estate sales, and the geographical expansion of the city. Common sense, urban theory, and statistical necessity affect the way these variables are actually entered into the regression equation, however. For example, common sense suggests that it will take at least a year for the effect of socioeconomic structural changes to register on the public sector. Policymakers responded to perceived changes in socioeconomic factors from previous years, but they were rarely in a position to know for certain what was going on during the current year. This was especially true during the nineteenth century, when the monitoring of socioeconomic indicators was far from the science that it has become today. For this reason, the values of port business, manufacturing density, real estate sales, and manufactured products are entered lagged by one year.

Urban theory suggests that total population is central to all of these developments, but precisely because it is, it is difficult for statistical reasons to enter it into the equation directly. Because population growth drove many of the socioeconomic changes in the city, there is a high correlation between population and the other socioeconomic variables. Thus when population is entered on the right side of the equation as an explanatory variable, it introduces a level of multicollinearity that makes it difficult to interpret the results of the equation. Rather than entering it directly, then, we control for population by dividing the dependent and quantitative independent variables by it. Thus the values of expenditure, manufactured products, business at the port, and real estate sales will be per capita values. Finally, statistical necessity requires dropping one of the three dummy variables measuring the changing size of the city, because the presence of all three in the equation would produce perfect collinearity among them and make it impossible for the equation to be calculated. For this reason, we will enter only the second and third dummies, and compare their effects with those of the first era.[42]

Because local operating expenditure is the portion of total local expenditure that the theory suggests fluctuated in response to these forces, the dependent variable in one of the tests is per capita local operating expenditure. The city's local operating expenditure averaged about 80 percent of its total expenditure during these years and included, in order of their share of the total, the salary and nonsalary expenditures of general government (police, fire, administration, and social welfare), education, streets, parks, and libraries (see chap. 2). However, expenditure is only one of the products of the fiscal process. In addition, there are revenue, assessed valuation, and the tax rate. Although the socioeconomic structural theory focuses exclusively on the explanation of the growth in expenditure, it is certainly possible that these variables enter the fiscal process at other points. To test this hypothesis, I regressed per capita revenue, valuation, and the tax rate on the same combination of variables. Table 15 lists the variables in the equations, along with their mean values, and the results are displayed in table 16. Because of the missing data for some of the variables, the statistical analysis can include only the years from 1870 through 1905.

Perhaps the most interesting result in the equations is the contrasting effects of socioeconomic structural development on expenditure and valuation. As noted earlier in this chapter, historians have assumed that socioeconomic structural development increases the demand for expenditure, not the potential supply of revenue. These equations indicate the opposite. None of the variables measuring industrial or commercial development has a statistically significant effect on expenditure, while

TABLE 15

VARIABLES IN THE EQUATIONS

Variable name	Explanation
EXP	Per capita operating expenditure (mean = $14.31)
REV	Per capita local revenue (mean = $13.66)
VAL	Per capita assessed valuation of real and personal property (mean = $987.58)
TAX	Tax rate per $100 of assessed valuation (mean = $1.19)
PORT	Per capita value of imports and exports at the port (mean = $277.07)
WORKS	Number of manufacturing works per 100 acres in the manufacturing districts (mean = 18.65)
MANVAL	Per capita value of manufactured products (mean = $231.24)
RES	Number of real estate sales per 100 population (mean = 1.63)
CITSIZE I	Acreage of the city 1870–1875
CITSIZE II	Acreage of the city 1876–1887
CITSIZE III	Acreage of the city 1888–1906

one in each category has a statistically significant positive effect on the valuation.

More specifically, in the case of per capita expenditure, only the city size variables have a statistically significant effect. This indicates that, compared with the average level of operating expenditure from 1870 to 1875, the levels in the second two periods of the city's growth were higher. In all these equations, the constant is the adjusted mean of operating expenditure during the first period of the city's growth, while the coefficients on the CITSIZE variables measure the difference brought about by the shift from the first to the second and the first to the third periods in the city's expansion. These figures indicate that, controlling for the effect of the other variables, operating expenditure averaged about $10.79 per capita from 1870 to 1875, about $13.23 between 1876 and 1887, and $13.56 from 1888 through 1905.

While this result might appear to confirm the relationship between city size and operating expenditure, it actually demonstrates that expenditure was stable despite the expanding size of the city. After 1875,

TABLE 16

REGRESSIONS OF PER CAPITA EXPENDITURE, REVENUE, ASSESSED VALUATION, AND THE
TAX RATE ON SOCIOECONOMIC STRUCTURAL VARIABLES[a]

Vars. and Stats.	EXP	REV	VAL	TAX
PORT (− 1)	−.0029	.0013	3.398[b]	−.0018[d]
WORKS (− 1)	.0207	.0653	14.45[c]	−.0040
RES (− 1)	.4691	.6777	− 127.70[c]	.1948[c]
CITSIZE II	2.436[d]	.6624	− 313.97[d]	−.4582[c]
CITSIZE III	2.7669[d]	−.1640	− 154.17	−.6281[c]
MANVAL (− 1)	.0058	−.0023	−.0776	−.00113
CONSTANT	10.792[b]	12.21[b]	188.49	2.22[b]
Adj. R-Sq.	.3039	.1656	.3439	.6188
Stan. Err.	1.311	2.1194	178.06	.2369
Est. Rho	.8952	.6879	.4810	.1083

[a] N = 35 (1870–1905).
[b] Significant at .01 level.
[c] Significant at .05 level.
[d] Significant at .10 level.

the opening of the Mission, Western Addition, and Outside Lands to settlement increased the city's area by a total of 7,847 acres (159 percent). The percent change in average expenditure from the first to the second and third periods was only about 23 percent, and that between the second and third periods was only 2.5 percent. In spite of this enormous increase in the city's settled area, then, per capita operating expenditure remained remarkably stable.

The stability of operating expenditure was not the result of a problem in the resource base, because some of the same forces of development that had no statistically significant impact on expenditure did have a significant and positive effect on the per capita assessed valuation of real and personal property. An increase of $1 per capita in business at the port brought about an increase of $3.39 per capita in the assessed valuation of the following year, while an increase of one plant per 100 acres in the manufacturing districts of the city brought about an increase of $14.45 in the valuation the next year. Meanwhile, the valuation per capita was $314 less in the second than in the first period of the city's growth, and it was inversely related to the number of real estate sales per 100 population, declining by $127 per capita when the number of sales increased by one per hundred residents.

The positive impact of the first pair of variables is both logically pleasing and historically important. As noted in chapter 2, San Francisco was known to have kept its assessed valuation relatively close to its "true" value. As more wealth was added to the city by its increasing business at the port or increasing density of manufacturing works, it is not surprising that the valuation increased. Furthermore, the positive effect of these variables on the valuation was better than one to one: a $1 increase in business at the port per capita caused a $3.38 increase in the valuation, and the addition of one plant per hundred acres in the manufacturing districts brought about a $14.45 increase. Previous historical accounts of urban fiscal policy, which usually have focused on expenditure only, have failed to consider that, logically, socioeconomic development was both a benefit and a cost to urban government. Indeed, these results suggest that in San Francisco it was more a benefit than a cost.

In light of these results, the negative impact of the second two variables is somewhat surprising. Again, one would expect the valuation to grow as the size of the city increased and more parcels of land were added to the tax rolls. Similarly, one might have expected that the valuation would rise when the number of real estate sales did. These results are somewhat less surprising, however, when compared with those in the equation analyzing the tax rate. To begin to interpret these results, we recall that the tax rate and the assessed valuation were negatively related; when the rate went up, the valuation went down, and vice versa (see chap. 2). At least in part, this relationship was the result of local officials' attempts to soften or obfuscate the effect of increases in either the valuation or the rate, by pairing an increase in the one with a decrease in the other. Thus it is not surprising that the socioeconomic variables that influenced the valuation positively influenced the tax rate negatively, and vice versa. In the tax equation, then, business at the port had a small but statistically significant negative relationship with the tax rate, while the number of real estate sales had a relatively large positive relationship. Meanwhile, the rate was lower in the second and third periods of the city's history than in the first.

The most interesting result of this equation is the strong positive relationship between real estate sales and the tax rate. What this indicates is that an increase of one real estate sale per 100 population brought about a $0.20 increase in the tax rate in the next year. This is interesting because the number of real estate sales was one of the most cyclical and most closely watched of the economic indicators available to nineteenth-century policymakers. These results suggest that when this indicator went up, local officials were emboldened to increase the tax rate, although they apparently fine-tuned the fiscal political effects of such an increase by counterbalancing it with a decrease in the valuation.

Taken together, the results of these equations demonstrate that socioeconomic structural development took a different path through the fiscal system than that suggested by most historical accounts written within the confines of the socioeconomic structural theory. Socioeconomic variables had their strongest positive effects on the assessed valuation, increasing the revenue-raising potential of the city's tax base. The tax rate, of course, mediated between the revenue base and the actual revenue raised. The rate was negatively related to the valuation and was affected positively by the most cyclical variable in the equations, the number of real estate sales per 100 population. The valuation was driven by the main engines of economic development in the city—namely, commerce and industry—while the more politically sensitive tax rate followed more closely the ups and downs of the business cycle. Apparently the effect of commercial and industrial development and the business cycle was exhausted by the time levels of revenue and expenditure were determined. None of these variables affected revenue significantly, and only the city size variables influenced expenditure, producing an effect that was positive but not dramatic.

Indeed, the impact of the city size variables on expenditure, valuation, and the tax rate was contrary to both theory and logic. Certainly there is nothing in the socioeconomic structural theory to suggest that the expansion of the city should result in either stability of expenditure or decrease in the valuation and the tax rate. Instead, both the theory and logic predict the opposite. Yet the results of the city size variables are consistent across the equations. Expenditure must at least remain stable if both the valuation and the tax rate decrease over time. While consistent, however, the results are not satisfying, because there is no convincing causal link between them and the expanding size of the city.

Because the three periods in the city's expansion are based on real estate and transportation records, they are not arbitrary, given the assumptions of the socioeconomic structural theory. However, the boundaries of the theory are arbitrary by necessity. The theory proposes that the correct way to carve up time is according to the pattern in the city's growth, and this is what we have done in the specification of this variable. As we have already seen, however, a competing political cultural theory suggests that the important change over time is from one sort of political ethos to another. Moreover, the political cultural theory proposes more explicit links between its explanatory variables and fiscal policy. Thus we turn to the test of hypotheses derived from that theory.

4

Testing the Political Cultural Theory

Historians have long thought that municipal expenditure would increase solely in response to socioeconomic structural factors only in a "world without social or political structure, power, dominance, and control," as Ira Katznelson put it.[1] Therefore, a political cultural theory has co-existed with the socioeconomic structural theory in the historical literature. The political cultural theory attributes aspects of the development of municipal government primarily to substantive differences in the policies of competing political regimes. Thus it suggests that different levels of municipal expenditure resulted primarily from the fiscal policies pursued by competing political regimes, and that these policies sprang in turn from differences in the leadership and constituency of competing political organizations.

If the socioeconomic structural theory is best summarized by Glaab and Brown's statement that there was "no way to avoid" the increasing range and scale of governmental activity "regardless of bosses and re-formers," then the political cultural theory is perhaps best outlined in Zane Miller's argument that the "astonishingly high cost of municipal improvements and services" in the developing American city was caused primarily by the attempt of urban politicians to resolve the "crisis of political leadership" by means of "patronage, special favors, and bribery." According to Miller's argument, municipal government, and thus expenditure, grew at least in part in response to political rather than social necessity. Although this implies that patronage, favors, and bribes were political tools available to all urban politicians, the political cultural theory has usually regarded the fiscal issue in urban politics as the classic confrontation between free-spending bosses and fiscally conservative reformers. The former are viewed as social service and welfare agents for their constituencies at "considerable cost to the taxpayers, generally"; the latter, as crusading for efficiency, economy, and good government, and threatening to "lop needed jobs off the payroll" in the process.[2]

ELEMENTS OF THE THEORY

These descriptions have characterized fifty years of historical writing on urban politics. Griffith, writing with more progressive spirit than scholarly objectivity, noted in 1927 that the problem of the political machine was not dishonesty so much as inefficiency: "The mediocre character of the political appointee, the loitering at work, the unnecessary multiplication of places for the spoils . . . all of these made the governing of many cities an outrage upon the common sense of the electorate." The reformers, meanwhile, represented the forces of "civic patriotism, desire for economy, or a search for better service." In 1977, Martin Schiesl described the sides similarly, noting that the "survival of the machines" depended on their continuing ability to "distribute public posts and social services to various groups in urban society." The reformers, in contrast, "believed that the growing expense of civic management was directly proportional to the degree of dishonesty and waste in machine administrations. By providing responsible officials with more efficient methods of control, they hoped to establish and maintain honest and economical government."[3]

According to most interpretations, these fiscal differences were the result of differences in the leadership, constituency, and thus political incentives of machine and reform politicians.[4] Machine politicians were just that—professional politicians interested in obtaining and maintaining political power, and willing to be "pragmatic" about the means by which they did so. They sprang from and rooted their politics in the ethnic neighborhoods at the center of the city, which frequently contained the neediest members of the urban population. They mobilized this population by means of incentives to political participation which attempted to meet those needs and which were both tangible (e.g., a direct payment for voting, a job) and divisible (i.e., available only to those who supported the machine). These incentives frequently were financed by the public sector—thus the unnecessary and/or overly expensive public works projects and the like—and this led to an expanded and hence more expensive public sector.

Conversely, the reformers were often not professional politicians but a coalition of various amateur groups united in their opposition to boss-ism, their commitment to efficient and economical government, or their objection to government by representatives of the lower classes. The leaders of these coalitions were distinguished primarily by their efforts to deny that they were, in fact, politicians; most declared that they were "above" politics and entered the fray out of a sense of moral obligation. To distinguish themselves from the professional politicians and to maintain a disparate constituency, reform leaders couched their political appeals in broad ideological terms. Their incentives, therefore, were both intangible (the idea of "good government") and nondivisible (e.g., civil service, which, theoretically at least, was available to all). Because they promised little in the way of material incentives, reformers were better able to control, if not cut, government expenditures. Indeed, the measure of their accomplishment was frequently the reduction of taxes, and this, of course, required the reduction of expenditure.

This political cultural theory is so familiar that it hardly needs further explication. What are worth more consideration are the serious problems with this theory. In the first place, historians have not established the links between constituency and leadership upon which this theory is based. Outside of a handful of tests of the Hays thesis, they have rarely compared systematically the ethnic or occupational backgrounds of the political decisionmakers supposedly representing the competing political movements and thus different political cultures. Instead, they have relied primarily on the characterizations of the social basis of the political leadership written by contemporaries with political ends.

Similarly, historians have accepted the terms of the fiscal debate as presented by the participants themselves. When Griffith, for example, criticized the inefficiency of the urban machine in 1927, he wrote from the perspective of a progressive reformer and shared the progressive faith that moral rectitude was on the side of reform. When he described the profligacy and inefficiency of the machine and the economy of its opponents, therefore, he reflected the positions taken in the contemporary debate. Moreover, as John Allswang has pointed out, this pro-reform position was characteristic of academic writing on the political machine until World War II. However, when Oscar Handlin criticized the elitism and inhumanity of reformers in *The Uprooted* in 1951, he did so from the standpoint of the machine politicians. It was, after all, Brooklyn Ward Leader Hugh McLaughlin and Tammany Boss Richard Croker on whom he relied for his fiscal portrait of machine politics.[5]

Thus the political cultural theory is at least potentially ideological in two senses. First, it presents the self-justification of both machine politicians and reformers. Second, as the post–World War II sea change in historical opinion indicates, it represents the attempt of historians themselves to legitimate different kinds of political economy. Just as the pro-reform opinion of pre–New Deal historians represented their own progressivism, so the anti-reform positions of early post–New Deal historians such as Handlin and Hofstadter represented their acceptance—indeed, defense of—the political economy of the New Deal. Both Handlin and Hofstadter clearly approved of the easygoing pragmatism of the machine politicians, especially their ability to avoid moralizing and get about the business of economic development and social welfare. Indeed, Hofstadter's admiration of the boss's "pragmatic talent" and the machine's essential "humanity" was paralleled in his praise of Franklin Delano Roosevelt's "opportunistic virtuosity" and of the New Deal's "triumph of ... human needs over inherited notions." More recently, the rising concern over the political and economic development of racial and ethnic minority communities has pressed the machine into contemporary service once again. In the wake of the Hays thesis, the machine now represents the apotheosis of community politics, since it rested "upon a mass lower class and working class base" and was involved with "issues of individual and group survival—in economic, social, and cultural terms." Reformers, in contrast, represent the elitist forces of centralization, who sought, as Hays put it, to channel political demands into "fewer centers of decision-making" and a "relatively small number of systems of human relationships."[6]

In part because it has served this doubly ideological function, the political cultural hypothesis has never been tested empirically. Instead, historians have "explained" these fiscal characterizations by means of a rather crude social determinism embedded in an overall functionalist framework. Most historians of both the machine and reform assume that once one has identified the social basis of support for an urban regime, one has also identified the nature of the regime's fiscal policy. This follows because of the essentially functionalist notion that political and social institutions persist because they fulfill certain functions for their supporters. As Alvin Gouldner has pointed out, the implicit slogan of functionalist analysis is, "Survival implies ongoing usefulness—search it out."[7] Dutiful historians contend, therefore, that because immigrants seem to have supported the political machine, it must have met certain of their needs; likewise, because municipal progressivism was essentially an upper-class affair, the policies of reform regimes must have represented the social needs of the urban upper class.

This framework begs many important questions, however. What was the reality, magnitude, or success of the putative social-welfare program of any political machine? How does one identify the class nature of reformist policy and link it to the social needs of urban elites? If political machines were meeting the social needs of the electorate, why did they fall? How did reform arise? Because of the variety of variables that intervenes between them, there is no necessary connection between a political movement's social basis and the nature of its policy. To believe otherwise is to deny the reality of political misrepresentation or exploitation and to assume that political institutions mechanistically reflect the social configurations that underlie them. Such an assumption is, of course, possible, but as Martin Shefter has written, it requires a commitment to "a species of social determinism that is the reverse of, but as strict as, that employed by only the most vulgar of Marxists."[8]

Questions such as these can be approached more profitably if the functionalist explanatory framework is rejected and the research strategy reversed. Rather than assuming that which needs to be proved, we begin here with the null hypothesis that there were no significant differences in the fiscal policymakers or fiscal policies of competing political movements in San Francisco from 1860 to 1905. To test this hypothesis, we establish the periods of predominance of certain political organizations (e.g., parties) or tendencies (e.g., bosses, reformers) by examining both secondary works on the city's history and municipal election data collected for this study. Using a collective biography of the city officeholders elected in these years, we determine whether there were important differences in the backgrounds of city policymakers during the eras of control by these organizations. Finally, we test the ability of these eras to explain the variation in the products of the fiscal process—expenditure, assessed value, revenue, and the tax rate—both alone and in the presence of the combination of socioeconomic structural variables which was shown to influence the municipal fiscal process in the last chapter.

As was the case in chapter 3, these investigations confound the expectations of historical theory. To begin with, predicted background differences among city officials in different political eras simply do not emerge. On the whole, city officials were remarkably similar in occupational and ethnic background. Moreover, by themselves, the political-era variables explain very little of the variation in fiscal policy. A combination of the socioeconomic structural variables from chapter 3 and the political-era variables does a better job of explaining this variation, but the results contradict the predictions of the political cultural theory. Controlling for the effect of socioeconomic and other political-era variables, the era of machine control of city government—during which there were more foreign-born and Irish officials than ever before in the city's history—has a statistically significant negative effect on fiscal policy.

SAN FRANCISCO'S TRADITIONAL POLITICAL HISTORY

Basing their work primarily on the political affiliations of mayors and supervisors, historians of San Francisco have divided the city's municipal political history into several major electoral eras, defined according to factors such as the nature of political leadership in an era, its characteristic political coalition, and the policies pursued during the era. These writers have outlined an early period of civic virtue, followed by a period of corruption and machine politics and a later era of reform.[9] In each case, they have made assumptions about the political and fiscal characters of the eras without investigating them systematically. To compare fiscal policy among these eras, it is first necessary to determine their validity, nature, and extent. This requires both a brief consideration of earlier portrayals of these eras and their comparison with municipal election data.

The electoral eras specifically identified by historians have included that of the local People's and Taxpayer's parties from 1856 to 1875; that of the Democratic party machine from 1882 to 1891; a local "era of reform" from 1892 to 1901; and the era of the Union Labor party from 1901 to 1909, after which partisan municipal elections were abolished. In the only analysis of San Francisco politics for the entire period from 1860 to 1905, Stephen Erie has suggested that these eras were related to one another in a cyclical fashion, according to the nature of their leadership and their fiscal policies.[10] According to Erie, San Francisco politics was a conflict between two elites representing different "political outlooks and social and economic groups." On the one hand were the "professional politicians, often from working class Irish back-

TABLE 17

POLITICAL AFFILIATIONS OF MAYORS AND SUPERVISORS, 1860–1875

Year	Party of mayor	Democratic supervisors	Republican supervisors	Independent supervisors
1860	P	3	0	4 P
1861	P	0	0	6 P
1862		0	0	5 P; 2 C
1863	P	0	0	4 C; 2 P
1864		0	0	3 P; 3 I–U
1865	P	0	0	5 P; 1 U
1866		3	0	4 U
1867	Dem.	3	0	4 U
1868		3	0	3 U
1869	I–TP	1	4	1 I
1870		4	1	1 TP
1871	TP	1	0	4 TP; 1 I
1873	TP	1	0	11 TP
1875	Dem.	9	0	3 I

Note: Independent party designations:

P = People's
TP = Taxpayer's
F = Fusion
C = Citizens
U = Union
I = Independent

grounds," who adopted an "inflationary political strategy, for every increase in city offices and expenditures could be turned to advantage." On the other hand were the "reformers," who were "most often Yankee business leaders dedicated to efficient and limited government," and whose political participation frequently was galvanized by the inflationary strategy of the "professionals."

Using the results of mayoralty and supervisorial elections between 1860 and 1905, shown in tables 17 and 18, we can begin to test the political cultural theory by determining the plausibility of these electoral periodizations.[11] As table 17 reveals, there can be little doubt of the electoral hegemony of the People's and Taxpayer's parties from 1860 to 1875. Until 1872, there was a municipal election every year, with the mayor and half of the board of supervisors standing in odd years and the rest of the board elected in even years.[12] In the seven mayoralty contests between 1860 and 1873, the People's or Taxpayer's candidates won in all but one. In the twelve supervisorial elections in this same period, these parties won half or more of the seats at stake eight times, meaning that most of the time there was a People's or Taxpayer's mayor and majority on the board of supervisors.

The People's party had been organized in 1856 by members of the Vigilance Committee, who had recently taken the law into their own hands, according to one of their partisans, in order to "secure political justice" and to correct the "abuses introduced by political tricksters from eastern cities" who had "robbed the property owners of millions upon millions." Having cleansed the Augean political stables, the committee members decided to organize what they called the People's party to prevent the government from again falling into the wrong hands. The first People's administration was, according to a sympathetic contemporary, "a marvel of economy," characterized by "an entire absence of ... partisan trickery, low scheming, and disreputable personal association." Although the party changed its name from People's to Taxpayer's to Union as the occasion demanded, succeeding administrations attempted to continue this tradition of economy and repute, and "with some minor changes and slight interruptions ... had control of the government until 1874."[13]

As table 17 also suggests, a loyal opposition was collecting around the Democratic party. In the election of 1875, the Democrats unseated the Taxpayer's candidates and ushered in an era of overall Democratic hegemony, which was to stretch almost uninterrupted to 1899, and to be epitomized by the reign of Democratic "Boss" Christopher Buckley from 1882 to 1891. From 1875 until the end of the century, Democrats captured the mayoralty nine times out of fourteen (64 percent), a majority of the board of supervisors eight times, and both the mayoralty and a majority of the board seven times. Moreover, in these years the Democrats reelected incumbent mayors four times, a feat matched by no other party. However, the Democrats were also wounded by the formation of an independent workingmen's party in 1877, and they were almost replaced by the Union Labor party after 1900.

The victors of 1875 were barely able to savor their triumph before the city began to slide into the depression of the late 1870s. Two well-known results of these depressed conditions were the labor and anti-Chinese violence of 1877–1879 and the formation of the Workingmen's Party of California (WPC) in San Francisco in September 1877. By all accounts, the Democratic municipal administration's response to the depression was a debacle. On the one hand, Democratic Mayor A. J. Bryant refused to use city government to do anything to ameliorate economic conditions, citing both lack of authority and lack of money, although he and the supervisors did petition the state legislature for permission to increase the size of the police force. On the other hand, Bryant and the supervisors cooperated to suppress the workingmen's protests and their party. According to one account, "leaders were arrested and jailed on charges which were thrown out of court . . . crowds were driven from the streets, indoor meetings were broken up . . . [and] the board of supervisors hastily enacted an ordinance which abridged the right of free speech."[14]

As table 18 suggests, these actions had two important political repercussions. First, the Democratic electoral takeover was aborted as workers and others deserted the party to vote for the Workingmen's and Republican candidates for mayor and supervisors in 1879 and 1881. Second, and more fatefully, this provided the occasion for Buckley's entrance into the higher councils of Democratic power.

According to Buckley's biographers, the wreckage of the Democratic party was nearly complete by 1882, when its leaders discovered that its rolls had shrunk from 22,000 to somewhere between 2,500 and 4,000 members. For this reason, the Democratic leadership handed the party over to Buckley, who was to run it (and, allegedly, the city) from then until 1891. From all accounts, including his own, Buckley was a boss in the classic mold. He was Irish-born, had worked first as a horse-car conductor, then advanced into politics via the saloon route. Along the way, he learned the technique of controlling both politics and policy so crucial to the success of bosses everywhere. Buckley organized forty-seven clubs distributed among the city's twelve wards. Each was headed by a trusted lieutenant, but beyond that, each "had more offices than actually needed" in order to provide what Buckley called "dignity" for his supporters. The clubs also supposedly "maintained supportive services for members and their families," functioned as employment agencies, and were the headquarters for electoral mobilization.[15]

With this organization, Buckley was usually able to obtain his "solid

TABLE 18

POLITICAL AFFILIATIONS OF MAYORS AND SUPERVISORS, 1875–1905

Year	Party of mayor	Democratic supervisors	Republican supervisors	Independent supervisors
1875	Dem.	9	0	3 I
1877	Dem.	7	0	5 TP
1879	WPC	0	12	0
1881	Repub.	2	10	0
1882	Dem.	12	0	0
1884	Dem.	1	11	0
1886	Dem.	9	3	0
1888	Dem.	11	1	0
1890	Repub.	0	12	0
1892	Non-Part.	11	0	1 Non-Part.
1894	People's	4	8	0
1896	Dem.	9	3	0
1898	Dem.	1	11	0
1899	Dem.	15	3	0
1901	ULP	9	6	3 ULP
1903	ULP	10	6	2 ULP
1905	ULP	0	0	18 ULP

Note: Independent party designations:
   I = Independent
   TP = Taxpayer's Party
   WPC = Workingmen's Party of California
   Non-Part. = Non-Partisan
   People's = People's (Populist)
   ULP = Union Labor Party

seven" (the number of supervisors needed to pass an ordinance) or "solid nine" (the number needed to override the mayor's veto of an action approved by the board). This being the case, he was able to guarantee the awarding of lucrative utility franchises to the highest bidders for his services. Meanwhile, he kept the tax rate low and avoided municipal indebtedness.[16]

Buckley's downfall came about not because of his malfeasance but, as William Bullough has pointed out, because of revolt within his own party. This revolt was based in part on the charge that he "sold out" the election of 1890 to the Republican machine of Martin Kelly, and in part on the ambition of insurgent leadership to take the Democratic party out of the saloon and into the drawing rooms of the San Francisco elite. The insurgents' weapon was the grand jury, which indicted Buckley in November 1891 for selling a street railway franchise.[17] In the meantime, Buckley had fled the city; the indictment was later thrown out by the state supreme court, and he returned to the area in 1894 to live out his days.

Bullough suggests that there is little evidence that Buckley "sold out,"[18] and whether or not he did is, ultimately, irrelevant. What is important is that the loss of the election and the subsequent indictment destroyed Buckley's political power and set off an intense struggle within the party. Moreover, the collapse of Democratic unity opened the way for an episode of party irregularity and the beginning of the era of "reform mayoralties" in the 1890s.

The Republicans' brief moment of glory ended in 1892 with the election of the mayoral candidate of the Non-Partisan League, Levi R. Ellert, along with eleven Democratic supervisors, in a wild seven-way race in which nine parties ran candidates for various offices. A similar free-for-all resulted in the election of Populist candidate Adolf Sutro and a Republican supervisorial majority in 1894. Ellert was a druggist, a former supervisor, and a renegade Republican. Sutro was a widely known self-made millionaire. Both campaigned against bossism and corruption and for honesty and economy, and lambasted their hostile or at least uncooperative boards of supervisors.[19] With historical perspective it can be seen that their real accomplishment was to unleash the spirit of reform, which was to be embodied in the person of James Duval Phelan, who was elected mayor in 1896.

According to Phelan's biographers, if a reformer had conjured up Phelan he could not have produced a more ideal San Francisco reform candidate.[20] The son of Irish Catholic parents (his father had been a Forty-Niner), Phelan was, at the time of his first campaign for the mayoralty, a thirty-five-year-old attorney who was dashing, honest, and enormously wealthy as a result of his family-owned banking and business pursuits. He was undoubtedly the most well-connected Democrat to that point in San Francisco history. Besides being Irish Catholic, he was president of the San Francisco Art Club and the local Native Sons of the Golden West, two important elite social organizations in the city. Phelan was also a founder, in 1891, of the Citizens Defense Association, an anti-Buckley reform group, and, in 1894, of the Merchants' Association, a businessmen's reform group that spearheaded campaigns in 1896 and 1898 for city charter reform. At the same time, he was president of the San Francisco Association of Improvement Clubs, an umbrella organization for the various neighborhood-improvement clubs. Given these affiliations, it is not surprising that Phelan was elected to three terms as mayor. His more lasting and fateful contribution to the city's political structure was the reform charter of 1900, which was approved with his vigorous backing at a special election in 1898.

William Issel has analyzed the charter reform campaign of 1896, which failed, and that of 1898, which succeeded, and has demonstrated that they conform to the Hays thesis of municipal reform. The charters were proposed and backed by alliances of social-register professionals and businessmen, and received their greatest support in the city's "newer and well to do districts." After losing in the general election of 1896, the reformers scheduled a special election on the charter in April 1898, in hopes that only proponents would be attracted to the polls. Thus the charter passed by two thousand votes, with only 32 percent of the electorate voting.[21]

The provisions of the charter were in the classic municipal reform mold.[22] It provided for a strong mayor, civil service, at-large election of supervisors, initiative and referendum, public ownership of utilities, and minimum-wage—maximum-hour provisions for municipal employment. Among the powers conferred on the mayor were the undivided authority to appoint and remove members of city boards and commissions, to suspend elective officials pending their trial on the mayor's charges by the board of supervisors, and to veto any ordinance the board passed unless fourteen of the now eighteen members of the board voted to override his veto. As a result of the charter, there was no doubt about the locus of executive power in municipal government. Indeed, it was the realization of this by the San Francisco working class which was to bring about Phelan's downfall and the end of this political era.

Having taken office in 1897, as the city's economy emerged from the depression of the previous years, Phelan had the good fortune to serve as mayor during an era of rapidly increasing prosperity, which facilitated his repeated reelection and the passage of the reform charter. The prosperity also stimulated union activity, which had come to a standstill during the depression. As the apparent strength of labor increased, it began to demand not only the usual wage, hour, and working condition improvements but also union recognition and the closed shop. Although employers had granted the usual demands, they balked at these new and more radical ones. In April 1901, they organized an Employers' Association to resist the pressure of labor by providing mutual aid during strikes and by encouraging firms that had signed "unreasonable" agreements to abrogate them.[23]

The test of this growing strength on both sides was the waterfront strike of July 1901, which ultimately involved sixteen thousand workers united in the City Front Federation and the full resources of the Employers' Association. Because neither side was willing to capitulate, the strike turned into a war of attrition that lasted from the end of July to the beginning of October. While it was stalemated, the strikers charged, on a variety of grounds, that police activity actually aided the cause of the employers.[24] Under the reform charter the mayor appointed the police commissioners, who in turn selected the chief of police. The strikers believed that Phelan could therefore influence the conduct of the police. He refused to do so, however, standing behind the policy of the police commission, which was headed by the president of the Chamber of Commerce.

Once again, then, as in 1879, the working class deserted the Democracy and the administration it had helped to elect and turned to independent political action, this time in the form of the Union Labor party. This party was the most significant factor in San Francisco politics during the first five years of the century, capturing the mayoralty three times and the board of supervisors once. The dimensions of its turpitude under the guidance of alleged "Boss" Abraham Ruef have been ably recounted by Walton Bean in *Boss Ruef's San Francisco*. For our purposes, it is more interesting to note that the party was an anomaly in the political history of San Francisco. In its own time it was scourged as a political machine, yet it was a pale imitation of Buckley's operation. It was not Irish and Democratic, and it had nothing of the organization of Buckley's machine. But it was not of the San Francisco reform tradition, either, being neither Yankee- nor elite-dominated.[25]

Its party roots, social bases, and political significance were, in fact, unique. Both Ruef and Eugene Schmitz, the musicians' union leader and Union Labor mayor from 1901 to 1906, were lifelong Republicans, Ruef having served as an aide to Republican Mayor George Sanderson during his mayoralty of 1890–1892. This Republican leadership ultimately managed to attract the support of areas of the city that had previously been Democratic strongholds. The party was rooted, however, in the traditional sources of Democratic support, the Irish and Scandinavian working class. Finally, although hardly known as a reform regime, the Union Labor party effected a fundamental reform: during its administrations, police were not used to protect strikebreakers or the property of employers during labor disputes. Under Schmitz, such support was sought and refused twice, during the carmen's strike of 1902 and the seamen's lockout of 1906.[26]

TESTING THE HYPOTHESIS

Taken together, these secondary accounts suggest five political eras in the city's electoral political history: (1) the era of the People's and Taxpayer's parties from 1860 through 1875; (2) an era of struggle for Democratic hegemony from 1875 to 1881; (3) the era of machine politics from 1882 to 1892; (4) the era of the reform mayoralties from 1892 to 1900; and (5) the era of the Union Labor party from 1901 to 1905, when the analysis ends because of the earthquake. These accounts also correspond with those of contemporary political actors. For example, Frank McCoppin, the lone Democratic mayor elected between 1860 and 1873, complained about the iron grip of the so-called reform parties in those years, while Bryant, the Democratic mayor elected in 1875 along with a majority of Democratic supervisors, made a special point in his inaugural that with his election the era of municipal control by the "regular" parties had arrived. Both Buckley and his Republican counterpart, Martin Kelly, wrote that the former's leadership in the Democratic party began with the election of 1882, and Kelly further noted that after 1892, bossism as he and Buckley had practiced it was dead in San Francisco, having been killed by reformers of various stripes. Finally, of course, both the Union Labor candidates and their opponents argued that the 1901 victory of Schmitz was the beginning of a new era in the city's politics.[27]

In addition to noting these changing political "cultures," contemporaries and historians have characterized these periods according to their fiscal policies. John Hittell, historian and partisan of the People's and

Taxpayer's parties, praised their economy, while Buckley himself testified that he was not above using fiscal policy for political advantage, and his biographer has suggested that he needed patronage posts. The reformers of the 1890s pledged economy, with Phelan promising a campaign to "eliminate extravagance" in his first inaugural address. The Union Labor party was less specific in its position on fiscal matters, although it might be surmised that the party followed an inflationary policy when possible, given the corruption of its leadership and the necessity of attracting supporters from the regular parties.[28]

To determine whether there were significant differences among the political personnel in the various eras, I compiled a collective biography of all men elected to the mayoralty, board of supervisors, and elected executive positions in the city from 1860 through 1905. For each officer the following information was collected: name, office, party, year of election, occupation, place of birth, and ward of residence at the time of election. The offices included were mayor, supervisor, assessor, county attorney, auditor, chief of police, coroner, county clerk, district attorney, public administrator, recorder, registrar of voters, sheriff, superintendent of schools, superintendent of streets, tax collector, and treasurer. Such officeholders, who actually made and executed the policy of urban government, are the crucial but frequently missing link between political culture and public policy. Rather than inferring this link, as is done in most studies, I analyzed the backgrounds of these officials to determine whether, as these variables measure it, there are significant differences among them.[29]

Overall, 46 percent (321) of the offices filled in these years were executive offices, 49.5 percent (340) were supervisorial positions, and 3.8 percent (26) were mayoralties. A total of 64 percent (437) of these offices were filled by members of the Republican and Democratic parties, 27 percent (185) by men affiliated with the People's, Taxpayer's, or Union parties, and 8.7 percent by those of other independent parties. At the time of their elections, these men came from 92 different occupations, the most frequent of which was "incumbent"; indeed, 28 percent (188) of these officials were incumbents. The next most frequent occupation, "lawyer," was a very distant second at 7 percent (47). When the occupations are categorized according to the Edwards-Thernstrom scale, adding a separate category for incumbents and other government officials, it is revealed that none of these offices was filled by unskilled workers, and only 5 percent (34) were filled by semiskilled or skilled workers. In contrast, 28 percent (128) were filled by persons holding high white-collar occupations, 28 percent (222) by those from low white-collar occupations, 28 percent (188) by incumbents, and 5.5 percent (37) by other government officials.[30]

Throughout these years, the officials were overwhelmingly native-born: 68 percent (442) were born in this country, while only 32 percent (208) were born abroad. These proportions are significantly different from the average of native- and foreign-born in the population, which were 58 and 42 percent, respectively. It is certainly true, however, that many of those born in this country were of foreign-born parentage, so the "ethnic" share of these officers is undoubtedly higher. It was not possible to obtain more detailed information on the parentage of the officials. Of those born in the United States, only 20 percent (86) were born in California, while 30 percent (135) came from northeastern states (101 from New York State alone), 29 percent (129) from New England, and 18 percent (81) from the South. Fully 40 percent (82) of those born abroad were born in Ireland, 27 percent (56) in Germany, and 26 percent (53) in England, Scotland, and British possessions. On average, the Irish were 10 percent of the city's total population and 24 percent of its foreign-born, while the Germans were 9 percent of the population and 22 percent of the foreign-born. The Irish-born were 12.6 percent of all officeholders, and Germans made up 8.6 percent. Overall, then, both of these politically active groups were represented among the officeholders at about the same level as they were present in the population. Finally, the officials came primarily from the central wards of the city rather than from its outer wards: 67 percent came from the central wards 1 through 10, while 32 percent came from wards 11 and 12, which were known during this period as the "suburban" wards.[31]

To determine whether these variables reveal significant differences among the officeholders during the five eras identified earlier, we can employ regression analysis with dummy variables to measure the statistical significance of differences in these background variables in each era. Five dummy variables correspond to the periods outlined earlier in this chapter. As in the case of the dummies created in chapter 3, the values of these variables are 1 during the era and 0 otherwise; thus the coefficient on each dummy measures the impact of the era on the dependent variable.

The dependent variables in the equations that follow measure aspects of the ethnicity, occupational background, political affiliations, and ward of residence of the officials, in accordance with the propositions of the political cultural theory. One of the foundations of this theory is that the native-born and foreign-born have different political cultures. We will test for statistically significant differences among the eras in the share of foreign-born officeholders. Because the stereotypical foreign-born political operator is Irish, the share of Irish-born officeholders is also a dependent variable.

A second foundation of the political cultural theory is social class, and occupational differences among the eras will be tested by using both percent of high white-collar and percent of low white-collar officeholders as dependent variables. A variation on this theme is that of center versus periphery. In the works of Richard Wade and Zane Miller, for example, it is argued that central city wards have political cultures different from those wards on the periphery. In San Francisco, the so-called suburban wards (numbers 11 and 12) surrounded the central city wards (1 through 10), so differences in location of officeholders in the eras can be determined by measuring the share of officeholders from the suburban wards.[32]

Although the political cultural theory considers two other aspects of officeholders only by implication, these aspects are worth analysis. The first is the level of incumbency. Because this was high overall among these officeholders, it is important to determine whether there were differences in the level among the eras. In the political cultural theory, this would be a measure of the professionalization of politics, in the "old style" sense of a professional politician, as opposed to the Hays thesis's sense of professionals in politics. Similarly, the share of officials elected from the major parties, as opposed to the various independent parties, may measure a professional as opposed to an amateur political outlook.

The definitions of these variables are repeated in table 19. The results of tests of the ability of the eras to explain class and ethnicity are given in table 20, and those for politics and geography appear in table 21. In both cases, the number of observations is thirty-one, which is the number of municipal elections—and thus of the officials elected at each—between 1859 and 1905 inclusive. Again, one less than the total number of era dummy variables will be entered into the equations to avoid perfect collinearity. It makes no difference statistically which is excluded, and I have excluded the era of the Union Labor party. Its effect

TABLE 19

VARIABLES IN THE REGRESSIONS OF OFFICEHOLDER CHARACTERISTICS
ON POLITICAL ERAS

Variable name	Explanation
%HWC	Percent of officials in high white-collar occupations at the time of their election (mean = 28.5 percent)
%LWC	Percent of officials in low white-collar occupations at the time of their election (mean = 28.2 percent)
%FORBORN	Percent of officials foreign-born (mean = 32 percent)
%IRISH	Percent of officials born in Ireland (mean = 12.6 percent)
%INCUM	Percent of incumbents among officials (mean = 27.9 percent)
%REGPAR	Percent of officials affiliated with the regular parties (mean = 64 percent)
%SUBWARD	Percent of officials living in suburban wards at the time of their election (mean = 32.6 percent)
PTP	Period of local reform parties, 1860-1873
IRREG	Period following collapse of local reform parties, 1875-1881
MACH	Period of control by national party machines, 1882-1890
REF	Period of control by Populist and progressive reformers, 1892-1899
ULP	Period of control by the Union Labor Party, 1901-1906

is not lost, however, but measured by the constant in the equation. When a regression equation contains only dummy variables, the constant is the effect of the excluded variable, while the coefficients measure the change produced by the shift from the excluded variable to one of the included ones. In this case, then, the comparison variable is the Union Labor era, and each of the other coefficients measures the change in the dependent variable associated with the shift from that era to another. To determine the individual effect of each era, then, the constant and the coefficient on each variable in succession are added. I have called this sum the estimate, and the estimates for each era for

TABLE 20
REGRESSIONS OF % HWC, % LWC, % FORBOR, AND % IRISH ON POLITICAL ERAS [a]

Vars. and Stats.	% HWC	% LWC	% FORBOR	% IRISH
PTP	.2410[c]	−.1962[b]	.0148	.0818[c]
IRREG	.2712[c]	−.0554	−.0178	.0448
MACH	.2628[c]	−.0125	.1508[c]	.1051[c]
REF	.2628[c]	−.0641	.0064	.0577
Constant	.0552	.3738[b]	.2850	.0646[d]
Adj. R-Sq.	.2306	.3661	.3263	.2044
Stan. Err.	.1510	.0330	.0910	.0638

[a] N = 31 (1860–1905).
[b] Significant at .01 level.
[c] Significant at .05 level.
[d] Significant at .10 level.

TABLE 21
REGRESSIONS OF % INCUM, % REGPAR, AND % SUBWARD ON POLITICAL ERAS [a]

Vars. and Stats.	% INCUM	% REGPAR	% SUBWARD
PTP	−.0855	−.3120[d]	−.5452[b]
IRREG	−.3166[d]	.1231	−.3766[b]
MACH	−.3074[c]	.4037[c]	−.2830[b]
REF	−.2948[c]	.3976[c]	−.1905[b]
Constant	.4722[b]	.5823[b]	.6570[b]
Adj. R-Sq.	.2951	.6236	.8842
Stan. Err.	.2025	.2654	.0747

[a] N = 31 (1860–1905).
[b] Significant at .01 level.
[c] Significant at .05 level.
[d] Significant at .10 level.

TABLE 22
REGRESSION ESTIMATES OF DEPENDENT VARIABLES FOR EACH ERA

ERA	% HWC	% LWC	% FORBOR	% IRISH	% INCUM	% REGPAR	% SUB-WARD
PTP	29.6%	17.8%	(29.9%)	(14.6%)	(38.6%)	27.0%	11.1%
IRREG	32.6	(31.8)	(26.6)	10.9	15.6	(70.5)	28.6
MACH	31.8	(36.1)	43.5	(17.0)	16.5	99.0	37.4
REF	31.8	(30.1)	(29.0)	12.2	17.7	98.0	46.7
ULP	(5.5)	37.4	28.4	6.5	47.2	58.2	65.7

Note: Parentheses indicate estimates that are not statistically significant.

every dependent variable appear in table 22. The interpretation that follows, then, is determined by the statistical results in the equations, but is built around the estimates in table 22.

The estimates suggest that, on the whole, the officials elected in these eras had a great deal in common. Perhaps the most surprising similarities among the eras have to do with the occupations of the officials. San Francisco officeholders were drawn from remarkably similar occupational backgrounds regardless of the political era in which they were elected. From 1860 through 1899, about one-third of all officials elected were drawn from high white-collar occupations. The exception to this rule was the Union Labor period, during which only about 6 percent of the officials were from high white-collar occupations. Although the four previous eras look similar, it is important to note that there were fewer persons in high white-collar occupations in the population during the first period, so that during that era officials from these occupations were most overrepresented. Jules Tygiel has pointed out that in 1870 the share of high white-collar occupations in the city was only 3.9 percent, which means that officials from these occupations were almost ten times more often officeholders than their share of occupations would predict during the years of the People's and Taxpayer's parties. In 1880 the high white-collar share of the occupational structure was 5.3 percent, in 1890 it was 5.1 percent, and in 1900 it was 7.4 percent, suggesting that in the other eras high white-collar occupations were overrepresented among officeholders by factors of six to seven.[33]

Overall similarity is also the pattern in the distribution of officials from low white-collar occupations. Among all officials elected, about one-third were from low white-collar occupations. From 1875 through 1899, the share of officials from these occupations fluctuated closely around this average. This share was higher than that of low white-collar occupations in the city as a whole. In 1870, 22 percent of the city's occupations were low white collar, in 1880, 24.7 percent; in 1890, 25.4 percent; and in 1900, 27.8 percent. Thus the first era was radically different from the others, with a share of low white-collar officials almost one-half lower than the other eras and—for the only time in the city's history—below the share of those occupations in the population. Just as the Union Labor period is low in high white-collar occupations, it is highest in low white-collar officials, followed closely by the machine era.[34]

In the case of ethnicity, the estimates for four of the five eras are quite similar. In fact, the coefficients in the equations on the first, second, and fourth era dummies are not statistically significant because a change from the Union Labor period to one of them makes little or no difference in the share of foreign-born officeholders. However, the machine era clearly distinguishes itself from the others, with 43 percent foreign-born officials. This era also fulfills its historical (and historiographical) destiny by having the highest share of Irish-born officeholders, although in the case of this variable, the distribution among eras was closer, with the first period running a close second to that of the machines. Again, it can be determined whether the foreign-born and Irish are over- or underrepresented in each era by comparing the shares of officials with those in the entire population. As we saw in chapter 3, the city's population was about half foreign-born in 1860 and 1870, 44 percent foreign-born in 1880, 42 percent foreign-born in 1890, and 34 percent foreign-born in 1900. These figures indicate that the foreign-born received their share of the officials during the machine era and were most underrepresented during the People's-Taxpayer's era. The share of Irish in the population was 17 percent in 1870, 13 percent in 1880, 10 percent in 1890, and 4 percent in 1900, so the Irish received more than their share of officials in all of the eras.[35]

Turning now to the measures of political culture within the political system itself—namely, level of incumbency and share of officials from the regular parties—it appears that the level of incumbency was highest when the share of officials elected by the regular parties was lowest, during the first and last eras. Ironically, this indicates that it was easier to be a professional policymaker during an era dominated by amateur or independent parties. Otherwise, the level of incumbency explained by the eras again displays remarkable stability during the middle three eras. The share of officials elected from the regular parties is also similar during the machine and reform eras.

Finally, the tests of share of outer-ward officials reveal little. As we saw in chapter 3, throughout these years the center of the city's population moved continually southward and westward, and hence into wards 11 and 12. The steadily increasing estimates over time indicate only that, as more population moved into these areas, more officials were elected from them. This is clearly a case where the dummies are simply proxying "time."

These differences among officials in occupational and ethnic background, levels of incumbency, and regular party affiliation are meaningful at this point only insofar as they permit assumptions about the character of fiscal policy in each of the five eras. We can summarize our characterization of these eras by combining these background analyses with the fiscal policies ascribed to the eras by contemporaries and other historians.

For example, during the era of the People's and Taxpayer's parties, men in high white-collar occupations were most overrepresented among officials, while men in low white-collar occupations and the foreign-born were underrepresented, and very few officials affiliated with the regular parties were elected at all. These characteristics suggest an era of low or at least cautious expenditure, given the propositions of the political cultural theory, and this, as we have seen, is what contemporaries and historians have said about the era. The only potential counter to this is the high level of incumbency, which might have encouraged more patronage expenditure to help keep the incumbents in office.

The era of irregularity was distinct from the other eras precisely because of its lack of anything to differentiate it from the other eras. During this period the levels of foreign-born, high white-collar, and incumbent officials were rather average. Its only real distinction was as the transitional era between control by independent parties and control by the regular parties. The fact that 70 percent of the officials elected in this era were affiliated with the Democratic or Republican parties contrasts with the 27 percent of the first era, but it is still about 25 percent lower than during the machine era. Although there are no assumptions about fiscal policies in these years in the historical literature, expenditure may have increased (1) because there was no overall party discipline over fiscal policy, as there was before and after this era; and (2) because the regular parties needed patronage to facilitate their wresting control of local government from the various independent parties.

The machine era distinguished itself as the most foreign-born and Irish, and thus as a period during which expenditure should be quite high, if the political cultural theory is correct. This is not what impressionistic analyses of fiscal policy in this period have suggested, however, for both Callow and Bullough contend that "Boss" Buckley kept expenditure low. A somewhat low level of incumbency and a high level of partisan competition, indicated by the increasing share of officials elected by the major parties, may have had a disciplining effect on fiscal policy.

Although the reform mayors of the 1890s accused their predecessors of extravagance, their campaigns did not revolutionize the ethnic, occupational, or partisan bases of officeholding and, in fact, resembled patterns in the machine era in every dimension except ethnicity. The political cultural theory would predict nonetheless that this would be a period of low expenditure.

Because it was boss-dominated and controlled by officials with almost no high white-collar representation, the Union Labor era should have been another period of high expenditure, according to the political cultural theory. But in this case, as during the machine era, it may have been necessary for the boss-dominated organizations to watch their fiscal policy carefully in order to maintain the political legitimacy necessary for other activities, such as the sale of franchises.

To test these hypotheses about fiscal behavior, I have again entered four dummy variables into regression equations analyzing per capita operating expenditure, per capita assessed valuation, per capita revenue, and the tax rate. Again, I have excluded one of the dummies, this time the first period, so that we will be comparing all other eras with the first. The results of the equations are displayed in table 23. Again, I have added the constant and coefficients to come up with measures of the

TABLE 23

REGRESSIONS OF PER CAPITA EXPENDITURE, REVENUE, ASSESSED VALUATION, AND THE TAX RATE ON THE POLITICAL ERAS

Vars. and Stats.	EXP	REV	VAL	TAX
IRREG	− 1.503	− .5872	− 135.33	− .6215[b]
MACH	− 1.284	− 3.584	− 290.85[c]	− .8802[b]
REF	− 2.228	− .5792	− 42.77	− .7055[b]
ULP	− 1.205	− .0207	2.810	− .7540[b]
Constant	15.73[b]	15.025[b]	1134.0[b]	1.835[b]
Adj. R-Sq.	.2627	.2903	.0320	.4614
Stan. Err.	1.371	2.0081	253.47	.2820
Est. Rho	.8703	.3427	.1678	.1014

[a] N = 35 (1870–1905).
[b] Significant at .01 level.
[c] Significant at .05 level.

TABLE 24

ESTIMATES OF PER CAPITA EXPENDITURE, REVENUE, ASSESSED VALUATION, AND THE TAX RATE BY POLITICAL ERA

Vars. and Stats.	EXP	REV	VAL	TAX
PTP	15.73	15.02	1134.0	1.835
IRREG	(14.22)	(14.43)	(998.67)	1.214
MACH	(14.44)	11.44	843.15	.9548
REF	(13.45)	(14.44)	(1091.2)	1.1275
ULP	(14.52)	(15.00)	(1136.8)	1.081

Note: Parentheses indicate estimates that are not statistically significant.

effects of each era on the dependent variable (see table 24). In these tests, as in chapter 3, there are thirty-five observations, ranging from 1870 through 1905.[36]

These results reveal both similarities and differences among the eras which confound the expectations of the political cultural theory; contradict Erie's argument, mentioned earlier, that there is a fiscal political cycle in the city; and raise serious questions about previous portrayals of the city's fiscal political history. On the whole, the eras after 1875 are more different from the era before 1875 than they are from one another. As the statistically significant estimates of the tax rate indicate, the average rate was always substantially lower after 1875 than it was before that time. The pattern in the estimates of the other fiscal variables is roughly similar, but most of these estimates are not statistically significant.

Part of the explanation for the uniformly lower level of taxation after 1875 is institutional. The political code of 1872, which secured the city's real-property tax base for the first time, allowed the tax rate to be lowered without cuts in revenue and expenditure. This effect is revealed in the similarities of the estimates of valuation, revenue, and expenditure for the years from 1876 through 1882, and 1893 through 1906.

This institutional effect does not explain the most striking and important difference among the eras after 1875, namely, the uniquely low and statistically significant average levels of taxation, valuation, and revenue during the machine era. This was the period during which major party machines allegedly controlled the policymaking of the most foreign-born and Irish-born officials in the city's history. The failure of this period to live up to the reputation for fiscal irresponsibility which contemporaries gave it and which some historians would expect is interesting, indeed.

In general, however, these political eras alone do not explain that much of the variation in the fiscal variables. To this point, we have been assuming that "all the world" is political culture, because these are the only variables entered into the equations. The analytic price paid for this exclusion of other elements of reality is revealed in the adjusted R^2 of the equations in table 23. This combination of political cultural variables alone explains about 26 percent of the variation in per capita expenditure, 30 percent of that in revenue, only 3 percent of that in the valuation, and 46 percent of that in the tax rate. Hence a good deal

TABLE 25

INDEPENDENT VARIABLES IN THE REGRESSIONS OF PER CAPITA EXPENDITURE, REVENUE, ASSESSED VALUATION AND THE TAX RATE ON POLITICAL CULTURAL AND SOCIOECONOMIC STRUCTURAL VARIABLES

Variable name	Explanation
PORT	Per capita value of imports and exports at the port (mean = $277.07)
WORKS	Number of manufacturing works per 100 acres in the manufacturing districts (mean = 18.65)
MANVAL	Per capita value of manufactured products (mean = $231.24)
RES	Number of real estate sales per 100 population (mean = 1.63)
PTP	Period of local reform parties, 1870–1876
IRREG	Period following collapse of local reform parties, 1877-1883
MACH	Period of control by national party machines, 1884-1893
REF	Period of control by Populist and progressive reformers, 1894-1901
ULP	Period of control by the Union Labor party, 1902–1906

of the variation in the dependent fiscal variables remains to be explained. As we saw in the last chapter, some of this variation is explained by socioeconomic structural variables.

To avoid the same mistaken separation of these theories for which I have criticized other studies, it is now necessary to test the joint effects of political culture and socioeconomic structure on these fiscal variables, by combining the independent variables used in chapters 3 and 4 in one equation. The variables used in this joint test are displayed in table 25, and include all those thus far discussed, with the exception of the city size variables, which are excluded from the joint test on the grounds both of theory and of the results in chapter 3. As I suggested there, at one level these theories disagree on the meaning of time in their explanations of the development of urban government. The socioeconomic structural theory contends that the physical size of the city grows over time, and so also must the city government. The political cultural theory contends that political regimes succeed one another and have varying effects on the growth of municipal government

TABLE 26

REGRESSIONS OF PER CAPITA EXPENDITURE, REVENUE, ASSESSED VALUATION, AND THE
TAX RATE ON POLITICAL CULTURAL AND SOCIOECONOMIC STRUCTURAL VARIABLES[a]

Vars. and Stats.	EXP	REV	VAL	TAX
PORT (− 1)	.0051	.0121	4.42[b]	− .0030
WORKS (− 1)	.0475	− .1191	− 2.09	− .0080
RES (− 1)	.1871	1.295[c]	− 91.70[c]	.3143[b]
MANVAL (− 1)	.0121[c]	.0148[c]	1.8373[c]	− .0008
IRREG	− 2.0356[d]	1.18	− 313.01[c]	− .1446
MACH	− 1.9084	− 2.639	− 199.38[d]	− .6338[b]
REF	− 2.907	4.13[c]	309.50[d]	− .3636[c]
ULP	− 2.0628	3.54	328.57[d]	− .5271[c]
Constant	13.853[b]	6.077[c]	462.36[c]	2.230[b]
Adj. R-Sq.	.2643	.5971	.8257	.7702
Stan. Err.	1.34	1.94	141.80	.2042
Est. Rho	.8737	− .2076	− .3809	− .2262

[a] N = 35 (1870–1905).
[b] Significant at .01 level.
[c] Significant at .05 level.
[d] Significant at .10 level.

over time, and hence on the level of fiscal variables as well. Obviously, one can only divide time in so many ways and still hope to have meaningful statistical results. In chapter 3 the effect of the city size variables was statistically significant but theoretically contradictory. Something was operating over time to keep expenditure almost stable and the tax rate declining, but there was no reason to believe that this factor was the expanding size of the city. A more likely cause, as we have just seen, was the effect of political culture. For this reason I have maintained the political cultural divisions of time in these equations, by entering four of the five political cultural variables into the equations.

Table 26 displays the results of the regressions of the fiscal variables on the socioeconomic structural and political cultural variables in combination. The statistics on these equations indicate that the combination does a better job of explaining the valuation, tax rate, and revenue than of explaining expenditure: it explains 82 percent of the variation in the valuation, 77 percent of that in the tax rate, 60 percent of that in revenue, and only 26 percent of the variation in expenditure.

The valuation was not only best explained by this combination but was also affected by more of the variables within the combination than any of the other fiscal dependent variables. As was the case in chapter 3, the valuation was again affected positively and significantly by business at the port and industrialization—this time, the per capita value of manufactured goods—and negatively by the number of real estate sales. Within the political cultural variables, all of which are statistically significant, the average level of per capita assessed valuation was lower in the second and third periods of the city's political history than in the first period, and higher in the fourth and fifth periods. This indicates a pattern of higher valuation per capita from 1870 through 1876 and again from 1894 through 1905, but lower valuation from 1877 through 1894, with a particularly sharp drop from the first to the second (1876–1882) period.

During the second and third periods of the city's political history—the years between the early and later reform periods—the socioeconomic and political cultural systems were at war over the valuation. Socioeconomic development drove the valuation up; political action appears to have attempted to keep it down. During the fourth and fifth periods of the city's history, these systems worked in tandem, with both socioeconomic and political variables influencing the valuation positively.

The mediating factor between the tax base and revenue was, of course, the tax rate, which also was affected by both socioeconomic and political cultural variables. Again the rate was positively and significantly influenced by the increase in real estate sales per hundred residents. An increase in the number of real estate sales brought about an increase in the tax rate the next year. This was counteracted, however, by the attempts of politicians to reduce the rate relative to that in the period 1870–1875. All political regimes after the first attempted to keep the rate low, with the largest reductions relative to the first period coming during the machine and Union Labor periods. Only during the machine era, however, was there a statistically significant reduction in both the valuation and the tax rate.

Of course, the relationships between the valuation and the tax rate

TABLE 27

ADJUSTED R² AND STANDARD ERRORS OF REGRESSIONS OF FISCAL
VARIABLES ON SOCIOECONOMIC STRUCTURAL VARIABLES ALONE, POLITICAL
CULTURAL VARIABLES ALONE, AND SOCIOECONOMIC STRUCTURAL AND POLITICAL
CULTURAL VARIABLES IN COMBINATION

Theory	Statistics	EXP	REV	VAL	TAX
SES	Adj. R-Sq.	.3039	.1656	.3439	.6188
	Stan. Err.	1.311	2.1194	176.06	.2369
PC	Adj. R-Sq.	.2527	.2903	.0320	.4614
	Stan. Err.	1.371	2.0081	253.20	.2820
SES + PC	Adj. R-Sq.	.2643	.5971	.8257	.7702
	Stan. Err.	1.34	1.94	141.80	.2042

carried over into revenue and expenditure, too. The positive and significant effect of real estate sales on revenue reveals that, on average,
the tax rate rose more than the valuation fell in the year following an
increase in real estate sales. Moreover, the positive relationship between
revenue and the value of manufactures reflects the positive relationship
between that variable and the valuation, a relationship not mediated in
a statistically significant fashion by the tax rate. Finally, the statistically
significant positive coefficient on the reform era suggests that the valuation increased more than the tax rate decreased in that period. The
effect of most of these variables was again exhausted by the time the
level of expenditure was determined. Expenditure was influenced positively by the value of manufactured products and negatively by the
second political era. In comparison with the first political era, average
per capita expenditure dropped significantly during the years 1876–
1882. However, this combination of variables explains relatively little
of the total variation in expenditure.

To compare the relative ability of political cultural and socioeconomic variables, alone and in combination, to explain the fiscal variables, table 27 displays the adjusted R² and standard errors of the three
sets of equations discussed thus far. Each of these statistics is relatively
independent of the number of independent variables in the equation,
and thus can be compared across equations containing different numbers of independent variables, as these do. On the whole, the comparison indicates that the valuation, revenue, and the tax rate are much
better explained by socioeconomic and political cultural variables in

combination than by either kind of variable alone. In the case of all three of these fiscal variables, the R^2 is highest and the standard error lowest in the equation containing both types of variables. Indeed, the combination has the somewhat ironic effect of clarifying differences among the political eras which were not statistically significant in the equations that included the political cultural variables alone. Expenditure, however, is not well explained by these variables, either alone or in combination. The standard errors of all the equations analyzing expenditure are remarkably similar, and combining these variables does little to increase the explanatory power of the equation. Thus important determinants of expenditure remain to be found.

Nonetheless, these results do indicate that, even in the presence of variables measuring socioeconomic structural development, variables indicating periods of different political cultures agreed on by both contemporaries and historians do have an independent statistical effect. Socioeconomic structural change is therefore a necessary but insufficient explanation of fiscal policy in San Francisco. Of course, the converse is also true; the political cultural variables alone do a poor job of explaining the valuation, for example, thus demonstrating the necessity but insufficiency of political culture in the explanation of fiscal policy.

Having established that both types of variables are necessary for an adequate explanation of fiscal policy, it is important to reiterate that neither type of variable has performed exactly as predicted by the theories. In San Francisco, socioeconomic development enriched the tax base rather than straining the treasury. Regimes in control in different political periods similarly minimized expenditure and the tax rate, and in the first and third periods in the city's political history, they worked to undercut the positive effects of socioeconomic development by lowering the valuation and/or the tax rate. Moreover, contrary to the predictions of the political cultural theory, the machine era was distinguished not by its profligacy but by its apparent penury. During this era, when there were more foreign-born and Irish-born city officials than ever before, there were statistically significant negative impacts on the valuation and the tax rate. During the reform era, in contrast, the valuation and thus revenue increased.

These findings demonstrate that political culture was a full partner— and at times a worthy adversary—of socioeconomic development in the formation of fiscal policy in San Francisco. Because they suggest that political culture was not simply an epiphenomenon of socioeconomic change, these results give us license to consider political culture in more detail. To do so, we must change our definition of political culture and our method of analysis.

The operational definition of political culture in this chapter has been a period of time during which a particular type of party (e.g., People's, Democratic) or type of organization within a party (e.g., machine, reform) has controlled the city's politics. This definition reflects the limitations of the theory we have been testing because, as already pointed out, the political cultural approach to urban political history operates by establishing periods of predominance of certain political tendencies and then attributing all actions taken during these periods to the predominant political actors, such as the "pragmatic boss" or the "bureaucratic reformers."

The political periods observed in this chapter have not been defined arbitrarily; their existence has been confirmed by both contemporary observers and historical analysis, and has been checked against local election results and the backgrounds of local officials. In other words, these periods were "real," and there were real differences in political personnel among them. These differences do not by themselves explain the differences or similarities in the fiscal variables we have discovered. We have established that during these eras there were statistically significant differences—and similarities—in fiscal policy. We have not established what it was within or among these eras that caused these differences and similarities.

To avoid the mistakes of the political cultural approach, we must now attempt to link our findings to the ideas held and actions taken by the political actors within and across these eras, concerning ourselves with the context of local political action, the "theory of the state" of local political actors, the institutional or electoral political influences on fiscal policymaking, and so on. Thus we turn from the estimation of statistical parameters to the analysis of political parameters, that is, to the ideological and institutional boundaries within which San Francisco policymakers actually operated.

5

Establishing the Boundaries: Political Institutions and Fiscal Ideologies, 1856–1882

In December 1918, the serialized memoirs of a widely known San Francisco politician began running in the San Francisco *Bulletin*, and in the first installment, the author considered the fiscal history of the city, paying great tribute to "a number of patriotic citizens" who, following the passage of the Consolidation Act in 1856, had labored to rescue the city from "the financial abyss." They were, he wrote, "men of affairs with wide monetary connections," the "counterparts of today's dollar a year men," and their great accomplishment was to bring the city out of "frenzied finance" to the "line of strict economy and the rapid retirement of its fiscal obligations."[1]

We met the men in question in chapter 4, as the leaders of the People's party, the local independent party that emerged as the political arm of the vigilante movement of 1856 and that represented the bipartisan political and fiscal outlook of the city's early native-born, merchant-led, interlocking elite. From 1860 to 1882, a tribute to these municipal founding fathers was never far from the lips of political orators; indeed, one would be hard put to find a single municipal campaign in which they were not invoked by some candidate or party laying claim to their mantle.

While there was nothing unusual in most politicians' genuflection before the People's party, there was something truly ironic in that of the memoirist just quoted, because he was none other than Christopher Augustine Buckley, the Irish-born alleged "boss" of San Francisco from 1882 to 1891 and, according to his detractors, the chief corrupter of the West, if not of the Western world. Yet had Buckley "bossed" in the 1850s instead of the 1880s, these same "men of affairs" whom he praised

116

might have seen to it that he did not live to enjoy the wealthy retirement that gave him the leisure to write memoirs.

Although ironic, Buckley's tribute was by no means disingenuous; he was being neither nostalgic nor rhetorical in his tribute to the fiscal founding fathers. On the contrary, after a life of corruption, Buckley clearly was attempting to go out on the side of the angels, and his choice of angels—the upper-class, fiscally conservative nonpartisans of the People's party—was sincere, despite the fact that they would by no means have reciprocated his compliments. Buckley nonetheless did share with the People's party, and with the first two generations of San Francisco political leaders, a set of ideas about the role of the public sector in urban society and about the relationship between politics and urban fiscal policy.

Almost regardless of party or persuasion, political actors in San Francisco between 1860 and 1882 shared a consensus on fiscal policy containing three principles—a low tax rate, low expenditure, and no indebtedness and thus the construction of capital improvements on a pay-as-you-go basis. However, the political significance of this consensus and the means of its enforcement were different during the first and second periods of the city's political history. From 1860 through 1873, local independent parties and their Democratic opponents shared the same fundamental principles of fiscal policy but battled furiously over whether the native-born "elites" of the independent parties or the foreign-born "common men" of the Democratic party should govern the city. After 1875, the decline of the independent parties left the local electoral political field open to the local branches of the "two great, national" parties, as they preferred to call themselves, and the strategy they adopted was to minimize their class and ethnic differences and focus instead on their fiscal policies.

During the first period, the independent party officials who controlled the city had a great deal of fiscal political legitimacy and autonomy because of their high status, their successful attempt to wrap themselves in the mantle of the vigilantes, and the relatively low level of controversy over fiscal policy. During these years, the setting of the tax rate and levels of expenditure was a more or less automatic process. Supervisors did not attack the auditor's estimates, and tax rates usually passed unanimously and were never vetoed by the mayor. While condemning high expenditure, the independents nonetheless authorized incremental annual increases in the cost of municipal government, so

that by 1876, real per capita local expenditure had increased 14 percent, from $16.18 in 1860 to $18.39 in 1876. At the same time, however, the independents were able to reduce the tax rate by about
50 percent because the city's assessed valuation increased by about
135 percent, primarily as a result of the political code of 1872 (see
chap. 2).

With the decline of the independent parties after 1873, appeals to
outright elitism and the common man began to appear less frequently
in the party platforms, and the ethnic and social backgrounds of Democratic and Republican municipal officials became more similar. Beginning in 1875, however, fiscal policy became more politicized as the
regular parties strove to prove that they were as reliable fiscally as the
independent parties, yet still different from one another. Supervisors
now began to demand cuts in departmental appropriations, the first
mayoral vetoes of the tax rate were recorded, and both parties adopted
the practice of lowering the tax rate in election years and raising it in
alternate years. Beginning in 1879, the Republicans attempted to codify
the newly politicized fiscal policy by including in their platform a pledge
to keep the tax rate at the level of $1 per $100 of assessed valuation.
The pledge, called the Dollar Limit, appeared in both platforms in the
municipal election of 1881, and by 1882 it began to have a dramatic
effect on municipal fiscal policy, driving taxation and expenditure steadily downward.

In this chapter, we investigate these developments during the years
1860 through 1882 by analyzing four main objects: (1) the fiscal ideas
of municipal politicians and the newspaper spokesmen of the political
parties; (2) the actual mechanics of the formation of fiscal policy by
the board of supervisors and the executive officers of the city; (3) the
social background of the municipal officials who actually made this policy; and (4) the fiscal products of this policy that we have been considering thus far—namely, expenditure, revenue, valuation, and the tax
rate.[2]

THE STRUCTURE OF POLITICAL ACTION, 1860–1882

Before moving on to a more detailed look at these factors, it is important to consider what we mean when we say that a fiscal consensus
developed in these years. When I use the term "consensus," I refer to

a set of ideas shared by political actors and their editorial spokesmen and fiscal policymakers. I do not contend that this set of ideas was widespread among the populace. Most analyses of urban political history in San Francisco and elsewhere assume that every election produces the sound of the authentic vox populi, but this seems so only because elections are abstracted from time and from the structure of political behavior. Placing the electoral history of the city in time and structure suggests that the municipal political universe of the city was small and not totally representative. Moreover, participation in local elections was less important to the parties and the voters than was participation in state and national elections.

The participation of San Franciscans in the political affairs of the city was structured by four main factors: (1) the requirements for the exercise of the suffrage; (2) the scheduling of elections; (3) the exertions of the parties; and (4) the behavior of the voters themselves, in the sense that, over time, repeated patterns became a structure of expected behavior. The effect of the first of these structuring factors was to narrow the social breadth of the electorate and thus blunt the utility of suffrage as an instrument of social protest, while that of the second and third was to raise or lower the size of the active electorate, depending on whether or not municipal elections were scheduled at the same time as state or federal elections.

While the United States has prided itself on its early removal of property qualifications for suffrage, it was only very recently that lengthy residency requirements were largely removed. In California, from statehood (1850) until 1880, it was required that a voter be a twenty-one-year-old male resident of the United States who had been a resident of the state for six months and of his election precinct for thirty days before the election in which he desired to vote. In 1880, this requirement was stiffened to require residence in the state for one year, in the county for ninety days, and in the precinct for thirty days. In 1894, a literacy requirement was added, requiring new voters to be able to read the constitution in English and to sign their names. Throughout these years, all voters were required to register before every general (i.e., statewide) election; if they did not, they became ineligible to vote.[3]

As we saw in chapter 3, mobility studies of San Francisco conducted on data from 1860 through 1900 have demonstrated that, as in other large cities, the rate of persistence from decade to decade averaged about 50 percent. At least in part for this reason, on average between

1875 and 1905, only a bare majority of males twenty-one and over were registered, and only a minority of these men actually voted for most offices. Between 1875, when registration statistics began to be kept, and 1905, when the last election before the earthquake was held, an average of 54 percent of the men twenty-one and over were registered to vote. This puts into perspective the very high level of participation once voters registered. Of those registered to vote, an average of 88 percent voted for president and governor, 80 percent for mayor, and 77 percent for supervisors. While these figures are quite high, what they mean is that, on average, 42 percent of men aged twenty-one and over voted for president, 37 percent for governor, 34 percent for mayor, and 31 percent for the board of supervisors. In San Francisco, then, the vaunted voice of the people was actually the voice of some of the people some of the time. Moreover, because studies have demonstrated that mobility is both age- and class-specific, it is likely that the core of the city's active electorate was older, more prosperous, and of higher occupational status than the male population as a whole.[4]

As the significant differences in voting for the various offices suggest, the higher the level of office at stake, in general, the higher the level of participation among registered voters. This relationship meant that fewer voters were mobilized when municipal elections were held alone than when they were held along with state or federal elections. These differences in participation were maximized during the years covered in this chapter because for most of this period, local, state, and federal elections were held separately. From 1860 through 1881, presidential elections were, of course, held every fourth year in November. State elections were held in September of odd years, with the governor elected every two years from 1859 to 1867, and every four years thereafter. Local elections were held annually from 1859 through 1871, with about half of the supervisors and half of the executive officers elected each time. From 1861 through 1866, municipal elections were held in May, separate from state elections. From 1867 until 1871, they were held in September, meaning that they coincided with statewide elections twice, in 1867 and 1871. In 1872, there was no municipal election in anticipation of a change in the system the following year to the election of all municipal officers together in September of odd-numbered years. This system was to continue until 1881. From 1860 until 1881, then, mayors were elected at times other than the governor or president seven out of twelve times.[5]

Because there are no continuing statistics on the number of registered voters or the number of males aged twenty-one and over before 1875, we must calculate our participation rate for these years by dividing the number of votes cast in an election by the total population. Between 1860 and 1881, this rate was 19 percent at presidential elections, 17 percent at gubernatorial elections, and only 15 percent when the mayor was elected alone. At elections when the mayor was elected with either the president or the governor, the rate for mayor rose to 17 percent, indicating that the "top" of the ticket increased votes for mayor, rather than vice versa. For purposes of comparison, after 1875 a rate of 48 percent participation among males twenty-one and over was equivalent to a rate of 19 percent per capita. Assuming that this relationship was stable over time, this suggests that the rate of participation in mayoral elections between 1860 and 1881 was about 40 percent of males twenty-one and over.[6]

The most significant factors in these variations in participation were the exertions of the parties themselves and the effects of straight-ticket voting, which was the rule in the state until the election of 1892. There is abundant evidence in the newspaper coverage of elections that the parties expended more time and money on the mobilization of voters at presidential elections than at gubernatorial elections, and that they expended the least of both at municipal elections held separately from others. There was more coverage of more events during presidential and gubernatorial election campaigns than during municipal campaigns because the parties sponsored more events, such as speeches, ratification meetings, and parades, during those elections. Moreover, in their role as partisan spokesmen, the newspapers editorialized more frequently and more emotionally the higher the level of the election. Because the parties controlled the printing and distribution of ballots and straight-ticket voting was the rule, high participation for president or governor meant higher participation for mayor, but as we have seen, the reverse was not true in these years.[7]

Furthermore, the mandates that mayors carried into office were by no means enormous. Between 1860 and 1881, mayors were elected on average by about twelve hundred votes (about 12 percent of the total vote cast). However, this majority was only about 7 percent when the mayor was elected alone, again indicating the important connections among the various levels of electoral action. The average majority also moved downward over time as the city moved out of the era of independent parties and into partisan mayoral politics. During the heyday of the People's party, from 1861 to 1866, when all mayoral elections were separate, the mean majority was 12 percent; from 1867 to 1873, it was 7.6 percent. In the election of 1875, which was the first time national party candidates captured both the mayoralty and the board of supervisors, the mayor did not receive a majority for the first time in the city's history, and from 1877 through 1881, the average majority was only 5.7 percent.[8]

Reading the newspapers alone, one would think that elections at all levels involved the clashing of gigantic armies of "the masses," "workingmen," "citizens," and "taxpayers." But as we have seen, these were all permutations of about 40 percent of all adult males. As great as the parties may have been, on the local level they were gladiators fighting in a very small arena, and the fiscal consensus they developed, to which we now turn, was by no means the cry of the masses. Political participation was simply not a mass activity in these years.

THE FOUNDATIONS OF FISCAL POLITICAL IDEOLOGY

Outrageous taxes were squeezed from the people but not spent on them. Instead they went "to buy fine horses for public thieves, luxurious living for hordes of gamblers and idlers, and fine raiment and showy equipages for impudent and brazen faced prostitutes." While the wives and daughters of the citizens slaved "over the wash tub," the "painted mistresses of public officers took the air in gilded coaches." The scene was not Rome in the days of Nero or Versailles under Louis XIV but, as recollected in the fevered phrases of local reformers, San Francisco from 1852 to 1856. According to these recollections, these were the years when the "gamblers, loafers, bummers, and the infamous of all sorts" ruled the city, led by "street walking, button holing, professional politicians" who had "bellies of big dimensions and no regular means of filling them" other than living off the public treasury. Having learned their trade "in the school of politics peculiar to New York," these men had moved to San Francisco, "seized her government, and held it struggling but helpless in their grasp." However, drunk with power, the "enthroned boodlers" finally counted too much "upon American patience," for the ultimate response to this corruption was "such a superb uprising of honesty against lawlessness and violence [as] the world had scarcely seen. Scoundrels were hung, deported, ejected; thieves were driven forth, the government rehabilitated, offices purified, and honest men resumed again the control of the city."[9]

Of course, the facts of 1852–1856 were slightly less dramatic than this. This account of those days is what I would call the Legend of Vigilantism, a creation myth composed of part fact and part fiction and used to rationalize a variety of political positions during the years 1860–1882. What the legend established was, most generally, a standard of civic performance by which succeeding political movements would measure themselves and one another, and a mantle that competing organizations would seek. More proximately, however, it produced a local political party, the People's party. In its original and later incarnations, this party would attempt to claim apostolic succession from the heroes of '56 and thus to dominate San Francisco politics during the years 1860 through 1875. It would do so by proclaiming greatly influential ideas about the nature of political leadership, the mechanics of political organizations, the legitimacy of party politics, and, most important, the fiscal behavior of the municipality. To understand the staying power both of the legend and of the party, as well as the obstacles that competing political organizations faced, we must briefly consider the events leading up to the founding of this party.

On May 14, 1856, James King, a popular crusading editor of a reform newspaper in San Francisco, was shot down in the street by a local politician whom he had been attacking in the columns of his newspaper. The shooting outraged the community, and within hours local notables called a meeting to determine a way to ensure "justice" for the attacker. By afternoon of the following day, twenty-five hundred men were enrolled by the so-called Vigilance Committee—a number that was to swell to six to eight thousand. Having drilled and armed themselves, the vigilantes marched on the jail on May 18, took the editor's assailant and another accused murderer from the local authorities, and returned them to vigilante headquarters for "trial." On May 2, the day of the editor's funeral, the vigilantes hung both men. By mid-July, when the committee ended its labors, hundreds of men had been detained and many "tried." As a result of these "trials," two more men were hung, twenty-five were ordered "deported," and others were simply driven out of town by threat. All of this was conducted illegally, under the eyes of the local authorities, who either supported the vigilantes or were outgunned by them.[10]

In 1851, a previous vigilance committee had disbanded after administering its "justice" to several malefactors. In 1856, however, the size of the movement, the number and magnitude of its acts, and the political importance of its opposition—the governor opposed it, and one of those arrested was a state supreme court justice—convinced the committee to go one step farther and form an organized political arm. In August a committee of twenty-one members of or sympathizers with the vigilante executive committee, styling itself the "People's Nominating Committee," went into session to prepare a ticket suitable to the vigilantes and their supporters for the November municipal election. The deliberations of the committee were conducted in secret, and according to H. P. Coon, one of the founders of the People's party who was nominated for police judge for the fall election, the committee resolved at the outset to nominate its candidates "from among those who did not desire, nor seek for an office, but who were known to be in full sympathy with the reform movement."[11]

The ticket was revealed on September 11, 1856, under the name of the People's Reform party. Its platform denounced the extravagance and lawlessness of the previous regime, but also criticized the failure of men of the "better sort" to do their civic duty and demanded that good men devote at least a few weeks of their time to public affairs. At least in part because its opposition was split between the Democrats and the Know-Nothing or American party, the new party was successful, winning the offices of mayor, sheriff, chief of police, assessor, police judge, and half of the members of the board of supervisors—enough to ensure that the party would control the organization of the new government required by the Consolidation Act, which had gone into effect the previous July. Because approximately half the municipal officers were elected annually after 1856, similar nominating procedures were followed in 1857 and 1858, and this procedure thus became institutionalized and a trademark of the party. Moreover, as Peter Decker has pointed out, the dominance of the party continued, for by 1860 former executives of the Vigilance Committee occupied positions as supervisors, city assessor, chief of police, city sheriff, under sheriff, deputy sheriff, deputy district attorney, harbormaster, and city treasurer, among other posts.[12]

Also institutionalized were the party's essentially elite nature and its fiscal conservatism. As Decker has demonstrated, the leadership of the vigilante committee of 1856 was dominated by the city's elite merchants. A total of 60 percent of the committee's executive committee consisted of merchants, and 90 percent of these were high-status importer-wholesalers. Of those who held civil or military offices with the committee, 70 percent were high-status general merchants, importer-wholesalers, bankers, brokers, manufacturers, or professionals. Most of the vigilante leadership simply moved over into the leadership of the People's party or, as we saw in chapter 4, chose officials like its founders.[13]

At the time of the uprising and thereafter, the vigilantes cited four reasons for taking the law into their own hands: (1) the extravagance of local government, (2) the incompetence and/or corruption of local officials, (3) the domination of politics by a local Democratic machine, and (4) the failure of judicial institutions. By "throwing the rascals out" beginning in 1856, the vigilantes eliminated the second and third of these problems, and their administration of "justice" solved the fourth, at least temporarily. The necessary last part of their "revolution" was implementation of the fiscal policy of the elites in municipal government, which was, to put it briefly, a policy of almost total fiscal restraint.[14]

According to contemporary estimates, expenses for city and county government under the People's regime dropped from $2.6 million in 1855 to $353,000 in 1857, and the local tax rate plunged 40 percent in the same period. Contemporaries claimed that the People's Reform party was a "marvel" of economy and attributed its political success in great part to its economical government. Later commentators, somewhat less taken with the party, noted that a great deal of the saving was brought about by the Consolidation Act itself, which, by combining city and county government, had eliminated duplicating city and county offices and set official salaries at a lower rate. Later observers also noted that the party's penuriousness affected vital services adversely. As a result of the cutbacks, teachers were laid off and children forced out of the schools, evening illumination of the streets was discontinued, street improvements were stopped, no significant government construction projects were undertaken, and most city business was conducted in rented buildings.[15]

Following up on all the claims and counterclaims of the 1856 era is difficult and unnecessary for our purposes. Roger Lotchin has successfully demolished vigilante claims that crime, government, and officials were all getting worse just before the vigilante uprising. Regarding the

claims of fiscal extravagance, he has made the important point that although the city and county governments undoubtedly ran up debts,
"nearly every kind of institution shared that dilemma." Indeed, the real
culprits in the "extravagance" of the pre-1856 period probably were
the instability of the city's tax base and the very high wages, prices,
and interest rates in the city brought about by the gold rush conditions.
The city and county governments were forced to pay gold rush prices
for goods and services but were unable to collect gold rush taxes because of the transience of the population, resistance to taxation, and
lack of legislation securing the tax base. The result was a revenue short-
fall made up by short-term borrowing at very high interest rates. Moreover, most of the borrowing was done to pay local merchants, firms,
and individuals, some of whom went to the state legislature to seek
legislation forcing the city to pay them. In such a situation, it would
have been remarkable if the city had remained debt-free.[16]

The point here is not that the People's party was (or was not) the
fiscal savior of the city, but that it claimed to be, thus playing its role
in establishing the Legend of Vigilantism. At the opening of the political
era that we will now consider, the components of this legend were:

That between 1852 and 1856 San Francisco had been ruled and plundered
by corrupt, extravagant politicians.

That in 1856 the citizens had risen up to "throw the rascals out" and had
succeeded politically by means of a nonpartisan, elite-led local organization that
selected its candidates by secret committee.

That the result of these procedures had been the moral and fiscal salvation
of the city.

Whatever the factual status of the legend in 1856, by 1860 it had
become a political "fact"—that is, an ideology to be reckoned with by
those in politics and municipal government throughout this period. Indeed, much of what followed, especially the battles over partisanship
and municipal fiscal policy and development, was defined within the
narrow confines of the vigilante legend. For those who claimed to be
successors to its promise, the challenge was to maintain and fulfill it;
for those who opposed them, the difficulty was creating a position of
political legitimacy against it.

As noted in chapter 4, the People's party controlled San Francisco
politics almost absolutely until 1866, when local elections were once

again joined with those of the state. In 1866 the supporters of the People's party declared themselves to be the Union party, which ran until 1869, when it was replaced by the Taxpayer's party. This, in turn, was unveiled in 1873 as the Republican party, the charge that the Democrats had been making about the "independent" local parties all along. At each one of these turns, however, the party's most vocal editorial supporters declared that the line from the People's party continued unbroken, and, until 1873 at least, the parties did maintain the defining characteristics of the original party.[17]

To the members of the People's party, their legatees, and their most zealous editorial supporters, the *Alta* and the *Bulletin*, the issue in municipal politics was a simple one: the people versus the politicians. Arrayed on one side were the nominees of the People's, Union, and Taxpayer's parties; on the other were the "professional" politicians, the "place hunters," and the feasters at the "public crib." Outside of the nonpartisan, local elite parties, in other words, there was nothing but corruption.[18]

According to its supporters, the virtue of the People's party was that its nominees "were selected only on the ground of their fitness and capacity," so that they had neither "friends to reward nor enemies to punish." For the "purely political" parties, however, "partisan services are of more weight than qualification," and politics are practiced for the "most selfish and sordid ends." The People's-Union-Taxpayer's nominees, then, tried to distinguish themselves from the rest (1) by refusing to hold an open party primary; (2) by nominating only the "best" men, who were not allegedly "professional" politicians; and (3) by declaring a focus on local issues and thus refusing to permit "extraneous political questions to blind us to local concerns."[19]

Already in the early 1860s, party primaries were notorious for their corruption and even danger, and this reputation was to grow as the century went on and primaries continued to be supervised only by the parties themselves. Because of the corruption of primaries, it was not difficult for the supporters of the People's party to legitimize the secret nominating committee procedure that distinguished the independent parties from 1860 through 1873. As the *Bulletin* put it, if San Francisco were to be governed by the selections of the primary system, the city would be "completely at the mercy of hired ruffians." Good men, it noted, had never attended primary conventions—in part because of fear for their safety—and thus the citizens lost nothing in not being able to select the candidates for the People's ticket. On the contrary, they gained, for the purified primary procedures—nomination by secret committee—guaranteed the right sort of candidates, according to the party's rubric, namely, that none be a "politician."[20]

In assessing the tickets of the independent parties, the declarations of the parties and their editorial supporters made it clear what non-partisanship really meant. In evaluating the People's 1866 ticket, for example, the *Bulletin* noted, as usual, that "no attention had been paid to the national politics" of the candidates, but also that all candidates are "old citizens, of established character and good reputation ... chosen from nearly all the leading businesses and professions." As such, the candidates were "thoroughly conversant with the great interests of the city." That this was a barely camouflaged endorsement of elitism was not denied; indeed, the assumption was that only those in the elite could have the background and the integrity to manage the city safely. As the *Alta* put it, it was only since the advent of the People's party that "the local government enjoys the confidence and respect of the community."[21]

In fact, the mayoral candidates of the independent parties reinforced their elite and nonpolitical image both in the way they dealt with their nominations and in their conduct in office. Two of the early mayors of the city gave dictations describing their public lives to historian Hubert Howe Bancroft, which have survived in their papers in the Bancroft Library. These two mayors were H. P. Coon, elected by the People's party in 1863 and 1865, and Thomas H. Selby, winner on the Taxpayer's ticket in 1869. Both emphasized that they had left a "higher" calling, or at least a more lucrative one, only at the importuning of their acquaintances. The usual electoral ritual included refusing the nomination of the committee when offered, but accepting it when a more dramatic appeal was made. In this manner the candidate proved that he had not sought the office, but instead, in the phrase of the time, that the "office had sought the man," and thus the nomination was "pure."

In Coon's case, he wrote, in accepting the nomination, he "resigned a [medical] practice already exceeding the official salary and only at the urgent request of friends and citizens of the People's Party." In fact, Coon maintained, he was nominated, refused the nomination, then accepted only after a "large" committee visited him and convinced him to run. Selby, an enormously wealthy merchant and manufacturer, was, if possible, even more reluctant, but as he wrote, "his many refusals of nomination were finally overcome by the persistent solicitations of the Taxpayer's nominating convention aided by the urgings of personal friends in all parties." To emphasize his nonprofessional status, at the end of his two years in office Selby donated his official salary to charity.[22]

As we saw in chapter 4, when this political era is compared with the others, there is a statistically significant overrepresentation of high white-collar occupations and native-born origins. An analysis of the relationships between occupation and party on the one hand and place of birth and party on the other indicates that in this era officials affiliated with the independent parties were overwhelmingly from high white-collar occupations and native-born. Between 1860 and 1873, a total of 230 officials was elected, of whom 42 percent (97) were affiliated with the People's party, 15 percent (36) with the Taxpayer's party, and 11 percent (26) with the Union party. Overall during these years, 31.7 percent of officials were from high white-collar occupations and 17.8 percent were from low white-collar occupations. However, among officials affiliated with the People's party, 41 percent were high white-collar and 12 percent low white-collar. Among Taxpayer's party officials, 38.9 percent were high white-collar and 38 percent low white-collar. Moreover, 43 percent of the People's officials, 16 percent of the Taxpayer's, and 65 percent of the Union officials were incumbents at the time of their elections, and many of them had originally entered politics from high white-collar occupations. By contrast, Democrats, who elected only 23 percent (53) of the officials, were 35 percent high white-collar and 22.6 percent low white-collar. Given that only 3.9 percent of the occupations in the city were high white-collar in 1870, these occupations were dramatically overrepresented among the officials in all parties, and most overrepresented by those of the early independent parties.[23]

A similar difference emerges in the analysis of ethnicity among officials in these years. Among all officials elected in this era, 70.2 percent (151) were native-born and 29.8 percent (64) were foreign-born. However, 78.5 percent of the People's party officials were native-born, as were 71.4 percent of Taxpayer's officials and 88.5 percent of Union candidates. By contrast, only 43.1 percent of Democratic officials were native-born. Therefore, at a time when almost half of the city's population and electorate were foreign-born, the native-born were remarkably overrepresented among the officers affiliated with the independent parties.[24]

As the editorial comments just quoted indicate, the independent parties were completely unembarrassed by the backgrounds of the officials affiliated with them and actually combined the themes of fiscal conservatism and elitism in their party platforms. In 1860, for example, the People's "Manifesto" declared only that "great and good results have been accomplished by the People's Reform Party.... Good order and Economy have superseded violence and prodigality in the administration of municipal affairs ... [and] more than $1 million have been annually saved to the city treasury." In 1863 the fiscal pledge was more specific, although general enough to have appeared in any platform of this period: "Every candidate has pledged himself to use his influence to prevent extravagance or waste of public funds or credit, to oppose the increase of salaries, and in general to carry out the principles of reform so wisely inaugurated by the People's Party."[25]

The "address" of the Taxpayer's party in 1869 combined these themes with those of nonpartisanship and elitism into what approaches the ideal independent platform in this period. Its genuflection before the vigilante legend declared that "no city in America was ever worse governed than the city of San Francisco during the absolute reign of the old parties," but that "as soon as our municipal affairs were disconnected from all party affiliation the reign of good order, peace, and prosperity was reestablished." Given this vision of the power of nonpartisanship, the party declared its support for "the absolute independence of the city government from all partisan control" and stated that "sitting with closed doors for the nomination of our ticket, we have felt in an especial manner the importance of this great duty." Refusing to apologize for its elitism, the party trumpeted its nomination of Thomas Selby, "a citizen with no stain upon his loyalty, a man of wealth, without suspicion of dishonest acquisition and a gentleman of the first business attainments, honor, and virtue."[26]

By claiming the mantle of elite tradition, nonpartisanship, honor, and economy, the independent parties kept their major opponents, the Democrats, on the ideological defensive and out of municipal power to any real extent until 1875. The Democracy was, after all, a national political party, so it could hardly portray itself as nonpartisan. More important, according to the vigilante legend, some of the most evil aspects of partisanship and extravagance in the pre-1856 period were exhibited in the Democracy. In fact, one of the precipitating factors in the vigilante uprising was the allegation of the elites that David Broderick, an Irishman and leader of the "Tammany" faction of the Democracy, had fastened a machine onto the city's government and was using local offices and expenditures to reward his mostly foreign-born supporters.[27]

Moreover, the Democratic party allegedly had dishonored itself during the Civil War. Because the party had a large "Chiv" (for Chivalry) faction that was sympathetic to the South, the Democrats were held in deep suspicion of disloyalty during the war, and this suspicion was confirmed by the arrest of one Democratic United States senator by federal authorities and the departure for the Confederate Army of leading state Democrats. When news of Lincoln's assassination reached San Francisco in 1865, mobs sacked the offices of the Democratic newspaper, and the militia had to be called out to maintain order.[28]

From 1861 through 1865, then, no Democratic ticket was presented in municipal politics. Instead, the People's nominees were faced by, in succession, "Fusion," "Citizens," and "Union" tickets. During these years, some Democrats supported these parties and others supported the People's party. Coon, for example, claimed that the "better element" of the Democracy supported the People's party in these years. In 1866, however, the People's nominating committee refused to nominate anyone who had voted against the Lincoln-Johnson ticket in 1864, thereby rendering the nonpartisan stance of the independent parties a non-Democratic one. This decision forced the Democrats both to rehabilitate their own party and to expose the "non-partisan dodge" of the others. To accomplish these tasks, the Democrats adopted three tactics: (1) they declared the correctness and responsibility of party politics; (2) they attacked nonpartisanship as either hypocritical or a "radical [Republican] dodge"; and (3) they attacked the elitism of the independents head on, declaring that the Democracy was the party of immigrants and workers.[29]

Given the setbacks the party had suffered and the hurdles it faced, the *Examiner* did not exaggerate when it noted that nothing so surprised the "radicals and the wealthier classes as the fact that, notwithstanding the fiery furnaces of trial through which the Democratic Party has passed, it remains indestructable." It survived because "the masses of the people espouse the Democratic Party... a party composed of the people themselves, animated at all times by the instinctive hatred of class legislation and pharisaical aristocratic assumption." If loyalty to the Democracy was simply a matter of instinct, however, then one marvels at the gallons of ink and columns of nearly hysterical rhetoric that the *Examiner* devoted to welding the "people themselves" into a fighting host. Moreover, one had to consider the essentially dismal showing of the party at the local polls. During the years 1860 through 1873, the Democrats took the mayoralty only once and elected only 24 percent of the board of supervisors, 24 percent of the most important executive officers, and 16 percent of the incumbents for any office.[30]

Unable to build a party from the top down, as the founders of the People's party had done, the Democrats set out to do so from the bottom up. Thus they built a party of workingmen and white ethnics united in their opposition to native-born elites on the one hand and to imported Chinese laborers on the other. Alexander Saxton has noted that by 1867 the Democrats in San Francisco and throughout the state had grasped "the Chinese issue" like a life preserver. The issue was the presence of Chinese laborers in San Francisco, and proposals on what to do about it ranged from banning further Chinese immigration to the more radical action of actually removing those who were already there. Indeed, one of the tasks of the party after 1867 was to keep the workingmen satisfied with the former rather than the latter solution. This mission failed during the depression of 1877–1879, when the Workingmen's Party of California emerged on the basis of the demand that "the Chinese must go" and successfully challenged the Democrats.[31]

This tactic was by no means the only one that Democrats used to appeal to the working class. Equally important were their anti-elite and ethnocultural appeals, both of which grew directly out of the San Francisco political situation. It was a fact, after all, that the local independent parties were led by members of the local native-born elite. The Democrats, in contrast, were not. Naturally, Democratic candidates and their editorial spokesman, the *Examiner*, made much of this. According to the *Examiner*, the "Democratic low taxation party was composed generally of the poor men of the nation" and was opposed by those representing "aristocratic principles ... and taxes upon the labor of the poor." On the local level, moreover, the independent parties stood against the worker's real interests. In the municipal election of 1870, for example, the *Examiner* noted that leaders of the Taxpayer's party "ridicule the anti-coolie movement, denounce and oppose all labor leagues, and take specific delight in stigmatizing as demagogues all those who stand by the laboring men in their legitimate efforts to better the condition of themselves and their families."[32]

These themes echoed through the speeches of Democratic candidates, both at the primary conventions and during their campaigns. An example is Matthew Canavan's nomination speech for chief of police in the municipal primary convention of 1868, in which he noted that during a previous term in the state legislature "he had worked for the best interests of the workingmen of San Francisco to which class he belonged," and added that he opposed corporations and monopolies "as against the poor man." Similarly, in his campaign for reelection in 1869, the city's first Democratic mayor since the war, Frank McCoppin, made a straightforward plea for the support of workingmen at the Democratic municipal ratification meeting. McCoppin was a supervisor but also a construction superintendent on the Market Street Railway, and he asked that "whenever you find one of your own class stepping out from the ranks and asking for promotion at your hands ... give it to him ... remembering that by sustaining him you elevate your own class."[33]

In San Francisco, because of the way in which class and ethnicity were intertwined, when one spoke to the workingmen, one also spoke to white ethnics, especially the Irish. Stephen Erie has estimated, for example, that in 1870, 84 percent of unskilled workers, 74.5 percent of semiskilled, and 59.5 percent of skilled workers were foreign-born. The largest group of foreign-born was the Irish, who made up 56.9 percent of all the unskilled workers, 35.3 percent of the semiskilled, and 21.8 percent of the skilled. Thus the second mainstay of the Democratic appeal was ethnicity.[34]

When the Democrats were on the offensive, their ethnocultural appeal consisted of attacking the threat or reality of sumptuary laws and "ethnicizing" the standard racist appeal. Indeed, there was nothing the *Examiner* liked better than connecting class and ethnocultural appeals. In the election of 1869, for example, the *Examiner* joined the issues of class, race, and ethnicity in noting that workingmen were under attack in their occupations, their nativities, and their recreations—in their occupations because they were threatened by "an invasion of Mongolians"; in their nativities because in the course of the campaign, the foreign-born, especially the Irish, had "been assaulted in disreputable language calculated to bring them to shame"; and in their recreations because they were attacked by a "set of bigots who, if they obtain the power, will establish sumptuary laws [and] tyrannical Sunday enactments." To emphasize these issues later in the same election, the paper reminded the Irish that the Taxpayer's candidate for sheriff had allegedly said that he "had rather see the Negroes vote, as a class, than the Irish," while also reminding the Germans that Thomas Selby, Taxpayer's candidate for mayor, was a member of the YMCA, which, the *Examiner* charged, was in favor of "a puritanical Sunday law modelled after that of New England."[35]

The last important Democratic theme of these years was that of party loyalty within the party and the importance of party outside of it. Borrowing the slogan of Ben Butler, the *Examiner* declared that the party was "an army where we may welcome recruits but must shoot deserters." After the county convention, all dissatisfaction among Democrats was to pass and the cry was to become "the ticket, the whole ticket, and nothing but the ticket," for to violate the rules of party organization was to "strike a blow at the very existence of the Democracy." This was in part a strictly opportunistic policy aimed at victory for the Democrats, and by no means at the local level alone. The idea was that, "for the party to maintain its supremacy," it had to be successful in the city as well as in the state government. Municipal failure would "endanger the success of the ticket next year when we have state officers, three members of Congress, and a legislature to choose." At a higher level of abstraction, the Democrats also claimed that it was the function of the party to guarantee responsibility in politics. When independent tickets were long gone, a "great, national party" would still be there to take responsibility for its acts. The so-called independent parties offered only the "security of broken pledges, a disbanded and demoralized party, a heterogeneous mass of irresponsible place holders."[36]

Thus the *Examiner* was especially harsh in its attack on the local independent parties, which it regarded as undemocratic and hypocritical. The Taxpayer's party, it argued, was "a myth, a sham, a cheat"; more generally, citizens did themselves a great disservice to "follow blindly the lead of the secret manipulators of committees of 10 or of 24, or any other band of conspirators who arrogate to themselves the sum of all the virtues" and deny the people the right to choose their own ticket at an open primary. Since "every man has some political beliefs," only hypocrites were independents. Hence every official position was also political, and a candidate who "feigns independence of political opinion" either "lacks the moral courage to avow his sentiments or he is a cunning trickster" and, in any case, unworthy to be trusted with the responsibilities of office.[37]

By contrasting party responsibility and nonpartisanship, the needs of workingmen and the pretensions of the elite, the rights of ethnics and appeals to barely concealed nativism, the Democrats carved out a place for themselves in the city's political culture. Precisely because of these appeals, the political cultural theory would predict that the Democrats' fiscal position would also contrast with that of the independent parties. In general, however, it did not. In their odyssey from the East or South to the West, local Democrats had not forgotten their Jacksonian roots and thus their mistrust of large or active government. Moreover, in this period the Democrats had other reasons for denouncing indebtedness and taxation, reasons that had little or nothing to do with local affairs. They were bothered by the national indebtedness resulting from the Civil War, which had been, as far as they were concerned, a radical project; so, too, was the current misuse of citizens' money in Reconstruction, which the local Democrats denounced as an object lesson in the danger of a too-active government. Finally, there was the greatest tax of all, the tariff, which supported much of this activity and which Democrats denounced regularly and shrilly during this period. To them, active government meant more power for their opponents (as in Reconstruction) or special privileges for corporations (as in the tariff). They extended the same logic to local and state levels. Thus in the party's first postwar campaign, in 1867, it called for the support of all those who would "cut down on the enormous taxes which are eating out the substance of the people" and who would have "an honest and economical administration." The Democrats maintained this position throughout this period.[38]

Despite their furious battles over the issue of who would govern, the Democratic and independent parties displayed surprising unanimity on the question of what to do with public resources. The best policy, they agreed, was to do as little as possible. This consensus was the all-pervasive general atmosphere in which fiscal policy was made; it was also the operational guide to the actual making of that policy when city officials set the tax rate, allocated expenditure, and contemplated indebtedness.

FISCAL POLICYMAKING UNDER THE INDEPENDENT PARTIES, 1860–1875

In his massive history of San Francisco published in 1912, John Young summarized the fiscal politics of this period with not a little condescension: "When the citizen found that the men chosen by the committee acting in secret had reduced expenditures he was satisfied. That was the good government test applied by the average voter of the period between 1856 and 1870." This was, Young continued, because the citizen was "merely looking for results and not thinking of theories of government." In fact, in this period "the good citizen of San Francisco was chiefly concerned about keeping down the tax rate and rarely gave thought to the desirableness of making the city a pleasant place of abode." Young's progressive-era assumption that the citizen of the 1860s should have been thinking about municipal improvements reflected his position that by "the exacting requirements of present day reformers," the performances "or rather non-performances of the men who held municipal office [in this period] will not demand ... high ... praise." It also reflected his refusal to admit that, even in his own enlightened era, there were still those who worried about the tax rate.[39]

Had Young looked more closely, he would have discovered that there was, indeed, a theory of government in this period, and that it was one that might have been found among some of his own contemporaries as well. The fiscal politics in this period began, as did all other politics, with Legend of Vigilantism as the touchstone of political economy. It continued beyond that, however, with a theory of taxation and property values, techniques for limiting debt, and some specific fiscal proposals embodied in the platforms of the competing parties.

As suggested in the previous sections of this chapter, the first principle of fiscal politics in this period was the burden of indebtedness left by the extravagance of the politicians who preceded the vigilantes in office. As the *Alta* put it in the municipal campaign of 1864, "for their dancing we are now paying the piper." According to the People's party and its supporters, the only concrete legacy of the rule of the politicians was a debt of several millions of dollars. Luckily, the People's party "took the reins" in 1856 and "held them with a firm hand ever since," reducing old obligations and contracting no new ones. Complaints about the debts, whatever their source, were not empty, for during these years the expenses of debt service were very high by comparison with later years. As we saw in chapter 2, in 1860, 46 percent of the city's total local expenditure was for debt service expenses.[40]

The result of this burden was that debt service sometimes almost doubled the tax rate. As the *Alta* noted in 1864, a rate of $1.035 on $100 of assessed valuation would have been sufficient for the ordinary expenses of government that fiscal year, but debt service added $0.67 to the rate, bringing it up to $1.705 for city and county purposes only, and to that another $0.90 had to be added for state purposes. The *Bulletin* fleshed out the rate for 1863 by noting that the taxpayer who owned a house and lot assessed at $5,000 that year would pay a total of $110 in real estate property taxes—$45 for state purposes, $10 for the local schools, $25 for debt service, and $30 for the general expenses of local government. Thus, it argued, the whole expense of the city, excepting the schools, was costing only a small amount more than did debt service, "yet some of our citizens appear to think it is of but little consequence whether the city elects men who desire to increase the debt."[41]

The indignity of paying for debt contracted by rascals was only half of the objection to high taxation, however. The other, more thoughtful objection was that high taxes, whether caused by high current expenditure or earlier indebtedness, lowered the value of local property. The logic of this position was straightforward and relied on the assumption that the value of property increased as the city grew: because high taxation supposedly tended to drive property owners out of the city and discourage others from coming, the effect of high taxes was to lower the value of everyone's property.

In 1861, the *Bulletin* noted the widespread and pernicious effects of high taxation, developing a crude—and inaccurate—multiplier effect model. To begin with, high taxes meant higher rents, which meant that workingmen could not save the money necessary to buy a home. This depressed property values. Moreover, if the "landlord has to pay half his rent to the tax collector, capital will not invest in houses, but seeks other channels"; this, too, affected the real estate market. (In fact, the situation was the opposite; in San Francisco, investment in speculative ventures like real estate was making the formation of industrial capital difficult, and thus probably retarding economic development.) Finally, high taxes served to limit local population growth. While a man "prospering here and able to own his own home writes to his brother or brother in law in the east such flattering accounts . . . that the latter is attracted to our city also," he whose savings were "eaten away by taxes would not attract friends to the city and thus again our population would be less." By keeping itself free from debt and committed to "economical" expenditure, San Francisco would stand at "the head of American municipalities," and "the light taxation following economical government" would cause the city to "grow and expand as no other city in America at this time can possibly do," the *Bulletin* editorialized in 1873.[42]

The independent mayors, of course, made much of their commitment to this sort of economic theory. Taxpayer's Mayor Thomas Selby (1869–1871) noted that "holding the veto power, he used it with telling effect against every encroachment upon the city treasury." His successor, Taxpayer's Mayor William Alvord, used the same theme to justify his veto of a $10 million subsidy to a "San Francisco and Colorado Railroad" in 1872:

Our aim should be to encourage men of modest means to make their homes here, by assuring them that no act of ours shall materially increase the public debt, ... that taxation shall be kept at the lowest possible rate, and they shall not be unnecessarily nor unjustly taxed.[43]

Given this rejection of indebtedness, then, the parties agreed that municipal improvements should be funded on a pay-as-you-go basis. Expensive municipal projects were not prohibited as long as their cost could be covered out of current revenues. Again, this was alleged to be an innovation of the People's party, the *Alta* declaring that "one of the most signal proofs of the economy of the People's Party [is] ... the fact that they pay as they go," but this position was also adopted by the Democrats. The *Examiner* noted that "the practice of liquidating obligations from present resources imposes a habit of economy and rigid inquiry into the necessity of the outlay," while the use of bonds "breeds carelessness, inattention, future financial difficulty, dishonesty and possible repudiation." This meant that municipal projects had to be done piecemeal if their construction was too expensive to be covered in the budget for a single year. Thus streets and sewers were built only in sections and never as systems, while a hospital, almshouse, industrial school, and city hall were built or expanded, and Golden Gate Park developed, all over a number of years. The city hall became something of a symbol of this technique, and the butt of later jokes, because it was begun in 1870 and built piecemeal for almost thirty years thereafter, depending on the amount of revenue available every year (which was none in some years). It was barely completed in time to be totally destroyed by the earthquake and fire of 1906.[44]

The consensus on no debt, pay-as-you-go, and low expenditure guided the annual setting of the tax rate, which was the centerpiece of fiscal politics in this period. As noted in chapter 2, the process for setting the rate was a straightforward one. After consultation with department heads about their expenditure during the current year and their needs in the upcoming one, the auditor proposed budgets for each activity. The auditor then consulted with the assessor for an estimate of the tax base for the coming year and, on the basis of his estimate of the revenue necessary to cover the estimated expenditure, proposed a tax rate. These estimates were presented to the finance committee for discussion, adjustment, and presentation to the full board of supervisors. The auditor had the power to accept or adjust the proposals of the department heads; the finance committee could do the same with the auditor's proposals; and, of course, the full board could do likewise with the finance committee's estimates. At each stage, expenditure in the current year was the basis for discussions of increases or decreases in the coming year. Approval by the full board sent the so-called revenue ordinance to the mayor for his signature or veto.

An official record of these negotiations was presented in the *Municipal Reports* only after 1881. Before that, the newspapers covered the process, and on the basis of these accounts, three aspects of the rate-setting process of 1860–1875 stand out in comparison with that of later periods: (1) the lack of controversy over or even discussion of the rate, (2) the essentially professional nature of the process, and (3) the resulting strategy of incremental increase in expenditure.

The power of the fiscal consensus was demonstrated by passage of the rate in these years almost without discussion and almost always by a unanimous vote. The most frequent phrase in the newspapers was merely that "the order providing for revenue for municipal purposes for the fiscal year ending June 30 . . . was passed without opposition." Even when a division of the vote was recorded, as occurred twice, there was none of the rancorous discussion of the issue characteristic of other controversial issues. And in contrast to later periods, the revenue ordinance was never vetoed by the mayor. The overwhelming political reason for this lack of dissension was the low-taxation, low-expenditure consensus shared by all the parties during this time—a consensus that was both reinforced by debt service payments, which kept the rate high without providing any new services to the taxpayers, and maintained by the overwhelming preponderance of independent party officials in the fiscal process.[45]

Another important reason for the lack of discussion lay in the nature of the process itself, especially the almost total reliance of the board on the auditor and department heads for advice. In its report of 1869, for example, the finance committee noted that "through the valuable aid of Mr. Harris, the Auditor, they have had before them much information in this matter and they believe that for the purposes of this city and county a levy of $1.25 on each $100 valuation will be sufficient." Although there is nothing startling about this process, its implications should be noted. Because the board relied almost wholly on the auditor, who in turn relied on the department heads for estimates of their needs, the setting of the tax rate was a completely professional undertaking, that is to say, an activity in which only government officials participated. According to newspaper accounts, during the years 1860–1875, not a single citizen or citizens group appeared before the finance committee or the board of supervisors to discuss the tax rate, although the meetings of both were open to the public for this purpose. The only persons who did appear before the board during these years were the representatives of various other city departments (the tax collector, school directors, etc.), who always sought increases in their budgets.[46]

The "professional" or at least "official" influence was heightened by the structure of the board itself. Combining both executive and legislative functions, as did most pre-reform urban legislatures, the board both set the appropriations of the various departments and oversaw the expenditures of those appropriations through its various subcommittees (e.g., finance, streets, health, and police). To facilitate their own supervisory tasks and to placate the departments under them, the supervisors logrolled between committees for appropriations for "their" departments. Thus the supervisors were pressured between their roles as the treasurers and administrators of the departments. They were also torn between their commitment to their official colleagues on the one hand and to their political goal of commitment to the economy on the other.

More important, these colleagues were professional in a sense that the supervisors were not. Of the 687 executive and legislative officials elected in San Francisco between 1860 and 1905, 33.4 percent were incumbents or other government officers at the time of their election. However, incumbency or other previous government experience was not evenly spread among all the officers. Only 23.3 percent of supervisors were incumbents or other officials at the time of their elections, compared to 42.5 percent of the executive officers. In the years from

1860 to 1875, 43.6 percent of all officials elected were incumbents or other governmental officials. Of the executive officers of the city elected in these years, 47.5 percent were from these backgrounds, while only 34 percent of the supervisors were incumbents or other officials.[47]

This difference was partly the result of the definitions of the offices themselves. Supervisors were part-time officials who were expected to conduct other business as well, whereas executive officers were full-time employees whose annual salaries ranged from $2,100 for the license collector to $8,000 for the sheriff. Moreover, for most of this period the staff budget for the board of supervisors was about $4,000 per year, while that of the license collector, who had the smallest staff among the elected executive officials, was five times that.

Long before "professionalism" became a reform ideology, then, San Francisco's executive officers were professional career politicians and bureaucrats. They faced the supervisors as full-time professionals forced to deal with part-time amateurs—and as politicians with political fiefdoms to maintain. By 1875, the staff budget of the assessor's office had already reached $50,000. What politically ambitious supervisor wanted that legion of clerks turned against him at the next election?

The result of these ideological and institutional factors was a fiscal politics of incrementalism. The budgetary process maximized the role of the departments and institutionalized the current year's expenditure as the basis of the next year's appropriation. Both the auditor and the supervisors considered only marginal increases for each department, and although this minimized innovation, it also minimized conflict and made it possible to spread small increases across all activities. This was a rational strategy for the supervisors to follow not only because they were part-time and overworked but also because they and the other officials were bound by (and committed to) a fiscal ideology that regarded any increase in expenditure with suspicion.

What this meant was not a fiscal "steady state" but steady incremental growth in local government, financed by increasing assessed valuations and decreasing amounts necessary for debt service. Furthermore, the domination of the fiscal process by officials meant that an ever-upward pressure was exerted on the budget; that growth occurred almost solely in response to official plans, rather than to the plans or appeals of citizens or outside interest groups; and that increasing expenditure occurred in the midst of a consensus against it. The municipal political candidate who advocated the growth of the public sector—or even

TABLE 28
CHANGES IN MEASURES OF FISCAL POLICY, 1860–1876

Category	1860	1876	Percent change 1860–76	Era mean
Per capita assessed valuation	$630.43	$1493.8	136	$1164.1
Per capita local revenue	16.461	16.26	−1.2	18.16
Per capita tax revenue	13.39	12.49	−6.7	15.063
Per capita cash on hand	.4577	3.225	604	3.207
Tax rate	2.25	1.11	−50	2.23
Per capita non-tax revenue	3.063	3.77	23	3.45
Per capita operating expenditure	8.825	18.786	112	15.22
Per capita School Fund expenditure	.00185	.0048	166	.0033
Per capita Street Fund expenditure	0	.0023	—	.0008
Per capita street lighting expenditure	.0006	.0015	150	.0018
Per capita police and fire expenditure	1.568	3.019	93.5	2.77
Per capita expenditure on official salaries	1.48	1.58	6.7	1.837
Per capita expenditure on social welfare	.8325	1.461	75	1.4016
Share of operating expenditure	54.5%	79%	46	69.5%

Note: All dollar values have been deflated by means of the price index explained in appendix A.

admitted that it was growing—was rare indeed. Thus government officials themselves helped to generate suspicion about their actions.

Listening to speech after speech on the evils of a large public sector, the San Francisco voter would have been right to be cynical, given the figures in table 28, which displays the changes in major categories of assessment, taxation, revenue, and expenditure from 1860 to 1876. These measures indicate that the city's ability to spend increased enormously in these years, as did the expenditure on most of its important functions. Most noticeable are the more than 100 percent increase in the city's per capita valuation; the significant increase in operating expenditure as a share of increasing total local expenditure; and significant increases in expenditures on schools, street lighting, police and fire, and social welfare. Although the tax rate dropped 50 percent in real terms, the valuation grew at a faster rate, which fueled increased expenditure. Thus per capita tax liability increased 17 percent, from $14.17 in 1860 to $16.58 in 1876.[48]

Although these changes were dramatic overall, they were incremental, with the exception of that in the assessed valuation. And because expenditures crept up on an annual basis, there was no dramatic moment or turning point in this growth. Municipal officials did not propose or even admit that anything should grow; taxpayers and newspapers complained that they were getting nothing for their money; and incrementalism was, as table 28 indicates, nickel-and-diming them to death. If this was the result of a no-growth consensus regarding municipal government, then the conservative taxpayer or public official must have lived in fear of the emergence of real "raiders" on the treasury.[49]

THE REGULAR PARTIES POLITICIZE FISCAL POLICY, 1875–1882

For those citizens and politicians who propagated or believed the independent party line, the political and fiscal moment of truth arrived in January 1876, when Democratic Mayor Andrew Jackson Bryant, nine Democratic supervisors, and seven (of fourteen) Democratic executive officers were sworn into office. As Bryant noted in his inaugural address, it was the first time since the Consolidation Act of 1856 that the candidates of a national party had carried the mayoralty and a majority of the board of supervisors. If, as the independents had warned, "merely partisan" rule brought only corruption and demoralization in its wake, then the first election of what I have called the era of irregularity was a harbinger of bad times to come. However, the dire predictions of the independents were not realized. Instead, the fiscal politics of this period codified the fiscal consensus in a truly effective limit on taxation that would drive the city's tax rate and expenditure to historic lows.[50]

In fact, the transition to regular party politics was a good deal smoother than the voices of doom had predicted, and the disappearance of the independent parties was the result not of a radical change in political culture but of shifts in the scheduling of elections in both 1867 and 1872. The first shift transferred the municipal elections to September of every year; the second eliminated annual elections and required that all city officials be elected every other year. These changes reduced the number of times when municipal elections were truly separate from others, and thus pulled the institutional rug out from under the independent parties.

In line with these new institutional realities, in the election of 1873, the Taxpayer's and Republican parties began a more open collaboration. The Republicans endorsed the local independent ticket. The *Alta*, the newspaper mouthpiece for the independent parties, urged former independent voters to cast their ballots for the statewide Republican candidates because "everyone knows that the great majority of the voters of the Taxpayer's Party have at all times been Republicans." Ironically, this charge had been made by the Democrats all along, although the *Alta* was transferring the "apostolic succession" to the Republicans, not admitting the Democratic charge.[51]

By 1875, the *Alta's* transformation was complete. During the election that year, it denounced nonpartisanship in terms usually employed only by the Democrats, declaring it the "greatest folly that a voter can commit," because by its nature a third party must be local and temporary. The paper did not explain its switch, other than to note that the Republican party was now "full grown," having reached the "age of full manhood." But its reference to the purely local nature of independent parties, which heretofore had been a virtue, suggests that the switch was in line with the changes in the election schedule.[52]

Whatever the reason, the resulting change in the partisan affiliation of the officials was dramatic. Between 1875 and 1881, for the first time since 1856, most offices were held by members of the regular parties. Of the 104 officeholders elected in 1875, 1877, 1879, and 1881, 38.5 percent (40) were Republicans, 31.7 percent (33) Democrats, 17.3 percent (18) Taxpayer's, and 7.7 percent (8) members of the Workingmen's Party of California. Democrats took the mayoralty and a majority on the board of supervisors in 1875 and 1877, Republicans took the board in 1879 and the board and the mayoralty in 1881, and the Workingmen's party took the mayoralty and a few of the executive offices in 1879.

The emergence of the "two great national" parties on the local scene also caused the officials elected by them to become much more alike in their occupational distribution. Of the 94 officials elected in this era for whom occupational information was available, 32 percent were from high white-collar occupations, 36 percent were low white-collar, and 23 percent were incumbents or other government officials at the time of their elections. Among the Democrats elected in these years, 36 percent were from high white-collar occupations, 26.7 percent from low white-collar occupations, and 26.7 percent were incumbents or other officials. Meanwhile, Republican officials were 34 percent high white-collar, 39.5 percent low white-collar, and 10.5 percent incumbents or other officials. Leaving aside the vagaries of electoral luck, the Democrats and Republicans were quite similar in their occupational backgrounds.[53]

The major parties were becoming more similar ethnically, too, because of a larger number of native-born officials elected by the Democrats. As previously noted, from 1860 to 1876, the majority of Democratic officials elected was of foreign birth; from 1877 to 1882, the majority was of native birth. Of the 100 officials for whom information on nativity was available, 73 were native-born and 27 were foreign-born. A total of 62 percent of Democratic officials was native-born, compared to 82 percent of Republicans, 76 percent of Taxpayer's, and 85 percent of Workingmen's officials. Although these differences are statistically significant, the important pattern is in the direction of similarity among the parties.[54]

The patterns of political participation established in the first era continued into the second, and they can be analyzed more closely in the latter because of the existence of registration statistics beginning in 1875. On average in these years, about 55 percent of men aged twenty-one and over were registered to vote, and about 85 percent of those registered (i.e., about 44 percent of the total) voted for president, 78 percent for mayor, and 75 percent for the board of supervisors. In this era, as before, the higher the top of the ticket, the higher the political participation. The only exception to this rule was the election of 1879, at which three parties—including the Workingmen's—and a new state constitution were on the ballot. This election had one of the highest rates of participation in the city's history, although the top of the ticket was only the governor.[55]

The shift from independent to regular parties made absolutely no difference in the ideology that surrounded fiscal policymaking in these years: the call was still for low taxation and expenditure, and for a pay-as-you-go procedure rather than indebtedness. The regular parties enshrined these principles in their platforms. When the Workingmen's party ran its independent municipal ticket in 1879, it followed suit, pledging to lower taxation and expenditure by requiring its candidates to accept only half of their salaries and return the other half to the city treasury.

The power of these fiscal political positions was reinforced by the economic difficulties of these years. As we saw in chapter 3, the years between 1875 and 1880 were hard ones for the city's economy, especially its commercial sector. Business at the port dropped 26 percent from 1875 to 1879, and the number of real estate sales plummeted 48 percent between 1875 and 1880. The decline in the manufacturing sector was less severe and of shorter duration but significant nonetheless. The number of men employed in manufacturing declined 6 percent between 1877 and 1880, the number of manufacturing works dropped 11 percent between 1880 and 1881, and the real value of manufactured goods declined 27 percent between 1877 and 1880. It was no coincidence, then, that these years saw the first mayoral veto of a revenue ordinance passed by the board of supervisors, the first appearance of nonofficials at the meetings of the supervisors' finance committee, the first lengthy debate over a nonincremental increase in expenditure for the police department, and the institution of the Dollar Limit on taxation.[56]

Avoidance of indebtedness was a particular theme in these years. Two-term Democratic Mayor A. J. Bryant condemned it in his second campaign, declaring that he believed that "if any mortgage was to be placed on my little house, I wanted to do it myself and not let the city do it." The *Bulletin*, at this time supporting the Republicans, declared that the future welfare of the city depended on "the extension of the principle [of pay-as-you-go] to all public improvements of whatever nature." And the Democratic platform of 1875 favored direct taxation rather than bonds for the improvement of Golden Gate Park, because "if taxpayers are made to feel the burden of its maintenance annually, instead of issuing bonds ... more and necessary attention will be given to the park expenses in the future."[57]

Indeed, in the setting of the tax rate and the allocation of expenditure, more scrutiny was being applied. In 1878, the finance committee of the board of supervisors made significant cuts in the auditor's estimates for the first time, carving $100,000 from the funds for schools, streets, and the police department for fiscal year 1878/79, which would begin July 1, 1878. The *Examiner* noted that "the general desire of the Board appeared to be to make whatever reductions were at all practicable," and that "they succeeded in materially lessening the heavy burden of the taxpayers."[58]

The following year, the mayor imposed the first recorded veto on a revenue ordinance passed by the board, after the first recorded intervention into the fiscal process of a nonofficial group. In June 1879, the auditor provided his estimates as usual, in this case expenditures requiring a tax rate of $1.48 per $100 of assessed valuation, and on June 17 the revenue order was passed to print. On June 25 a group styling itself the "Executive Committee" of the "Real Estate Protective Association" objected to the estimate, noting that "in such stringent times as these . . . with no prospect of immediate relief, the Committee believe it incumbent upon you to forgo all improvements not immediately necessary, and to continue all appropriations within the narrowest limits allowable." The proposed rate was already $0.21 lower than the previous year's rate of $1.69 in current dollars, but on July 1, Mayor Bryant vetoed the rate, noting that "everyone wants to economize," so that it was not a year to "extend improvements." He proposed reductions in expenditure on streets and for the new city hall. The result was a revised rate of $1.37, which represented reductions from the previous year of $0.17 for the General Fund, $0.11 for the street department, and $0.10 for the new city hall building project.[59]

In 1880 the supervisors cut $429,225 from the auditor's estimates, much of it from streets, schools, and the new city hall project, but to finance a doubling of the police force, they raised the rate to $1.57 per $100 of assessed valuation for fiscal year 1880/81. This increase in the tax rate brought the realtors back in 1881. This time, city officials were out in force, too. Both the police and fire chiefs appeared at the finance committee hearing in 1881 to urge that their appropriations not be reduced, and one of the school directors argued that, given the increase in students and the need for new schoolhouses, the school fund appropriation should actually be increased over the auditor's estimate of $750,000, to $820,000. The complaint of the schools was by no means unjustified because the auditor's estimates for schools had been the target of reductions every year since 1877, and the School Fund's share of the tax rate had dropped from $0.20 in the rate set in 1877 to $0.17

in 1880, while average daily attendance in the schools had increased from 24,889 students in 1877 to 29,092 in 1881.[60]

Regardless of these changes, the real estate representatives denounced the pleas from officials for more. Patrick Magee, editor of the San Francisco *Real Estate Circular*, declared that "arguments to raise the appropriations in each department are heard, but none to cut them down," and he reminded the board that in setting the tax rate they were also setting the price of real estate, because the real estate market was adversely affected by a high tax rate. Republican Supervisor James Whitney, who was a physician, proposed that it was the poor condition of the streets, not the taxes, "which depreciated the price of real estate." In response, the realtors immediately shouted, "No, the taxes do it." Auditor John Dunn reinforced the realtors' point when he complained that none of the department heads had even been willing to discuss a reduction in the previous year's expenditure during his negotiations with them. In the end, the board went to work lopping amounts off the estimates, taking $68,000 from departmental salaries on the General Fund, $65,000 for streets and sewers, $100,000 from the School Fund, and eliminating all appropriations for work on the new city hall. This resulted in a rate of $1.15, a reduction of $0.42 from the rate of the previous year. Among the other cuts, this lower rate included a reduction of almost one-half in the share of the tax rate going for schools, from $0.17 to $0.09.[61]

Those familiar with the history of American urban development may be somewhat surprised by the continuing cuts in expenditures on streets and schools. Surely streets were important to the economic development of the city and, as David Tyack has pointed out, schools were the one public service widely used by urban residents. But San Francisco officials hewed to the line of the fiscal political consensus, not to some vague public service ethic, and for reasons both pragmatic and institutional, cuts in streets, schools, and long-term projects like the city hall made life within that consensus easier for them. As we saw in chapter 2, the costs of opening and grading streets were assessed to property owners along those streets. The city's task was merely to maintain the streets after they were built. Deferring street expenditure, then, was deferring street maintenance and cleaning, not necessarily halting the expansion of the city. Work on the new city hall, too, was easy to postpone for politicians who knew they would never occupy it anyway, and even the patronage advantages of employment on the project were out-weighed by the necessity for a low tax rate.[62]

The relationship between the board and the schools was more insti-tutional. By charter, the board of supervisors controlled school expen-diture by setting the share of the tax rate—not to exceed $0.35—which was to go for that purpose. Meanwhile, the administration of the ex-penditure from the School Fund was the responsibility of a separately elected board of school directors. Thus the state of the schools was the responsibility of someone other than the supervisors, and repeatedly in these years, the supervisors merely passed the political football along to the school directors by setting a school tax rate low enough to be fiscally safe but not necessarily high enough to finance the improve-ments in education that the school directors requested.[63]

In spite of the scrutiny of the supervisors, the threat of the mayor, and the intervention of businessmen, however, the growth of expen-diture and the tax rate seemed inexorable. In 1881, the *Examiner* noted that "the taxpayers of San Francisco are tired of paying heavy taxes, but they are more weary of seeing those taxes so continuously and grossly misapplied." One could, of course, find such an editorial almost every year from 1860 to 1905, but this time there were grounds for com-plaint. In current dollars, the tax rate had been only $1 per $100 in fiscal year 1875/76; for fiscal 1880/81, it was $1.57. It edged upward by means of an electoral cycle in the rate, according to which tax rates were lower in election than in nonelection years. Between 1875 and 1881, rates in election years were an average of $0.31 lower than those set in nonelection years. Moreover, those who felt that the problem was excessive salary expenditure had a point. As the figures in table 29 demonstrate, in real per capita terms, the only major categories of ex-penditure that grew (i.e., in which real total expenditure increased more rapidly than population between 1877 and 1881) were those for police and fire and for official salaries—specifically, in the case of the latter, those for the deputies and clerks of the executive officials.[64]

As we have already seen, the pressure for growth in the patronage positions around the executive officers was constant, incremental, and for the most part systemic; there was no fiscal moment of truth at which it was decided that the number of clerks in city government should grow. This incremental growth was not the case for police and fire expenditure, which grew primarily because of doubling the police force

TABLE 29

Changes in Measures of Fiscal Policy, 1877–1883

Category	1877	1881	1883	Percent change 1877–81	Percent change 1881–83	Era Mean
Per capita assessed valuation	$1314.8	$729.19	$659.16	−44.5	−9.6	$897.2
Per capita local revenue	20.37	13.93	10.29	−31.6	−26	14.36
Per capita tax revenue	17.27	12.08	8.448	−30.0	−30	12.145
Per capita cash on hand	4.153	3.364	1.8781	−18.8	−44.1	3.325
Tax rate	1.463	1.276	1.000	−12.8	−21.6	1.201
Per capita non-tax revenue	3.093	1.845	1.848	−67.6	0	2.47
Per capita operating expenditure	17.08	12.92	10.62	−24.4	−17.8	13.99
Per capita School Fund expenditure	.0036	.0029	.0025	−19.4	−13.8	.0030
Per capita Street Fund expenditure	.0018	.0008	.0006	−55.6	−25	.0012
Per capita street lighting expenditure	.0014	.0009	.0007	−55	−22	.0009
Per capita police and fire expenditure	2.487	2.850	2.625	14.6	−7.9	2.646
Per capita expenditure on official salaries	1.62	1.89	1.29	16.7	−31.7	1.4953
Per capita expenditure on social welfare	1.439	.7952	.7129	−44.7	−10.3	.9272
Share of operating expenditure	70.6%	81.7%	69.9%	15	−16	75.4%

Note: All dollar values have been deflated by means of the price index explained in appendix A.

after lengthy debate during the 1877/78 fiscal year. This jump in police expenditure, along with the continual growth in patronage salaries, raised expenditure to the level where the parties themselves adopted the Dollar Limit to reform their own previous practices. We can conclude our look at fiscal policy from 1877 to 1882 by turning to the decisions to expand the police force and to impose the Dollar Limit on taxation.

Most who have written about the 1878 expansion of the police in San Francisco have done so with the intention of proving that an elite controlled city government during the troubled times following the "July Days" of rioting and the renaissance of vigilantism in 1877. Within this framework, the doubling of the size of the local police force has been seen as a terrified city government's response to turbulence from the working class below and demands from the local vigilante elite above. Although there is truth in this interpretation, it does not tell the whole story, or even the most interesting part. Looked at more carefully throughout the nine months during which the expanded force was a fiscal political issue, it is clear that the decision exemplifies both the relative autonomy of the local public sector from the demands of the elites and the power of the fiscal consensus to discipline even the demands of the elite.[65]

On July 21, 1877, the city received word of the deaths of forty persons in Pittsburgh in rioting connected with the great railroad strike. Organizations sympathetic with the strikers called a meeting for the night of July 23 in support of the strike. As the meeting ended, sections of the crowd broke off and rampaged through Chinatown, burning buildings and ultimately killing one person. Convinced that the city's 150-man police force was inadequate, local elites organized a Committee of Public Safety, enrolled three thousand men, and engaged in a heated battle with anti-Chinese rioters on the night of July 25, during which five more persons—all white—were killed. By July 29, the immediate danger had passed and the "troops" of the committee were dismissed, although the committee itself remained in session.[66]

On July 31, the executive committee of the Committee of Public Safety met with representatives of local banks to discuss expansion of the city's police force. The plan transmitted by the committee to the board of supervisors the next day called for the addition of 150 policemen to the existing 150-man force, with local banks paying the salaries of the new police until the city received authorization from the state legislature to do so. There were two catches in the offer, however. First, the supervisors were required to pledge the faith of the city to repay the bankers as soon as possible, and second, the executive committee of the Committee of Public Safety was to select the 150 new men. These were not mere details. By law, the supervisors were not permitted to pledge the full faith of the city without the permission of the legislature, and the legislature would not meet until January 1878. Moreover, appointments to the police force were customarily made by the police commissioners with the advice of the supervisors. The bankers' proposal, therefore, violated both fiscal and political practices.[67]

By mid-August, supervisors were objecting to both of these provisions. Thus the ordinance that passed on August 20 authorized the appointment of 150 additional officers and the acceptance of the bankers' money, but neither pledged the faith of the city nor reserved the right of appointment to the Committee of Public Safety. This time, the bankers and the committee balked and again demanded that the committee choose the new officers. On September 12, therefore, the board indefinitely postponed action on a proposal giving the power of appointment to the committee. Because a new board of supervisors had been elected the week before, this postponed the issue until the installation of the new board in January.[68]

January brought both a new board of supervisors and a new session of the state legislature, and one of the first actions of the board was to resolve that the members of the San Francisco delegation in the legislature "use their best efforts to secure such legislation as will authorize an increase in the police force of 150 additional men." Negotiations between city officials and the city's legislators resulted in a bill reorganizing the police commission and raising the size of the force to 400 officers (i.e., 250 new ones). This bill passed the legislature on April 1, 1878.[69]

Like most bills expanding the size of the city's work force, this one did not require the city to raise the size of the force to 400 men; rather, it permitted this to be done, and the supervisors undertook the task carefully. On April 8, 1878, acting on a recommendation from its own health and police committee, the board authorized the appointment of 100 new officers, less than half of the 250 positions granted by the legislature. On April 12, the police commission requested permission to add another 150 men to the force. The request was supported by the most fiscally conservative of the local newspapers. The *Bulletin*, which usually opposed any increase in municipal expenditure, editorialized that "nothing could tell more to increase the feeling of security than to fill out the police force to 400 in all," while the *Alta*, reflecting on the disorders of the previous July, said that "a strong, anti-communistic police force is needed. Let us have the full police force as allowed." Because the local elite had first proposed the expansion of the police, there was little doubt of its support for the expansion. Indeed, there probably was more unanimity about this plan than about any other for fiscal expansion in the first twenty-five years of the city's existence under the Consolidation Act.[70]

Nonetheless, the supervisors balked, and they explained why they did so strictly in terms of the fiscal consensus. The lines of debate were laid down on May 6, when the resolution authorizing the 150 additional officers came up for the first time. Fred Gibbs, a native-born merchant elected as a Taxpayer's supervisor from the eleventh ward, noted that "the press was unanimous and all the principal taxpayers . . . were anxious to have the appointments made." Yet Robert Haight, a native-born commission merchant who had been serving on the school board at the time he was elected supervisor on the Taxpayer's ticket, opposed the increase, noting that "the people were over-taxed and rigid economy was necessary": "I oppose this," he said, "because I oppose increased taxation." A vote to postpone action on the measure for one week carried seven to four, with three Democrats and four Taxpayers voting to postpone and three Democrats and one Taxpayers (Gibbs) voting to take immediate action.[71]

When the debate continued the next week, it was unusual in both length and detail. Nearly every supervisor wished to record a position on the issue. This time Henley Smith, vice president of the Pacific Transfer Company and supervisor for the fifth ward, moved that the police commissioners' request for 150 additional officers be approved. The proposal lost by seven to four, with the same four voting for it as had voted against postponing action on the issue the week before. At this point, Edwin Danforth, a warehouse proprietor and Taxpayer's supervisor for the fourth ward, proposed a compromise of 75 additional officers, noting that the whole force would be needed "by and by," but that "the city should go slow in this matter." Haight agreed to this, and Martin Mangels, German-born Democratic supervisor for the second ward, also supported 75 additional policemen but refused to go higher, given the state of the city's "treasury box." James Rountree, Democratic supervisor for the sixth ward and a wholesale grocer, capped the discussion by noting that as a city taxpayer for twenty-six years, he believed he "knew what the people wanted as well as anybody and 75 would be sufficient for the present." The authorization for 75 additional officers passed unanimously, and at the end of the fiscal year 1877/78 (July 1878), the strength of the police force stood at 325.[72]

In some grand scheme of things, of course, an agreement to split the difference on a proposal to increase the police force would not be that significant. But in the context of fiscal politics in San Francisco, to say nothing of the events of 1877–78, it was of great importance. By delaying and resisting the demands of the Committee of Public Safety in the fall of 1877, the supervisors demonstrated that they were not just a tool of the elite. By rejecting the counsel of both the elite and the newspapers in 1878, they demonstrated their allegiance to the fiscal consensus. Moreover, the supervisors who refused the addition of the full 150 officers were part of the elite: all of those who voted against the 150-man increase were well-to-do merchants. Mangels, who had rejected the full increase so forcefully, was one of only 343 persons in the city holding personal property assessed at between $10,000 and $20,000. Only one other official elected in 1877 even had more than $5,000 in personal property.[73]

The caution of the supervisors was well-founded, because in more than doubling the police force, they had to raise the share of the total tax rate going to the General Fund (from which the police were funded) from $0.52 in 1878 to $0.91 in 1879, and the total tax rate for city purposes from $1.20 per $100 of assessed valuation to $1.69 per $100 of assessment. In doing so, the supervisors helped to set off a genuine tax revolt in the city.[74]

Ironically, the incentive for the revolt came from the Workingmen's party, some of whose supporters had been suspected of precipitating the rioting that had led to the expansion of the police force in the first place. The party had been organized in September 1877, too late for the municipal election of that year, so it presented its first municipal platform and ticket in time for the election of 1879. Although in January 1878 representatives of the party had demanded that the city finance public-works projects to help unemployed workers, when the party entered the municipal political arena itself, fiscal restraint was the order of the day. In its 1879 municipal platform, the Workingmen's party pledged to lower expenditure and the tax rate by requiring its candidates to accept only half of their official salaries, donating the remainder to the city treasury. If all its candidates had been elected and all had done this, the savings would have been about $250,000 per year.[75]

Local newspapers scoffed at the offer, doubting the ability of the Workingmen's candidates to carry through on their pledges. Nonetheless, the idea set some candidates in the other parties to thinking. The *Bulletin* noted that the pledges were "specific and to the point," and added that the Republicans would "enter the race badly handicapped" if they were not equally "precise and definite." Because the "main local question at this time relates to taxation," the *Bulletin* recommended that the Republican county committee pledge its supervisorial candidates to the position "that during this administration the tax levy shall not exceed $1 on $100 [of assessed valuation] for local purposes." The editor argued that such a pledge was realistic because twice in recent years the rate had been that low, and it did not require "niggardly economy." "Supernumeraries" would have to be discharged and "barnacles" removed, but on the present assessment, the $1 rate would provide more than $2 million in revenue, the paper argued. Most important, the pledge would allow the taxpayer "to calculate the maximum which he would have to set aside for taxes during the next administration"— and, it might have added, to calculate precisely how closely the supervisors kept to their pledge.[76]

The *Bulletin* editorials proposing, explaining, and defending the Dollar Limit appeared on August 6 and 7, 1879, and on August 12, the Republican county convention adopted it. In doing so, the *Bulletin* announced, the Republicans took the city into a new "era of specific pledges." The old platform generalities of "economy and retrenchment" had long ago "gone to mere molasses intended to catch flies," the *Bulletin* argued; with specific pledges there would now be "fewer avenues of escape for city officials."[77]

For their part, the Democrats answered with one of the "glittering generalities," the *Bulletin* attacked: a fiscal plank in the platform promising to "materially reduce the expenditure in every department so as to largely decrease the present rate of taxation." Because of the emergence of the Workingmen's party and its attempt to capture exactly the same constituency as the Democrats, the election of 1879 was a debacle for the Democrats that no fiscal pledge could have averted (see chap. 4). The Workingmen's party elected its mayoral candidate, while the Republicans took all twelve seats on the board of supervisors.[78]

The failure of the Democrats to adopt the Dollar Limit, combined with their electoral failure, undermined the *Bulletin's* high hopes, however. There were no references to the limit when the tax rates were set in 1880 and 1881 by the supervisors elected in 1879. Because the limit was proposed by the parties, it could only be enforced by partisan competition, and it was not until the election of 1881 that this emerged. In this election the Democratic, Workingmen's, and Republican parties all endorsed the limit, and now the Democratic *Examiner* sang the praises of the specific pledges: "We have entered upon a different era now, for with specific pledges no one elected to office can go back on his constituents without incurring the stigma of dishonesty, faithlessness, and falsehood." Nonetheless, the election was again a Republican triumph, giving that party both the mayoralty and ten-to-two majority on the board of supervisors.[79]

Now that the Dollar Limit was a multiparty pledge, its effect on the supervisors was remarkable. Under the pressure of the pledge and facing a municipal election (1882 was the first year of the new system of elections in even years, so there were municipal elections in September of both 1881 and 1882), the supervisors elected in September 1881 met as a committee of the whole in June 1882 with the explicit goal of reducing the auditor's estimates to the point where a tax rate for the next fiscal year would be in the range of $1. The committee of the whole cut more than $400,000 from the auditor's estimates and answered objections to their actions by reference to the limit. Again, streets, sewers, city hall work, and schools felt the budgetary axe. The school directors had asked the auditor for $848,000 from the board, but knowing the board's perchant for trimming the request for the schools, the auditor cut this estimate to $700,000. When the president of the board of school directors appeared to ask for a restoration of the funds, Republican Supervisor Henry Molineaux replied that the board "would gladly give $850,000 if it could, but that it is impossible to get away from the pledge of the nominating convention." In the end, the supervisors raised the appropriation to $750,000 but the precedent of appeal to the Dollar Limit as a justification for reduction had been set.[80]

Also set by this first board was the precedent for the interpretation of the limit. Although the language of the pledge implied a total tax rate of $1, this first board interpreted the pledge to mean $1 for the ordinary running expenses of government and an additional amount—mandated, in fact, by the laws authorizing bond issues—for sinking funds and interest accounts that comprised debt service expenditure. Therefore, the final result was a total rate of $1.2063: $1 for "the general expenditure of Municipal Government," as the supervisors put it, and $0.2063 for debt service.

In praising the limit, the *Examiner* had warned that there were still those who regarded pre-election promises as "the merest chaff." This first board under the limit (and most of the boards thereafter) demonstrated that it was not composed of this sort of man. Moreover, the board's action had an effect, as table 29 demonstrates: having increased until 1881, expenditures on official salaries decreased 31 percent by fiscal year 1882/83, which was the first year under the limit. Even the heretofore sacrosanct categories of police and fire funds and official salaries were no longer growing faster than the population.[81]

Just when it seemed that the city would nickel-and-dime itself to death with incremental expenditure, the party system roused itself to put the brake on even this marginal growth in municipal government. The Dollar Limit was a genuine fiscal political innovation, but it would have been unthinkable outside the context of the fiscal consensus. In some ways, it was the apotheosis of that consensus, but because it was, it looked backward rather than forward. Indeed, even as it was being imposed, politicians were coming of age who would undermine and finally destroy it.

6

Enforcing the Boundaries: Political Institutions and Fiscal Ideologies, 1882–1896

The importance and pervasiveness of the Dollar Limit in the city's fiscal political history after 1882 is made clear by simple observations from both the input and the output sides of fiscal policymaking. To begin with, the limit was never absent from the platforms of the major parties during the ten municipal elections from 1882 through 1899. Thereafter, it did not need to be in the platforms because it was mandated in the city's reform charter, which took effect in 1900. Moreover, in all but one of the seventeen reports of the finance committee to the board of supervisors presented between 1883 and 1899, the Dollar Limit was cited explicitly as the guiding principle of fiscal policymaking, and in all but two of those reports, the tax rate proposed fell well within its guidelines. Thus the limit was continuously salient in both fiscal politics and fiscal policy during these years.[1]

As this prominence suggests, in the 1880s and 1890s the question, "Who governs?" had been almost completely supplanted by the question, "How shall public resources be authoritatively allocated?" However, the answers provided by the fiscal political system before and after about 1892 were remarkably different. "Boss" Christopher Buckley typified the fiscal political position of the 1880s in his statement that "the safest test of good government is the number of cents out of the dollar which the taxpayer earns he is permitted to retain for his own purposes." Union Labor Mayor Eugene Schmitz reflected the reformed fiscal outlook of the 1890s in his position in his 1901 campaign that "for every dollar taken from the people in taxes they should be given a dollar's worth of services." Although the difference between these two statements may seem slight, the movement from the first to the second was the result of almost twenty years of political struggle.[2]

From 1882 through about 1892, the parties agreed that that government was best which spent least, and they institutionalized this position in drastic limits on the growth of the city's assessed valuation, in combination with the Dollar Limit on taxation. Local politics in these years was intensely partisan and highly competitive, and the parties attempted to distinguish themselves from one another by platform pledges for taxation and assessed valuation which revealed the property-tax-based "price" for municipal government should their candidates be elected. Under the pressure of this price competition, political leaders of both parties had forced taxation, valuation, and expenditure down to their lowest levels in the city's history by 1887.

Support for this position began to erode in the late 1880s and early 1890s under the pressure of demands from neighborhood and businessmen's groups for municipal improvements. Beginning in 1891, representatives of neighborhoods outside the boundaries of the "old city" began to appear at the annual allocation meetings of the finance committee to demand the municipal expenditure necessary to extend services into their areas. By 1894 these neighborhood groups had federated into a citywide organization and were joined by the Merchants' Association, a citywide group of high-status businessmen. Recognizing the potential for a political coalition based on promises of benefits from an expanding public sector, Democratic politican James D. Phelan, who had been instrumental in founding both the Merchants' Association and the citywide improvement association, took over the political leadership of the reform movement in his 1896 mayoral campaign. His victory set the stage for an even more intense campaign for a new charter and bonds for municipal improvements in the late 1890s.

The fiscal positions of both the 1880s and the 1890s were the result of the possibilities and necessities of political action, rather than of the functional necessities of urban development. Politicians of the 1880s competed within the framework of the Dollar Limit because of the highly competitive partisan political atmosphere and the power of the preexisting fiscal consensus. Reformers attacked the limit itself in the 1890s, because they conceived of themselves as political insurgents out to destroy the preexisting fiscal consensus and thus gain political power. Because of this political focus, we will now consider the electoral political ground on which the fiscal political culture of the years 1882–

1905 was built. Having laid out this ground here, however, we will discuss the lengthy and complicated fiscal political debate in these years in two parts. The remainder of this chapter focuses on the years from 1882 through 1896, and we examine the years from 1897 through 1906 in chapter 7.

THE STRUCTURE OF POLITICAL ACTION, 1882–1905

As we saw in chapter 5, the most fundamental factor structuring the participation of San Franciscans in electoral politics was the legal framework within which the suffrage was exercised. Between 1882 and 1905, this framework was changed three times: the schedule of elections was changed twice, and the actual means of voting was revised in important ways. The municipal election of 1881 was the last election held separately from state and federal elections until the very end of the century. Beginning in 1882, municipal elections were shifted to November of even years, and from then until 1898, municipal elections coincided with either gubernatorial or presidential elections. The former occurred in 1882 and every four years thereafter; the latter, in 1884 and every four years thereafter. In the reform charter passed in 1898, municipal elections were once again shifted to odd years, and after 1899, when this change took effect, municipal elections were held separately from others.[3]

In addition to these changes, in 1891 the state legislature passed the Reform Ballot Act, which introduced the so-called Australian or secret ballot, beginning with the election of 1892. The act brought about three major changes necessary to institutionalize the secret ballot: (1) it required that the state take over from the parties the responsibility for printing and distributing the ballots; (2) because this was the case, it required that all parties appear on the same ballot and thus, for the first time, permitted real split-ticket voting, although straight-ticket voting was still possible; and (3) because the state printed the tickets, the act institutionalized a procedure for getting on the ballot, requiring that parties or slates seeking a place on the ballot either (a) have received 5 percent of the total vote cast at the preceding election, or (b) present petitions signed by a number of qualified electors equaling 5 percent of the total vote cast in the jurisdiction in which they wished to run. This meant that the major parties automatically qualified for the new ballots in 1892. Other groups had to go the petition route; given the turnout in San Francisco in the election of 1890, they were required to find 2,775 electors to sign their petitions. In 1893 the legislature reduced the 5 percent rule to 3 percent. This change meant that insurgent slates in the election of 1894, for example, had to find only 1,823 electors to sign their petitions.[4]

Somewhat surprisingly, the overall patterns in electoral participation from 1882 through 1905 remained remarkably similar to those for 1960 through 1881. On average, between 1882 and 1905, about 55 percent of males aged twenty-one and over were registered for presidential elections, and about 51 percent were registered for gubernatorial elections. Once registered, voters maintained a high level of participation. An average of about 88 percent of registered voters voted for president, 86 percent for governor, and 80 percent for mayor. However, this meant that only about 49 percent of males twenty-one and over voted for president and about 45 percent for governor. Between 1882 and 1898, when local elections were held with either presidential or gubernatorial elections, the level of participation in the mayoral election varied with the top of the ticket; about 48 percent of males twenty-one and over voted for mayor in a presidential election, while about 45 percent did so in a gubernatorial election. After 1898, when the inflating effect of the state and national elections was withdrawn by the separation of municipal elections from others, the participation of the city's eligible males in mayoralty elections dropped to its true level, which was about 41 percent on average. These figures are almost identical to those for the years 1870 through 1881, for which we have comparable figures. Then about 48 percent of eligible males voted for president and about 44 percent voted for governor. When the mayor was elected with the governor, about 44 percent voted for the mayor, while about 40.5 percent of eligible males did so when municipal elections were held separately from others. Despite changing issues and political organizations over time, then, political participation remained the acitivity of a minority of males twenty-one and over in these years.[5]

Within these overall similarities, however, were significant differences in levels of political mobilization, participation, regularity, and competition among the three time periods from 1882 through 1905, defined by the changes in the schedule of elections and the mechanics of voting. Tables 30, 31, and 32 display averages of these variables from 1882 through 1890, when elections were combined and the parties printed

TABLE 30

ESTIMATED AVERAGE SIZE OF THE REGISTERED ELECTORATE AND PARTICIPATION OF REGISTERED VOTERS, 1882–1905

	1882–1890	1892–1898	1899–1905
Presidential elections			
Registered/Males 21	52.7%	58%	51.1%
Voting/Males 21	48.4	49.3	46.4
Voting/Registered	93.6	86.8	82.5
Gubernatorial elections			
Registered/Males 21	48.4	52.9	51.1[a]
Voting/Males 21	44.7	46	43.5[a]
Voting/Registered	92.5	86.3	85.1[a]
Mayoral elections			
Registered/Males 21	50.1	55.4	58.6
Voting/Males 21	45.3	48	41.9
Voting/Registered	91.2	86.5	71.5
Supervisorial elections			
Registered/Males 21	50.1	55.4	58.6
Voting/Males 21	46.6	43.8	37.8
Voting/Registered	92.8	79.1	65.2

[a] For 1902 only.

straight-ticket ballots; from 1892 through 1898, when elections were combined and the effects of ballot reform were felt; and from 1899 through 1905, when elections were separated. These data indicate that although municipal politics was always quite competitive, during the 1880s the electorate was smaller, more partisan, and more highly mobilized, while after 1892 it was larger, less regular, and less highly mobilized.

The data in table 30 reveal that the size of the electorate and the level of participation of registered voters were inversely related over time at all levels, even when elections were held together. As measured by the share of males twenty-one and over who were registered to vote, the electorate was smallest from 1882 through 1890 and larger thereafter, while the share of registered voters who voted was highest from

TABLE 31

AVERAGE MEASURES OF POLITICAL REGULARITY, 1882–1905

	1882–1890	1892–1898	1899–1905
Number of tickets in the field			
Presidential	2.5	3.0	4.0
State executive	3.0	4.0	4.0[a]
City executive	2.8	5.4	3.75
City legislative	2.6	4.75	3.75
Share of total vote going to regular parties			
Presidential	98.5%	97.4%	92.4%
Gubernatorial	89.9	92.8	96.4
Mayoral	87	61.3	52.4
Supervisorial	96.9	75.9	70.3
Winning local ticket same as winning top of ticket			
Supervisors	5/5	2/4	n/a
Mayor	4/5	0/4	n/a

[a] For 1902 only.

TABLE 32

AVERAGE SHARE OF TOTAL VOTE GOING TO WINNER, 1882–1905

	1882–1890	1892–1898	1899–1905
Presidential	52.9%	51.7%	58.5%
Gubernatorial	50.1	52.8	56.3[a]
Mayoral	47.2	53	50.6
Supervisorial	51	42.1	44.5

[a] For 1902 only.

1882 through 1890 and lower thereafter. In other words, from 1882 through 1890, political organizations maximized the participation of enrolled voters without expanding the size of the enrolled electorate; after 1892, they expanded the size of the enrolled electorate but failed to maintain as high a level of participation among enrolled voters. This difference in the size of the eligible electorate was not an artifact of institutional change in the method of registration. From 1878 until the end of the period under consideration, registration was conducted within the precincts according to procedures that remained essentially the same.[6]

More relevant reasons for the expansion in the size of the eligible electorate—and perhaps for the decline in the core active electorate—are revealed in table 31, which displays three measures of political regularity in these years: (1) the average number of tickets at the different electoral levels; (2) the share of the total vote at each level going to the regular (i.e., Democratic and Republican) parties; and (3) the number of times that the winners at the lower levels of the ticket (i.e., mayoral and supervisorial) were of the same party as the winners at the top of the ticket. These data indicate that local politics was always less regular than state or national politics; however, it was remarkably more regular between 1882 and 1890 and remarkably less regular after 1892, when the share of votes going to regular party candidates dropped, the number of tickets in the field rose, and the tie between the top of the ticket and local offices was broken to a great extent.

As shown in table 31, local politics was quite regular from 1882 through 1890, but much less so after 1892, when the average share of votes for mayor going to the regular parties dropped by 25 percent and that for supervisors dropped by 20 percent. Similarly, the average number of tickets on the local level was almost twice as high after 1892 than from 1882 through 1890. Perhaps even more disappointing from a party regular's point of view was the disconnection after 1892 of the electoral fate of local officials and that of the candidates at the top of the ticket. In the nine elections from 1882 through 1898 at which municipal and other officials were elected together, the party controlling the board of supervisors was the same as that winning at the top of the ticket (i.e., gubernatorial or presidential candidate) seven out of nine times, and the party of the mayor was the same four of nine times (see table 31). This type of regularity reached its peak from 1882 through 1890, when four out of five mayoral elections and all supervisorial elections went the same way as the top of the ticket. This regularity dropped dramatically after 1892, when the winning supervisors were the same as the top of the ticket only half of the time, and the winning mayor was never of the same party as the top of the ticket.[7]

Although local politics was more regular before 1892, even in the years of high regularity, parties controlled the city by a mere razor's edge. This is obvious from table 32, which displays the share of the total vote going to the winners at each level of electoral activity. Closely contested elections were definitely the rule between 1882 and 1898, when candidates at all levels won by bare majorities at best. Moreover, at least in part because of this closeness, there was a tendency for the partisan outcomes to swing somewhat unpredictably.

At the local level, Democratic dominance was clear, but again, because of the influence of the top of the ticket before 1892 and party irregularity thereafter, this dominance was not continuous. Democrats won the mayoralty seven times, Republicans once, and nonregular party candidates five times. Democrats won the majority of the board of supervisors eight times, Republicans four times, and the Union Labor party once. However, the Democrats held both the mayoralty and the board of supervisors only five times (in 1882, 1886, 1888, 1896, and 1899), and only once back-to-back. As table 32 reveals, this was in part the result of the degree of competition at the local level; elections for mayor and the board of supervisors were even closer than those for president or governor. Indeed, on average, mayoral candidates did not win by majorities between 1882 and 1890, and the party controlling the board of supervisors did not receive a majority from 1892 through 1898.

We can take a closer look at this pattern of competition on the local level in table 33, which displays the party of and share of the total vote going to both the winner of the mayoralty and the majority on the board of supervisors from 1882 through 1905. If we define a decisive municipal election as one in which a single party won both the mayoralty and the board by a majority, the first decisive election in these years was in 1882, the next in 1899, the last in 1905. Between 1882 and 1899, in particular, the potential for crises of political legitimacy was great, given the minority mayoralties in 1888, 1890, and 1892 and the minority boards of supervisors from 1892 through 1896.

Politics in these years was, then, a hard-fought battle among a minority of the city's eligible males. Between 1882 and 1890, the battle was fought between well-drilled armies of roughly even strength whose

TABLE 33

SHARE OF TOTAL VOTE GOING TO PARTY OF WINNER
IN MUNICIPAL ELECTIONS, 1882–1905

	Mayor	Majority of board of supervisors
1882	Dem. 52.9%	Dem. 58.5%
1884	Dem. 53.5	Rep. 45.6
1886	Dem. 53.5	Dem. 46.4
1888	Dem. 38.3	Dem. 51.3
1890	Rep. 37.9	Rep. 53
1892	Non-Part. 31	Dem. 37.7
1894	People's 52.1	Rep. 40.5
1896	Dem. 46	Dem. 35.8
1898	Dem. 51.9	Rep. 54.3
1899	Dem. 56.8	Dem. 53.5
1901	ULP 42.8	Dem. 33
1903	ULP 45.7	Dem. 35.7
1905	ULP 57	ULP 53.5

Note: Independent party designations:
    Non-Part. = Non-Partisan
    People's   = People's (Populist)
    ULP   = Union Labor Party

votes were determined more by the "top" of the ticket than by the municipal "bottom." Beginning in 1892, this well-disciplined warfare dissolved into political guerrilla war as more tickets entered the field and the electorate became larger and less reliable. There were both costs and benefits to the post-1892 political situation. With sometimes as many as six or seven slates in the field, municipal elections after 1892 came close to being chaotic, and the participation of registered voters dropped, as a result of both the increased complexity of the act of voting and the removal of the parties as the sources of ballots and voting instructions. Yet the decline of partisan loyalty and of the top of the ticket as the determinants of political action set off a search for a new basis on which to build political coalitions within the expanding electorate. It was the reformers who recognized the possibilities for using promises of benefits from an expanding public sector as the cement for these new coalitions.[8]

THE DOLLAR LIMIT AT ITS ZENITH, 1882–1892

The potential for political chaos in the 1890s was far from the minds of the San Francisco politicians of the 1880s, who entered the decade with a rather smug sense of themselves as genuine fiscal political reformers. After all, by imposing the Dollar Limit they had just "solved" the thorny issue of ever-increasing taxation and expenditure. Given their lights, these men had a right to be smug, because the limit was a genuinely innovative response to the widespread demand for fiscal responsibility. It introduced into the city's politics a measurable standard of commitment to the fiscal consensus, and thus a new era of fiscal responsibility, and it demonstrated to contemporary critics that the political system could reform itself. As the *Bulletin* pointed out, now that the limit was in place, "if the Mayor will do his duty, if passably honest Supervisors can be obtained, if the connivance of the latter with bureau officers (to increase their allowances) can be prevented, we can have under the existing laws all the economy that is necessary or desired in the administration of local government."[9]

Buckley would later take credit for the Dollar Limit, but its rise and fall were by no means attached to his. The limit would have been unthinkable outside of the twenty-year fiscal political consensus from which it emerged and which, in essence, it codified. More concretely, as we saw in chapter 5, the pledge emerged in 1879 from the Republican party and was in the Democratic platform by 1881, the year before Buckley claimed to have introduced it. Buckley was politically "dead" by 1891, but the limit continued long after that. It was less the iron grip of a boss than the lead weight of the fiscal consensus of the first twenty years of the city's history that was responsible for the introduction of the limit, and it was the sharp edge of partisan competition that maintained and enforced it.[10]

When they introduced the Dollar Limit, the leaders of the parties did not intend to use it to kill the goose that laid the golden egg. Although they believed in limited government and set out to act on that belief, they did not intend to stop the steady incremental growth of the local budget that had been characteristic from 1860 through 1880. Buckley, for example, admitted in his memoirs that the Democrats adopted the limit, "forecasting that with the expanding assessment roll the revenues would increase in proportion to the greater needs of a growing population." What he meant was that, although the tax rate would remain constant at $1, the city's assessed valuation would increase, and thus revenue available for the expansion of local government would grow.[11]

What Buckley and others had not counted on was the dynamic of partisan competition. Once both parties put the Dollar Limit into their platforms in 1882, it lost its power to differentiate them from each other. Apparently recognizing this, the Republicans upped the political ante in 1884 by combining the limit with a ceiling of $200 million on the assessed valuation. In essence, this was a pledge that, if elected, the Republican candidates for the board of supervisors would accept a total assessed valuation not to exceed $200 million in their capacity as the county's board of equalization. In current dollars, this was pledging a reduction of $53 million (20 percent) from the total valuation for the preceding fiscal year. Of course, this also meant corresponding reductions in individual assessments. In combination, the limit on taxation of $1 per $100 of valuation and the limit on total valuation of $200 million meant that the Republicans were pledging to run the city on a total revenue raised from taxation of $2 million.[12]

To do this, the platform not only called for general cutbacks but also, for the first time, included a specific limit on one of what were then called the "major" patronage offices. These offices included those of the sheriff, county clerk, auditor, assessor, tax collector, and superintendent of streets, and they had the largest budgets for staff. The specific pledge of the 1884 Republican platform was to limit expenses for the county clerk's office to $6,000 per month ($72,000 per year). In current dollars, this would have been a reduction of only $3,000 from the previous year, but of more than $20,000 from the year before that.[13]

In response, the Democrats pledged a tax rate of $0.975, with no limit on the assessment. They outdid the Republican pledge for the county clerk's office by $500, promising to run it at $5,500 per month. In the subsequent election, the Republicans took the board and about half of the executive offices, while the Democrats took the mayoralty and the other half of the executive offices. Because James G. Blaine also carried the city for the Republicans and ran ahead of the Republican supervisors, it cannot be said that the valuation limit was the decisive factor in the local election. Nonetheless, from 1882 until 1899, no platform was without some limit on the total assessed valuation, and the platforms became more competitive in this regard and more specific about the parties' limitations on some of the patronage offices.[14]

Noting the similarity of the parties on the Dollar Limit in 1884, the *Bulletin* said that the parties were "practically a unit" and declared that "no party can hope to live in this community which is not sound on that proposition." More important, the limit was regarded as the fiscal salvation of the city regardless of the state of the local political culture. Commenting on the complaints of many about the "boss rule" of the parties, the *Bulletin* declared that "there is a silver lining to the cloud [of boss rule], dark as it may appear at the moment. The One Dollar Limit on taxation for general purposes is safe, no matter what party, or combination of parties, wins. That is a great point gained."[15]

The editorialist was more correct than he knew, because the parties were emulating their colleagues in the private sector and introducing cutthroat price competition in the public sector. In essence, the platform limits on taxation and assessment together established the tax-based price of municipal government for the next two years. The object of the platforms was to match or undersell the political competition by means of the assessment pledge. Building on the 1884 assessment pledge, the parties jockeyed for competitive fiscal position, pledging a slowly increasing valuation. In 1886, for example, the Republicans pledged an assessment of $220 million, the Democrats $215 million; in 1888, both pledged a $230 million assessment. In 1890, both parties introduced the innovation of an increasing two-year pledge, with the Republicans promising a limit of $250 million in the first year of their administration (if elected) and $275 million in the second. The Democrats pledged to match this in the first year and undercut the Republicans in the second, promising a total assessment of $260 million then. Both parties also kept the lid on the hapless county clerk, pledging a limit of $6,000 per month for the expenses in that office in every platform until the end of the century. At various other times, they pledged to cut or limit staff expenditures in the offices of the superintendent of streets and of the board of supervisors itself.[16]

It was, of course, easy to make these pledges. The more important question is whether they worked. In fact, they did. The evidence for this is seen in both the use of the limits in the setting of the tax rates and expenditure levels in these years, and in the other measures of fiscal policy that we have been considering thus far.

The status of the Dollar Limit as the guiding light of fiscal policy-making was dramatically confirmed in the first report of the finance committee after the election of 1882. Meeting in June 1883 to set fiscal policy for the coming fiscal year, the committee declared that its task had been guided by the "fact that the people have uniformly decided, irrespective of politics, that taxation should not exceed $1 on each $100 valuation of property," and thus it worked to come within the limit. It did so by reducing the already low auditor's estimate of expenditure by $191,000, through cutting all the major patronage offices but making the largest cuts—$25,000 and $80,000, respectively—in the Street and School funds. The committee noted that these cuts were made despite "the opinions advanced by representatives of the departments," who "strenuously urged for an increase of the amounts determined upon." The result of the committee's labor was a rate of $1 for "ordinary expenses" and $0.20 for debt service, which was unanimously approved by the board and signed by the mayor.[17]

Sentiments like these were displayed in every report of the finance committees from 1883 until 1892. The 1884 committee declared that the limits opened a "new era of the management and control of municipal business," while the committee of 1889 began by restating the pledges of the platform under which it had been elected and concluded by noting that the "pledges exacted have been complied with, and, apart from special pleading on behalf of many appropriations, there can be no question but that they are ample."[18]

Even those committee members who personally opposed the limits paid tribute to them in practice. In 1885, for example, the Republican-dominated finance committee declared that "every fact which has been presented to your Committee in reference to the public needs ... affords indubitable evidence that the pledge of the so-called One Dollar Limit which was forced upon us and upon the convention which nominated us, was the offspring simply of insane public clamor ... inconsiderate and detrimental to the public interests." Nonetheless, the members declared that they would not "deviate from the pledge which they have made to observe it," and the rate they presented was only $0.9091 for the ordinary expenses of government. Moreover, the members were willing to make such a complaint only in a nonelection year.

The next year, this same committee delivered up a $1 tax rate without so much as a whimper.[19]

Whether they liked it or not, then, the supervisors never wavered from observance of the limit. Had they wavered, however, the limits could have been enforced by Dollar Limit men in the executive branch of local government. For example, Washington Bartlett, the attorney elected mayor on the Democratic ticket in 1882 and 1884, declared in his 1882 campaign that the Dollar Limit was "the most important" pledge in the platform because "a people has the clear and indisputable right to say what portion of their [sic] means shall be taken" for taxation. After two terms as mayor, Bartlett ran for governor in 1886, and campaigned in the city on the position that San Francisco's economy had recovered from the depression of the late 1870s because of the Dollar Limit. Since 1882, he said, capital had revived, new enterprises had been undertaken, and new buildings erected: "I claim that these happy results were largely achieved by... setting the 'Dollar Limit' to the greed of those in power," he declared, "and insisting that the property owners had rights which must be respected."[20]

Elected along with Bartlett in 1882 were two Democratic supervisors whose later political careers would also reinforce the limit. One was Edward B. Pond, a self-proclaimed capitalist who was elected supervisor from the Sixth Ward in 1882 and 1884, and who succeeded Bartlett in the mayor's chair in 1886 and 1888. Pond was chairman of the first two finance committees after 1882, and he enforced and praised the limits, arguing that "my experience has taught me that a pledge is often of great assistance in constraining a weak officer and has been found in the past [to be] the only means of giving the people any relief in matters largely in their interest."[21]

The other man elected in 1882 was Fleet Strother, the Eighth Ward supervisor who would go on to be elected auditor in 1884 and reelected to that position in 1886 and 1888. Strother introduced the tradition of the letter of transmittal of the auditor's estimates of expenditure for the upcoming fiscal year, and in these letters he defended the limits steadfastly and, at times, poetically. In the first of these, in June 1885, Strother noted that "the desire for economical administration of government has been unequivocally expressed by all the late political municipal conventions. Whatever, therefore, may be the view as to the policy of increasing municipal expenditure, it does not seem to come within the scope of the officers of the municipality until such time as the people evince and express a desire therefor." For this reason, then, the estimates Strother presented to the finance committee were already Dollar Limit estimates. It was to be his policy annually, from then on, to present estimates of expenditure "under the pledge in the platform of the party which was endorsed by the people."[22]

When attacked in 1890 by those in favor of more municipal expenditure on improvements, Strother delivered a stirring defense of the limits. Conceding that "the wants of our municipal government have been very emphatically urged and represented by the public press ... and the impression seems to be that more liberal appropriations should be provided," he contended nonetheless that "the question as to the power to be exercised in face of the pledges declared to be a solemn obligation, which should be sacredly kept, remains and, like Banquo's ghost, will not down. The will of the people is the measure of the power to be exercised and is the rule and guidance of this department."[23]

If necessary, then, fainthearted supervisors could have been buoyed up by a Dollar Limit auditor preparing estimates of assessment, taxation, revenue, and expenditure for the finance committee, and by Dollar Limit mayors ready to wield the veto against limit-breaking rates of taxation or levels of assessment. However, between 1882 and 1892, this was never necessary. In striking contrast to the years between 1876 and 1881, when the mayor's veto or veto threat was an important tactic in the new politicization of the tax rate, during this later period the mayor never vetoed or even threatened to veto a tax rate proposed by the board. The platforms had already taken care of that problem; once the magic limit was reached, no one was expected to do more.

Under the pressure of and unanimity behind the limits, then, expenditure, revenue, and taxation dropped to historic lows in real terms by the end of fiscal year 1886/87. Table 34 displays the changes in the measures of fiscal policy that we have been following thus far. Looking first at the percent change between fiscal 1883/84 and 1886/87, we see that almost every indicator declined or barely held its own. The per capita real assessed valuation remained stable, while the tax rate dropped about 13 percent, tax revenue dropped 23 percent, and per capita operating expenditure remained stable. Within the major components of operating expenditure, stability or decline was also apparent. Per capita school expenditure increased a mere 4 percent, per capita street expenditure decreased 25 percent, per capita police and fire expenditure remained stable, and even the much maligned category of

TABLE 34

CHANGES IN MEASURES OF FISCAL POLICY, 1884–1893

Category	1884	1887	1893	Percent change 1884–87	Percent change 1887–93	Era mean
Per capita assessed valuation	$720.4	$722.35	$1027.1	0%	42%	$832.44
Per capita local revenue	11.38	9.13	12.28	−19.7	34	10.93
Per capita tax revenue	9.430	7.235	10.190	−23.3	40.8	8.86
Per capita cash on hand	1.793	2.093	2.599	16.7	24	2.557
Per capita total local expenditure	13.85	11.45	15.31	−17.3	33	13.780
Tax rate	1.0169	.8860	.9259	−12.9	4.5	.9504
Per capita non-tax revenue	1.946	1.878	2.0936	−2.5	10.2	2.070
Per capita operating expenditure	10.61	10.56	14.84	0	40.5	11.99
Per capita School Fund expenditure	.0025	.0026	.0031	4	19.2	.0027
Per capita Street Fund expenditure	.0008	.0006	.0012	−25	100	.0009
Per capita street lighting expenditure	.0007	.0007	.0008	0	14	.0007
Per capita police and fire expenditure	2.725	2.713	3.1150	0	14.8	2.828
Per capita expenditure on official salaries	1.19	1.1376	1.26	−4.4	10	1.197
Per capita expenditure on social welfare	.7004	.7967	.6253	13	−21.5	.6932
Share of operating expenditure	78.6%	88.9%	93.6%	13.1	5.3	85.3%

Note: All dollar values have been deflated by means of the price index explained in appendix A.

official salaries declined 4 percent on a per capita basis. The city was barely balancing its budget by relying on increasing nontax revenue and its cash reserves.

Beginning about 1886, however, significant strains in the consensus on the limits began to appear. Political leaders and newspapers began to question the wisdom of constantly postponing street work, refusing to increase educational expenditure significantly, and making no improvements of a permanent sort. Because of the political power of the limits, however, the position of these groups was ambiguous; they wanted improvements, but they also wanted the limits, and the amount of expenditure on improvements that they would back was minimal. Less ambiguous were the neighborhood improvement groups, which began to spring up around 1885 and which by 1891 had invaded the budget meetings of the board of supervisors both to demand the extension of municipal services to their areas and to denounce the limits.

As already noted, by 1885 there were municipal politicians ready to denounce the limits. The report of the Republican-dominated finance committee of that year noted that while public economy was "doubtless the surest safeguard of public prosperity," there was a wide difference between "public economy and public parsimony, and public prosperity can never follow when the policy persists of making the latter stand in the place of the former as its sham representative and makeshift." The supervisors noted that a "great and growing" city like San Francisco required "large expenditures" for streets and sewers, the extension and embellishment of public parks, the erection and repair of public buildings, and more facilities for public education, and they denounced a fiscal policy that "scrimps and pinches" regardless of public wants as "shortsighted if not humiliating and disgraceful." Yet this fine rhetoric came to naught in the actual fixing of the limit, because this committee, too, dared not break the Dollar Limit pledge it denounced.[24]

Nonetheless, the Republicans continued this theme in the campaigns of 1886 and 1888, arguing that "recent events have . . . shown that the expenditure of the municipal government must necessarily increase with the growth of the city." Declaring that "Republicanism is synonymous with progress," the version of the 1886 platform originally introduced at the municipal convention called for a $1 limit on taxation but no limit on the assessment, because "revenue for the proper administration of the city government must be increased." The next day, however, the convention amended the platform, maintaining the declaration but including a limit of $220 million on the assessment. In 1888, the Republican platform again proclaimed that "we cannot fail to recognize the universal demand by the people for better streets and sewers, more and better schoolhouses, increased facilities for putting out fires, and improved parks, and we declare it to be the policy of the Republican party to furnish these growing necessities as the increase of the city demands them." Nevertheless, the platform called for a $1 rate on a $230 million limit.[25]

The Democrats, meanwhile, stood fast with the limits, in both their general statements and their specific proposals. In 1886 they answered the Republican attack on the limits by recalling "with pride and satisfaction that the Democratic Party were [sic] the first to adopt in good faith and subsequently observe the one dollar limit of taxation ... and they claim credit for having compelled the Republican Party to follow in the wake of this great municipal reform." In 1888 they declared again for the "solemn obligation" of the Dollar Limit. It goes without saying that the limit was found in both platforms, along with an assessment pledge of $215 million in 1886 and $230 million in 1888.[26]

Although neither party was completely against municipal improvements, neither would step forthrightly out of the consensus on the limits to finance them. In 1888, for example, the Republican platform allowed expenditure on improvements outside of the limits only if "each public improvement is appropriated by unanimous vote of the Supervisors and approved by the Mayor." This was an attempt to insure the party against political risk for stepping beyond the limits, but it also guaranteed that there would be no improvements. That year, the Democrats similarly pledged to use the extra revenue produced by the $15 million increase in assessment over the previous fiscal year to finance specific improvements, including $150,000 for streets and sewers, a police patrol service, additional fire hydrants, and more money for the public schools. However, at the 1 percent rate, an increase of $15 million in the valuation produced only $150,000 in additional revenue, enough to finance only the first of the listed improvements.[27]

By 1890 the chairman of the Democratic municipal convention, R. B. Mitchell, would declare that it was time to make San Francisco the "Paris of America," but the platform proposed only a $20 million increase in the valuation, which meant only $200,000 in additional revenue. Politicians like Mitchell and others were definitely moving in the direction of improvements, and this brought about gradual increases in the assessment. But they could see no dramatic way around the limits and no well-organized or visible coalition for improvements that would support an assault on the limits.[28]

In fact, when politicians looked to another significant source of organized political opinion, the newspapers, what they saw was advice that was always contradictory and sometimes simply irresponsible. Because the *Examiner* was the voice of the Democracy and Democrats controlled city government for most of these years, the *Examiner* was probably the most influential paper in the city. It, too, began to be disillusioned with the limits in 1886, but like the politicians it frequently criticized, the *Examiner* found it impossible to move forthrightly away from the fiscal consensus around the limits.

In the space of one month during the municipal election campaign of 1886, the *Examiner* declared that the limits on assessment and taxation were starving the fire department and thus jeopardizing "millions of property every day," but then declared that "no property holder should willingly consent, under any circumstances, to be liable to an unlimited tax on an unlimited valuation." During the election of 1888, the paper demanded that the Democratic platform "repudiate the 'Dollar Limit' as it is worshipped and understood by the . . . mossbacks." What it meant, however, was that the $1 limit on a $215 million assessment pledge should be raised to $1 on "not less than $230 million," an increase that would have resulted in only an additional $150,000 in the city treasury.[29]

In repeatedly calling for "progress" without "license," the paper was calling for the age-old dream—something for nothing. It urged the political conventions to construct pledges "liberal enough to allow the city to make a little progress," but it did not repudiate the tiny incremental increases in the valuation or the maintenance of the $1 limit on those increases. Instead, it constantly demanded that funds be reallocated from salaries to "permanent improvements." As it put it in 1889, "the less that can be put into current expenses and the more that can be put into permanent improvements, the better the people will be satisfied."[30]

Like many others, the *Examiner* wanted both low taxation and municipal improvements. Unlike some others, it was occasionally honest enough to admit the irresponsibility of its opinion. An editorial published during the tax-rate setting process in June 1891 demanded that the supervisors both keep the limits and bring about municipal improvements, but rejected responsibility for prescribing how this was to be done: "How? That is none of our business. . . . They [the supervisors] put their own noses to the grindstone and now we insist that they keep them there until they are satisfactorily sharpened."[31]

To point out the inconsistency and irresponsibility of this position is not to deny its difference from that of previous periods. Before 1886 newspapers of whatever persuasion rarely encouraged improvements, but after that time it was a regular bipartisan occurrence. The Republican *Chronicle* made the same points, editorializing in 1892 that it was "time to drag the city out of the rut into which it has fallen and to put it on the highway of progress and prosperity." Here again, however, the changes had to be made within "proper and necessary limitations." This "new" position of both politicians and newspapers, then, was both backward- and forward-looking: on the one hand, it approved of some municipal improvements; on the other, it was still suspicious of the ability of government to carry them out efficiently, and was thus unwilling to hand the local leaders a "blank check."[32]

Less ambiguous in their support of municipal improvements were the so-called neighborhood improvement clubs that began springing up in 1885 to encourage the improvement of municipal services in their areas. The improvement groups were introduced to the city in a rather condescending story and editorial in the *Examiner* of June 1889. At that time, the paper said there were eight of the groups in existence, although another source has identified two more not mentioned in the story. All were outside the 50 and 100 vara areas of the old city and, although each club had specific improvements in mind for its area, all shared similar philosophies and long-run goals. The groups worked to have streets and sewers in their neighborhoods accepted for maintenance by the city and to have police, fire, and educational services extended to their areas, but they relied on self-help and subscription among their members to finance most of the improvements. Therefore, by 1889, their existence had resulted in no significant direct costs to the city for the improvements.[33]

As an example of the groups in action, the *Examiner* considered the 16th Street Improvement Club, which had recently organized its members to finance the extension of 16th Street. They had done this by taxing themselves $1.50 per front foot of property owned on the street, in order to purchase the needed property and lay out the street. We can recall from chapter 2 that the costs of "opening" a street were assessed against adjacent property owners in just this fashion. When the city "accepted" an opened street, it assumed the responsibility for its maintenance. The club had simply accelerated the process by facilitating the organization of adjacent property owners. Other clubs were working in similar fashion to extend streets and sewers in their areas, to "assist one another in the removal of nuisances," and to encourage private sector companies to extend street railways into their areas.[34]

The *Examiner* praised the public-spiritedness of the clubs, noting that the particular improvements they carried out were less important than the public spirit they fostered. According to the editorial, the clubs were a welcome relief from those who constantly obstructed progress. For the "rousing and crystallizing of opinion the local improvement club is potent," the paper noted, adding that "it is an old saying [that] if each would sweep before his own door the village would be clean."[35]

It was not surprising that the clubs were all outside the 50 and 100 vara areas of the old city, because it was within these two areas that most of the physical locations for urban services, such as firehouses, police stations, schoolhouses, and paved and accepted streets were found. As we saw in chapter 3, beginning in the 1880s, the population of the city began to move rapidly outside of these boundaries to the west and south and into precisely those areas complaining about the lack of services. Because expenditure for most purposes had barely reached its pre–Dollar Limit level by 1893, there was little or no money through most of the decade for the geographical expansion of these services to the "suburban districts," as these areas were called.

Nor was it surprising that the self-help philosophy of the improvement groups was relatively short-lived. The good that the groups could do with their own funds alone was limited, indeed. More important, if there really was plenty of money for improvements, as the newspapers claimed, it was only a matter of time until the groups would try to shift the funds in that direction. In June 1891 improvement groups made their first foray into the allocation process by appearing at the meeting of the finance committee of the board of supervisors, where appeals from department heads and from the public were heard. Speaking were representatives of the Richmond District in the city's northwest corner and of the 16th Street Improvement Club in the Mission District. The former group requested appropriations "liberal enough" to extend services to its area, while the latter requested the completion of a large sewer on Brannan Street that would drain its area. In that regard the leader of the 16th Street group said that "in a matter of such gravity as this the question of taxation percentages should, if necessary be lost sight of.... Dollar Limit pledges are all very well, but I do not think you gentlemen can shift upon anyone else the responsibility for the health of the city." When the finance committee made its report to the board a week later, $60,000 had been appropriated for the sewer project.[36]

Now, the Dollar Limit had by no means been transgressed; the appropriation was made within the limit. The importance of the project was not that it was an attack on the limit, but that it was the first time a nongovernmental group had received a specifically appropriated request from the board of supervisors. Others had asked for and received funds from the board, but none had appeared at the annual tax-rate and expenditure-allocation meeting to ensure that their funds would be included in the next year's budget. Although neither the supervisors nor the improvement groups realized it, they had set a precedent in the history of the city's fiscal politics. The moment was not without its irony, however, because appearing at the same meeting was a citizens group urging the board not to forget the Dollar Limit.

Following the law that nothing succeeds like success, the improvement groups were back the following year, this time from other parts of the city. Along with the fire chief, school directors, and other city departments, representatives of the Panhandle and the Alamo Square improvement clubs appeared. The first group requested $75,000 for better streets around the panhandle of Golden Gate Park; the second, $15,000 to improve the square after which the club was named. Requests for projects totaling $90,000 do not seem like much in the larger scheme of things, but the finance committee was not working in the larger scheme. In fact, the previous year's assessment had been $311 million and the next year's was estimated to be $340 million. This meant a total increase of $29 million, of which 1 percent or $290,000 was available for additional revenue. Thus the clubs' requests were for about one-third of the additional tax-based revenue for the fiscal year.[37]

Listening to these demands, in combination with those of the departments, Republican Mayor George Sanderson made a surprising proposal. He said he was in favor of breaking the Dollar Limit pledge "if the needs of the city required it." His Republican colleague and chairman of the finance committee, Levi Ellert, disagreed. Although Ellert recognized the necessity of the desired appropriations, he was "not in favor of breaking his pledge." In the end it was Ellert who carried the day, at least in part because it was he who wrote the finance committee's report. The report included the requests of the improvements groups in the budget, but it also lionized the Dollar Limit and denounced the practices of the groups. Noting that "the importunities of associated bodies of citizens requesting special or increased appropriations for various purposes" were "duly considered," Ellert explained that, nonetheless, "the united efforts of those citizens were misdirected in this, that the Board having limited powers could not entertain any proposition looking to an expenditure in excess of what had been contemplated and by which the members were bound."[38]

According to Ellert, the political parties had forseen just such pressure when they imposed the limits as a means of "protecting the taxpayers against such importunities," and for this reason, the question of discretion in expenditure was vested not in the board but "in the political conventions that adopted the platforms with the limits." Therefore, he argued, if citizens desired increased expenditure and believed that it was in the public interest, it was their duty to "have the platforms so molded as to provide for what is desired." In the meantime, he wrote, the policy of limits was, on the basis of experience, "wise and judicious" and "the only safety against oppressive and unwise taxation." The limits controlled the board, prevented "specious or meritorious demands for a violation of this obligation from having any force or effect," and relegated demands for improvement "to the political conventions of the people, who determine in their platforms all such issues."[39]

In essence, Ellert was telling the improvement groups to work "within the system," because he recognized that they were a threat to the finely calibrated fiscal procedure that the parties had created. He was correct, of course, that the platforms bound the supervisors to a limited increase in expenditure, and as we have seen, the platforms after 1886 became increasingly specific about exactly what was to be done with that extra expenditure. Because this was the case, any extraordinary or unanticipated demands—from executive officers, improvement groups, or others—were intolerable, in that they paved the way toward pledgebreaking. By means of the pledges—and probably, in these years, the power of nomination—the parties could control the supervisors and the executive officers. But neither parties nor policymakers could control the improvement groups, whose continued existence and fiscal persistence threatened to overload a system that had not responded to outside groups historically and could not keep on doing so now because of the fiscal scarcity imposed by the limits.

Ellert's advice to the groups to go into the conventions and work for change was farcical, however. San Franciscans were convinced that the party conventions were corrupt and boss-dominated, and they were right. Although there were elections of delegates to the conventions, these were easily manipulated, as "bosses" Buckley and Kelly admitted in their memoirs thirty years later. Even if they were not corrupt, the conventions were dominated by successful municipal politicians themselves. Both by belief and by practical political experience, these men were unwilling to do anything about the limits. Thus it is very unlikely that the improvement groups would have accomplished anything by going to the conventions, other than diluting their threat to partisan fiscal political business as usual.

Had they done so, however, it is worth considering what manner of men they might have met. Who were these municipal policymakers who continually put political pledges before social needs? First, the officials elected to municipal offices in these years were activists in the regular political parties. In the elections from 1882 through 1890, for the first and only time in the city's history, every single elected official was affiliated with either the Democratic or the Republican party; there were no successful independent candidacies. Moreover, Democratic officials predominated in these years, with 58 percent of officials elected being Democrats and 42 percent Republicans.[40]

Second, these officials were foreign-born to a greater extent that ever before or after in the city's history. As we saw in chapter 4, the only statistically significant differences between officials elected in this era and the other eras defined thus far was the share of the foreign-born in this era. Of the 125 officials for whom the information on nativity was available, 44 percent (55) were foreign-born and 56 percent (70) were native-born. Because the share of foreign-born in the city's population was exactly 44 percent in 1880, this was not an overrepresentation of the foreign-born but the one and only time in the city's history that the foreign-born received their share of elected officials. They received this share primarily from the Democratic party, because 66 percent of foreign-born officials elected in these years were Democrats, compared with only 34 percent who were Republicans. The relationship between nativity and party was statistically significant in these years for the last time in the city's history.[41]

Finally, the officials were from a relatively wide range of occupational backgrounds. A total of 31 percent of the officials elected in these years were from high white-collar occupations, 35 percent were from low white-collar backgrounds, 22.7 percent were incumbents or other government officials at the time of their elections, and 7 percent were skilled workers. Following the trend of increasing occupational similarity between the parties established in the last chapter, there was no statistically significant relationship between party and occupation; occupations were spread through the parties in approximately the same proportions as they were through the population of officeholders. As was the case in earlier years, there was a statistically significant relationship between occupation and office held. Executive officers were more likely to come from high white-collar occupations, while supervisors were more likely to come from low white-collar occupations, and there was more incumbency among the executive officers than among the supervisors.[42]

This information indicates that the restrictions on the growth of the public sector in these years were imposed by foreign-born, Democratic, and low white-collar officials—precisely the ones that the political cultural theory predicts would espouse an expanding public sector. Indeed, because the charter located ultimate budgetary power in the board of supervisors, it was these predominantly low white-collar individuals who, year in and year out, kept the lid on demands, whether they came from high white-collar executive officers for increased departmental appropriations or from various interest groups for specific improvements.

Of course, these men were not totally unsympathetic to the call for improvements. As we have seen, when the newspapers and politicians spoke of "permanent improvements" in these years they meant, among other things, expenditures on streets and sewers, schools, and police and fire services. As we saw in table 34, from fiscal 1883/84 through fiscal 1886/87, streets and schools were, as the finance committee of 1885 put it, the "sacrificial offering to the policy of the 'Dollar Limit.'" In these years real per capita school and police and fire expenditures barely held their own, while street expenditures dropped 25 percent. The supervisors continued to postpone street work because it was only maintenance, and they barely raised school expenditure because it was the political problem of the school directors, not the board of supervisors.[43]

Between fiscal 1886/87 and 1892/93, however, the per capita value of almost every indicator in table 34 increased, and a good deal of the increase went for improvements. While the tax rate remained stable, the real per capita assessed valuation increased 42 percent and per capita tax revenue increased 41 percent. The supply of revenue increased, as we have seen, because the parties gradually increased their pledges for total assessed valuation. Much of the new revenue went to meet the demands for improvements. The real per capita value of spending on schools increased almost 20 percent, on streets 100 percent, and on police and fire 15 percent, while the amount for official salaries increased only 10 percent. Municipal policymakers were responding to requests for increasing expenditure to the limits of their political pledges. But the response was too little too late to prevent the formation of a pro-improvement coalition that would attack the entire pre-reform political system.

ATTACKS ON THE "SILURIANS," 1892–1896

Throughout the late 1880s and early 1890s, the newspapers and other political actors began increasingly to use the term "Silurian" to refer to those they felt were the opponents of municipal improvement. During the campaign of 1888, for example, the *Examiner* called for a municipal policy that "will not be agreeable to the silurians" but that would instead be "fully abreast of the public opinion which demands that San Francisco shall be made a modern city." In 1890, the chairman of the Democratic municipal convention announced that "the watchword of today is progress. The people are tired of the Silurian policy." In 1891, the *Examiner* declared that "the best ally of the silurians in the work of keeping the city stagnant and dilapidated" was "Boss" Buckley, because the "sticky fingers" of his retainers in city government discouraged the people from voting the liberal taxes necessary for municipal improvement.[44]

The reference to the Silurians was geological. The Silurian period of geological history is that from 405 to 435 million years ago, the fourth oldest period of the Paleozoic era. It is believed that it was during this era that the earliest land plants and animals emerged, and Silurian plants and fishes are the oldest preserved. The Silurian system was named in 1839 by the Scotsman Sir Roderick I. Murchison, so the term was available as a way of describing one's political enemies as "prehistoric" for the rest of the nineteenth century. However, it was not until 1892 that the use of the term in the San Francisco context was fully explained. During the 1892 debate over the tax rate, the *Examiner* identified the enemies of progress in the city at some length, attributing the lack of municipal improvements to "a small class of men whom we call silurians. They are of the same breed as the persons who in the east are known as 'mossbacks' and 'clams.'" Continuing, the editorial declared:

Our silurians are for the most part old and rich. They possess much real estate, which they hold idle until the growth of the community shall have made it very valuable.... They are the foe to improvement which would cost them anything and regard the tax-gatherer as a personal enemy and a highway robber. These silurians have opposed the park, opposed decent pavements, opposed new sewers, opposed new schoolhouses, opposed everything, in short, that the city has needed and has had to be taxed to pay for.[45]

The notion that a cabal of rich old men with vast real estate holdings controlled the city's fiscal politics was, as we have seen, ridiculous. The truth was that the Silurians were everywhere and everyone, including the newspapers, political leaders, and others who, in demanding "liberality without prodigality," effectively paralyzed municipal government and guaranteed that only slow and incremental progress would be made on municipal improvements.

Between 1892 and 1899, San Franciscans worked for improvements and managed to break this paralysis, but they did so in stages. Between 1892 and 1896, the momentum of fiscal political action shifted almost entirely outside of municipal government. While the party platforms continued to present the limits and the mayor and supervisors enforced them, the campaign for improvements gained momentum. Improvement groups spread, reorganized, and continued to appear in force at finance committee hearings. A grand jury investigating municipal government in 1894 denounced the limits, and the same year a newly organized businessman's group called the Merchants' Association began to agitate for "efficiency and improvement" in municipal government. In 1895 the state legislature intervened in the city's fiscal process by bringing the assessed valuation under the supervision of the state and promptly raising it to compensate for the politically maintained limits of the past. It was the achievement of Democratic reformer James D. Phelan to weld together the apparently disparate elements of the pro-improvement

forces and to channel their energy into his own campaign for the mayoralty in 1896. His victory brought the pro-improvement forces inside
city government for the first time, giving them strategic heights in the
war against the Silurians.[46]

Attacks on the Silurians were also facilitated by two other changes
in the city's political and economic structure over which it had no
control. The first of these was the Reform Ballot Act, the consequences
of which we have already considered in detail. As a result of the act,
which took effect in 1892, the number of municipal slates in the field
increased; split-ticket voting was facilitated; the share of the vote going
to the regular parties decreased; and the political fate of local politicians
was, to a great degree, disconnected from the fate of the top of the
ticket. Although 96 percent of the officials elected in the municipal
elections from 1892 through 1899 were from the regular parties, the
margins by which they were elected were seldom as great as in the
1880s. This was particularly true for the supervisors; in the elections
of 1892, 1894, and 1896, the "winning" party on the board received
only 37, 40, and 35 percent of the vote, respectively.

As great a threat to political legitimacy as these minority boards might
have been, they were an even greater threat to fiscal stability. As a result
of this heightened political competition, incumbency on the board of
supervisors almost disappeared during the 1890s, and with it the fiscal
benefits of veteran supervisors facing executive officers continuously
hungry for larger budgets. As we have seen, throughout the city's history the level of incumbency was higher among executive officers than
among the supervisors. Among all officials elected between 1860 and
1905, 43 percent of executive officers were incumbents or other government officials at the time of their election, while only 23 percent of
the supervisors held such positions. Among the officers elected between
1892 and 1899, the shares were 45 percent for executive officers and
only 6 percent for supervisors—by far the lowest level of incumbency
among supervisors in the city's history. With each board having to learn
the fiscal ropes from scratch every two years, its dependence on the
executive officers was heightened, as was the probability that more
money would go for salaries and less for improvements.[47]

The drama of the crisis of the old political system was matched by
the second change, the collapse of the city's economy. As we saw in
chapter 3, the city's economic history in the nineteenth century was
punctuated by two depressions, one extending from 1875 through

1880, the other from about 1892 through 1897. By the early 1880s, the city had pulled out of the first depression and was on its way to a decade of substantial economic growth, according to the indicators of economic development that we have been using. According to the figures of the city assessor, the number of manufacturing works in the city increased 16 percent between 1880 and 1890, while the number of men employed in those works increased 14 percent and the real value of manufactured goods increased 122 percent. Meanwhile, the real value of imports and exports at the port increased 33 percent and the number of real estate sales increased 186 percent.

Primarily as a result of national economic conditions over which the city had little or no control, beginning in 1891 these same indicators began a sharp downward plunge that led them to pre-1880 levels by the mid-1890s. Measuring from pre-depression peak to mid-depression trough, business at the port dropped 38 percent in real terms from 1891 through 1895, and real estate sales dropped 68 percent from 1891 through 1897. But the sector of the local economy that was hardest hit was manufacturing, in which the number of plants declined 13 percent between 1891 and 1895, the number of men employed dropped 35 percent between 1891 and 1897, and the real value of output dropped 50 percent from 1890 to 1897.

Both contemporaries and later historians agree that the political regularity of the 1880s was reinforced by the prosperity of that decade. The threat of insurgency from "below," such as that during the late 1870s, was minimized by the expanding economy. But so, too, was the threat from "above": while business was good and tax rates and assessment kept within the limits, local business leaders cared little about local politics. There was, for example, no ongoing organization of businessmen interested in municipal affairs during the 1880s.[48]

In the 1890s, of course, this economic stability was lost. As the economy collapsed, city government faced pressure on both the supply and the demand sides of fiscal policy. On the supply side, the collapse of the real estate market and the closing of manufacturing works threatened the assessed valuation, while the loss of jobs undermined the ability of small property holders to pay their taxes at all. On the demand side, difficult economic conditions brought increasing pleas for municipally financed relief measures—all of which were rejected—and for increased governmental efficiency and thus lower cost. Given this economic context, it was not surprising that the reformers built their campaign on promises both of increased efficiency in local government, and thus lower cost, and on increased municipal improvement activity, and thus the creation of jobs and restoration of prosperity.

Meanwhile, as the political and economic systems collapsed around the parties, they continued to split fiscal hairs in their platforms for the elections of 1892 and 1894, emphasizing minor differences in rates of taxation and valuation and proposing improvements without providing the means to pay for them. The possibilities of the Reform Ballot Act were realized in wild scrambles for municipal offices and in differences between the tops and bottoms of the tickets. In 1892, for example, there were seven candidates for mayor and five slates for supervisor. The Democrats took the city for Cleveland and got the majority on the board of supervisors, while the mayoralty went to former chairman of the finance committee and renegade Republican Levi Ellert, who ran on a nonpartisan ticket. Running on the Republican ticket in 1894, Ellert was defeated for reelection by Adolf Sutro, a local millionaire who ran on the Populist ticket. In this election the practice of ticket splitting was readily apparent, because Sutro won along with the Democratic gubernatorial candidate and a Republican majority on the board of supervisors.[49]

Neither Ellert nor Sutro proposed significant fiscal innovation, so neither played a very active role in the budgetary process. Although Ellert proclaimed that he was "not a silurian," he also admitted that he had no overall plan for San Francisco because "the city is not ready for anything of the kind." He favored improved streets and sewers and opposed "niggardliness" for parks, the fire department, and the school department, but he also supported the Dollar Limit and pay-as-you-go financing for public improvements. Sutro's fiscal ideas harked back even further. In a pre-election interview, he declared that the "best government we have ever had before or since" was that immediately after the Vigilance Committee of 1856, which, he recalled, had eliminated "ballot box stuffers" by "hanging a few" and driving others out of the country. His proposal for dealing with contemporary official corruption was the same: "a vigilance committee and a number of judicious hangings."[50]

The fiscal political agency of the mayors was hardly needed, however, because of the amount of fiscal action elsewhere. At the first meeting of the finance committee in the Ellert administration, the improvement groups served notice that they were not going to disappear. Representatives of three separate improvement groups and the newly formed, citywide Federation of Improvement Clubs attended the meeting, demanding the extension of more fire protection into the suburban districts and indicating that the appearances of the clubs were now going to be annual.[51]

The next year, a grand jury empaneled to analyze the activities of municipal government blasted the limits on taxation and assessment and blamed them for the failure of the city to make improvements. It must have been with a sigh of relief that city officials received the report in September 1894, because it revealed that the grand jury had found no significant evidence of malfeasance. Instead, the report focused on the lack of municipal progress, declaring that the board of supervisors had kept to its limits, but "only at the sacrifice of needed work." "There is no systematic sewerage system, a great many parks are unimproved and have been for years, principal streets are unattractive and in a wretched condition." The problem was the system of limits on taxation and assessed valuation:

We do not believe in the cobwebbed and dust-stained expression of the Dollar Limit, which limit should not be upon any stated sum, but upon the assessed valuation of the taxable property of the city. We believe that expenditure of money to meet the wants of this government should be provided, whether below or above the Dollar Limit, and we believe that such tax will be cheerfully met by the people and appreciated in the beneficial results obtained.

The report concluded that prompt action was necessary to put the city "in a condition that will compare favorably with other cities in this country" and that, if necessary, bonded indebtedness should be incurred to support the improvements.[52]

In October 1894 another significant fiscal political actor appeared at the first public meeting of the Merchants' Association. The group had been organized the previous April by 47 businesses in the city, including that of James D. Phelan, and by the time of its first regular public meeting its membership had increased to 350 firms; two years later it would include 657. Its purpose was explained at the first meeting as the attempt to "beautify and healthify [*sic*] San Francisco, make it attractive to strangers and pleasant to its residents, and thereby increase its business and add to the value of property."[53]

Like the improvement associations, the Merchants' Association started off with a relatively harmless, apolitical, and cost-free, do-it-yourself project. In October 1894 the association bid on and received the city's contract for street sweeping for one year, to demonstrate more efficient and more effective techniques for performing the work. According to the association and its supporters, the street-sweeping project was a total success. With this success under its belt—and closely following the paths of the improvement associations—the association plunged deeper into fiscal politics. By the summer of 1895, it was considering whether to recommend that the city bond itself to pay for improvements. In June 1896 members of the association appeared at the finance committee meeting to present an "economy plan" to the board of supervisors.[54]

Although the report was based on an allegedly thorough analysis of the city's operations on a department-by-department basis, nothing in its recommendations was startling. It affirmed the Dollar Limit and called for a reduction in the number of clerks in city government, along with a more cost-efficient method for the purchase of municipal supplies. Noting that "no matter what the political complexion of those in control there is generally [fiscal] dissatisfaction," the report did propose that the city stop trying to fund both current expenses and improvements out of the same tax levy. It recommended that municipal expenses be divided into two categories, current outlay and extraordinary outlay, with the former paid from current income and the latter (including expenses for sewers, streets, park improvement, etc.) paid for by means of bonds. The report concluded, however, that the issuance of bonds would be impossible until the city received a new charter.[55]

The demands for improvements put forward by the grand jury and the merchants were not totally lost on fiscal policymakers, and signs of declension from the faith in the limits began to appear even among the supervisors after 1892. After the finance committee report of 1892, there was never again a detailed exposition of the party pledges or an eloquent defense of the limits. The pledges remained in the platforms, but they were no longer as obvious or compelling a guide to fiscal practice. A more important sign was the complaint of the finance committees after 1892 that bureau officers were ignoring their budgets and overspending their appropriations. The committees of 1893, 1894, and 1895 each complained of this, citing in particular the election commissioners, county clerk, and superintendent of streets for hiring deputies, clerks, and so on and demanding payment for them beyond the budget authorized by the supervisors. In fiscal year 1892/93, for example, these overruns amounted to $300,000. When, in 1893, the board refused to pay these salaries, a chief clerk in the office of the registrar of voters took the city to court for his salary. The state supreme court ultimately ruled that salaries authorized by the state legislature, whether approved by the supervisors or not, had to be paid. What this meant was that if the legislature had created a position and the bureau head had filled it, the salary had to be paid. Cooperation by the bureau heads with economy moves by the supervisors was, thereafter, strictly voluntary. It was probably true that this had always been the case. That it had never been tested in court before was powerful testimony to the ability of party discipline to impose fiscal stability.[56]

An even more flagrant attack on the limits occurred in 1895, when the supervisors actually broke the Dollar Limit. That year, the finance committee presented recommendations requiring a rate of $1.47 on an assessment of $320 million, and the full board raised even that rate to $1.56, an increase of $0.56 over the rate for the previous year. Far from being "cheerfully appreciated," as the grand jury had predicted, the proposal for increased expenditure, much of which was to go for improvements, was denounced in the newspapers, vetoed by the mayor, and even criticized by the finance committee itself.[57]

As we have already seen, it was not unusual for the tax rate to be raised marginally in nonelection years. Some increase, then, was not surprising, but the size of this increase was startling. Taking the cry for improvement at its word, the board doubled the amount in the rate for the Street Fund, intending $100,000 of the increased funds raised to go for the improvement of public squares; tripled the amount in the rate for the new city hall building, in hopes of completing that monument to the pay-as-you-go philosophy within the fiscal year; added $0.09 to the rate for new public buildings, including a home for dipsomaniacs and a new criminal justice building; and added to the General Fund the money for seventy-five new police officers.[58]

In submitting the estimate, the members of the finance committee warned that the rate was high, and when the full board increased the rate, two of the members of the finance committee protested, arguing that "it is unfortunate that your honorable board deems it imperative to carry out a policy that will result in the imposition of a very high tax rate." Conceding that "many if not all of the projected improvements should be made," they asked that some be postponed or done piecemeal so that the tax rate would not oppress the taxpayers at a time when "they are unable to meet such a burden as is contemplated." However, the authors of this report were the only two dissenters when the rate came up for passage.[59]

The negative reaction to the rate was almost instantaneous. The *Examiner* blasted it, noting that it was 50 percent greater than the rate the board had pledged to keep. The newspaper declared that the rate should arouse "astonishment and indignation" and would have the most unfortunate effects just now, when "business is just reviving from the depression of two years." Mayor Sutro, too, denounced the levy as an outrage and moved immediately to veto it. It was only then that the city learned that the mayor had lost his veto power because of legislative action earlier that year. To force the issue into the courts, Sutro vetoed the ordinance anyway at the end of September, but the opinion of the state supreme court two months later let the rate stand and confirmed the permanent loss of the veto power.[60]

It turned out that the mayor's veto over the tax rate had been lost in 1895, at the same time that the state board of equalization's power to adjust the city's assessed valuation was confirmed. Prior to 1895, the city conducted its assessment and taxation procedures in accordance with the Consolidation Act, as amended by the state legislature in 1873/74 (see chap. 2). Because of this preexisting act, the city was exempt from the portions of the state constitution of 1879 implementing a new, statewide revenue system. In particular—and fortunately, from the standpoint of the city's taxpayers—the city was exempt from the oversight of its local assessment by the state board of equalization. Although the state board could and did intervene to adjust the city's valuation for purposes of state taxation, it could not change the valuation for local purposes. It was in part for this reason that the local parties could pledge levels of assessment; in all other counties of the state, pledges for assessment could be overturned by the state board.[61]

When the state legislature again revised the revenue laws in 1895, it acted to bring the city out of this anomalous position by repealing the section of the Consolidation Act regarding the assessment and taxation procedures in the city and county. Now San Francisco was required to set its tax rate by September 1, instead of June 30, and its valuation of property was for both local and state purposes, and thus subject to the scrutiny of the state board of equalization. It was no secret in Sacramento that the city's political parties had attempted to control the increase in property valuation, so the state board moved immediately to make up for its lost opportunities by raising the city's overall valuation by 15 percent in 1895 and 20 percent in 1896. Because the repealed section of the Consolidation Act covered all revenue procedures, it also contained provisions for the mayoral veto of the tax rate, a power unique to San Francisco because of its dual status as both a city and a county. When the state supreme court ruled in November 1895 that the new revenue acts took precedence over the Consolidation Act, the veto was lost. It was not restored until the legislative session of 1897.[62]

Although the loss of the mayoral veto received an enormous amount of publicity at the time, it was a critical but by no means fatal blow to the fiscal system, because during times of political regularity the parties were able to impose the Dollar Limit without the need for the mayoral veto. Much more significant in the long run was the loss of complete local control over property assessment. Its effect was twofold. It was, first of all, the death knell of assessment limits imposed by the party conventions. Although the limits continued to be proclaimed by the parties, they were meaningless because city officials could not risk the sudden increases imposed by the state board. When the city was called to Sacramento to defend itself from a proposed adjustment by the state board, it was required to prove that its assessed valuation had been following recent trends in the private real-estate market. The choice for local politicians, then, was clear: allow for more or less natural and usually incremental fluctuations in assessed valuation, or be subjected to unpredicted and significant increases imposed by the state board. The second effect followed from this. The state legislature had done what no local politician had dared to do. It had eliminated limits on assessment and thereby freed the city's ability to produce revenue. Because of the state's action, the city's coffers were now in a position to bulge, and the opportunity for municipal improvement was finally at hand.[63]

During the debate on the tax rate of 1895, the *Examiner* had attacked the supervisors by comparing them unfavorably with Buckley. Having previously denounced Buckley as an ally of the Silurians and an intolerable load on the Democratic party, the paper now waxed eloquent about his virtues. According to one of its editorials, the current board had "done what Buckley in the height of his power and insolence never dared to do—perhaps, to do him justice, never wanted to do." For all of his crimes, the paper argued, Buckley was a man of his word, and when he promised that his supervisors would keep the taxes within a certain limit, they did so: "The present gang [of supervisors] bids fair to accomplish the seemingly impossible feat of making people regret the fallen boss."[64]

What the *Examiner* and others really yearned for was not the "boss" himself but the fiscal and electoral stability that had been characteristic of the city before 1892. Fiscal and electoral insurgency was making the city's political system resemble a bicycle tire with a bulge in it. As political slates and fiscal demands multiplied, the bulge grew larger and the tire seemed smaller. By failing to assimilate the pro-improvement forces, the regular partisan system was in deep crisis, and its leaders lacked a contemporary solution. However, the man partly responsible for creating the crisis had been abroad in the city for several years proposing his solution. His name was James D. Phelan.

By 1896, James Duval Phelan had already been a significant figure in local politics for many years, although he was only thirty-five years old (see chap. 4). He was, as the *Examiner* noted, "young, gifted, and rich," and he put all of his gifts and a good deal of his money into municipal affairs beginning about 1885. Phelan was the son of an Irish-born Forty-Niner and mainstay of the Democratic party who had made a fortune as a merchant and then multiplied it by moving into banking and real estate. With little need to worry about a livelihood, the younger Phelan had education and experience unique among the Irish-American politicians of the city in this period. He was graduated from the Jesuit college in San Francisco in 1882 and then trained at the Hastings College of the Law there. When his education was complete, he embarked on a one-year grand tour of Europe, much of which he devoted to the examination of municipal conditions in the great cities there, reporting his observations in articles sent back and printed in the *Examiner*. Upon his return he took over the management of his father's affairs, becoming president of his father's Mutual Savings bank when the elder Phelan died. Between about 1885 and his nomination in 1896, he was active in the reform wing of the Democratic party, serving as chairman of the Young Men's Democratic League and as a member of the Citizens' Defense Association, a nonpartisan group devoted to the prevention of electoral corruption and to the campaign for the Reform Ballot Act. Service in these organizations made Phelan a natural for membership in the so-called reorganized Democracy that helped to overthrow Buckley and purge his supporters from the party.[65]

Phelan's more broadly civic activities included founding membership in the Merchants' Association and first presidency of the Federation of Improvement Clubs. In 1896 he was also president of the city's Bohemian Club and of the Art Association, and he had been executive officer of the California World's Fair Commission, which had organized the California Mid-Winter Fair in 1894.[66]

With these connections, it is hardly an exaggeration to say that Phelan was almost a one-man political movement. In particular, his leadership in both the Merchants' Association and the improvement clubs allowed him to tap the skills of the business elite and the membership of the neighborhood organizations. He offered the same qualities to both sorts of supporters—responsible leadership provided by himself as mayor, and more benefits from a rationalized and thus more efficient and effective municipal government brought about by a new charter.

The opening gun of Phelan's campaign to mobilize the pro-improvement forces behind his mayoral campaign was fired in September 1896 in a speech entitled "The New San Francisco," which he delivered at the opening night of the Mechanics Institute Fair. Reports claimed that the audience was electrified by the thirty-five-year-old's declaration that it was time for the city to accept its destiny as the metropolis of the West, and that, to do so, it would have to revamp its government and reassess its fiscal priorities. Because Phelan had been appointed head of the Citizens' Charter Association by the Merchants' Association a month earlier, it was not surprising that he called for a new charter. Moreover, because he had been a member of the faction of the Democratic party that had helped topple Buckley and had purged his supporters from the party twice since the Boss's fall, it was not surprising that the speech contained the usual blasts against municipal corruption. What was surprising and historically significant was Phelan's wholehearted embrace of municipal improvement and his attempt to explain how the entire city would benefit from fiscal expansion.[67]

In fact, the speech contained almost all the themes Phelan would articulate and elaborate in the six campaigns that lay ahead of him— three for the mayoralty, two for a new charter, and one for bonds for municipal improvements. Thus it is worth examining in some detail. In essence, Phelan argued that although nature had richly endowed San Francisco with a beautiful natural location and a great harbor, a spirit of provincialism and "incivism" had developed in the city which prevented it from reaching its manifest destiny. There were signs, however, that this era was over and that San Franciscans were awakening to the "duties of the hour." The challenge was to restore public confidence, seize the moment, and move ahead.[68]

According to Phelan, because of the discovery of gold in California, the early settlers in San Francisco came only for fortune and there was no "community of interests" or "civic pride in the founding of a commonwealth." Later, when there was the opportunity for such a commonwealth, the city was "pillaged by her custodians," the elected leaders of the city. As a result, for many years the city had lacked "confidence and courage" and had "groveled in a slough of self-depreciation." A change was evident now, however, in the work of organizations like the Merchants' Association and the improvement clubs, which, "taking a broader view, convinced themselves that, provided man but supplements what nature had done, San Francisco may yet become the pride of the American continent."[69]

Among the tasks at hand, then, was restoration of public confidence in the city's government by recognizing that a city's prosperity reduces itself to a "question of science—sanitary, engineering, education, and governmental." According to Phelan, the citizens of San Francisco were well aware of the "inadequacy of their present government; of its corruption and of its disgrace." Thus a charter was needed to ensure "local autonomy, executive independence, and systematic organization under a wise civil service."[70]

Having reformed government, it would then be necessary to reject the counsel of conservatism and kindle the spirit of enterprise in the city. The enemy was, again, the Silurian, the "class of people who oppose conservatism to progress," who "would not brush cobwebs off their house lest the roof should fall." A great city spends "vast sums for drainage, for streets, for the protection of life and property, for schools, for museums, for galleries, for parks," Phelan said, "and becomes a well equipped exposition, or market, or emporium." Therefore, it was necessary to stir the public spirit of the people, to "teach them that these objects are desirable, not only for their health, comfort, and lucrative employment" but for "the delight and pleasure of strangers who shall be attracted to their city, and thus add to their municipal and individual prosperity." He declared that "civic capacity will follow close upon the footsteps of civic pride."[71]

PORTENTS: THE MUNICIPAL ELECTION OF 1896

It was no surprise that Phelan was nominated for mayor by the Democrats a few weeks later, and the new model Democracy under Phelan's control revealed itself in its platform as well as in his nomination. The platform, one of the longest in the city's history, contained twenty-two planks and something for everyone. For the improvement block there were exemption from the Dollar Limit of work on squares and parks; a call for a plan of sewer improvement; better paving and cleaning of streets, including the repaving of the city's main street, Market; and a call for municipal ownership of utilities. For labor there were a two-dollar minimum wage for city street work, the first minimum wage of any kind proposed for city work; a call for white labor and California materials on city work; and a call for a ten-hour maximum day for those "employed in stores or in close confinement." For ethnics there were the denunciation of the injection of religious bigotry and intolerance into politics and a condemnation as "un-American" of the American Protective Association. There was even a provision for "equal traffic rights for wheelmen" (bicyclists). Although appeals for improvement were typical in these years and the Democratic party historically had attempted to appeal to ethnics in its platform and nominations, this was the first time that the platform of any regular party had contained "class" appeals such as those involving minimum wage or maximum hours.[72]

Benefits to labor were also a part of Phelan's own campaign. However, labor was but one of the groups that he promised would benefit from a "progressive administration tempered with enlightened economy." Repeating this theme over and over in his campaign stops, Phelan declared that election of the Democratic ticket would mean that the citizens were ready to "turn your back on Silurianism and Silurian methods," but he did not advocate an overly active public sector. His first task, he said, was to restore confidence in the public sector by means of a business administration in city hall that was at once "energetic and economical." If it were not wasted keeping "hangers on in idleness," there was, he claimed, "enough money each year to give the city good streets and permanent improvements" and to permit city policies to be "liberal to the suburban districts." Tax increases in the past had been the result of "extravagance and waste" on the expenditure side and an unwillingness to force corporations—especially public service corporations—to pay their fair share of taxation and a proper share of their franchise-generated profits into the city treasury. By "checking all waste" and seeing to it that "the heritage of the people were not given away to corporations," Phelan planned to finance improvements and keep taxes low. The return of confidence in the public sector would encourage private-sector enterprise, and money spent on municipal improvements would go to the workingmen. In combination, then, the public and private sectors would restore prosperity to the city. "We need a revival of good times... and I think a clean and careful administration of the city's affairs is best calculated to restore it," Phelan declared. Once confidence was restored, "improvements, manufacturing, and public works will be inaugurated and lucrative employment given to our people, laborer, mechanic, and merchant alike."[73]

In his call for low taxes and minimum waste, Phelan stood squarely within the fiscal consensus of his political predecessors. More than a decade before, Mayor Washington Bartlett had declared that lower municipal expenditure and taxation had pulled the city out of the depression of 1877. However, in suggesting affirmative action by the public sector—improvements and public works providing "lucrative employment to our people"—Phelan was stretching the consensus to its limits. The consensus was not only a no-growth consensus, it was a no-benefit consensus that argued that there were no benefits to be received from action by the public sector—only costs to be paid. Improvements had been grudgingly approved before because they were demanded by a specific neighborhood or needed for "a great and growing city." They had never been proposed to provide direct economic benefits to the citizenry.[74]

In the meantime, however, Phelan understood that all this was academic under the old charter. Therefore, at least until mid-October of 1896, he threw his lot in with a campaign for a new charter that would also appear on the ballot on election day. This most recent campaign for a new charter had begun in the fall of 1894, when the freeholders to form a new charter had been elected. All of the freeholders elected were high-status local businessmen—86 percent of them were listed in the city's social register—and at least four of the fifteen would hold office in the Merchants' Association by 1897. With these kinds of interconnections, it is not surprising that the freeholders leaned heavily on the Merchants' Association for ideas on a new charter, and that an "interlocking directorate for reform" was organized among the freeholders, the Merchants' Association, and an ad hoc Civic Federation headed by one of the freeholders. Nor is it surprising that the charter document produced by the freeholders called for centralization of authority in the mayor, civil service, and "business principles."[75]

Although there was opposition to several of these provisions of the charter, its undoing was a much less significant and relatively obscure section relating to the school department and requiring that teachers in the city's public schools be public high school graduates. In late June 1896, the Reverend Peter Yorke, a Catholic priest who was editor of the newspaper of the Archdiocese of San Francisco, *The Monitor*, blasted the charter as "supremely vicious" because of the school section, which demonstrated that the "trail of the APA [American Protective Association] is visible across it." The school requirement meant, Yorke wrote, that "if a parent wishes to educate his child where he believes best, he is to be punished by having that child debarred from teaching in the public schools." While it was doubtful that the requirement had emerged from an APA plot, it was a remarkably damaging provision in a charter about to be presented to an electorate with a large and highly mobilized Irish-Catholic membership.[76]

In an apparent attempt to woo back this contingent of the electorate, the Merchants' Association appointed Phelan head of a Citizens' Charter Association in August 1896. From that position—and for some time after his nomination for mayor—Phelan campaigned actively for the charter, declaring that without it he would be merely a "good figure-head." This was true, of course, because without the power of the veto, the only power remaining to the mayor was that of moral suasion. Phelan also defended the school section valiantly, arguing both that it had been misinterpreted and that the section was unconstitutional and would not be enforced in any case. By mid-October, however, Phelan began to abandon the charter's sinking ship, declaring repeatedly that "the charter stands or falls by itself and the mayor stands or falls by himself." He wanted a new charter, but he wanted to be mayor more.[77]

When the election was over, Phelan had received 29,066 votes—more than any of the six other candidates for mayor but still only 46 percent of the total vote cast. The new charter went down to defeat, at least in part from lack of interest. Only 45 percent of those registered to vote in the election voted on the charter, compared with 85 percent who voted for mayor and 80 percent who voted for supervisors. Of those that did vote on the document, 47 percent favored it and 53 percent opposed it.[78]

In their post-election analyses, both Yorke and the *Examiner* attributed the defeat of the charter to the objectionable school clause. For this reason, however, neither felt that the cause of charter reform was dead; all that was necessary for success was that the reform movement broaden its social base. The *Examiner* declared that "the essential thing this [next] time is to conciliate all the genuine friends of honest government." This time there could be no clause in the charter "which any well-meaning class of citizens can honestly consider a grievance." Moreover, "all important elements of our population" had to be represented on the board of freeholders, the work of the board had to be done in public, and "all opinions" had to be heard. Yorke was even more specific in his demand that the reform forces realize that "this city is not made up entirely of merchants and does not exist for the well-to-do alone." On the contrary, he argued, "the laboring man, the tradesman, the artisan, have as much stake as the merchant prince," and therefore "any association which is working for the good of the city must open wide its ranks and gather in all its classes."[79]

This, of course, was precisely what Phelan and the Democrats had been trying to do in their platform and in his campaign. In fact, the fervor with which they had courted the workingman's vote was surprising, given Phelan's patrician background. There was no altruism in this plea for support, however, just good electoral political sense. Phelan and the Democrats appealed to workers because since 1888 the mayoral prospects of the party had been wounded by a self-proclaimed workingman's candidate whose campaigns belied the image of the all-powerful political machines of the 1880s, defied the odds for a significant insurgent candidacy during the era of straight-ticket party regularity, and demonstrated the existence of a significant undercurrent of dissatisfaction with politics as usual. For all these reasons, we turn to look at the candidacies of C. C. O'Donnell, M.D.

Denounced by his contemporary partisan opponents as a maniac and a throwback, and ignored by historians since, O'Donnell nonetheless ran for mayor in each election from 1888 through 1896, and through 1892 he averaged almost 30 percent of the vote cast. This was an extraordinary accomplishment for a candidate who ran without a ticket and without any coverage (other than denunciation) from the local newspapers. It was O'Donnell's candidacy that produced the minority mayoralties from 1888 through 1892 (see table 33), and it was his candidacies that kept the Democrats out of the mayoralty after 1888, because his support came increasingly from Democratic ticket-splitters. In the elections of 1888 and 1890, when straight-ticket voting was still the rule and O'Donnell was the only significant independent candidate, 26 percent of those who voted for the Democratic presidential ticket split for O'Donnell, while 28 percent of those voting Republican did so. In 1890, 43 percent of those voting for the Democratic gubernatorial nominee split for O'Donnell for mayor and only 23 percent of those voting Republican did so. After 1892, when there were more independent candidacies, O'Donnell still received significant shares of the total mayoral vote: 29 percent in 1892 and 21 percent in 1894.[80]

In 1877, O'Donnell was, along with Dennis Kearney and others, one of the founders and heroes of the Workingmen's Party of California (WPC). Born in Maryland in 1834, O'Donnell had moved to San Francisco in 1850 and practiced medicine, although his political enemies would later claim that he was trained as a veterinarian and made his living as an abortionist. For reasons that are not completely clear, he joined the new Workingmen's party as it emerged in the fall of 1877 and quickly became one of its leaders and most incendiary orators. As we saw earlier, the major slogan of the party was "the Chinese must go," but its analysis of the Chinese situation also included the monopolists of land and capital who brought the Chinese to the city and the state in the first place. O'Donnell in particular attacked the employers of the Chinese and threatened in one speech that if they did not do something about the Chinese, the seventeen thousand workmen in the WPC in San Francisco would make Jackson Street run "knee deep in blood." At other times he urged workers to take city hall and "hold it against hell," and he proposed mounting cannon on Telegraph Hill to blow the ships bringing Chinese to San Francisco "out of the water." For these and similar statements, he and the other leaders of the party— none of whom shrank from bloodthirsty rhetoric—were arrested for incitement in the fall of 1877, but then tried and acquitted in January 1878. As a hero and martyr of the party, O'Donnell was elected a WPC delegate to the state constitutional convention in June, where, according to the historian of the convention, he revealed himself to be "unpopular even with his own group ... and notably lacking in judgment in matters of diplomacy."[81]

By the time of the municipal elections of 1879, O'Donnell had apparently fallen out with the WPC, for he ran for coroner as an independent against the WPC ticket. In 1882 he again ran for the same office as an independent and lost, but in 1884 he was back as a Democrat and won with a higher vote total than that received by the winning Democratic mayoral candidate. With this win under his belt, he was off on an apparently quixotic series of campaigns for higher office, including one for governor in 1886 and five for mayor from 1888 through 1896.[82]

Throughout the late 1880s and early 1890s, O'Donnell's symbolic appeal harked back to the glory days of the WPC. As self-proclaimed leader of the San Francisco Anti-Coolie League, O'Donnell kept himself before the public eye in the "off season" by purchasing advertisements in the newspapers announcing his incendiary speeches on the Chinese question. In a rare bit of publicity during the campaign of 1894, he continued his critique of the class situation in the city, declaring that the municipal fiscal problem stemmed from the failure of the rich to pay their taxes. He claimed that more than $1 million of the property of the rich escaped taxation and that, if elected mayor, he would force the "millionaires and corporations" to pay their taxes, thus eliminating the need for the city's fiscal "pinching."[83]

Historians analyzing the social basis of the WPC have argued that what success the party had in 1879 came from the defection of local workingmen from the Democratic party. No one has analyzed the social basis of the O'Donnell candidacies, and because of redistricting in the midst of his campaigns, it is unlikely anyone will be tempted to do so. It can be said, however, that O'Donnell's yoking together of attacks on the Chinese and on the rich represented working-class political consciousness circa 1879. It is likely that his candidacies were the voice of unresolved class issues stemming from that period but lacking more current political expression.[84]

Whatever psychic satisfactions O'Donnell may have offered his supporters, he had none of the material incentives (improvements, jobs, etc.) offered by Phelan, and in their first test of electoral strength, in 1896, the new working-class politics crushed the old. In the worst showing of his political career, O'Donnell received only 1,737 votes against Phelan, just 2.6 percent of the total. This meant not only that he was defeated but also that he was ineligible, according to the terms of the Reform Ballot Act, to have his name automatically listed on the ballot at the next election. He was never a serious candidate for mayor again.[85]

Phelan won in 1896 only because he had wooed the O'Donnell supporters back into the Democratic ranks. If O'Donnell had received even as large a share of the mayoral vote as he had in 1894—his worst showing to that point, at 20 percent of the total—Phelan would have been defeated by his leading Republican opponent. This lesson was not lost on Phelan. In his next three election campaigns, he would continue and even increase his appeal to the working class, adding its numbers to those of his more natural allies in the reform movement, the improvement clubs, and the Merchants' Association.[86]

7

Redefining the Boundaries: Political Institutions and Fiscal Ideologies, 1897–1906

In the years from 1897 through 1905, the proponents of municipal improvement routed the Silurians and transformed the municipal fiscal political consensus. Whereas the politicians of the 1880s and early 1890s came to power on the basis of pledges to minimize the growth of municipal government, those of the late 1890s and thereafter attacked the penuriousness of their predecessors and promised benefits to all from municipal improvements financed by an expanding public sector. The triumph of this new view was dramatically symbolized in a 1902 vote by the supervisors to suspend the once-sacred Dollar Limit for that year in order to raise more money for improvements.

The pioneer of this new fiscal political approach was, of course, James D. Phelan, who was mayor of the city from 1896 through 1901 and, just as importantly, political leader of the coalition for municipal improvement, which included the Merchants' Association, neighborhood improvement groups, and workingmen. While it lasted, this coalition was a political juggernaut that won the mayoralty for Phelan in 1896 and 1898, a reform charter for the city in 1898, victory for Phelan and his hand-picked slate of supervisors in the first election under the new charter in November 1899, and passage of bonds for municipal improvements a month later. Phelan maintained the alliance among these potentially strange political bedfellows by means of promises of benefits from the public sector which could come only after a new charter and a reform administration under that charter were in place. By thus postponing the day of political reckoning, he was able to focus the attention of these groups on the common political enemy rather than on differences among themselves. However, while he depended on the neighborhood and labor groups for electoral support, he relied more and more heavily on the Merchants' Association for leadership of the various reform campaigns and evaluation of proposals for municipal improvement. Therefore, by the time he took office in 1900 under the new charter, the association was the senior partner in the coalition and almost an informal branch of government.

The junior partners in the coalition quickly became aware of their status during Phelan's first—and last—term under the new charter. The neighborhood improvement groups were disappointed to learn that Phelan was more interested in fully staffing the new agencies created by the charter than in embarking on a wide range of neighborhood improvements, and they were surprised that he publicly rebuked them for expecting everything to be done at once. From their perspective, the first budget under the Phelan administration revealed that he, too, would spend more money on salaries and less on improvements, despite his promises to do the opposite. Phelan alienated his labor support even more dramatically during the summer of 1901 by assigning police officers to escort nonunion wagons during a strike of unionized teamsters. The result was a sympathetic strike of all waterfront workers in the city and the complete disaffection of labor from Phelan and the reform movement.

The strike was the catalyst for the organization of the Union Labor party and the election of its mayoral candidate, Eugene Schmitz, in 1901. However, the party's persistence and the reelection of Schmitz twice thereafter are best understood as a revolt of the junior partners of the improvement coalition. Schmitz promised both "equal representation" in city government to labor and "less on salaries, more on improvements" to the neighborhood groups. The first promise was rightly perceived as radical within the context of the city's politics, because it entailed the removal of the Merchants' Association from its privileged position in local policymaking and its replacement by representatives of labor and other groups. Within the new consensus on improvement, however, there was nothing radical about Schmitz's second pledge; in fact, the conservative fiscal image he created provided an important shading of his perceived radicalism on the labor issue. Neither Schmitz nor other members of the party promised fiscal political measures designed specifically to benefit the poor or the working class or to hamper the efforts of capital. Indeed, Schmitz located himself on the conservative side of the new consensus by vetoing every budget approved by the supervisors from 1902 through 1905, thereby setting the record for mayoral vetoes in the city's history to that date. Each veto message attacked salaries and applauded improvements.

Ironically, whatever their other political differences, Phelan and Schmitz faced the same challenge of answering both the general demand for more public benefit at less cost and the specific conflicting demands of bureau heads for more personnel, of businessmen for more efficiency, and of neighborhood groups for more improvements. The triumph of the new view of municipal government did not signal an end to the controversy over fiscal policy. On the contrary, by broadening the definition of acceptable fiscal policy and mobilizing more groups into political action, those favoring improvement had widened the bases of fiscal political conflict. In these years, the boundaries of acceptable fiscal behavior were redefined, but the promise that this redefinition would lead to a permanent peace on the fiscal battlefield was an illusion.

THE DESTRUCTION OF THE OLD FISCAL POLITICS, 1897–1899

After winning the mayoralty in November 1896, Phelan hit the ground running as both mayor and charter reform leader in January 1897. On January 4, he delivered a wide-ranging and detailed inaugural address to the board of supervisors. Three days later, he asked the Merchants' Association for a list of names from which he could select a "Charter Committee of 100" which, with him at its head, could renew the campaign for a new charter. There was a fundamental conflict of interest in Phelan's occupancy of these two positions, however, because to justify the need for a new charter he had to demonstrate as mayor that "good government" was impossible under the old charter. Therefore, while carefully guarding his position as mayor, Phelan set out to undermine the legitimacy of the old system in general and the board of supervisors in particular, by denouncing its extravagance, inefficiency, and corruption.[1]

The major themes of both campaigns were revealed in his inaugural address, which focused on the need for a new charter, economy, and improvements. Phelan declared at the very outset that "no municipal progress is possible on broad and enduring lines until the present laws are superseded by a charter embodying the correct principles of municipal government." In the meantime, then, little more than a holding action was possible, and the theme of that action was to be "economy without parsimony." Diagnosing past problems of municipal economy as having resulted from "waste and extravagance" in expenditure and the shifting of the tax burden away from public service companies, Phelan demanded that the supervisors cut expenditure and, in their function as a board of equalization, increase assessments on corporations. At the same time, he declared that the city should finance improvements. Specifically, he contended that "the suburbs of the city should have the fostering care of the municipal authorities," the public schools should receive "the generous support of the municipality," and streets and parks should be improved. He concluded, however, with a reiteration of the Democratic platform's fiscal pledges calling for a $1 tax rate on $310 million assessed valuation, exclusive of debt service (the city's total indebtedness when Phelan took office was $186,000) and park improvements. This meant that the city was to be operated on tax-raised revenue of $3,380,000, a decrease of $710,000 from the current fiscal year. He admitted that this "forced upon the board the necessity of retrenchment," but he claimed that he was sure this could be done without "impairing the efficiency of the public service."[2]

Phelan's demands for retrenchment fit perfectly into what was becoming a familiar reform pattern. He denounced extravagance everywhere, but when it came down to cases, his examples of this extravagance could hardly bear the load of his charges. Analysis of the specific expenditure cuts he called for and his charge of extravagance in the school department demonstrate this. In his inaugural, Phelan declared that expenditure in the county clerk's office needed to be cut by about $58,000, and that other official salaries were inflated by about 25 percent overall. At $24,000 a year, janitorial service for city hall was too high, as were expenditures of $29,730 on the city's contingency fund and at least $250,000 for supplies. Yet even if the supervisors had made all of these cuts, the total savings for the next fiscal year would have been $485,000—little more than half of the total necessary to meet the pledges, and about 7 percent of the total expenditure in that fiscal year. While these cuts were not insubstantial, they hardly justified Phelan's implication of large-scale waste in local government.[3]

Another example of this tactic was his charge of extravagance in the school fund. Without calling for a cut in the public school budget, Phelan pointed out in the inaugural that "in 1883–84 there were 31,578 pupils, average attendance, with 714 teachers with salaries of $657,824.

In 1895–96, with 32,436 average attendance, there were 928 teachers with salaries of $872,311, that is, an increase of 858 pupils had been attended by an increase of 214 teachers at an increased expense of $214,487 for teachers' salaries." Phelan quoted this verbatim from a grand jury report; it had been a staple during the campaign for the new charter and was absolutely true in the statistics that it quoted. But it was wrong both in the meaning of the statistics it quoted and in the statistics it chose to quote.[4]

To begin with, simple arithmetic with these figures indicated sound fiscal management: the school board had added personnel instead of increasing salaries. The average salary per teacher in current dollars was $921 in 1884 and $939 in 1896—an increase of only about 2 percent over a twelve-year period. More important, however, Phelan knew very well that the force driving educational expenditure was not the average daily attendance of students but the number of school-age children in the city. It was on the basis of the number of school-age children, determined by the city's annual school census, that the state subsidy to the city's school fund was based. Moreover, this state subsidy covered more than 60 percent of total school expenditure on average (see chap. 2). In 1884 the state's share was 69 percent; in 1896 it was 64 percent. The number of school-age children in 1884 was 63,029, while in 1896 it was 71,822. Considering this as the proper base for determining per pupil expenditure (because this determined much of the supply of revenue), salary expenditure per pupil was $10.43 in 1884 and $12.14 in 1896, an increase of $1.71 or 16.4 percent. For the twelve fiscal years in question, then, this meant an annual increase of $0.1425 per child per year.[5]

These figures indicated good management, not mismanagement. The school board was taking the increasing funds from the state and hiring more teachers. By keeping salaries stable, the board increased the number of teachers by almost 30 percent while per pupil expenditure increased only half that much. This was not pointed out by Phelan and the other reform groups, because their essential purpose was not to evaluate municipal government objectively but to delegitimize it so as to support the necessity for a new charter. To do this, they made simultaneous demands for services and economy and then refused to credit the pre-reform system when it met them.

Phelan's next attack on that system came in 1897, during the process of setting the tax rate, when he and the *Examiner* initiated a $2 tax-rate scare. Phelan's election had, of course, been a boon to the improvement clubs, and at the first finance committee meeting of his administration, in 1897, the groups were out in force, proposing thirty-two improvement projects at a total cost of $1,648,500. The list included citywide projects, like $300,000 for improvements in the city and county hospital, along with neighborhood improvement projects, such as $5,000 for improving Bernal Park near the Mission District. After hearing the pleas of the improvement groups, the finance committee proposed a tax rate of $1.02 on the $320 million assessed valuation, which included none of the improvements. But the committee did attach a list of the improvements to its report, with notice that including them in the budget would raise the tax rate to $1.67. When the report was presented to the board, finance committee member Lawrence Devany noted that the figure for the improvements and the higher rate were not intended to be submitted to the board but were "thrown out to see just what the people would stand in the way of taxation." In essence, the supervisors were asking the Merchants' Association, the improvement clubs, and the citizens at large to put their money where their mouths were and declare how much they were willing to pay for the improvements they requested.[6]

To their credit, some representatives of the improvement clubs understood the problem. At a meeting of representatives of the clubs called to discuss the proposed improvements and the tax rate, one leader noted that "the supervisors are placed in an anomalous position, for we go to them and ask for this and that improvement and they don't like to offend the Mission people, nor the Merchants' Association, nor the police department, nor, in fact, any body of citizens who present requests for money for maintenance or improvements; but when they come to make up their estimates, including all these good things . . . all of us who have asked for these improvements raise an outcry."[7]

This, however, was the minority opinion. Most speakers at this meeting repeated the reform line, demanding "the heaviest cuts in departmental expense" and "higher assessments of public service corporations," and holding the supervisors to their pledges for taxation and assessments. In the end, they passed a resolution declaring that "an increased rate of taxation beyond the amount of said $1 pledge would at this critical period, be a menace to the reviving progress of this city." The strength of the unambiguously pro-improvement forces at the meeting and, perhaps, of those who understood the role of the clubs in the supervisors' dilemma was revealed in the vote on the resolution. It passed by only a one-vote margin of sixteen to fifteen.[8]

Throughout the discussion at the improvement club meeting, speakers assumed that the $1.67 rate was already a reality, and the *Examiner,* the Merchants' Association, and Phelan himself did nothing to disabuse the city of this notion. By this time the steadfast ally of both Phelan and charter reform, the *Examiner* blasted the "plunderers" and "pledge-breakers" on the board who had proposed the levy, declaring one day that "at least $1 million" could be saved on salaries and another day that "at least $1.5 millions was wasted" on salaries. In a separate story, the *Examiner* quoted F. W. Dohrman, head of the Merchants' Association, as saying that "I know and every taxpayer knows, in a general way, that at least $1 million a year might be saved for improvements." Phelan, too, warned against a high rate, but declared that nothing could be done without a new charter: "What we want is a new organic law and a bond issue for permanent improvements. We want a charter first and then a Board of Supervisors in whom the people have confidence."[9]

Phelan's reference to an untrustworthy board of supervisors arose out of a third project to delegitimate the old system during 1897, an attempt by reform forces to obtain a court order removing the elected board of supervisors on the technicality that they had not set water rates by the legally specified deadline. Beginning in 1881, state law required that the board of supervisors set the rates for water service charged by the Spring Valley Company, the private supplier that served the city. The setting of the rates was a rancorous affair, requiring that the board determine the financial status of the company and set a rate allowing it a reasonable rate of profit. In 1897, when the board's water committee began its work, committee members determined that the water company had not given them sufficient information on which to set the rate, so they asked for more. Because of this request, the committee's work continued past the deadline specified by the law for setting the rate, which was the end of February.[10]

No complaint was raised about the delay until the full board rejected the water committee's proposal for a 20 percent reduction in water rates, a proposal that the water company disagreed with, too. Phelan and others blasted the board for this action and implied that it was the result of bribery. A month later, George Fitch, chairman of the Non-Partisan party that had endorsed Phelan for election in 1896, sued to have the board removed for malfeasance for missing the February deadline for setting the rate. The case was assigned to Judge William T. Wallace, a well-known friend of reform who had empaneled the grand jury that had indicted Buckley in 1891. On September 15, Wallace removed the supervisors from office on this obvious technicality. After consultation with the Democratic governor, James Budd, Phelan moved rapidly to appoint a new board, including on it the four supervisors who had supported the decreased water rate, along with a number of local notables, including F. W. Dohrman, Joseph Britton, and James Denman, all of whom were members of the Charter Committee of 100 and prominently identified with the reform cause. Acting under orders from Phelan, police officers drove the recalcitrant old board out of the supervisorial offices in the city hall and installed the new. The old board sought its own relief in the courts, in the form of an appeal of Wallace's ruling and an order declaring it the real board until the appeal was heard. On October 7, the order was handed down reinstating the old board until the hearing of the appeal. Almost a year later, the state supreme court ruled that Wallace's decision had been wrong because officials could not be removed by means of civil suit.[11]

For three weeks, nonetheless, the city was treated to the spectacle of two boards of supervisors attempting to make policy. The most important job of the supervisors at this time of the year was the setting of the tax rate, and on September 21, both boards dutifully issued their rates. That of the old board was $1.18; that of the new was $1.15. The allocation of the rates was identical, except that the new board cut $0.03 from the amount of taxation on the $100 of assessment going to the General Fund to add more fireman. The "millions" wasted on salaries had not been touched by the blue-ribbon board. As for the water rates, they remained the same through 1899. In 1900, the reform board elected with Phelan in the fall of 1899 under the new charter finally reduced the rates, but only by 10 percent. A compromise 10 percent reduction was not considered in 1897. These decisions underline the political dimensions of the crisis in 1897; having set out to destroy the old system, the reformers had to refuse to accept its every act, even if their own actions were little different.[12]

The battle over the water and tax rates and the dual boards had been played out against the counterexample of the quiet efficiency of the charter reform campaign. In July 1897, the Committee of 100 picked by Phelan began meeting to discuss the outlines of a new charter, and to consider a slate of freeholders and a strategy for obtaining electoral approval of the new charter. Although the committee as a whole and its twenty-two subcommittees on various reform issues were firmly in the control of local economic elites, the committee was more representative of the varied interests of the city than the pro-charter organizations in 1896, as well as more self-conscious about its representative nature. Only 43 percent of its members were listed in the social register, and its membership included five skilled or semiskilled workers; the editor of the *Coast Seamen's Journal,* an influential labor newspaper; and P. H. McCarthy, a carpenter who was head of the city's Building Trades Council.[13]

In the fall of 1897, the committee proposed its nominees for the board of fifteen freeholders who would actually shape the charter and present it to the electorate. This time, too, the freeholders were dominated by high-status businessmen and professionals and members of the Merchants' Association. Also included was P. H. McCarthy, who was widely regarded as a conservative leader of labor, but a labor leader nonetheless. There had never been a labor representative on the four boards of freeholders elected previously in the city's history, and there was none on the fusion ticket for freeholders which ran against the reform slate.[14]

In presenting this slate of candidates for the board of freeholders to the city, the Merchants' Association *Review* noted that the freeholders had been nominated by a convention—the Charter Committee of 100—comprising "representatives of all classes and callings in the community, irrespective of political affiliations." It also attempted to minimize differences between businessmen and wage earners, arguing that the "truest division of a community was into workers or drones, taxpayers and taxeaters." The first worked for "industry, economy, and progress"; the second, for "idleness, extravagance, and retrogression." The "highest ambition" of the former was "to maintain and operate city government honestly and efficiently," while that of the latter was to "run the city hall as a private institution for the subsistence of officeholders." Wage earners and businessmen needed to be sure that they supported a board of freeholders "determined to frame a municipal charter for the benefit of the taxpayer."[15]

The Merchants' Association campaign to woo workingmen to the side of the charter by lumping them with businessmen in the "taxpayer" class was not done out of genuine recognition of the demands of labor, but because of the perception shared by the *Examiner,* Yorke, Phelan, and others that reform could not win without a three-cornered, non-ethnocentric coalition including business, improvement interests, and labor. It is very likely that P. H. McCarthy was intended to be a token and symbolic representative of labor, and it was the demands of electoral competition that created the strange bedfellows of capital and labor in the reform movement. Nonetheless, such a self-consciously pluralistic coalition was unique in the city's history to this point. With Phelan again leading the charge and blasting the opposition slate of freeholders as tools of the bosses and corporations, the reformers elected all fifteen of their freeholder candidates by an average margin of about fourteen hundred votes.

Although the freeholders were not bound by the suggestions of the Committee of 100, they nonetheless relied heavily on the reports of the committee's subcommittees in the preparation of the new charter. The document that the freeholders presented to the city in March 1898 contained something for nearly everyone. For those interested in "business principles," the mayor's power was significantly increased, civil service was instituted, budgetary controls were improved, and the Dollar Limit was maintained. For those worried about a "despotism" in the mayor, the new charter maintained eleven of the elected executive offices that had existed under the Consolidation Act, expanded the board of supervisors from twelve to eighteen members elected at large, required that all appointed boards and commissions be bipartisan, and provided the initiative. The improvement block received the exemption of debt service and park expenses from the Dollar Limit, the removal of limits on the assessed valuation, the expansion and professionalization of the fire department, an elected school superintendent more susceptible to pressures for expansion of the system, a provision promising that the city would acquire and operate its own public utilities, and the consolidation of all construction, repair, street lighting, and street work into a single Board of Public Works. Finally, for labor interests the charter provided a two-dollar minimum wage and an eight-hour maximum day for all municipal employment and on all contract work let by the city.[16]

Phelan and his allies again cranked up the campaign machinery to win the special election on the charter to be held on May 25, 1898, but this time the coalition was complete. Phelan stumped the city with the leaders of the Merchants' Association and improvement clubs when that was necessary, and with P. H. McCarthy of the Building Trades Council and pro-labor editor James Barry where they were necessary. Neither of the latter had favored the charter proposed in 1896. Just as important, this time there was no offending clause in the charter, and on May 21, four days before the election, the Catholic priest Yorke declared that the charter was "entirely free from bigotry and injustice," thus freeing Catholic friends of reform to vote for it. It was only necessary for Phelan and his allies to repeat over and over again in speeches that the charter meant the end of control by bosses and of subservience to public service corporations and the beginning of an era of prosperity and improvement that would benefit all. The culmination of the working-class version of the campaign came in an emotional rally of workers two days before the election, at which Phelan and McCarthy together extolled the virtues of the charter, with the labor leader proclaiming that the minimum-wage and maximum-hour provision meant that it was a "charter that would benefit the common people."[17]

On the day of the election, only 26,969 voters turned out, about 32 percent of those registered at the last general election. The charter passed by a vote of 14,389 to 12,625, receiving 54 percent of the vote cast. Although the turnout was low, the vote was decisive in the context of recent margins; not since 1882 had any city candidate or proposal received 54 percent of any vote cast. More important, however, was the spread of the approval through the city. In his analysis of the vote in the city's eighteen assembly districts, William Issel has pointed out that it lost in only six of them, and in two of those a shift of a few votes would have produced an affirmative decision. Among the districts, it appears that the factor most likely to determine passage of the charter was the level of home ownership, a variable that cut across class and ethnicity. The charter swept every assembly district outside of the old city (i.e., the 50 and 100 vara areas) and won in four of the districts within the old city, too. All of these areas had high levels of home ownership, and they included the two working-class districts in which "appreciable numbers owned their own homes." The districts in which the charter lost were transient, waterfront working-class areas in which the level of home ownership was low. Citywide, the rate of home ownership was about 24.1 percent. However, home ownership was not just a privilege of the upper class. Jules Tygiel's analysis of home ownership among workers in San Francisco found that 27 percent of his sample of carpenters, teamsters, and laborers who had families owned their homes: 41 percent of the carpenters, 21 percent of the teamsters, and 15 percent of the laborers.[18]

Because of the passage of the charter, the next elections, in November 1898, were to be for one-year terms—and "lame duck" terms at that, because 1899 was the last year under the Consolidation Act. Both parties as well as Phelan recognized this and stressed continuity and preservation rather than the great visions of the reform campaigns. The party platforms were essentially identical. Both included the Dollar Limit on a $350 million valuation, imposed expenditure restrictions on the county clerk's office, and endorsed the new charter and some of its specific provisions, including municipal ownership, fairer assessment to increase the tax rolls, and the minimum-wage–maximum-hour guarantee. The Democracy did attempt to identify itself as the party of reform. But Phelan also defined the task of the campaign conservatively, repeating on the stump that the coming year was "a critical year, a clean up year," the last year under the "loose provisions of the Consolidation Act," and thus a year in which the city had to have "officials you can trust."[19]

For their part, the Republicans bitterly denounced the Democrats for taking all the credit for reform, noting that during the charter elections reform had been nonpartisan but was now claimed to be a Democratic achievement. The *Chronicle* also attempted to portray Phelan as merely a new political boss, referring in particular to his attempt to oust the supervisors and demanding the "utter repudiation of the usurper." Far more powerful than these appeals, however, were pro-Republican stands related to the Spanish-American War and the revival of prosperity, for which the Republicans and McKinley took full credit. Against this and the explicit call of local Republicans to support the national administration by voting the straight ticket, Phelan and the Democrats were almost helpless.[20]

In the event, the election was a striking victory for the Republicans, who took almost every citywide race, including all but two of the executive offices and all but one of the twelve seats on the board of supervisors. Phelan won the mayoralty with 51 percent of the vote, which was the same share of the total received by the Republican gubernatorial candidate in the city's vote. He was elected, in other words, by both loyal Democrats and ticket-splitting Republicans. The *Examiner* was correct to regard his victory as a personal tribute to him. "The war enthusiasm and the desire to uphold the federal administration gave the Republicans a general victory," it noted, but the voters also "remembered what Mayor Phelan had done for the city."[21]

After his inauguration, Phelan immediately moved back into the safe waters of nonpartisan reform by accepting the suggestion of F. W. Dohrman of the Merchants' Association that the organization "appoint committees of competent men, familiar with our conditions and surroundings, to study the material wants of the city [and] ... prepare an economical but progressive plan" for the last year under the Consolidation Act. Acceptance of the plan was not only a recognition of Phelan's debt to the Merchants' Association—and an indication of things to come regarding the municipal power of the organization—but also an attempt by Phelan to protect himself from any suspicion of partisan action in the nine months remaining before the next election.[22]

In March the supervisors added their own agenda to this project by asking the Merchants' Association to evaluate the various proposals put forward by the improvement groups. Although noting that "the board is the sole judge of what should or should not be done," the supervisors nonetheless requested the "advice of our businessmen to ascertain under the pledge exacted as to the limit of taxation, what provision should be made to meet the expense, if the wants are indispensable, and whether the funds therefore should be raised by the issuance of bonds or in the tax levy, without reference to the so-called Dollar Limit." This, of course, allowed the board the safety of nonpartisanship, as well as the displacement of one of its most difficult tasks—balancing the demands of the departments and the improvement groups—onto the Merchants' Association.[23]

To complete the task, the association appointed thirteen committees manned by high-status businessmen to consider everything from the major departments of city government to "Public Buildings and Institutions." The task of the committees was to determine the income and expenditure for every city activity and, in particular, to determine whether any of the expenses could be abolished immediately or whether they would be reduced or abolished by the new charter. This could be determined because half of the fiscal year 1899/1900 was under the Consolidation Act and the other half was under the new charter. This was the chance the reformers had claimed they were waiting for;

now they could reclaim the "millions" wasted on salaries that Dohrman, the *Examiner,* Phelan, and others had so often complained about, and use the money for improvements.[24]

The reports of the committees, presented in August 1899, would have been a bombshell if presented a year before, but then, such reports would not have been presented a year earlier. The first interesting finding was that there were no expenses of government to be abolished and almost none to be reduced. Careful scrutiny revealed a reduction of only $37,000 in estimated expenditure between the last six months of the old charter and the first six of the new. This was 0.7 percent of the total estimated expenditure for the year. More important, under the platform pledges, once the "necessary appropriations" for government purposes were made, there was no money for improvements. The report noted that the new charter excluded parks, squares, grounds, and debt service from the limit, and that under its provisions, even with the limits, there would have been $500,000 for these improvements. The merchants recommended waiting until the first full fiscal year under the charter to determine how this money would be expended. They also proposed considering bonded indebtedness, as permitted in the charter, for such purposes as new school buildings, repaving of streets, and new sewers, a new city and county hospital, and a new public library. But they postponed concrete proposals for bonding until later.[25]

The irony that one of the first acts of the reform coalition was to confirm the honesty of the pre-reform era was completely lost on the merchants and politicians involved in these efforts, but it cannot be ignored by the historian. In concluding their report, the merchants claimed that they had considered the requirements of the various departments of the city "conscientiously, impartially, and with due consideration of existing conditions." Having done so, they concluded what the pre-reform politicians had contended all along: (1) that little money was wasted on salaries, and (2) that the limits on taxation and assessment made large-scale improvements next to impossible. The merchants did not want "their" municipal government entering the era of the new charter underfunded, so they made no cuts and offered no explanation about why they had demanded this of the ancien régime.[26]

Two months later, Phelan and his reform supporters again swung into electoral political action, as the campaign of 1899, the first for a full two-year term under the new charter, got underway. Victory for Phelan and the reformers in this election was important, both symbolically and structurally. As the first election under the new charter, the 1899 race had the symbolic aura of the beginning of a new era. Moreoever, Phelan and his supporters defined it that way, calling the election a referendum on reform and on his plans for a progressive program for the city. Equally important, because of the new authority vested in the mayor by the charter, the winner of the election would structure the new government through his appointments to the many commissions and other posts created by the charter. Because appointment to the boards and commissions was designed to last beyond one mayor's term, the victorious mayor would control the trajectory of city government for its first four years or more.

In platform and principle, there was again no proclaimed difference between the parties in 1899. When the platforms were unveiled, they were almost identical. Both promised to enforce the new charter, both approved of bond issues for a variety of municipal improvement projects, and both pledged the $1 limit with different assessment pledges—$360 million for the Democrats and $375 million for the Republicans. Both upheld the minimum-wage–maximum-hour provision of the charter, approved of municipal ownership of public works, and listed a long series of permanent improvements to be carried out. When the Merchants' Association presented its own "Plan for Municipal Improvement" in October, it noted that its proposals had received a "courteous recognition" by "both of the great political parties" and noticed that nearly all of the provisions of its plan were "incorporated in the municipal platforms" of both parties. The association's *Review* declared that both parties were to be "congratulated upon the general excellence of the platforms," which were "far superior to the average municipal platforms heretofore presented at city elections." Returning the compliment, both mayoral candidates read and applauded the Merchants' Association plans at various points in their campaigns.[27]

There were differences between the candidates standing on these platforms, however. The Democrats again presented Phelan for an unprecedented third term as mayor. The Republicans sought a man of overwhelming social and economic prestige as well as political experience, and they found him in Horace Davis, a millionaire miller who had been a two-term Republican congressman and a former president of the University of California. Davis was a Harvard-educated easterner who had come to San Francisco in 1849 and become a millionaire through the processing of wheat by 1879, when he was listed in the city's first elite directory. It was in that year, too, that he was elected to Congress on the Republican ticket. The peak of Davis's social and political prestige had come, in other words, when Phelan was only eighteen years old.[28]

The mayor's race was therefore between two well-bred millionaires, but the contrast in their political images was such that citizens and newspapers alike were not wrong to view the election as a final conflict between the old and the new in both electoral and fiscal politics. Coming to political maturity in an era when gentlemen did not seek office, Davis did not seek the mayoral nomination and did not campaign vigorously. Moreover, he offered not proposals but character, as in the old days. Stressing his background as a successful businessman, he declared that "I have shown in my own affairs such business capacity as will give you confidence in me." Having been first elected in the days of straight-ticket voting, he campaigned heavily on the national issue, declaring that Republican national policies had returned prosperity to the city and asking the voters: "Are you going to turn your back on this national policy? How can you expect people on the other side of the continent to interpret it if they hear that the Democrats have been endorsed by the great commercial city of San Francisco?" On the one occasion when Davis spoke on the municipal issue, he merely read the Merchants' Association municipal platform and said that he agreed with it. Finally, and perhaps most important, he urged a policy of municipal fiscal conservatism, thus harking back to when an expanding public sector had been viewed with suspicion. Noting that for half a century San Francisco had been one of the few cities with little or no bonded debt, Davis declared that "to some progressive minds like that of Mr. Phelan, there may be more of shame than of pride in that regard, but to my mind prosperity in the past, freedom from debt and low taxes prophesy well for the future." The Republicans had reached deep into the past for a man of probity and accomplishment. What they had found was a Silurian in the truest sense of the word, a man whose sense of himself and of fiscal and electoral politics in the city were about a generation out of date.[29]

Symbolically, then, Phelan was the antithesis of Davis. To age he contrasted youth; to aloof superiority he contrasted a warm and vigorous campaign style; to partisanship and the national issues he contrasted four campaigns in which he had minimized partisanship for the sake of nonpartisan reform; and, most important, to conservatism in both style and proposal he contrasted progress. Although Phelan introduced no remarkably new issues into the campaign, his statements on conservatism and progress, nonpartisanship and the benefits of municipal improvements were undoubtedly the boldest he had ever made as a candidate. He set this tone in his acceptance speech at the Democratic municipal convention in October, when he simply read conservatives out of the party. Arguing that San Francisco was young and eager to be progressive, Phelan asked the convention to "let no relics of the past stand in her way. Let there be no question of conservativism when progress is in our platform," he declared. There were those in the city who were attached to the old order of things, he admitted, but "we have left them out of our platform."[30]

On the stump, Phelan contrasted his vision of an affirmative policy with that of the preexisting, negative fiscal consensus in terms very much like those argued in this book. The men of the early days who "simply fought abuses and pursued a negative policy," Phelan said, "were satisfied if the city hall was not looted and the taxes kept down." But today the city wanted an "affirmative policy." The fight for the charter, he thought, had unleashed a spirit that was unknown in earlier times but that now demanded "the accomplishment of something which will redound to the prosperity of the city and the happiness of its people."[31]

Such an affirmative policy was based on the construction of improvements that would bring direct and indirect benefits to all residents of the city. A "progressive program" included the building of schoolhouses and a new hospital, a new sewerage system, and a complete parks system, among other things. Most directly, the building of these public works would "give employment to labor and circulate money," Phelan said. More generally, however, the improvement of the city would bring new resources to the city which would enrich all. As Phelan put it, "when we have made our city sanitary and our schools fit ... we will draw a population and every accession will pour into the veins of trade new blood and new energy, and with the growth of the city based upon such a new foundation, every man, woman, and child, especially in industrial employment, should feel and enjoy the benefit."[32]

Phelan's reference to the benefits to labor was not just incidental; indeed, he reviewed the specific benefits of municipal improvements to workingmen so frequently on the stump that the *Chronicle* finally accused him of demagoguery. As part of the newspaper's contrast of "economical" Republicanism with the extravagance of the Democrats, it noted that Phelan proposed "inaugurating a boom in San Francisco" by heavily taxing property to promote "real or fancied improvements." According to the *Chronicle*, Phelan told workers that they "need not bother themselves about the amount that an improvement . . . will cost, because their concern is to see new work created." This was true, in that Phelan's campaign in the working-class districts consisted entirely of promises to workers of both more care from city services and more jobs from improvements. Phelan repeatedly declared that "every man who swings a hammer seems ready to endorse our policy, as it means benefit to labor when put in action." According to Phelan, workingmen supported the Democracy because "the workingmen want new school buildings for their children, they want to know . . . that the city is properly drained; for health and work are inseparable." Phelan tried to protect himself from the charge of demagoguery by issuing a disclaimer at every talk that "I have not urged to laboring people that I have advocated these things because it would give them work; it would be demagogic to make such an argument." Yet the disclaimer was always embedded in a list of promises of benefits from public sector projects which included "employment to labor."[33]

The appeal to labor was clinched again by appearances by P. H. McCarthy, Phelan's labor ally in the charter fight. In his campaign speeches for Phelan in 1899, McCarthy stressed the significance to workers of both the direct benefits of improvements and Phelan's willingness to make labor a partner in city affairs. The city was now poised at the edge of an era of improvement, McCarthy said, during which a "condition will prevail of which the laboring population will be the direct beneficiaries." The man who brought this condition about, McCarthy declared, was Phelan, who personally advocated the incorporation of minimum-wage and maximum-hour provisions in the charter but, more important, "called labor into his councils." "He has placed labor upon the same footing with the banker, merchant, and capitalist; he has heeded labor's requests and he has complied with them; he has elevated labor to the position of advisor in civil matters, and he has proven himself Mayor of the entire people," McCarthy concluded.[34]

On the day before the election, the *Examiner* summarized the issues, both real and symbolic, in an editorial entitled "For Progress or Silurianism." The editorial argued that the questions to be decided in the election were two: "First—Shall the city be run on the lines laid down by the friends of the new charter or on the lines laid down by those who opposed that instrument? Second—Shall the new government stand for progress or Silurianism?" The answer was delivered when the voters gave Phelan a victory in every assembly district in the city, totaling 56 percent of the vote, a margin of victory for a mayoral candidate not seen in the city since 1867. Elected along with Phelan were fifteen of the eighteen Democratic supervisors, who averaged 53 percent of the vote, and seven of the eleven executive officers elected under the new charter, including the district attorney, the assessor, and the city and county attorney. The *Examiner* exulted that the victory meant that the city was "turned in the path of progress and that silurianism is left behind," and even the *Chronicle* had to admit that "the result is so decisive that it will be admitted without further cavilling that San Francisco is anxious to embark on the municipal career marked out for it by the successful candidate."[35]

Spurred on by the vote for Phelan, later the same month the board of supervisors authorized two elections on bonded indebtedness for municipal improvements to be held in December 1899. The first issues, passed on December 27, called for the expansion and extension of Golden Gate Park and the beginning of a large park in the Mission District, at a total cost of $4.5 million. The second, passed on December 29, called for three separate projects, including $4.6 million for sewers, $1.4 million for the construction and repair of schoolhouses, and $475,000 for the construction of a new city and county hospital. The total of more than $11 million in bonds added $0.05 per $100 of valuation to the tax rate. The passage of the bonds was almost a foregone conclusion after Phelan's election victory. Although there was controversy over bonding the city for "ornaments" like the Golden Gate Park extension, the park bonds passed with a comfortable 73 percent of the vote. The school, hospital, and sewer bonds passed with an even larger majority of 96 percent each. Any Silurians left after Phelan's victory were certainly routed by these votes. The headline in the *Call* trumpeting the passage of the first bonds acknowledged this: "BY A TREMENDOUS MAJORITY THE VOTERS OF THE CITY DECLARE IN FAVOR OF PARK EXTENSION AND DECREE THE PASSING OF A HISTORICAL SILURIANISM."[36]

THE CRISIS OF THE NEW FISCAL POLITICS, 1900–1906

The reform campaign and the new charter shifted the ground on which fiscal policy was made, but it remained a battleground nonetheless, and the hope that the reform coalition had held for a sort of permanent peace in fiscal politics was definitely a delusion. If the choice of the pre-reform fiscal world had been between spending and saving, in the reform world it was among projects on which to spend. The momentum toward improvement was not lost. Indeed, its symbolic victory over economy was confirmed in the suspension of the Dollar Limit in 1902. However, battles continued over what, exactly, constituted an improvement, and just how and how quickly improvements were to be accomplished. Therefore, after 1900, boards of supervisors, executive departments, and improvement groups continued to battle one another for shares of increasing revenue. Despite their differences in background, support, and political style, Phelan and his Union Labor party successor, Eugene Schmitz, faced the same issues of fiscal politics.

Much of this conflict was based on the disparity between the promises made by the reform coalition and Phelan's ability to deliver on these promises in his first and last administration under the charter, from January 1900 to December 1901. The coalition had succeeded by mobilizing new groups into political action by promises of benefits from an expanding public sector. Of course, the reformers had not proposed any specific timetable for the delivery of these benefits. Nonetheless, all the promissory notes signed during the reform campaigns came due on January 1, 1900, when both Phelan and the new charter came into power. The Merchants' Association wanted economy, efficiency, and improvements; improvement groups wanted more expenditure on neighborhood improvement projects, less on salaries and citywide projects; and labor wanted services, jobs, and the maintenance of the equal status its leadership thought it had achieved by its service in the reform coalition.

Unfortunately, the real world of post-1900 fiscal politics prevented delivery on all these promises. Built into the charter were significant new or increased old salary costs of administration, which meant that there was less money for improvements initially. Moreover, contrary to what the reformers had implied when they were insurgents, San Francisco, like Rome, could not be rebuilt in a day, so neighborhood projects could only be done a few at a time, if at all. This meant few funds for the increasing number of improvement groups whose lengthening lists of projects made it look like the city was falling farther and farther behind in its commitment to neighborhood improvement. Finally, when "push came to shove" between labor and management during the waterfront strike of 1901, Phelan made clear what many suspected all along— that labor was to be a junior partner in the reform coalition.

In the exhilaration following the 1900 inauguration of Phelan under the new charter, interests both inside and outside of local government upped their fiscal demands significantly, and by the end of the budgetary process, the outside groups were in rebellion. The new administration took office in January, and the auditor began preparing budget estimates for the coming year almost immediately. Total expenditure for the current fiscal year, ending on May 30, 1900, had been estimated to be about $5.4 million. For the coming fiscal year, the departments alone requested $7 million and the improvement groups $507,000 more. The auditor was able to trim the departments down to about $4 million in his estimates, but because he did not include the full amount for the improvements, he was denounced for his efforts. A meeting of the Federation of Mission District Improvement Clubs resolved that "the auditor has been too generous to the taxeaters and has shown little regard for the taxpayers."[37]

The argument of the Phelan administration was that additional expenditures required by the charter to initiate new services or to improve old were, in a sense, improvements. For example, the fully professionalized fire department instituted by the charter required an increase of $120,000 in the first full year under the new charter. Each of the new boards and commissions also had start-up costs for salaries and staffs, ranging from about $8,000 for the civil service commission to $12,000 for the newly paid school directors. Even the expenses of the mayor and the board of supervisors went up by about $5,000 each. More important, and ultimately more controversial, were the expenses of the massive new board of public works, which under the new charter was charged with responsibility for all street and sewer work, all public engineering and construction, and all repairs and lighting of public buildings. Salaries for employees of the board—not including wages paid on specific projects—would require about $100,000, including $20,000 for the commissioners of public works and their assistants. Many of these salaries were simply reallocated from the departments, such as streets and street lighting, that were merged into the board. The difference was that now, massed together as they were, the salary expenditures were easier to attack.[38]

Caught between their desires to staff fully the new agencies, begin citywide improvement projects, and still keep the tax rate low, Phelan and the board of supervisors rejected the specific, neighborhood-level improvements proposed by the clubs and followed their own lights, approving a budget without them. In fact, Phelan finally rebuked the neighborhood groups, noting that "it goes without saying that every need or aspiration of the people cannot be gratified in one fiscal year." Furthermore, he argued that the supervisors had scrutinized the departments so carefully that "I do not believe that a single unnecessary employee is on the payroll."[39]

This conflict between improvements and salaries was the theme of the budget controversy the next year, too. Again the improvement clubs appeared with a list of demands. However, the auditor and the supervisors had come close to agreement on their estimates, with the major increases going to charter departments, including $168,000 more to the board of public works, $60,000 to the fire department, and $100,000 to the school department. Again the Mission Federation of Improvement Clubs attacked the salary expenditure, this time in the health department and the board of public works. The total appropriation for the former was $63,000, of which $56,735 was for salaries. For the latter, the total appropriation was $812,196, of which more than $150,000 went for salaries. This time even the Merchants' Association jumped on the salary complaint. In May, during the budget-setting process, the Merchants' Association *Review* published an article on the first full year under the charter which noted that "a just criticism of the administration of the present Board of Public Works and Board of Health is their appointment in some cases of superfluous deputies and clerks." The departments were allowed by charter to create new appointments within the limits of their appropriations, subject to the approval of the civil service commission. The latter commission had already disapproved of some of the new positions, but in actions reminiscent of the pre-reform days, the respective boards had refused to eliminate them.[40]

Stung by this criticism, Phelan himself took space in the *Review* in July 1901 to extol the results of the "first fiscal year under the charter." According to Phelan, the charter had proved its worth. The tax rate was down and there was more money for improvements. Indeed, he listed specific improvement projects in the budget for the next fiscal year, including $317,313 in street and sewer work, $218,485 in improvements to public buildings, and $120,000 for construction of public buildings. These were all within the Dollar Limit. Outside of it was an additional $280,000 for parks.

Many of the improvements Phelan listed had been demanded earlier by improvement groups. About half of the street and sewer work was scheduled for the suburban areas, and the funds for construction of public buildings included money for police, fire, and school buildings in the same areas. Other improvements that Phelan listed (e.g., typewriters for the recorder and assessor, new furnishings for city hall offices, and a "steel tank" for the almshouse) were padding added to the improvements list that he would very likely have denounced in his insurgent days. Moreover, the money for these projects did not appear magically. The assessor had raised the assessment roll by $30 million for the next fiscal year. Therefore, even though the tax rate was reduced by $0.055 from the previous fiscal year, tax-based revenue was expected to increase by $132,000. In other words, the tax rate had dropped but overall tax liability had increased.[41]

The major themes in these new conflicts over salaries versus improvements had been summarized in an editorial in the *Examiner* during the allocation process in 1900. Then the newspaper had denounced the budget approved for the next fiscal year with sadness and disillusionment, noting that "the budget is a disappointment to the people of the city," because it contained "not one notable improvement." On the contrary, "practically the whole of the increase is eaten up in salaries of one sort or another." Given the promises of the reformers that they would cut salaries to pay for improvements, "it was hoped," the paper noted, "that the Supervisors would . . . be able to reduce the expenses of most of the offices. This hope has been disappointed." In contrast to its stance during the pre-charter period, however, the paper did not attribute this to dishonesty. Rather, it was the "product of good nature which has been unwilling to refuse the requests of the departments or to force a cut in the number of employees." The paper explained that the "supervisors do not like to offend the officeholders with whom they are in daily contact, therefore the taxeaters get most of the money and the people get less."[42]

As the consistently positive measures of change in table 35 indicate, the city's fiscal world had changed by the end of fiscal 1901/02, and in the directions that the *Examiner* and others had requested. In real terms, every measure of the city's fiscal activity had increased more than population. Valuation and revenue were up more than 6 percent, and operating expenditure was up more than 16 percent. Moreover, expenditures on the School Fund, Street Fund, and uniformed services

TABLE 35

CHANGES IN MEASURES OF FISCAL POLICY, 1894–1902

Category	1894	1902	Percent change 1894–1902	Era mean
Per capita assessed valuation	$1051	$1121.7	6.7	$1095
Per capita local revenue	12.92	13.743	6.34	14.71
Per capita tax revenue	10.739	12.013	11.92	12.73
Per capita cash on hand	3.852	5.009	42.1	4.572
Tax rate	1.000	1.048	4.8	1.133
Per capita non-tax revenue	2.187	1.729	−26.4	1.96
Per capita operating expenditure	13.19	15.371	16.5	15.84
Per capita School Fund expenditure	.0029	.0035	20	.0033
Per capita Street Fund expenditure	.0010	.0012	20	.0013
Per capita street lighting expenditure	.0008	.0007	−12.5	.0008
Per capita police and fire expenditure	3.352	4.159	24	4.1121
Per capita expenditure on official salaries	1.1397	missing	missing	1.382
Per capita expenditure on social welfare	.5945	.6515	9	.6961
Share of operating expenditure	90%	99.7%	10	93.9%

Note: All dollar values have been deflated by means of the price index explained in appendix A.

had all increased more than had total operating expenditure. Perhaps the most interesting symbol of the change came in the average tax rate, which was $1.13. It had been only $0.95 during the years when the limit held undisputed sway.

The criticisms of Phelan were remarkably unfair, but it is hard to feel much sympathy for Phelan because he was, in essence, hoist on his own petard. The criticisms were unfair because improvements were being made and the salaries about which the *Examiner* complained were financing activities that the city government had not undertaken before but that the electorate had approved by passage of the new charter and the election of Phelan to administer it. From the beginnning of his first term as mayor, Phelan had declared that city government should "care for the health, the comfort, the education, the property, and the general well-being of the people." Such a government cost money. In fact, during the campaign for the charter, the auditor had estimated that the new charter would cost more than $1 million more to administer than the Consolidation Act. Phelan and the reformers did not deny this, but neither did they emphasize it. Instead, they denounced even the necessary administrative expenses of the old system, and thus created an atmosphere in which all salary expenditure, even that authorized by a reform administration, was suspect. Moreover, the reformers implied that the passage of the charter would somehow magically resolve the hard issues of allocation. In reality, it aggravated those issues because more groups felt entitled to more benefits from the public sector. Phelan was, therefore, reaping a harvest of disillusionment that he and the reformers themselves had sown.[43]

It is possible that Phelan realized this and wearied of it, because by the time he wrote his defense of the first year under the charter in July 1901, he had already announced that he would not run again for mayor. At that time, too, he was embroiled in the waterfront strike of 1901, which would produce bitter disillusionment with the reform coalition and with Phelan himself, and which would lead to the election of Union Labor candidate Eugene Schmitz as Phelan's unlikely successor and mayor of the city through the earthquake.

We may recall from chapter 4 that the issue in the strike was the closed shop. The strike began with a lockout of teamsters who refused to work with nonunion men during a convention in the city, and by the end of July it had spread to a strike of all waterfront workers who worked with the teamsters, on behalf of the union shop demand. From the start, an employers' association opposed the strike, and the Merchants' Association joined in the opposition to the closed shop. At a special meeting of the association called to discuss the "labor problem" in September 1901, former president F. W. Dohrman declared that "although the present state of industrial war was to be regretted, it would end only if the union leaders would fully recognize the constitutional right to labor whether the laborer was a member of a union or not." This was exactly the position that Phelan took when he authorized the use of police to convoy nonunion wagons through the streets. As he explained in his valedictory address as mayor, he was obligated to use police to protect nonunion labor because of the "constitutional right" to work. It was necessary, he said, for the police to "uphold the law and to see that every citizen might pursue his daily work without molestation."[44]

In doing this, Phelan signed his political death warrant with the labor movement, whose leaders, like Andrew Furuseth of the Coast Seamen's Union, argued later that "if the governing power of the city had been exercised properly, the recent strike would not have extended beyond the teamsters. It was because they [the employers] knew they held the executive power of the city in the hollow of their hands ... that the strike was continued." The result, of course, was the hasty formation of the Union Labor party (ULP) and the call to the city's workingmen to "vote as they had marched on Labor Day" so that there would be "some hesitation in the future about the kind of treatment that they [the employers] propose to administer to men who have quit work because they have a grievance." The party's mayoral candidate, Schmitz, won the election of 1901 in a three-way race and was reelected two more times before the earthquake.[45]

The Union Labor party was born in controversy, and it has lived on in controversy among historians, who have had a difficult time reconciling its erstwhile political radicalism with its fiscal orthodoxy. Both contemporaries and historians agree that the fiscal policy of the party was completely orthodox within the terms set by the Phelan administration. Rather than blazing new—perhaps even class-conscious—fiscal trails, Union Labor Mayor Schmitz and, later, his Union Labor colleagues in city government followed the same fiscal lines laid down by the businessman's reformer Phelan, stressing improvements over salaries, commitment to the Dollar Limit, and fulfillment of the terms of the charter regarding public ownership of utilities.[46]

Nonetheless, in the context of 1901 San Francisco, the appeal of the party was distinctly radical, because in demanding "equal representation" for labor the party proposed a radical attack on the plans of the reform coalition. From the outset of the 1901 campaign, Schmitz declared that the issue in the election was "representation." Over and over again he said that the time had come for workingmen to demand representation in the affairs of the municipality. As he put it in a speech to the Pressmen's Union, "this is a fight for representation. It is a fight for the representation of the workingman in the government of this city." Schmitz denied that he proposed a class government, and he rejected "dividing the people into classes." Rather, he was in favor of "equal representation for employer and employee, for capital as well as for labor and equal protection for all."[47]

It was possible for Schmitz to call for the support of labor without calling for a class government because the reform coalition had done so before him. However, within the terms of the reform coalition, his call for equal representation for labor was profoundly radical. Although Phelan had essentially mobilized the labor interest politically, neither he nor his business allies had ever intended to do so on an equal basis. Labor and the improvement groups were to be the foot soldiers in a campaign commanded by Phelan and the Merchants' Association; they were to be acted upon, to be grateful for the benefits they received from reform government. This was made clear both before and after the charter, when the suggestions for municipal improvements produced by the improvement clubs were evaluated by the Merchants' Association and then ultimately rejected by Phelan. A similar situation arose during the teamsters lockout and, later, the waterfront strike. In essence, Phelan referred the labor issue to the Merchants' Association for evaluation. The answer of the association was no closed shop and the use of the police to support the employers' organization.

The depth of bitterness that labor leaders felt toward Phelan and the reform coalition was exactly proportional to the degree to which Phelan had convinced them that they were equal partners. In fact, the Merchants' Association had always been "more equal" than the others in the reform coalition, and the call for equal representation for labor entailed a diminution of the influence of business in municipal government. This was the "radicalism" of Schmitz's 1901 campaign, and this is why I agree with Jules Tygiel that the labor vote for Schmitz was a "class conscious" act within the real possibilities of politics in San Francisco. Moreover, this act had true benefits for the labor movement. The election of Schmitz meant the end of the status of the Merchants' Association as an informal branch of government and the end of the use of police to protect strikebreakers.[48]

Neither Schmitz nor the other leaders of the party or the local labor movement had a "theory of the state," however, that called for the use of fiscal policy to aid the working class or, conversely, to "harm" business. It is ironic that the first mayoral candidate in the city's history to quote from the *Wall Street Journal* was Schmitz. Moreover, when Schmitz tried to justify his record in 1905, during his third campaign, he used statistics on real estate sales and the holdings of banks to prove that he had been good for business. All of this was necessary, most immediately because of the opponents he called "calamity howlers," who argued that if he were elected—or, ultimately, reelected—business in the city would be ruined. More fundamentally, however, Schmitz's radicalism was not fiscal.[49]

In declaring that "for every dollar taken from the people in taxes they should be given a dollar's worth of services," Schmitz located himself firmly in the reform (as opposed to pre-reform) fiscal consensus. Mayors before Phelan would never have made such a statement, as we have seen. Yet within that consensus, the tone of Schmitz's campaigns was on the conservative side. Although he favored "every public improvement," including "good streets, free parks, a new municipal sewerage system, better schoolhouses, and a permanent improvement fund," he also pledged to "cut off the ornamental salaries and to turn money now used in paying them that such money shall count for public goods." According to Schmitz, municipal government was a "business institution," and therefore required "honest and conservative administration."[50]

Schmitz demonstrated his fiscal conservatism by vetoing the budget proposed by the supervisors every year from 1902 through 1904. Each year the pattern was the same. Schimtz proposed that the supervisors cut salary expenditure in some departments, the supervisors refused to do so, he vetoed their budget, and they, in turn, passed it over his veto. In 1902 and 1903 the supervisors unanimously rejected his cuts, and in 1904 the three Union Labor supervisors on the board who had been elected in 1903 voted to sustain Schmitz's veto. His veto message argued the same thing each year: there should be less money for salaries and more for improvements. In 1902 he told the supervisors that "for a long time" it had appeared to him that "far too large a proportion of the monies raised by taxation are expended in salaries and far too little in permanent municipal improvements." In 1903 he said that his proposed cuts would "go far toward reconciling our taxpaying citizens toward bearing their proper burden of taxation."[51]

Every year, however, both the amounts and the targets of Schmitz's cuts demonstrated that his protests were more than a little ritualistic. In 1902 he recommended cuts of $134,000; in 1903, $172,000; and in 1904, $53,615. Each year the cuts were composed largely of a clerkship here and a clerkship there, with the bulk coming from the board of health and the board of public works, which were targets for the complaint of "too much salary expenditure" already identified by the Merchants' Association, improvement groups, and others in Phelan's first term under the new charter. With these cuts (which were rejected in any case), Schmitz demonstrated his fiscal conservatism and separated himself from the policies of the board. Like his predecessors who complained about salaries, he did not alter the budget's priorities fundamentally. Nonetheless, his projection of a conservative image in fiscal affairs was an important shading of his starkly radical image in political affairs.[52]

Even had Schmitz intended to do something surprising fiscally, he lacked the political control necessary to do so for his first two terms, and the earthquake interrupted his third term, when he did have that control. Schmitz and the Union Labor party did not control city government until after the election of 1905, which was a complete sweep of every municipal office by the ULP. The new administration took office in January 1906, but had barely begun its work when the city was devastated by earthquake and fire in April of that year. Prior to that, because of high levels of incumbency under the new charter, it could almost be said that Schmitz was a figurehead for what were, in fact, Phelan administrations.[53]

As we saw in chapter 4, the city officials elected in 1901, 1903, and 1905 were different from those in the four other political eras in two ways that were statistically significant: among these officials there was a low level of high white-collar occupations and a high level of incumbency. Both were artifacts of the charter. By separating municipal elections from others, the charter removed the effect of the top of the ticket and hence the source of much of the turnover in municipal electoral fortunes. Levels of incumbency were highest during the Union Labor era, next highest during the era of the People's and Taxpayer's parties; during both eras, municipal elections were separate from others (see chap. 4). In addition to separating elections, the charter increased the size of the board of supervisors by 50 percent. This had two effects. Because historically, supervisors had come predominantly from low white-collar occupations, this increased the pool of likely low white-collar winners. Moreover, by increasing the number of supervisors and detaching them from the wards, the charter increased the value of city-wide name-recognition, and therefore the advantage of incumbency. This advantage was spread evenly among the elected officials. For the only time in the city's history, from 1901 through 1906 there was no statistically significant difference between levels of incumbency and type of political office held. Overall, 47 percent of officials elected in these years were incumbents, compared with 48 percent of executive officers and 47 percent of supervisors.[54]

Among these incumbents, holdovers from Phelan's administration elected in 1899 were a significant portion of the officials in Schmitz's first two terms as mayor. Among the eleven executive officers elected with Phelan in 1899, five were reelected with Schmitz in 1901, and three of these were elected again in 1903. Among those three were the very important offices of assessor and district attorney. Among the supervisors elected with Phelan, eight were reelected in 1901, along with two more appointed by Phelan to fill unexpired terms. Seven of these ten were reelected in 1903. In 1901 the executive officers elected with Schmitz were four Democrats, six Republicans, and two members of the Union Labor party.[55]

In fact, there were radical fiscal changes going on in these years, but Schmitz could take little credit—or blame—for them. The first of these was the radical increase in the city's assessed valuation. An aggressive revaluation policy of reform Assessor Washington Dodge, first elected in 1898 and reelected in 1899 and 1901, increased the city's personal property valuation by 72 percent between 1899 and 1900. Also, the state board of equalization had stepped in in 1904 to force an additional 30 percent increase on the city, so by fiscal 1905/06, just before the earthquake, the city's total valuation stood at $525 million, an increase of 28 percent from the first full year under the charter and of 50 percent from the last full year under the Consolidation Act. This change is apparent in table 36; in real per capita terms, the valuation increased almost 15 percent from fiscal 1902/03 through 1906.[56]

TABLE 36

CHANGES IN MEASURES OF FISCAL POLICY, 1903–1906

Category	1903	1906	Percent change 1903–06	Era mean
Per capita assessed valuation	$1085.4	$1246.5	14.8	$1163.5
Per capita local revenue	14.985	16.20	8.1	15.06
Per capita tax revenue	13.315	14.47	8.7	13.345
Per capita cash on hand	5.99	12.79	113.5	10.068
Tax rate	1.16	.9907	−14.5	1.054
Per capita non-tax revenue	1.669	1.726	3.4	1.70
Per capita operating expenditure	16.091	16.089	0	16.13
Per capita School Fund expenditure	.0034	.0036	5.8	.0034
Per capita Street Fund expenditure	.0011	.0016	45.4	.0013
Per capita street lighting expenditure	.0007	.0005	−28.5	.0007
Per capita police and fire expenditure	4.393	4.536	3.25	4.50
Per capita expenditure on official salaries	missing	missing	missing	missing
Per capita expenditure on social welfare	.6584	.6909	4.9	.6763
Share of operating expenditure	99.7%	81.7%	−18	94.4%

Note: All dollar values have been deflated by means of the price index explained in appendix A.

The second radical change was the transformation of the Dollar Limit from a ceiling over to a floor under the tax rate. Once the limit was institutionalized in the charter it disappeared from the party platforms, along with the limits on assessed valuation. Because it had been partisan competition that forced the rate downward, the removal of that pressure allowed the limit to float upward more freely. Added to this, of course, was the charter-based exclusion of expenditures for parks from the limit. Under the new charter, the lowest the tax rate ever reached in current dollars by 1906 was $1.076, which consisted of the Dollar Limit for regular expenditures, the $0.07 allowance specified in the charter as the maximum for parks, and the $0.006 for debt service on the few remaining outstanding bonds issued in the 1870s. Even in the fiscal year when the state board raised the assessment by 30 percent, the tax rate decreased only 12 percent from the previous year and did not go below the new minimum of $1.076. In real terms, the average rate was $1.05 (see table 36).[57]

As a result of the increasing valuation and the stable or increasing tax rate, the taxes levied by the city increased significantly in these years, as did its ability to spend and its actual expenditure. Taxes levied increased from $4.6 million in 1901 to $6.1 million in 1906, an increase of 32 percent. Total local expenditure in current dollars increased apace, rising from $4,770,900 during the first full fiscal year under the charter to $7,436,000 by 1906. In real per capita terms, as table 36 shows, operating expenditure remained almost stable, while the share of debt service expenditure increased as the city began to build its sinking funds for the improvement bonds issued in these years. Within the category of operating expenditure, per capita school and street expenditures increased again, in the case of the latter, by 45 percent. Although the vast majority of this operating expenditure went for salaries and other expenses of the departments, a good deal was also going for improvements. In the budget of fiscal 1903/04, for example, 65 percent of the $6.1 million was allocated for salaries, but there was also $350,000 for specifically listed improvements. The next year this total had risen to $500,000, and the finance committee of the supervisors listed the projects proposed by improvement clubs—totaling $438,000—and seven others proposed by city offices. Typewriters for city officials were not included in these lists, as they had been by Phelan in 1901.[58]

However, the most expensive and most symbolically important of these improvements came in 1902, when the board of supervisors, in preparing the budget for fiscal 1902/03, appropriated $630,000 for work beginning the new county hospital and for repairing schoolhouses, and voted unanimously to suspend the Dollar Limit to do so. The background to this decision was the bond campaign of 1899, which we have already reviewed. In December 1899, voters had approved bond issues totaling more than $10 million for a variety of improvements, including a new county hospital and the building and repair of schoolhouses. In June 1900, friendly suits testing the legality of the bond issues had been instituted before the state supreme court. In the spring of 1901, the court ruled that because the bonds had been voted upon under the old charter they could not be issued under the new. The money for the first year of the sinking funds and interest accounts for the bonds—about $210,000—had already been collected and was allocated to other improvements during fiscal 1901/02.[59]

It was expected, of course, that the bond issues would be reintroduced soon, but when the supervisors began the budget process for fiscal 1902/03 in the spring of 1902, Democratic Supervisor Peter J. Curtis introduced an ordinance to set apart $0.075 outside of the Dollar Limit to finance the beginnings of work on the new county hospital. All agreed that the present hospital was "a disgrace to the city," Curtis said, echoing a point made repeatedly during the bond campaign, and that the city "should provide a proper place for the sick poor at the earliest possible date." His proposal set off a flurry of editorial and improvement-group comment, all favorable. A month later, however, Republican Supervisor Horace Wilson introduced a similar ordinance calling for $0.075 outside of the Dollar Limit for the repair of school buildings, arguing that the charter permitted the board to set aside the Dollar Limit in case of emergency and that the condition of the schools was such an emergency.[60]

The introduction of both ordinances set the stage for a battle on two fronts: over which proposal should be approved, and over what the charter meant by an "emergency" that justified suspension of the limit. Interest groups for both sides flocked to finance committee hearings. The school directors, teachers, and improvement groups favored the school proposal, and the *Examiner* editorialized that the schools were more important at the time than the hospital. Physicians, supervisors on the board's hospital committee, and advocates for the poor such as the Paulist Fathers, St. Vincent de Paul, and the Salvation Army supported the hospital proposal.[61]

The full board of supervisors discussed the proposals over two meetings, considering both the merits of the proposals and the legality of the suspension of the limit. It was obvious from the outset that none of the supervisors was hard-hearted enough to attempt to compare the merits of one proposal against another. Both were important, both had been approved by large majorities in the bond election, and the expenses of both would already have been included in the tax rate had the court not thrown the bonds out. What opposition there was to the proposals either stemmed from or was camouflaged as concern for legal propriety. The new charter declared that "in case of any great necessity or emergency" an ordinance passed by the unanimous vote of the supervisors and approved by the mayor could supersede the Dollar Limit. The argument against the proposals, made by Republican Supervisor George Sanderson, was that an "emergency" as contemplated by the charter did not exist because there had been no "calamity." If a school had burned down, then there would have been the "necessity" contemplated by the charter, he argued. Democratic Supervisor Samuel Braunhart replied that Sanderson's construction of the charter was not "liberal." Braunhart would vote for the measures, he said, because the state supreme court had held that "the legislative body is the supreme and final judge of what is an emergency and a necessity."[62]

Following up on this interpretation, Democrats Augustus Comte and Henry Brandenstein argued that both the charter and "the people" supported this more liberal interpretation. Brandenstein decried the "fetish which some were inclined to make of the Dollar Limit." The charter, he said, "gives us the right to go outside of the limit and leaves it to the exercise of our honest judgement and our proper discretion to decide when we shall avail ourselves of the exceptional privilege." Comte argued that what the people wanted was an honest but "not parsimonious" administration of city finances. The charter was made to "prevent dishonest expenditure of the people's money," he said, but also to provide for "the needs of the people and an honest administration." Taking what he called the "broad and liberal view" of the issues, he said, "this Board can make no mistake in passing the ordinances." In the end, both passed unanimously and the tax rate for the next fiscal year was set at $1.226, accordingly.[63]

The symbolic effect of this vote was to end the era of the Dollar Limit. Since 1882, "bosses" and "reformers," storm and strife had come and gone, but, as its partisans declared often enough, the limit remained. It had been evaded, of course, and its status as the leading principle of fiscal policy had been declining for some time, but it had never before been repudiated formally and on the record. Its death was foreordained by the victory of the reform argument that the city had to abandon the "negative" policy of the past, which was symbolized by the limit, and adopt the "positive" policy of the present, which would be brought about by the end of limits on assessment, the opening of loopholes within the limit, and even by the suspension of the sacred limit itself in case of "emergency."

Moreover, the city continued to move rapidly in this direction. In September and October 1903, the city again considered bonded indebtedness, voting on issues totaling $18.5 million and approving $17.5 million of them. In 1904 the supervisors unanimously approved an ordinance for a charter amendment to be submitted to the people calling for another $0.15 per $100 of assessed valuation outside of the Dollar Limit for a "permanent improvement fund." In 1905 the budget proposed for the next fiscal year included a record $670,000 within the limit for seventeen specific permanent improvements, including an appropriation of $350,000 as the down payment for purchase of a privately owned traction line that would mark the city's first venture into municipal ownership of public utilities.[64]

By the time of the earthquake, in other words, the city was well on its way into a fiscal world that the politicians of the 1880s would not have recognized. It was this world that Buckley criticized when he wrote in his memoirs that under the guidance of the reformers the city's finances had "fallen entirely into the hands of irresponsibles" and had gone from bad to worse "with a rapidity that I can only call queer." It was not the rapidity of this change but its enormity that struck Buckley as odd. The accomplishment of the reformers was a fundamental transformation of the idea of responsibility in fiscal politics. Politicians of the 1880s were, first and foremost, responsible to the municipal political conventions and to their platform pledges. Listening attentively to the proclamations of the conventions, these leaders turned a deaf ear to pleas for municipal policy based on vaguely defined social needs. For men like Buckley, Blake, or Strother, there was no need greater than the need to keep the tax rate and assessed valuation low. Against this overriding necessity, all other requests were simply special pleading. In contrast, reform leaders like Phelan, Schmitz, and others declared that they would take responsibility for all aspects of urban life, including, at the minimum, as Phelan put it, the "health, the comfort, the education, the property, and the general well-being of the people." This responsibility, they claimed, required a government that was reorganized, more expensive, and more continuously involved in municipal life, and that permitted them to identify and respond to social needs rather than to the demands of partisan political conventions.[65]

Nonetheless, the reformers, too, were politicians, and this fact must not be ignored. The expansion of municipal government after 1900 did not occur by means of an automatic "internalizing of the externalities" of urban industrial growth, as some historians have suggested. The reformers and their successors built and maintained a political coalition based on groups excluded from the old fiscal politics, and they held it together by means of promises of benefits from an expanding public sector in the new fiscal politics. If, as Buckley implied, the new system opened a fiscal-political Pandora's box, it was human hands that opened it, not "hidden hands."[66]

8

Reconciling Theory and Practice in San Francisco

If the fiscal political world we have visited in the last three chapters ultimately seemed strange to some of its participants, it is stranger still to strict adherents of what I have called the socioeconomic structural and political cultural theories of the development of the urban public sector. Where these theories predict chaos, we have found order; where they predict growth, we have seen constraint. Most important, where they portray a smooth functional fit between socioeconomic or political "needs" and the development of the public sector, we have found a fiscal political system that stubbornly refused to do its historic duty.

The account of fiscal policymaking just concluded has differed from the predictions of these theories because it has emphasized the role that institutional structure, political strategy, and fiscal ideology played in the shaping of the public sector in San Francisco. The socioeconomic structural theory argues that it is socioeconomic development that drives the growth of municipal government. Thus it grants little or no autonomy either to institutions or to political actors; rather, both are overwhelmed by socioeconomic forces and respond more or less automatically to needs and demands. Conversely, the political cultural theory argues that it is the political ethos of competing political regimes that determines the development of the urban public sector, thus granting political actors almost total autonomy to act on behalf of their political clients. In this theory, "bosses" and "reformers" are abstracted from all structure, whether institutional, socioeconomic, political, or ideological.

In chapter 1, I noted that the problem of functionalist theories such as these is not that they are necessarily wrong, but that they are poorly specified and ahistorical. The variables the theories do include are not

239

well defined, important variables are excluded, causal links among the variables are not made, and hence the operation of the general theory in any particular historical situation is not clear. The understanding of the fiscal process in San Francisco which we have now achieved does not, therefore, reveal that socioeconomic structural development and political culture had no influence on fiscal policy, but that their meaning, effects, and point of entry into the fiscal process are different than these theories propose.

In this chapter, we use this understanding to build and test a final statistical model of fiscal policymaking in San Francisco. We begin by recapitulating the arguments of the preceding chapters and reconsidering earlier statistical models in light of these arguments. Then we test a new model of this process and consider the implications of its results for the history of San Francisco and for the major propositions of the two theories in question.

RECAPITULATING THE ARGUMENT

San Francisco policymakers were both more autonomous than predicted by the socioeconomic structural theory and less autonomous than predicted by the political cultural theory. Without realizing it, they resisted the demands created by socioeconomic development, but they were by no means free to deal with political clients in any way they chose. Instead, their conduct of the public sector was embedded in a specific institutional framework, informed by a well-developed set of ideas about appropriate fiscal policy, and constrained by the necessity to produce a policy that was politically strategic. For most of the nineteenth century, however, local leaders did not rail against the limitations on their policy initiative. On the contrary, the public sector was bound by chains that the policymakers themselves had forged.

At the level of institutions, these men insulated themselves—and the city's fiscal policy—from the vicissitudes of change in either socioeconomic structure or political culture. They did this by creating and maintaining fiscal institutions that, by charter and by custom, enshrined an incremental style of fiscal policymaking. By charter, we may recall, the budgetary process began in February with reports to the supervisors on the expenditure and activities of the various departments during the current year, along with requests for changes in funding for the next.

Thus the reference point for fiscal policymakers was past activities, not future needs. For most of this period, too, the only participants in this process were other elected municipal officials, who were, for the most part, content with small increases in their budgets because they, too, were subject to an electoral political discipline. Outside groups that might have been more authentic carriers of demands generated by socioeconomic structural development were not regularly involved in the fiscal process until the 1890s.

The satisfaction of insiders with small increases and the tardiness of outsiders to involve themselves in the policymaking process were the results of an ideological boundary on fiscal politics. Participants in the fiscal political debates developed an ideology that rationalized a no-growth position on the public sector. In practice, this meant that only marginal increases in the city's budget were tolerable. Although the Dollar Limit was the clearest operational measure of this ideology, the limit existed and persisted only because of the widespread, preexisting belief that little or no good could come from the expansion of local government. For many, such expansion was a positive evil.

As the century progressed, these institutional and ideological influences on fiscal policy suffered different fates. The central thrust of the reform movement was the argument that a larger, more efficient public sector would better serve the needs of all, and the political coalition behind reform was cemented by means of promises of benefits from the public sector. By 1902, when the Dollar Limit was temporarily suspended, the belief that government expansion was a positive good was more widespread among policymakers, although the incremental basis of fiscal policymaking continued to serve as an anchor on this expansion until the earthquake. Whereas earlier politicians had used previous values to demonstrate their frugality and later ones stressed their commitment to services or improvements, both justified their policies by reference to the past.

At the outer edge of these boundaries was yet another, composed of political strategy and the opportunities provided and constraints imposed by the schedule of elections and the rules for exercise of the suffrage. One short-term effect of political strategy was to force fiscal policymaking into an electoral cycle corresponding to whether or not a fiscal year was an election year. For this reason the tax rate or expenditure was in several cases higher in nonelection years and lower in election years (see chaps. 5, 6, and 7). Whatever a given administration—or official within that administration—hoped to accomplish with fiscal policy, it had to be accomplished within two years, only one of which was free from the pressure of an election campaign in which the tax rate and the state of the public purse were bound to be an issue. In general, then, the short-term, politically strategic politician tried to stay within reasonable boundaries of past behavior, avoid outraging the fiscal consensus, and avoid making substantial increases in the tax rate or expenditure in election years. Defined in this way, there was a political ethos operating in the city, but it was based on the calculus of political self-interest, not on the necessities of the poor or of immigrants.

These more or less short-term strategic decisions were also affected by long-term changes in politics, which widened or narrowed the possibilities for policy initiatives, assuming one had any. The five political eras we have identified in the city's history were a reality, but the motor of change from one to another, and the fiscal political possibilities within each era, were not the result of changes in political ethos, as previous historians have assumed. The movement from one period to another was accomplished by changes in the schedule of elections or in the mode of exercising the suffrage, and the policy possibilities within each period were influenced by the level of competition and party regularity.

From 1860 through 1873, independent parties controlled the city's politics because municipal elections were separate from other elections most of the time. For this reason, this era was characterized by a low level of political competition, a high level of incumbency among officials, and a low level of politicization of fiscal policy. During these years, the foundations of the public sector were laid and municipal expenditure per capita began its seemingly inexorable rise. The "two great, national" parties were able to enter the local political arena after 1873 because off-year municipal elections were eliminated and municipal elections coincided with state elections every other time. Both to establish their fiscal political reliability and because of increased competition, politicians in these years began to politicize fiscal policy through supervisorial cuts, mayoral vetoes, and, finally, the Dollar Limit.

From 1882 through 1890, municipal elections were always held at the same time as other elections, and party-printed, straight-ticket ballots were the rule. These procedures introduced full-scale partisan political competition into every municipal election, producing high levels of political regularity and competition and historically low levels of taxation and expenditure. The effect of the 1892 Reform Ballot Act was to damage the party system by multiplying the number of tickets in the field, detaching the fate of local candidates from the top of the ticket, and decreasing party regularity and incumbency. In part because of these changes, between 1892 and 1899 the political conventions lost control over fiscal policymaking and the political salience of the Dollar Limit declined. Simultaneously, the demands for improvements increased and the mayor temporarily lost his veto. While the old electoral political system was staggered, reformers reorganized both fiscal and electoral politics by forming the pro-improvement coalition and campaigning for the reformed charter.

The two most important political changes brought about by the new charter were the separation of municipal elections from others and the election of supervisors at large. The first change introduced the possibilities of both an exclusively municipal politics and independent political action. The second restored a high level of incumbency among the supervisors. From the first fiscal year under the charter, 1900/01, until the earthquake, the Phelan and Schmitz administrations carried out the reform program in fiscal politics which was made possible by these new political conditions.

The inclusion of these political, ideological, and institutional influences not only broadens the analysis by adding more information but also specifies it by clarifying relationships among the fiscal variables and thus helping to identify the point of entry into the policymaking process of nonfiscal variables. The institutional framework within which fiscal policy was made set in motion a causal path through the fiscal variables from the valuation, which was least influenced by the other fiscal variables, to the expenditure, which was most influenced by other fiscal variables. Along this path, socioeconomic, ideological, political, and fiscal influences affected some of the fiscal variables directly, others only indirectly.

This path properly begins with the valuation, which was the only fixed value in the policymaking process. The assessor passed the value of the valuation on to the auditor, and there is no evidence that the auditor ever went back to the assessor with a request to raise the assessment, thus enabling the city to raise more revenue to cover more expenditure. The causal arrow from the valuation to the other fiscal variables went only one way. Moreover, tests in chapters 3 and 4 suggested that the valuation was the fiscal variable most strongly and positively affected by socioeconomic variables such as business at the port and manufacturing, which represented the two cornerstones of local economic development.

As indicated by the attempts in the 1880s and 1890s to minimize the increases in the valuation from year to year, the valuation was not immune to purely political influence. However, it was by no means as politicized as the next variable on the causal path, the tax rate. As we saw in chapter 2, the valuation and the tax rate were negatively correlated, which means, within this causal framework, that when the valuation increased, the tax rate decreased. It did so because it was the most closely watched and politically sensitive of all the fiscal variables. In earlier statistical tests, the tax rate was the fiscal variable most strongly affected by the political eras, while among the socioeconomic variables it followed the trend in real estate sales, the most cyclical of the socioeconomic variables. The historical account in the last three chapters indicates that the rate was frequently lower in an election year than otherwise, and also lower during the years of the Dollar Limit.

The direct influence of these socioeconomic, ideological, and political factors became indirect in the determination of the levels of revenue and expenditure. Because local revenue was, in part, simply the product (in the mathematical sense) of the tax rate and the valuation, all direct influences on the valuation and the rate affected the revenue indirectly. However, there is no evidence that any of these variables had direct effects on the revenue. On the contrary, revenue appears to have been simply the sum of its parts—namely, the taxes raised on the base; revenue from fees, licenses, and fines; and the amount of cash on hand at the end of the preceding year. The amount of revenue available, in turn, obviously had a direct effect on the level of expenditure in a given year. Because revenue carried within it the direct effects of socioeconomic development on the valuation and of political strategy on the tax rate, it also carried the indirect effects of these factors to expenditure. However, earlier statistical tests demonstrated that neither socioeconomic nor political variables directly explain much of the variation in expenditure, and this suggests that the direct influence of these variables was mediated by the other fiscal variables.

Both statistical and historical evidence from the preceding chapters suggests that this is a reasonable representation of the role of these variables in the fiscal process. To determine whether or not this was the way the process typically operated, and to understand the relative weight of the influential variables, we must turn again to statistical tests. The coefficients in a regression analysis reveal the effects of the independent variables on the dependent variable at their means, or "on average." In the case of variables arranged in time-series, as these are, regression analysis reveals these effects in the "average" year. The statistical analysis that follows does not determine whether, say, political strategy affected fiscal policy, because we already know from our historical account of fiscal policymaking in San Francisco that, on occasion, it did. Instead, statistical analysis tells us whether these effects were important on average, and how important they were compared with those of other influences.

The variables available for this analysis include all those we have used this far: the fiscal variables themselves, the measures of socioeconomic structure, and the political-era variables. But our understanding of the political-era variables is different now, as just indicated, so the last period must be redefined. The political-era variables do not measure differences in political culture but in political structure, and the changes in political structure brought about by the new charter were the same for all administrations under it, whether headed by James D. Phelan or Eugene Schmitz. The last era in the city's political history within our time span should thus extend from fiscal year 1900/01 through fiscal year 1905/06, which were the years in which fiscal policy was controlled by officials elected under the new charter. And the preceding era should extend from 1893/94 through 1899/1900, which were the last years controlled by officials elected under the old charter, though also under the banner of reform.

In addition to these variables, we use measures of the past behavior of government itself; the components of local revenue; the electoral political discipline to which all officials were subject; and the most significant production of the city's fiscal ideology in these years, the Dollar Limit. Values of the fiscal variables lagged by one year will control for the effects of past fiscal decisionmaking. Variables composing the revenue in this test include the per capita values of cash on hand at the end of the previous fiscal year, non–property-tax revenue, and the product of the tax rate times the valuation. To determine whether the coincidence of a fiscal year with an election year was a constraint on fiscal policy, I created an election-year dummy variable that is 1 in an election year and 0 otherwise. The coefficient on this variable measures the difference in fiscal variables produced by the presence of an election year. Similarly, the Dollar Limit variable is 1 when the limit was in effect and 0 otherwise. The limit was present in all party platforms from 1882 through 1899, and in the city's charter thereafter. However, the new charter institutionalized new exemptions from the limit, provided for its legal suspension, and changed the character of the political competition that had enforced it. For these reasons, the "real" Dollar Limit was the one originated and enforced by the party platforms during the fiscal years from 1883 through 1900.

The path through the fiscal variables just discussed suggests that the valuation is affected by its own value in the preceding year, the election-year dummy variable, the five political-era variables, and the lagged measures of socioeconomic structural development included in earlier tests—namely, per capita business at the port, per capita value of manufacturing, the number of real estate sales per 100 population, and the number of manufacturing works per 100 acres in the city's industrial districts. The valuation carried the indirect influence of all these variables forward in its effect on the tax rate, which was also affected by its own value in the previous year, the election-year dummy variable, the political eras, and the number of real estate sales per 100 population. The direct influences on the tax rate and the valuation were carried forward into the revenue, which was affected by the per capita values of the product of the rate and the valuation, current expenditure, cash on hand at the end of the previous year, and non–property-tax local revenue. The per capita expenditure was affected indirectly by all of these variables, but directly only by the revenue and its own previous value. All of these variables are listed and defined in table 37. The results of the equations are listed in table 38, in which lagged values of the variables are indicated by the "(−1)" suffix. In these equations, the excluded political-era variable is that of the new charter (1901–1906). This means that the coefficients for the included eras measure the difference in the adjusted means of the dependent variables during the new charter era and each of the others. There are few surprises in the results.[1]

The variables with a statistically significant effect on the valuation include the lagged value of the valuation itself, business at the port, and the value of manufactures on the positive side; and they include the lagged value of real estate sales per 100 population, the election year, and the second and third eras of the city's political history on the negative side. Business at the port and the value of manufactures pumped

TABLE 37

VARIABLES IN THE EQUATIONS

Variable name	Explanation
EXP	Per capita operating expenditure (mean = $14.31)
REV	Per capita local revenue (mean = $13.66)
VAL	Per capita assessed valuation of real and personal property (mean = $987.58)
TAX	Tax rate per $100 of assessed valuation (mean = $1.19)
CASH	Per capita value of cash on hand at the close of the fiscal year (mean = $3.43)
OREV	Per capita value of non-property-tax local revenue (mean = $2.09)
TAXVAL	Per capita value of the tax rate times the assessed valuation (mean = $11.68)
PORT	Per capita value of imports and exports at the port (mean = $277.07)
WORKS	Number of manufacturing works per 100 acres in the manufacturing districts (mean = 18.65)
MANVAL	Per capita value of manufactured products (mean = $231.24)
RES	Number of real estate sales per 100 population (mean = 1.63)
PTP	Period of local reform parties, 1870–1876
IRREG	Period following collapse of local reform parties, 1877–1883
MACHINE	Period of control by national party machines, 1884–1893
REFORM	Period of control by Populist and progressive reformers, 1894–1900
CHARTER	Period of new city charter, 1901–1906
ELECYR	Election year, yes/no
DOLLIM	Period of Dollar Limit enforced by local platforms, 1883–1900

TABLE 38

FINAL MODEL OF THE POLICYMAKING PROCESS[a]

Vars. and Stats.	VAL	Vars. and Stats.	TAX	Vars. and Stats.	REV	Vars. and Stats.	EXP
VAL(−1)	.1930[a]	TAX(−1)	.2845[d]	EXP	.4224[b]	EXP(−1)	.6375[b]
PORT(−1)	3.33[b]	VAL	−.0007[b]	CASH(−1)	.1099	REV	.2607[c]
MANVAL(−1)	1.30[c]	RES(−1)	.1575[b]	OREV	.1832	Constant	1.593[d]
RES(−1)	−68.18[c]	PTP	.2639[d]	TAXVAL	.3401[b]	Adj. R-Sq.	.7990
WORKS(−1)	5.66	IRREG	.0730	Constant	2.894	Rho	−.1044
PTP	3.723	MACHINE	.0386	Adj. R-Sq.	.7547		
IRREG	−398.06[b]	REFORM	.5127[b]	Rho	−.0550		
MACHINE	−321.81[c]	ELECYR	−.0967				
REFORM	80.22	DOLLIM	−.3770[b]				
ELECYR	−264.44[b]	Constant	1.422[b]				
Constant	−108.84	Adj. R-Sq.	.8509				
Adj. R-Sq.	.9186	Rho	−.2228				
Rho	−.7944						

[a] N = 35 (1870–1905).
[b] Significant at .01 level.
[c] Significant at .05 level.
[d] Significant at .10 level.

value into the next year's valuation, which increased $3.33 for every $1 increase in the former and $1.30 for every $1 increase in the latter. When the valuation itself went up $1, the next year's valuation increased by $0.19. Conversely, in an election year the valuation was an average of $264 lower per capita than in a nonelection year; it was lower in the years 1876–1883 and 1884–1893 than under the new charter; and it was higher by $68 per capita when real estate sales were lower by 1 per 100 population.

The valuation carried these influences within it in its negative effect on the tax rate, which was also affected negatively by the Dollar Limit and positively by its own lagged value, the number of real estate sales, and the first and last two periods in the city's history. When the valuation for the current year went up by $1 per capita, the tax rate went down by $0.0007. When the rate itself increased by $0.01, it increased the next year by $0.0028. The rate was lower by $0.37 under the Dollar Limit than otherwise. The coefficient on the election-year dummy variable had its expected negative sign but was not statistically significant, perhaps in part because electoral political pressure on the tax rate was highest under the Dollar Limit, and controlling for the limit, as this equation does, may wash out the effect of the election year. Yet when real estate sales increased by 1 per 100 population, the tax rate increased by $0.15 the next year. The tax rate was also higher during 1870–1876 and 1893–1900 than under the new charter, although it was high then, too, as the positive and significant coefficients on the political-era variables and the constant indicate.[2]

The product of the rate and the valuation had its expected positive effect on revenue, along with the level of expenditure in the current year. An increase of $1 per capita in the former brought about a $0.34 increase in revenue, and a similar increase in expenditure produced an increase of $0.34 in the revenue. Expenditure, of course, was influenced positively by the revenue and also by its own previous value. The determination of the level of expenditure in any year began with the levels of expenditure in the previous year. A $1 increase in the lagged value of expenditure brought about a $0.64 increase in current expenditure, an effect greater than that of a $1 increase in revenue in the current year, which brought about a $0.26 increase in current expenditure.

The negative relationship between the valuation and the tax rate in these equations reflects the tension between the socioeconomic and political influences on the city's fiscal policy, as well as the different roles that these fiscal variables played in the mediation of these effects by the city's policymakers. The assessed valuation did capture some of the wealth created by commercial and industrial development. Commerce and manufacturing were not only of great significance to the economic development in the city but were also to some extent countercyclical to each other (see chap. 3). When business at the port was down during the depression of the 1870s, manufacturing was up; when manufacturing plunged during the depression of the 1890s, business at the port suffered less and rebounded more quickly. In part because it was driven by those variables, the valuation was negatively related to the number of real estate sales per 100 population. This does not mean that a decline in real estate sales caused a rise in the valuation, but that the valuation stayed high when the number of real estate sales dropped.

The tax rate, in contrast, was influenced positively by this cyclical and closely watched variable. When the number of real estate sales per 100 population increased by 1, the tax rate for the next year could increase by $0.15, other things being equal. The different responses to this variable by the valuation and the rate have both economic and institutional explanations. The valuation was not only driven by other socioeconomic variables but was also "sticky" in the downward direction because it was based on real estate prices, which, like all prices, are slow to fall. The lag between a decline in real estate activity—which is what the number of sales measures—and real estate prices might very well be significantly longer than one year, because of this stickiness of prices. The tax rate, by contrast, was both more sensitive to short-term fluctuation in commercial activity and stickier in an upward direction. A decline in real estate sales in one year could bring the realtors into city hall demanding tax relief in the next (see chap. 5). For political reasons, it was easy to lower the rate and hard to raise it at all. Nevertheless, it was easier to raise the tax rate when times were thought to be good, and the number of real estate sales was one way in which the quality of the times was measured.

In the average year, then, controlling for previous decisionmaking and with other things being equal, the more stable and "sticky" valuation tracked the main engines of economic growth in the city, while the tax rate, which was more flexible in a downward direction, tracked a shorter cycle in the business economy. However, as the political variables indicate, an average year in which other things were equal was rare indeed. The coefficient on the election-year dummy variable indicates that in an election year the valuation was lower than otherwise. The assessor, too, was an elected official, after all. Moreover, the coefficients on the eras of irregularity and of the political machine indicate that the valuation was lower in these years (1876 through 1893) than in the era under the new charter, which is the excluded comparison era in both of these equations. The coefficient on the Dollar Limit indicates that it was doing its job of holding down the tax rate from 1883 through 1900. Even so, the rate crept up slightly from 1893 through 1900, when the limit was still the declared policy of the municipal platforms, and more substantially after the new charter, when it was no longer enforced by partisan competition. Given all these political limitations, opportunities for real growth in one or both of these fiscal variables occurred, on average, only in nonelection years before 1876 and after 1900, which were the years when separate municipal elections facilitated independent political action, encouraged a strictly municipal policy, and reduced the politicization of fiscal policy.[3]

The mediation of these influences by the valuation and the tax rate produced one of two statistically significant influences on the revenue, which was itself one of two statistically significant influences on expenditure. The product of the rate and the valuation, along with the plans for expenditure for the same year, explained $0.76 of every $1 of the revenue, other things being equal. In turn, the revenue available, along with figures on last year's expenditure, accounted for $0.89 of every $1 of expenditure per capita.

The adjusted R^2 for each of these equations, which ranges from a high of 0.9186 for the valuation to a low of 0.7547 for the revenue, indicates that they explain more of the variation in each of the fiscal variables than any of the other combinations we have tested, despite the fact that those combinations contained more independent variables than some of these do. Less is more in this model, because it (1) includes the effects of institutional, ideological, and political variables which were missing in earlier tests, and (2) follows the proper path from one fiscal variable to another. The most important evidence for the propriety of this path is historical; this is the way the system actually worked. However, there is a small bit of symbolic statistical confirmation for the model presented here, which conceives of the valuation as the main carrier of long-term socioeconomic effects, the tax rate as the carrier of shorter-term economic and political effects, and the revenue and expenditure as products of the influences of the policymaking process itself. Standardized measures of the relative influence of the independent variables in each equation indicate that the valuation was most strongly influenced by business at the port; the tax rate, by the era of reform; the revenue, by the current year's expenditure; and expenditure, by its own lagged value. In the end, expenditure was the most incremental fiscal variable, although it is important to note that this presentation of the process is not, strictly speaking, an incrementalist one.

As we have seen, incrementalism was built into the city's fiscal system, both because previous levels of expenditure were the basis on which estimates for coming years were made and because, in general, increases in expenditure or taxation and assessment were marginal. Political scientists have long been aware of the effects of this incrementalism and have proposed an incremental theory of the development of fiscal policy. Among others working within this framework, John P. Crecine and Aaron Wildavsky have argued that the budget is an "internally determined event" in which available revenue, previous levels of expenditure, and system inertia are the major influences. According to Wildavsky, "the largest determining factor of the size and content of this year's budget is last year's budget." This perspective has found its way into the historical literature in J. Rogers Hollingsworth and Ellen Jane Hollingsworth's 1979 study, *Dimensions in Urban History*. After examining the expenditures of mid-sized American cities in 1900, they agreed with Wildavsky and others that "excepting moments of crisis, budget decisionmaking operates to produce a process of incrementalism in public expenditures."[4]

As John Jackson has pointed out, the key to incremental theory is the belief that changes in revenue are "exogenous" and made independently of expenditure decisions. Incrementalists like Crecine argue that tax rates are adjusted to increase revenue only occasionally, whereas the amount of revenue is routinely fixed before expenditure is planned. Thus observed changes in expenditure are simply a function of changes in revenue, which are distributed according to "very stable rules of thumb."[5]

As useful as such a perspective may be for explaining the routinized world of contemporary policymaking, it does not closely resemble the situation in San Francisco. I have argued that the valuation was exogenous to the other fiscal variables, but the tax rate—and thus the revenue—was not. Adjustments to the tax rate to produce more or less revenue continued right up to the end of every fiscal year. Moreover, the entire process was subject to political influences at every stage. In San Francisco, therefore, it is appropriate to say that the measure of change in fiscal policy was incremental, in that the starting point for the next year's policy was always the current year's. But the fiscal policymaking process was not incrementalist in the sense proposed by the present-day theory of incrementalism.

An incremental or marginal approach to fiscal policymaking was a constant in San Francisco, but the interesting and important point of this analysis is that, controlling for this influence, other factors also played a role there. Socioeconomic development poured a potential river of revenue into the fiscal system. Under the pressure of electoral political pressure and fiscal political pledges, however, the city's policymakers dammed and directed this flow in strikingly similar fashion, with the ultimate goal, for at least most of the nineteenth century, of reducing it to a trickle. Because fiscal policy responded not to the logic of socioeconomic structural change but to the calculus of political advantage, the task of fiscal policymakers was not to manage scarcity but to create it: to find a level of assessment, taxation, and thus revenue and expenditure which reflected not the city's great potential to finance the growth of the public sector but a demand for low taxation. This required turning off the supply of public resources created by the city's development. Election-year strategies and the politicization of fiscal policy generally reduced the valuation. The same electoral pressure and the platform pledge of the Dollar Limit kept the tax rate low, and by the time expenditure was authorized, the potential abundance for the public sector was eliminated. For most of these years, policymakers looked not forward to the needs of the city but backward, both to the higher expenditure in the early years of the city's history and, more immediately, to recent values of fiscal variables, which dictated the range within which marginal increases were politically tolerable.

The waves of socioeconomic development crashed against this political dam continuously and at times lapped over the top, as in the late 1890s, when the coalescence of economic and political crises led to increasing taxes. The dam did not break, however. Rather, its sluice gates were opened by reformers, who eventually bypassed the old fiscal political system in the 1890s, then destroyed it by means of the new charter as the new century opened. As both historical and statistical evidence indicate, between 1876 and 1899, the valuation and/or the tax rate were held down by political influences. Both were unleashed after 1901 by the new charter, and thus the historic tension between socioeconomic development and political strategy was reduced. After the new charter, politicians were still influenced by electoral pressure, of course, and the rate and valuation remained lower in an election year than otherwise. But they were never again as low as they had been. The reform coalition promised that the new government would respond more fully to the needs of a growing city. This meant that thereafter, for better or worse, governmental growth and socioeconomic change were mixed in the same raging torrent.

RECONSIDERING THE POLITICAL CULTURAL THEORY

By specifying the point at which socioeconomic development entered the fiscal political system, our analysis has reformulated but by no means discarded the socioeconomic structural theory. It has not done the same for the political cultural theory, which seems irrelevant to the San Francisco situation, no matter how twisted or patched. In San Francisco, bosses and reformers did not act in accordance with this theory. On the one hand, much of their behavior seemed to be shaped by similar institutional, ideological and political strategic factors. On the other hand, within the framework of political opportunity created by those factors, the bosses and reformers acted in ways opposite to those predicted by the political cultural theory: Irish-born bosses spent less; elite reformers spent more. In San Francisco, the patron saint of the public sector was not the rumpled old politician but the high-powered downtown businessman. Is this contradiction between theory and practice the result of peculiarities of the case or problems with the theory?

Not surprisingly, I lean toward the latter interpretation. The contradiction stems from the fact that the political cultural theory is based entirely on supposition. In fact, the theory is based on three major assumptions that have been challenged by recent research, both in San Francisco and elsewhere. First, it has assumed that lower-class culture in general and ethnic cultures in particular lacked the organizational, financial, or cultural resources to deal with the needs of the lower class or the foreign-born, and hence that these groups had to turn to the public sector—especially machine politics—for their sociability and social welfare services. Second, the theory has assumed that occupational mobility was blocked for immigrants and others, so that it was necessary for political actors to create an alternate route of social mobility funded by patronage. Third, and most important for this study, this theory has assumed that political culture of the sort we have been analyzing as the result of fiscal political ideology and action was somehow either epiphenomenal or artificial, but in any event not as important as social needs or political ethos.

Recent work of historians of ethnicity and mobility in San Francisco and elsewhere has completely repudiated the first two of these assumptions. Ethnic historians have revealed a variety of family and ethnic-group strategies for economic and cultural survival, which may very well have mitigated or removed the need to turn to politics for either organizational stability or social services. In Robert Burchell's careful study of the Irish in San Francisco to 1880, for example, he finds an extensive network of familial, religious, and ethnic organizations meeting the economic and cultural needs of this group, which was a mainstay of the Democratic party. Although the party was an important organization to the Irish, it was not the most important such organization, and there is no evidence that there was a greater need to obtain sociability via politics during the 1880s than at any other time. In fact, Burchell argues that by 1880, the Irish were fully integrated into the city's social and political structure. It is his argument, too, that the Irish had no particular need for patronage-sponsored social mobility because their rate of occupational mobility was comparable to that of other groups and their rate of home ownership was, in fact, higher than other groups.[6]

Similarly, work in the history of social mobility in San Francisco and elsewhere has revealed that occupational and property mobility was available to immigrant and working-class males on a wide scale. These studies suggest that those who stayed in one place long enough to "count" politically—to become, for example, part of the 50 percent of eligible males who voted regularly in San Francisco—were older, more occupationally mobile, and more likely to own property. However, the process by which these small occupational and property gains were consolidated was a difficult one, usually requiring the mobilization of all family members into the labor market and, even then, the practice of what Stephan Thernstrom has rightly called "ruthless underconsumption."[7]

This work raises important questions about both the need and the desire of urban residents for the expansion of the public sector. Within the precariously balanced family economy of the small, urban property-holder, any proposal for the expansion of the public sector had to be balanced against the only definite, direct, and concrete consequence of that expansion: higher property-tax liability. Similarly, in the calculations of the urban politician, the benefits produced by the creation of a few new patronage positions had to be balanced against the political costs of raising the property-tax liability of thousands of small holders like those who sat on the board of supervisors.

As we have seen, San Francisco politicians were well aware of these calculations, and they built a political culture on this basis. These men did not float in the imaginary world of unlimited fiscal resources that the political cultural historians appear to occupy. Rather, they hammered out fiscal policy between numerous rocks and hard places created by intense political competition and a political culture in which fiscal scarcity was a virtue. For this reason, the results of this analysis repudiate the third assumption of the political cultural theory. Fiscal political culture—represented in the platforms, campaigns, finance committee reports, and political decisions of this period—was a strong and autonomous force in the city's fiscal politics and a bulwark against the expansion of the local public sector. Moreover, it was a force constructed by real political actors who were willing to postpone the satisfaction of social needs or the construction of the "Paris of the West" forever, if necessary.

The most recent application of the political cultural theory to the history of San Francisco is in William Bullough's 1979 biography of Christopher Buckley, *The Blind Boss and His City*. Bullough's careful account of Buckley's life and richly detailed analysis of the inner workings of the city's Democratic party during the 1880s make this book an important contribution to the history of the city. His explanation of the differences between "bosses" and "reformers" in the city rests not on his own indefatigable research, however, but on an almost ideal typical restatement of the political cultural theory. According to Bullough, "the latent functions of the Democratic machine in San Francisco furnished to the urban working classes services which official agencies were unprepared to render: relief, employment, sociability, and alleviation of the anomie characteristic of life in the industrial city." For their part, however, the reformers who replaced Buckley offered no "tenable alternatives to the machine's services"; they "took the political organization out of the employment and welfare business, but they offered no official programs or policies to replace these critical functions of the machine." Moreover, Bullough argues, either by chance or by design, the reform programs "reduced citizens' identification with and participation in municipal government and politics, for better or worse."[8]

When Buckley identified his greatest accomplishment as the putative leader of the city's politics from 1882 to 1891, however, he did not cite the provision of the proverbial Christmas turkey or of a "place where any bloke can come for help," as other bosses—or their raconteurs—might have suggested. Rather, Buckley named his maintenance of the Dollar Limit. "When I introduced the Dollar Limit pledge into the Democratic platform," he wrote, "I must confess that I builded [sic] far better than I knew." Neither Buckley nor his Republican counterpart, Martin Kelly, ever claimed to operate a social welfare business; one searches their memoirs in vain for the "Plunkitt of Tammany Hall" type of stories of social welfare provisions. In fact, they and the other leaders of their parties would have been astounded at such a notion, especially if it involved increasing municipal expenditure. They saw their function as that of protecting the taxpayer's purse by minimizing municipal expenditure, including patronage expenditure, and thereby keeping tax rates and assessed valuations low. The political organizations of the 1880s simply were not in the employment or welfare business on a large scale, so it cannot be said that the reformers took the political organizations out of that business.[9]

In the realm of political participation, the story also seems different. During the 1880s, the political machines mobilized registered voters (with a healthy assist from the new election dates), but they did not expand the size of the electorate as a share of eligible males. During the reform era, the share of registered males increased, while the participation of those registered decreased. This decline, however, was apparent beginning in 1892, when the effects of the Reform Ballot Act, a statewide reform, were first felt. When municipal elections were separated from other elections as a result of the reform charter, participation in municipal elections dropped, but only to the levels that were typical historically for municipal elections held separately from others.

Phelan and his cohorts did not smash a preexisting social welfare system inadvertently funded by the public sector, nor did they introduce or reintroduce anomie or political alienation into the city. But neither did they rescue the city from a municipal government that was either hopelessly corrupt or inefficient. Neither contemporaries like the grand jury and the Merchants' Association nor later historians have discovered evidence of serious or widespread municipal corruption in these years. In fact, the evidence considered in this analysis is the opposite; in the main, and given their lights, municipal officials in the 1880s and 1890s did the best job they could. Moreover, there is no evidence that city government was becoming less (or more) efficient in the 1890s. The complaints about too much spent on salaries were perennial; they could be found in any year after 1860, just as they are to this day. When we look at where the money went in the 1890s, a good deal of it went for improvements. The salary categories of real growth were not for deputies and clerks in the executive offices but for the police and fire departments, which were growing in response to demand from outlying districts for more protection. Historically, both by custom and politics, the city government had responded to requests from inside rather than outside itself. When confronted with continuing demands from outside, the government did what it could, but it continued to place first priority on the reproduction of or marginal increases in the services to which it was already committed, depending on the amount of resources available in a given year.

While it was neither hopelessly corrupt nor pathetically inefficient, local government was, in fact, paralyzed between the demands for increasing expenditure on improvements and citizens' unwillingness to pay the taxes necessary both to continue everyday government operations at current levels and to embark upon those improvements. The reformers did not solve this problem; on the contrary, they set out to aggravate it. By simultaneously emphasizing the corruption and inefficiency of local government, encouraging the improvement groups and other organizations to demand even more from the local treasury, and promising everyone that substantial benefits would come only from a city government under their control and organized under a new charter, the reformers delegitimized the preexisting municipal political system and enthroned their own.

In explaining his downfall, Buckley noted that while he was boss, "what I really had to fear was the silent ill will of men of intellect and power—men who had the skill to plan deeply and the ability to execute their plans." Without naming names, Buckley would have had to include James D. Phelan in this category, because Phelan was certainly the youngest and perhaps the most brilliant of those who ousted Buckley. More generous and more specific—perhaps because he was less personally stung—Republican "Boss" Martin Kelly called Phelan "the real founder of modern political history in San Francisco."[10]

When Kelly said this, he referred specifically to Phelan's role in the 1898 passage of the reform charter. Although the victory of the charter was not solely the result of a personal crusade by Phelan, it would not have succeeded without the backing of this phenomenally popular and successful young mayor. However, this was the least of his contributions to "modern political history" in the city. More important in the long run were his transformation of the political image of the mayor and his development of a pluralistic reform coalition.

Phelan was the first mayoral candidate in the city's history to admit that he sought the party's nomination and to conduct a vigorous, city-wide campaign for the mayoralty. In accepting the party's nomination in 1896, Phelan declared that it was "no honor to accept a nomination to go out to the people and then to wait until they come to you." On the contrary, he pledged to the Democratic ratification meeting that he would "go out to them" and "convince them that your policy is in their interest." Accordingly, he set out on the first truly citywide campaign in the history of San Francisco. In 1896 this campaign took him to two or three meetings a night from mid-September until early November, so that by the end of the campaign he had spoken at scores of gatherings. In one week of the campaign, he spoke to meetings that were estimated to have attended by twelve thousand people. He continued this pattern through four more campaigns as well.[11]

Because Phelan sought victory for himself and his reform ideas, he was much more conscious of the necessity of building a political coalition than his predecessors had been. Although a lifelong Democrat, Phelan considered himself an insurgent within his party as well as an enemy of the Republicans and of the entire old system of municipal electoral and fiscal politics. As such, he felt required to go outside the parties and build a coalition of groups that were left out of politics as usual—namely businessmen, improvement groups, and the working class. The one thing that Phelan had to offer to each of these groups which did not immediately require difficult choices among them was benefits from an expanding public sector. Businessmen had little or nothing to do with politics, but were easily convinced that they got nothing from their taxes. "Suburban" homeowners, represented by the improvement groups, had concrete evidence that they got little for their taxes; even some of the city's basic services had yet to be extended to their areas. Moreover, when these groups appealed to the supervisors, they were frequently advised to "work through the system," although the system was paralyzed by its commitments to limits on taxation and assessed valuation. Workers, in fact, had received nothing specific from the parties since the end of the campaign against the Chinese in the early 1880s. However, the grievances of these groups, as real as they were, were politically latent; although socioeconomic development "produced" workers, businessmen, and neighborhood expansion, it did not point them in the direction of the public sector.

Because Phelan's papers for the period before the earthquake no longer exist, we do not know how he came to recognize the political possibilities in this situation. But from his campaign in 1896, we do know that he set out to build the latent potential of those estranged from the municipal system, and that his goal was a manifest, powerful coalition based in part on promises that each of the elements of the coalition would receive benefits from a better-managed, efficient, and expanding public sector. Whether or not Phelan realized it, he won in 1896 by bringing O'Donnell supporters back into the Democratic fold and eliminating this sort of "left wing" opposition. Having personally led the "right wing" of the reform movement (i.e., the Merchants' Association and improvement clubs), he set out to woo the "left" by offering both symbolic and real rewards to labor. Thus reform in San Francisco was forced, because of its politically insurgent status, to be pluralistic in its class and ethnic bases. Although elites led the movement, it won because it mobilized groups that had been neglected by the pre-reform system.

It was Phelan, not the bosses, who had "a broad pluralistic understanding" of municipal politics, and Phelan who introduced into the city's political history a cross-class political organization mobilized on the basis of pre-election promises of group-specific benefits from the public sector. It was because of this coalition that Phelan won an unprecedented three terms as the city's mayor, along with victories for a reform charter and bonded indebtedness for improvements. Even the denouement of the reform movement after 1901 supports this interpretation, because the bitterness against Phelan and his allies, which resulted in the victories for his Union Labor party successor, rested in the improvement groups and the labor movement. These were fiscal-political interest groups that Phelan himself had mobilized into action. The bargain that Phelan and the other elite reformers thought they had struck with the city's electorate was this: "You let us run the government and we will respond more fully to your needs." The Union Labor party challenged Phelan and his allies over the definition of the "us" in the bargain, not over the terms of the bargain itself.

In hindsight, the bargain seems Faustian, because it brought with it the potential for unlimited fiscal obligation, interest-group elitism, bureaucratic politics, and hitherto unimagined levels of government intervention in a wide array of activities. Armed with this hindsight, historians have ransacked the past in search of an urban political world in which the needs of both politics and society were better met. Under the banner of the political cultural theory, they have abstracted the history of the urban public sector from the political context in which it must be understood, lionizing men of limited vision who were willing to ignore social needs to maintain political power and denigrating men who took genuine political risks to open up politics and the public sector. Naturally, both "bosses" and "reformers" sought political power, but it is an injustice to the past to ignore this in one case and lament it in the other.

Furthermore, in creating a past in which there was a smooth fit between politics and society, urban historians have implied that urban government "worked" once, but does so no longer. Yet contemporary urban government looks different from past urban government only if we ignore the fiscal constraints, bureaucratic interests, and struggles for power that were just as problematic then as they are now. The current call for the old party system is symptomatic of the triumph of this nostalgic view of urban politics and, in particular, of the politics of the urban political machine. Alas, as always, we can neither take refuge from the present by retreating into the past nor improve the present by imagining the past.

9

Reconciling Theory and Practice in General

At the end of a lengthy case study, the reader has the right to wonder about the typicality of the case; the author, however, has the duty not to exaggerate it. Unfortunately, the wisdom of this principle has been recognized only slowly by urban historians. They long ago admitted that "all the world" is not Philadelphia, Newburyport, or Lynn, but they have usually failed to resist the temptation to write as if it were. The result has been a tradition of conclusions to works of urban history in which a case originally chosen because of its proximity, available documentation, or fame as a site of important events or previous analyses becomes transmogrified into the epitome of its historical epoch. Clifford Geertz called this technique the "Jonesville-is-the-USA 'microcosmic' model," and correctly pointed out that it is so fallacious that "the only thing that needs explanation is how people have managed to believe it and expected others to believe it."[1]

By declaring a case study to be a microcosm, historians err in two ways. First, they deny the need for the genuinely comparative research that would really determine the typicality of the case, and, second, they fail to appreciate the fact that a historical case study can be important—typical or not—if it is structured in a way that tells us something both about history and about the way we think about history. As Geertz has said, small facts can speak to large issues if they are made to do so. However, the way they are made to do so is not by means of specious arguments about the typicality of the case, but by the conscious structuring of the analysis by means of theory.[2]

The focus of this chapter is not, therefore, on the typicality of San Francisco's history so much as on the place of my analysis of San Francisco's history in the stream of urban political historiography. Whether or not San Francisco was typical of other cities of its time, this analysis of San Francisco is typical of recent work in urban political history, which takes a more critical approach to the frameworks of the past while still working within them. The challenge to this work is to stop providing new answers to old questions and to move toward new frameworks for new questions. This chapter considers the staying power of the old frameworks and proposes a possible new approach to the subject.

THE PROBLEM OF TYPICALITY

Before turning to these issues, however, let me deal briefly with the issue of San Francisco's "typicality." As pointed out in chapter 3, I have not argued that San Francisco was somehow typical or representative of other cities of its size, nor do I intend now to sneak this argument in through the back door. I would like to know whether San Francisco's fiscal political history was typical, but there are neither the data nor the literature necessary to prove this systematically within the confines of this study.

The problem of data is twofold. Good data exist, but they are relatively unavailable; conversely, the census data that are easily available are relatively bad. The data with which one could accurately determine whether the fiscal policy of San Francisco (or any other city) was typical do exist, in volumes similar to the *Municipal Reports* of San Francisco which were issued by many American cities during the late nineteenth and early twentieth centuries. Time-series of fiscal data similar to those employed in this analysis could be collected from these volumes for some subset of cities comparable to San Francisco. The collection of these data alone would be a lengthy task, but that would be only the first and lesser hurdle. The second and more daunting obstacle would be the task of rendering these series comparable—that is, controlling for the different levels of service responsibility among cities at any one point in time and the changes in those levels within cities over time. Genuinely comparative fiscal history would be both enormously time-consuming and enormously important. I believe that such work should be done, but confess that I have not done it.[3]

The problems of comparability in these data are not solved but aggravated by what might at first glance appear to be conveniently available and useful compilations of urban fiscal statistics by the census bureau. An example of one such compilation demonstrates the problems with this source. In 1891 the census office issued a bulletin on "The Receipts and Expenditures of One Hundred Principal or Representative Cities of the United States." San Francisco was included in this analysis among the cities of the "First Class" (those with populations of more than 200,000). Detroit, with an 1890 population of 205,876, was the smallest city in this group, while pre-consolidation New York City, with an 1890 population of 1,515,301, was the largest. San Francisco's 1890 population was 298,997, which made it the eighth largest among these cities. The fiscal data in the bulletin attempted to compare the "ordinary" expenses and receipts of the cities. In the case of the former, these included expenditures on libraries, schools, fire, health, lighting, police, charitable objects, streets and bridges, sewers, public buildings and improvements, parks and public grounds, other salaries, water works or use of water, interest on debt, and miscellaneous.[4]

According to these figures, the average per capita ordinary expenditure for these fourteen First Class cities during the fiscal year ending in 1890 was $19.57. The standard deviation among the cities was $7.48, and all but four were within one standard deviation above or below the mean. Cleveland and New Orleans were more than one standard deviation below the mean, and their averages of $11.06 and $11.69 per capita, respectively, made them the least costly cities in this group. On the other end were Boston and New York, which were more than one standard deviation above the mean at $35.94 and $32.30 per capita, and therefore the most expensive cities in the group. San Francisco ranked almost exactly in the middle of the distribution among these cities, as the seventh most expensive, with per capita ordinary expenditures of $18.86, just $0.71 less than the average. It would seem hard to be more typical of cities of its size than that.

It would, however, be risky to conclude this or anything else on the basis of this report—or any other report produced by the census bureau before 1903—because of two important problems in the collection of data: (1) inconsistency between local and federal categories, and (2) failure to control for different statutorily determined levels of service responsibility among cities. To make some sense out of the welter of fiscal data, the bureau imposed its categories on the reports of the cities. According to the report, this recategorization was "in every case approved by the proper municipal officer or no objection was made thereto." One suspects that the latter was the case in more cities than not; in any case, the correspondence between local and federal categories was loose at best. For example, it has been impossible to determine how the expenditure categories of San Francisco were recombined in the census report.[5]

A more important problem was different levels of service responsibilities. Where services were provided at a level other than the municipal, "it was found impracticable to include their amounts." This was a reasonable strategy, but it led to the placement of zeros in those expenditure categories for some cities, and had, therefore, a dramatic effect on the per capita figures. Among the cities of the First Class, it appears that the remarkably low-cost cities, Cleveland and New Orleans, were so because they paid little or nothing for schools, which were an enormous component of the budgets of other cities. Cleveland, in fact, paid nothing for schools (neither did Cincinnati, which suggests county or state responsibility in Ohio), and New Orleans spent $182,000, which was less than $1 per capita. In contrast, the most expensive cities, Boston and New York, provided the full array of services, had no zeros in any category, and included the expenses of county government in their totals.[6]

The point here is not to nitpick at this essentially laudable attempt to collect information, but to point out that because of these problems the figures are almost useless for comparative purposes. One shudders to see that Superintendent of the Census Robert P. Porter offered the survey as a basis on which policy could be made, writing that "the figures given should suggest to the citizens of those places where such conditions exist a careful inquiry as to the causes of such extraordinarily high per capita expenditures." Use of these figures to determine what an "extraordinarily high" level of expenditure was would have been wrong then; their use to determine typicality now would simply compound the problem. Porter wrote more wisely, earlier in his introduction, that "few who have investigated the subject have an idea of the difficulties encountered in every step of this inquiry."[7]

Despite these problems of data, San Francisco could be put in a fiscal political context if there were a sufficient number of studies of fiscal politics elsewhere. Alas, there are not. Instead, as Jon Teaford has written, although the question of finance is basic to the history of all municipal policies, "the topic is one of the most neglected," and "historians have written blithely about waste, incompetence, and inefficiency in city government without ever testing these generalizations against the municipal ledgers." I have already indicated my differences with both the few recent quantitative historical analyses of fiscal policy and the numerous nonquantitative works on the topic. Fortunately, the tide is turning away from these approaches in the works of a handful of historians, including Teaford himself. This recent work does not prove that San Francisco's fiscal history was typical, although it does suggest that the city's experience was similar to those of some other cities.[8]

Undoubtedly, Teaford has worked the most assiduously among urban historians to prove that municipal government was no "simple struggle between a citywide party boss with a diamond shirt stud and a malodorous cigar and a good government reformer with a Harvard degree and kid gloves." His monument to this effort is his 1984 book, *The Unheralded Triumph: City Government in America, 1870–1900*, which will certainly become the standard interpretation of the development of municipal government in these years.[9]

Teaford's method is different from that employed here. His analysis ranges widely but is essentially anecdotal, and his case study cities—primarily New York, Chicago, Boston, Philadelphia, St. Louis, and Baltimore—are not compared systematically or, for the most part, quantitatively. Nonetheless, by looking carefully at these cities and placing them in a national context, he fashions a convincing narrative of the development of municipal government in these years. In spite of these methodological differences, his arguments in the areas of the city-state relationship, the class backgrounds of municipal officeholders, the patterns in fiscal policy, and the role of political machines are strikingly similar to those made here.

For example, Teaford, too, argues that, in general, state legislatures were not the enemies of cities but provided "necessary flexibility" for them, and he finds that city councils were dominated by low white-collar groups, while high white-collar groups dominated executive offices. On the question of fiscal policy, his analysis indicates that San Francisco followed a general pattern closely. Teaford argues that the "watchword of the age" between 1870 and 1900 was "economy," not expenditure, and that in these years pay-as-you-go was "one pillar of the general policy of fiscal conservatism," while low taxation was the other. In these cities, too, he contends that the "purple prose image of evil omnipotent party machines distorts the reality of nineteenth century politics." In fact, he argues, "party leaders proved influential in municipal government but were not tyrannical figures with unlimited power."[10]

Some of these arguments are also confirmed in the very systematic work of sociologists M. Craig Brown and Charles N. Halaby, who have explored the history and fiscal effects of machine and reform municipal governments using detailed data on local politics and fiscal policy collected from the thirty largest cities in America in 1900 for the period 1890 through 1940. These authors contend, too, that compared to later years, those from 1890 through 1910 were characterized by low per capita expenditure for these cities, despite the fact that these were the years when machine regimes were found most often. Based on this observation, they argue that "the squandering boss is obviously a caricature," and prove this in a sophisticated quantitative analysis of the patterns of fiscal policy in these cities, including San Francisco. Their analysis demonstrates that, controlling for other important environmental variables, political machines alone have no substantial impact on expenditures. This finding makes sense, given their further argument that the typical urban machine was "factional" rather than "dominant." In most cities with machines, several ward-level machines competed for dominance and the all-powerful, citywide machine was quite rare, being more typical after 1920 than before that time.[11]

Missing in the analyses both of Teaford and of Brown and Halaby is the interaction between fiscal and electoral politics that I have emphasized here. Its absence is most apparent in their attempts to explain (as opposed to describe) the fiscal restraint characteristic of these years or, for that matter, the end of this restraint later on. Brown and Halaby suggest that the image of urban fiscal politics they prefer is one of "machines struggling to dominate and govern cities in the face of political competition and the complexities created by social change." However, they do not investigate how the political system structured this competition, nor do they consider forms of competition outside the boss-reformer dichotomy, such as the simple but intense partisan competition that went on regardless of bosses and reformers.[12]

Teaford, however, contends that the "chief foe" of municipal solvency was "neither the corrupt politician nor the wasteful alderman, but, instead, the boom-bust economic cycle of the late nineteenth century"; thus he argues that expansive municipal programs began in the good economic times, while constriction and extreme economies were the rule during the bad. Specifically, according to Teaford, many cities found themselves overextended when the depression of the late 1870s hit, so that they were forced to be frugal thereafter. But as indebtedness contracted earlier in the century was paid off, more money was available for the expansion of municipal functions and services in the late nineteenth century.[13]

This argument explains the initial contraction, but neither its persistence nor the later expansion. In San Francisco the national pattern was replicated, as economy was imposed after 1880 and as the money used previously for the retirement of debt was spent for additional services. However, both the imposition and persistence of the economy moves—enforced by the Dollar Limit—were a response to political conditions, not just economic ones. Moreover, the issue of the 1890s was not just the incremental growth made possible by the reduction of debt service expenditures, but a totally new conception of the role of the public sector and the nonincremental change which that redefinition presaged.

With the exception of this emphasis on electoral politics as an important independent variable, our arguments about fiscal policy (the dependent variable) are quite similar. Whether or not San Francisco was typical of other cities, my analysis is typical of this other new work. This similarity is the result of a shared attitude toward theory as much as of new findings in history. These works are similar because they are tests of theory rather than simple applications of the preexisting explanations of the development of municipal government. Teaford's book is a direct test of the progressive-era contention that municipal government was a "conspicuous failure." Reflecting their training in sociology, Brown and Halaby confront most directly the image of the machine proposed by sociologist Robert Merton. My study, of course, is a test of the main adaptations of the functional theory made by historians.

On the one hand, this new, more critical approach to these frameworks is to be welcomed. On the other hand, the theoretical limitations of our work should be admitted, too. These works are tests of the earlier frameworks, not reformulations of the role of politics and government in American urban life. We continue to honor the old frameworks by wondering whether municipal government was a "success or failure," whether bosses were "good or bad," whether reformers were "democrats or dictators." But these time-honored questions have less to do with urban political history than with the contemporary political concerns of those writing about it. This point is widely recognized for the first generation of professional urban historians, much less so for the generation—including Richard Hofstadter, Oscar Handlin, and sociologist Robert Merton—whose writing shaped the agenda for the urban political history of the 1960s and 1970s.

EXPANDING THE BOUNDARIES OF URBAN POLITICAL HISTORY

As pointed out in chapter 4, there has been little disagreement that early historical accounts of municipal government were influenced by the political commitments of historians. As David Hammack has noted, a "patrician elitist" theory of urban power, which conceived of the "master conflict" in urban politics as between the "rich, well-educated, and good on the one side and the corrupt and ignorant on the other," was transmitted from James Bryce's *American Commonwealth* through the work of Arthur M. Schlesinger, Sr., to the first generation of professional urban historians. These analysts shared the position of progressive reformers themselves that American urban politics was dominated by corrupt political machines, and they took as their task the explanation of this dominance. Writing within this framework, Schlesinger attributed bad urban government to the "avarice of big business, the venality of the bosses, and the indifference of the better class."[14]

Undoubtedly the most significant event in urban political historiography after World War II was the rejection of this patrician elitist theory and the subsequent rehabilitation of the political machine by Handlin, Hofstadter, and Merton. These authors responded to the progressive contention that municipal government was a "conspicuous failure" by arguing that it was a "latent" success, via the political machine. Their argument was based not on new historical research but on a reinterpretation of the urban political past influenced by their contemporary political commitments. In essence, the new view of the machine—which I have called the political cultural theory—was part of an attempt to legitimate the political economy characteristic of the New Deal–Fair Deal tradition.

A good place to begin a brief consideration of this issue is with Michael Rogin's now rather neglected 1967 book, *The Intellectuals and McCarthy: The Radical Specter*. Ostensibly an analysis of the political roots of McCarthyism, Rogin's book is also a brilliant analysis of the postwar turn toward pluralism in the writings of sociologists, political scientists, and historians. Drawing on the writings of such diverse thinkers as sociologists Seymour Martin Lipset and Edward Shils and historians Hofstadter and Handlin, among others, Rogin summarized the shift toward pluralism in the opening paragraph of his book:

Modern pluralism emerged as American intellectuals, many ex-radical, responded to the events of their youth and the pressures of the 1950s. The rise of communism and fascism in Europe had forcefully suggested the similarities between the extreme right and the extreme left and the dangers of mass movements. The moderate New Deal, on the other hand, succeeded in giving American capitalism a reasonable and stable basis. Thus drastic social change seemed not only terribly dangerous but also unnecessary.[15]

According to Rogin, the pluralists thought that the way to protect liberal political economy from its conservative and radical opponents was to redefine American political theory and American political history in such a way as to represent interest-group liberalism as the natural and positive outgrowth of social and economic development in the United States. At the heart of postwar pluralism, therefore, was a theory of industrialization and its effect on American society and politics. This theory rejected both the conservative position that industrialization destroyed traditional loyalties, thus introducing alienation and a "mass" society, and the radical argument that industrial capitalist development introduced new forms of oppression. For the pluralists, the effect of industrialization was to fragment power, introduce social complexity, and, ultimately, require "rational, instrumental politics."[16]

This theory held that at one time there had been a situation of what Robert Dahl would later call "cumulative inequality" in the United States, in which there was a single, interlocked, socioeconomic, political, and at times religious elite. However, the effect of industrialization was to destroy the socioeconomic basis of this elite by creating new sources of economic power, generating greater social complexity, and permitting a larger population. Immigration and urbanization added further to this socioeconomic complexity, and together these changes broke the elite interlock and multiplied the bases of political power. As a result American society became a mosaic of groups. For those who understood and accepted these changes, the "rational" approach to politics was one rooted in political conflict among self-interested groups whose goals were short-term, pragmatic, negotiable, and capable of being fulfilled within the existing framework of social and political institutions of

American society. Agreement on these conditions formed a consensus on the political "rules of the game," and competition among the many groups maintained a rough political equilibrium. Therefore, according to the pluralists, the state was not dominated by any one group and was not an institution over and against society. Rather, its structure was a mosaic of accepted interest-group demands, and its controls shifted from one group to another as various political coalitions gained and lost power.[17]

According to the pluralists, the enemies of this smoothly functioning political system were those who rejected its prescriptions and practiced "irrational" or "ideological mass politics." Such political leaders or movements rejected the consensus on the rules of the game by making "moralistic" or absolute demands that could not be fulfilled within the system itself, or, worse, by practicing political "utopianism" and demanding change in the system itself. Conservatives who yearned for a return to preindustrial society or radicals seeking a socialist utopia frequently made such demands. Just as frequently, such demands were based not on the desire for concrete improvements in society but on "generalized resentments" and "projective rationalizations arising from status aspirations and other personal motives" that stemmed from the "deeper layers of the personality." In essence, for the pluralists, pragmatic interest-group politics was "rational"; all other political practice was "irrational."[18]

In the immediate postwar years, the enemies of pluralism were seen by liberal intellectuals to be the so-called radical right, a loosely defined group containing supporters of Joseph McCarthy's attacks on communists in government, older style isolationists who rejected the expanded international role the United States had assumed after World War II, and those who hoped to "roll back" the institutional legacy of the New Deal. According to their critics, these political actors and movements could not accept the reality of a complex, modern, industrial world power, so they made moralistic or irrational attacks on its most prominent political advocates or symbols.[19]

It was to defend this new political reality that Hofstadter undertook to rewrite American political history since 1890 in pluralist terms in his justly famous book, *The Age of Reform*, which was published in 1955. According to Hofstadter, liberals of the 1950s found themselves "far more conscious of those things they would like to preserve than . . . of those things they would like to change," and thought, therefore, that they could better serve themselves in the "calculable future by holding on to what we have gained and learned . . . than by dismantling the social achievements of the past twenty years."[20]

Hofstadter's contribution to this effort in *The Age of Reform* was his attempt to rewrite the political history of modern America in liberal terms, and thus defend the New Deal–Fair Deal political tradition from its "moralistic" critics on the right and the left. Focusing on the three great reform movements since 1890—Populism, Progressivism, and the New Deal—Hofstadter took as his historiographical target the widespread belief that the New Deal was the "analogue and lineal descendent" of Populism and Progressivism. In fact, he argued, the New Deal was fundamentally different from both. Populism and Progressivism were "moralistic binges" carried out by status-anxious farmers and members of the middle class who were unable to accept the changes in their status brought about by industrialization, immigration, and urbanization. These movements were the last gasps of the "indigenous Yankee-Protestant political tradition," which was based on "middle class life" and which held that individual political action should be disinterested and that public life should be run "in accordance with general principles and abstract laws and apart from and superior to personal needs."[21]

Opposed to this tradition and emerging out of the industrialization, urbanization, and ethnic differentiation of the United States was a competing system of political ethics. Founded on the "urgent needs [of the immigrants] that so often grew out of their migration," this developing tradition rejected a moralistic approach to politics, "interpreted political and civic relations chiefly in terms of personal obligation," and, in particular, "placed strong personal loyalties above allegiance to abstract codes of law or morals." The New Deal was rooted in this second ethos and represented a "triumph of human needs . . . over inherited notions and inhibitions." Rejecting moralism, ideology, and status anxiety, the New Deal simply went about the business of grappling with politics and society as it found them in depression-ridden 1930s America.[22]

For Hofstadter, the cockpit of the conflict between these competing political ethical systems was the city, in which "bosses" and "reformers" competed. Thus he had to reinterpret this conflict and link the New Deal to the political machines rather than to the reformers. Luckily for Hofstadter, the definitive book on this topic had already been written by Handlin. Among the many topics taken up by Handlin in *The Uprooted*, his 1951 history of immigration in America, was that of "Democracy and Power," and it was here that he created lasting stereotypes of bosses and reformers which reversed the patrician elitist theory of urban politics. Hofstadter's portrayal of the political machine was based almost completely on Handlin's.[23]

As I argued in chapter 1, for both Handlin and Hofstadter, the free-spending boss was the hero, the tightfisted reformer the villain. The boss expanded the public sector to meet human needs; the reformers, as Handlin put it, rarely paused "to consider what were the needs and interests of a new citizen." They spoke high-mindedly of efficiency, system, and economy, but to the immigrants, these abstract principles were not worth the suffering they entailed if men had to be laid off from municipal government to accomplish them.[24]

I have reviewed these portrayals of bossism and reform in more detail earlier, and there is no need to reconsider them further here. What is important to reemphasize is the presentist attempt to read the New Deal back into the political machine and to portray the bosses as Franklin Delano Roosevelt "writ small." Hofstadter's admiration of the boss's "pragmatic talents" and the machine's essential "humanity" was paralleled in his praise of FDR's "opportunistic virtuosity" and the New Deal's "triumph of . . . human needs over inherited notions." Handlin argued that it was the machine that "opened to the immigrants the prospect that the state might be the means through which the beginnings of security could come," although it was not until the New Deal that immigrants were no longer "divided by the necessity of choosing between their own machines and reform," because by then reform had changed so that it could "swallow up their machines, bosses and all."[25]

Both Handlin and Hofstadter won the Pulitzer Prize in history for their books, in 1952 and 1956, respectively, and given both this prestige and the absence of intellectually legitimate opponents, it was not surprising that their interpretation soon reigned supreme among historians. Moreover, the influence of their view was widened by its simultaneous codification as a sort of "law" of functional sociology in the 1949 and 1957 editions of Robert K. Merton's classic text, *Social Theory and Social Structure.*[26]

In the now justly famous first chapter of the 1949 edition of *Social Theory and Social Structure,* Merton undertook to codify and exemplify functionalist theory. A distinction he was particularly interested in making was between what he called "manifest" and "latent" functions. The former, he wrote, were "those objective consequences for a specified unit (person, subgroup, social or cultural system) which contribute to its adjustment or adaptation and were so intended"; the latter were "the unintended and unrecognized consequences of the same order." Merton argued that the employment of such a distinction offered many advantages to social science. It clarified the analysis of seemingly irrational social patterns, directed attention to theoretically fruitful fields of inquiry, and precluded "the substitution of naive moral judgements for sociological analysis." It was to demonstrate this last point that Merton offered his famous analysis of the "latent functions" of the political machine.[27]

According to Merton, the first of these latent functions was the organization of power in an atmosphere in which political authority was legally fragmented by state laws or city charters that minimized executive authority. Having accomplished this centralization of power, the machine then fulfilled other functions for "diverse subgroups." For what he called the "deprived classes," it humanized and personalized assistance; for those with limited opportunities for social mobility, it provided an alternate route; and for business, the machine provided political privileges that stabilized the economic situation and thereby facilitated the maximization of profits.[28]

Merton did not rank these functions according to their importance to the machine or to the various subgroups. Nonetheless, his description of machine-style politics—strikingly similar to those of Handlin and Hofstadter—implied that service to the deprived was at the heart of the machine's persistence. According to Merton, machine politicians realized that the voter was primarily "a man living in a specific neighborhood, with specific personal problems, and personal wants." Therefore, public issues were "abstract and remote," private problems "concrete and immediate," and it was not through the generalized appeal to large public concerns that the machine operated, but "through the direct, quasi-feudal relationships between the local representatives of the machine and voters in their neighborhood."[29]

Like Handlin and Hofstadter, Merton also saw in the New Deal the reflection of this sort of political practice. Merton was more subtle in his admiration for the New Dealers—he kept it in a footnote—but he was obviously similarly impressed. In describing the way the machine "humanized and personalized" aid to the needy, he contrasted professional social workers with the precinct captain. The former were perceived by clients to be legalistic snoopers, while the latter "asks no questions, exacts no compliance with legal rules of eligibility, and does not 'snoop' into private affairs."[30]

To exemplify this point, Merton added a footnote in which he turned not to the many stories of such actions by machine politicians but to the "open-handed and nonpolitical distribution of unemployment relief" in New York state by Harry Hopkins during the governorship of Franklin D. Roosevelt. In the anecdote that Merton related, Hopkins was criticized by regular welfare agencies for having handed out work tickets to the unemployed without sufficient investigation of the eligibility of the applicants. Hopkins was alleged to have told the agencies to "go to hell," thus again sustaining the "triumph" of needs over inherited notions in a process similar to that he would use as national coordinator of unemployment relief under Roosevelt as president.[31]

The uncanny similarity of the accounts of Handlin, Hofstadter, and Merton was shaped not only by their shared commitments in the political present but also by the source they shared for their understanding of the urban political past. None of these works was based on primary research, of course; instead, from the scores of accounts of bossism and reform written during the progressive era, all three of these authors based their analyses on *The Autobiography of Lincoln Steffens*. Merton cited Steffens's autobiography as the source of his information regarding the latent functions of the machine. Handlin did not use footnotes in *The Uprooted*, but the quotations regarding the machine were taken verbatim from Steffens. Hofstadter, of course, based his account on Handlin, and therefore on Steffens, along with William Riordan's *Plunkitt of Tammany Hall*, a collection of pro-machine statements attributed to a subleader of New York's Tammany Hall.[32]

This choice was not just a coincidence. Steffens's account appealed because, as Christopher Lasch has pointed out, its objective in its own time was the same as that of these authors thirty years later—namely, to demolish the moralistic pretensions of middle-class reform and exalt in its stead the pragmatic, pluralistic, humanitarianism of machine politicians. In his interpretation of Steffens in *The New Radicalism in America*, Lasch has argued that for Steffens there were "strong" men who accepted the harsh facts of life as they found them and who proceeded to act upon them, and "weak" men who idealized existence by theorizing about it. Steffens decided early on that he preferred the strong "bad" men to the weak "good" ones, the crooks and bosses to the reformers. In the stories collected in the *Shame of the Cities* (1904) and retold in the *Autobiography* (1931), Steffens set out to prove that the bad bosses were in fact "good," while the good reformers were in fact "bad." Thus he portrayed the bosses as pragmatic, self-conscious, and essentially humane in order to protest the "hypocrisy of middle class morality."[33]

The dubious achievement of the functional approach was to base a presentist portrayal of the political machine on the work of an author who openly declared his sympathy with the machines. Despite this fundamental error in historical method, the "new" Merton-Handlin-Hofstadter rehabilitation of the political machine via Steffens swept the fields of American history, sociology, and political science, where it remains the reigning paradigm today. John Allswang has summarized the prevailing attitude toward the political machine in his aptly titled book, *Bosses, Machines, and Urban Voters: An American Symbiosis*, published in 1977. According to Allswang, the machines rested on "a mass lower class and working class base which was involved with issues of individual and group survival—in economic, social, and cultural terms," and the machines persisted because they were better able to respond quickly and directly to the needs of the "very large number of dependent or semi-dependent people in the American cities."[34]

The triumph of this view of the machine also silenced the generation of commentators on the urban political scene, from Bryce to Schlesinger, who held the patrician elitist theory of urban political history. Their theory was admittedly arrogant, unsympathetic to immigrants, and moralistic. But also embedded within it was a powerful critique of the political status quo in turn-of-the-century urban America. The research agenda suggested by this critique pointed toward analysis of the urban power structure, the relationships between business and politics, and the myriad ways in which the urban political system was dysfunctional.[35]

By trivializing this literature as status-anxious moralizing, Handlin, Hofstadter, and Merton prevented this critique from being developed further. Rather, they shifted the agenda of urban political history away from the examination of the urban power structure and the role of local government in that structure and toward the enumeration of the alleged functions of the machines, especially their services to the immigrant masses. Their purpose was not to better understand the political history of the American city but to create a usable past for liberal political economy, by linking the expansion of the state under the New Deal to the humane and pragmatic machine politicians, and by linking the opponents of the New Deal political tradition to a succession of moralistic opponents of pragmatic politics.

Thus the functional theory of urban politics is best regarded as a moment in recent intellectual history, not as a window on urban politics in the past. Moreover, functional theory did not abolish "moralism" from urban political history so much as substitute another version. Under the aegis of the patrician elitist theory, historians denounced the corruption of the machines and praised the virtue of reformers, whereas those writing within the functional framework praised the pragmatism of the machine and denounced the moralism of the reformers. In both cases the framework was presentist, however, and the history of urban politics was refracted through the lens of the contemporary political commitments of its analysts.

If a wise historiographer had argued this convincingly in, say, 1960, the shape of urban history might be different today. Such an author did not appear, and hence the functional theory has been carried forth, even by some of the best urban historians. For example, the work of Samuel Hays revived but did not revolutionize the field because it, too, was limited by the functional framework (see chap. 1). Hays accepted uncritically the portrait of machines—a term he used interchangeably with the "ward system"—presented by Handlin, Hofstadter, and Merton, but revised their image of the reformers. For Handlin and Hofstadter, the machine was the perfect political adaptation to the urban environment, whereas the progressive reformers were politically impotent moralizers. Ignoring those cities in which reform succeeded politically, Handlin and Hofstadter essentially jumped from the period of machine domination to the New Deal. Because Hays accepted the Handlin-Hofstadter position on the machine but focused on places where reform "won," he was compelled to explain the "defeat" of the "perfect" local system. To do so he adopted a functionalist interpretation of the effect of "industrialism" on American society and politics.

Hays's turn to the social analysis of reform was thus born of the need to contrast one functional necessity (the machine) with another (the reform movement as a response to industrialism). He answered the question about how the reformers won by focusing on what he called the "systematizing and organizing processes inherent in industrialism as the dynamic force in social change in modern life." This focus revealed that the modernizing forces of science and technology produced cosmopolitan tendencies in the late nineteenth century, which gave rise in turn to "a structure of relationships in which cosmopolitan elements, corporately organized, looked upon local life ... as parochial, narrow, and unenlightened," while local communities considered cosmopolitan influences and their bureaucracies to be "imperialistic, dictatorial, and destructive of established values." Nonetheless, initiative now moved upward to extra-community forces. Within this framework, then, the reformers triumphed, because it was a functional necessity of the newly organized and systematized society that they do so. Their triumph was not automatic and not without conflict, but its outcome was predetermined.[36]

Building on Hays's work, a more simpleminded application of the "response to industrialism" framework has rejected any concern with the political history of the American city as a sort of moralistic atavism. The prevailing view of urban politics is thus at least twice removed from reality. It began, as we have seen, with a functional analysis of the machine, grew to a functional analysis of reform out of the necessity to explain the downfall of the machine, and it is now a functional analysis of the entire process of development of urban politics. Moreover, the study of urban political history continues to carry a heavy political load. What I have called the socioeconomic structural and political cultural variants of the functional theory share the attempt to rationalize the growth of the state in America, for if an expanded public sector was either "humane" or "inevitable," its status should be non-controversial.

If the functional theory is really not about urban history but about the legitimacy of and proper techniques for the growth of the state in American life, then as urban historians we lie in a procrustean theoretical and historiographical bed that we did not make. This recognition is both liberating and terrifying, however. On the one hand, it is clear that we need not continue to organize urban political history around the battles between progressive and New Deal intellectuals. The terrifying flip side of this recognition is that if we abandon the functional framework, having lived so long in its shadow, we may lack any organizing principle for urban political history.[37]

A developing field of interest to historians suggests a rubric through which urban political history can and should proceed, however. As already noted, the implicit subject of postwar urban political history was the legitimacy of the expansion of the state in American life. Recent work suggests that an explicit focus on statebuilding would enrich the study of state and local government, at the same time that a state and local focus would enrich the study of statebuilding.[38]

When we look over the field of urban history, we see a somewhat stunted subfield of political history, a once flourishing but now somewhat quiescent subfield of social mobility, a growing subfield of community studies of labor, and a richly detailed and still growing subfield devoted to urban institutions such as schools, police, and hospitals. All are related in theory, but only rarely so in historical practice. Mobility influences political participation, the political parties and political system help define the meaning of class, and urban institutions develop in part in a fiscal political context, but because of the segmentation of these areas of study these connections are seldom carefully made.[39]

Indeed, when we look at recent work on the building of the nineteenth-century state in America, we find either an ignorance of statebuilding on the local level or an attempt to link all levels of the federal system into the same pattern of development. Stephen Skowronek's interesting book, *Building a New American State* (1982), exemplifies the first tendency in its argument that "the exceptional character of the early American state is neatly summarized in the paradox that it failed to evoke any sense of a state." But this is true only if one looks for the state where it is supposed to be (at the national level) rather than where it was (at the local and state levels). In fact, the federal system did not obstruct the development of the state in America so much as locate it at a level below the national. The American state was built "from the bottom up," as it were—namely, from the local and state levels to the national level—and many of the political struggles for control of government and debates over the proper role of government were conducted in city halls and state legislatures.[40]

The advantage of Morton Keller's massive *Affairs of State* (1977) is its awareness of statebuilding as an issue up and down the federal system. The disadvantage of his analysis (aside from its rather meager explanatory framework) is his attempt to force the polity at all levels into the same pattern of growth, so that local, state, and national government appear to develop in lockstep. Statebuilding activities at the different levels of the federal system experienced different rates and periods of expansion and contraction because of obvious differences in the political and social contexts of the different levels. Skowronek suggests that among the stimuli to the development of the national state were crises, class conflict, and increasing social complexity. All of these affected the different levels of the federal system differently.[41]

A focus on statebuilding could give necessary political content to urban history and necessary local context to the history of statebuilding. Such new work would have to be different from existing work in both focus and approach. For example, within a statebuilding framework, the specifically local focus of urban political history would have to give way to the parallel and contrasting patterns of development in both state and local government. The recognition that nineteenth-century legislatures were more facilitators of than meddlers in urban government has carried with it the realization that the contemporary distance between local and state government was not felt as intensely in the nineteenth century. On the contrary, in large cities like San Francisco, the legislature was almost regarded as just another branch of local government. Thus the proper study of statebuilding at this level should focus on the division of labor between local and state government and on changes in this division over time.

New work would also be required to have a more political focus. The focus of social historians on what Michael Katz has called the "institutional state"—institutions of mental health, education, justice, and public welfare—must give way to a broader concern with the political context for the emergence of all institutions in the state. Katz is correct that the key question is, "Why did the institutional state emerge at the time and in the manner it did?" But his belief that the answer will be found through the explanation of "the origins and founding of institutions and the shift from reform to custody" suggests that he conceives of institutions too narrowly. The interesting and fundamentally important fact is that these social institutions emerged at the same time as political institutions such as widespread suffrage, the mass party system, and the seminal bureaus of state and local governments. The challenge is to explain the nearly simultaneous emergence and mutual legitimation of all of these institutions, in addition, of course, to their change or persistence over time.[42]

Such a political focus will require a turn—or return—to some of the topics of the old political history, such as the suffrage, the party system, and the nineteenth-century policymaking process. The new social history has ignored these topics, and as J. Morgan Kousser has pointed out, the "new political history has not yet absorbed all the useful lessons of the old." In particular, as Richard L. McCormick has explained, the new political history has thus far been unable to link political participation and policy formation. However, the clear role of the political system in structuring the policymaking process in San Francisco suggests that this link can be found if one looks for it. Both the significance of this influence and the links between participation in local, state, and national elections further support the necessity of a politically focused, supra-local, statebuilding approach to these issues.[43]

If San Francisco is a good example of it, the state we discover with this work will be far from the functionalist dream. It will exist for most of the nineteenth century in a poisonous anti-state atmosphere in which every request for its expansion will be blasted as a "political job." It will be restrained by competing political agendas, restrictive fiscal ideologies, and vested bureaucratic interests. Because of these restraints, it will respond poorly to forces outside of itself, be they rich, poor, or otherwise. What growth it will experience will be more incremental than nonincremental, and change in that pattern will come about through political action—or the political interpretation of social change—and not just through social change alone. Our task will be to explain this recalcitrant subject, rather than to await the epiphanies of our own theoretical constructs.

Restoration of the state at the subnational level to a "controversial" status does not require the substitution of one moral standard for another. The proper response to the argument that the growth of the public sector was "functional" is not that it was dysfunctional, but that this position robs historical analysis of everything important in political history—power, ideology, conflict, the state itself. Living in the era of the gigantic state, one can hardly debate the point that it is crucial to understand its growth and the political process by which that growth was accomplished and legitimated.

In fact, the political events of the 1980s have provided both the opportunity for a new interpretation of the role of the state in American life and a demonstration of the necessity for such an interpretation. The collapse of liberalism as a political and intellectual movement has called into question the explanation of the state developed in the 1950s and

1960s, thus opening the field intellectually. The disorganization of liberal politics—once claimed to be the "natural outgrowth" of American development—provides an object lesson about what happens to those who use the past to rationalize their version of the present. It is not that they are condemned to repeat the past; the problem is more poignant than that. They cannot face the future.

Appendixes

Appendix A

THE "GREENBACK" ERA IN SAN FRANCISCO
AND ITS EFFECT ON PRICES

Although historians and others have written a great deal about the various ways in which San Francisco has been anomalous, one anomaly that has received less attention has been San Francisco's refusal to abandon the gold standard during the "greenback" era in American monetary history from 1862 through 1878. As is well known, one of the ways the federal government financed the Civil War was through the introduction of so-called greenback paper currency into the economy beginning in 1862. The result was an immediate and almost incredible inflation of the currency. As Wesley Mitchell has pointed out in his study of this issue, while the price of a gold dollar in greenbacks averaged $1.13 in 1862, by 1864 this had risen to $2.03, and it did not decline completely until 1878. All of the national price indexes produced by economists to enable others to convert "current" dollars into "real" dollars for comparison over time or among locations assume that this inflation occurred everywhere. The problem for this study is that, because of the force of both custom and law, this did not occur in California. Throughout the greenback period, California in general and San Francisco in particular remained on the gold standard.[1]

The California constitution of 1849 set this process in motion by banning the issuance of currency by banks in the state. But as Walton Bean has pointed out, this constitutional prohibition of "soft" money was typical of most states organized after the Panic of 1837. Of more local importance was the sheer plenitude of gold. From the time of the Gold Rush onward, gold dust or gold coin became the accepted currency in California. Thus the suspension of specie payment by New York banks in December 1861 and the subsequent issuance of the greenbacks by the federal government set off something like a currency civil war between California and the federal government, in which leaders of both the private and public sector in California did everything they could to prevent the circulation of the greenbacks in the state.[2]

The first gun in this war fired, fittingly enough, by the tax collector for the city and county of San Francisco, Ebenezer Washburn, who announced in 1862 that he would not accept legal tender notes in payment for state and county taxes. There were two good, personal reasons for his announcement. First, the tax collector was paid on commission, so if he collected less he received less, and the devalued greenbacks certainly meant less. Second, and perhaps more important, the tax collector was billed by the assessor for a certain amount of taxes expected, and was held liable for explanation of that amount not returned. In case of problems with the currency, his liability would be increased. More important, Washburn had the force of law behind him, because in an act unrelated to this controversy, the state legislature had, in 1861, passed a law requiring the payment of state and local taxes in the "legal coin of the United States." Washburn's ruling was immediately challenged in the courts, but in part because of the 1861 law, it was upheld by the state supreme court in July 1862 in a decision that not only validated his action but also declared that United States notes could not be accepted as payment for state and county taxes.[3]

With the public sector thus protected, the San Francisco private sector moved to protect itself, too. In November 1862, the merchants of the city met and resolved not to "pay out or receive the legal tender at any but the merchant [i.e., the gold] rate." The agreement also provided sanctions for those who failed to follow it. To further solidify this position, the merchants lobbied the state legislature for a law called the Specific Contract Act, which passed in 1863 and allowed parties to any contract to specify the type of money to be used in a transaction. Naturally, San Franciscans wrote these contracts to require gold payment. Given both these formal and informal supports for the gold standard, Peter Decker has stated flatly that "greenbacks did not circulate" in the city during the Civil War.[4]

Although the Specific Contract Act was repealed after the Civil War, it protected California from the worst of the inflation, which occurred from 1863 through 1865. It also set a monetary standard that appears to have carried through the rest of the greenback era. For example, when the Bank of California collapsed in 1875, the San Francisco *Bulletin* noted that the impact of the collapse was mitigated by the fact that Californians traded exlusively in gold. Bean has noted further that for decades after this, "even large financial transactions were likely to be conducted in piles of gold coins," and Young pointed out that, even as he wrote his history of San Francisco in 1912, the use of paper money in ordinary business was "very unusual."[5]

The state legislature continued to protect the public sector throughout the greenback era. As a result of the controversy preceding and following the Specific Contract Act, it reaffirmed, in 1864, that taxes would be paid "exclusively in the gold and silver coin of the United States." Moreover, it rejected several attempts to repeal the contract act, including one supported by Salmon P. Chase, secretary of the federal treasury, who telegraphed the legislature that "the California gold law is against national policy." In 1872, when the political code of the state was organized, taxes were again required to be paid in "legal coin of the United States." In fact, it was not until 1880 that the legislature declared that "legal tender notes shall be received at par in payment for taxes." Of course, by that time the inflationary threat from the greenbacks was over.[6]

Given this behavior on the part of both the private and public sectors in California during these years, it is most probable that there was no greenback era in California, and almost certain that there was none in San Francisco. In the case of San Francisco's government, it is clear that it was required to accept only coin for the payment of taxes. Given the proclivities of local contractors and workers, it most likely paid only coin for goods and services as well. It follows, therefore, that the "current" value of the city's revenues and expenditure during this period should not be deflated by a price index but inflated to reflect the higher "real" value of this coin.

Unfortunately, there is no price index based exclusively on prices in San Francisco—or, for that matter, in the region—for the entire period of 1860–1905. Thus it is necessary to turn to a national index. The index selected here is that constructed for the years 1774 through 1974 by Paul A. David and Peter Solar, called the Brady-David-Solar (BDS) index. In the years covered by this study, the BDS index simply links together the indexes of other historians, but David and Solar have provided a thoughtful explanation of these linkages, not to mention the most thoughtful consideration of the overall meaning of price indexes that I have encountered. Like all other national indexes, however, this one significantly deflates the real value of current dollars during the greenback era.[7]

Because it is not even a remote goal of this study to comment on relative prices in San Francisco, I have adopted a jury-rigged solution to this problem. In his classic study of the economic effects of the greenbacks, Mitchell has provided tables of average prices of gold in greenbacks and of greenbacks in gold in New York for 1862–1878. Price indexes for these years normally deflate dollar values, based on an approximation of the price of gold in greenbacks. I decided to pursue the opposite procedure, substituting for the values of the BDS index the average price of greenbacks in gold for each year given by Mitchell. In this way I have inflated the value of San Francisco's dollars during these years. Thus the index for this study uses the BDS values for 1860–1861 and 1879–1905, and the prices of greenbacks in gold for 1862–1878. In chapter 2, I reported most values in real as opposed to current form. In later chapters I consider both, because the historian of fiscal politics must be concerned both with what really happened (and thus the real values of currency) and with what politicians and voters thought or claimed was happening (and thus with current values).[8]

Appendix B

SOME ASPECTS OF REGRESSION ANALYSIS

Among the things that historians do, the most important may well be investigating the relationship between cause and effect in a particular situation. Indeed, if one were to strip away or boil down the narration in historical studies, the remainder would be a list of causes for a particular effect, be it an event, a cultural transformation, or what have you. A great deal of historians' work consists of the compilation and evaluation of these causes, and much historical argument concerns competing lists of causes or the rank order of causes within a single list.

These "inventories of causes," as sociologist Hubert Blalock has called them, are useful but usually imprecise. They do not reveal how powerfully the combination of independent variables influences the dependent variable, and they only rarely assess the relative weight within the combination of each independent variable. If the variables can be quantified, and if the functional relationship between the combination of the independent variables and the dependent variable is linear—that is, can be expressed mathematically as a straight line—then one is justified in using a multiple regression equation to answer these questions.[1]

Multiple regression analysis, therefore, is the statistical equivalent of typical historical work. The differences, of course, are in the nature of the variables, which must be quantitative, and in the criteria of proof, which are statistical. The regression equation describes the linear relationship between a dependent and one or more independent variables. The line produced by the equation is described by the constant, which locates the point at which the line crosses the Y axis (and which is of little or no interest to us), and by the coefficient, which measures the movement of the dependent variable along the line by estimating the change in the dependent variable predicted by a change of one unit in an independent variable. The proper interpretation of a coefficient in the multivariable or multiple regression equation is as the effect of a one-unit change in one independent variable, measured while holding the other variable(s) constant. This is what is meant by "controlling for" the effect of another variable statistically.

The statistics accompanying the results tell us with what amount of confidence we can reject the null hypothesis (i.e., that there is no relationship between the dependent and the independent variables). For example, the t-ratio, which is the ratio of the regression coefficient to its standard error, tells us with what degree of confidence we can reject the null hypothesis that the coefficient actually equals zero, and thus that there is no statistical relationship between the dependent and independent variables. To use this statistic, we specify a critical value of the t-ratio below which we will not reject the null hypothesis, and then check the ratios in each equation against the percentiles of the t-distribution. Throughout this book I have adopted the 0.10 minimum acceptance level, and have indicated the coefficients that have t-ratios at that level or above. A t-ratio significant at the 0.10 level or above means, roughly, that we reject the null hypothesis with 90 percent confidence.

The R^2, or coefficient of determination, measures the proportionate reduction of error in explaining the dependent variable brought about by knowing the independent variable(s). In other words, it indicates the percentage of variation in the dependent variable that is explained by the independent variable(s). The remainder of the variation is assumed to be the result of measurement error, of the effect of variables left out of the equation, or of the fact that the regression process is a simplification of reality, so that we are unable to explain it all. The normal R^2 increases with the number of independent variables in an equation. Therefore, throughout this study I have reported the adjusted R^2, which controls for the number of independent variables in the equation and permits comparison of the results of equations with different numbers of independent variables.

Because regression analysis is a useful tool for historians, we are fortunate to have an accessible introduction to the subject in Roderick Floud's *An Introduction to Quantitative Methods for Historians* (1979). Floud's book is particularly relevant to the present work because it is an introduction to quantitative methods for the analysis of data arranged in time-series, as are the data in this study. Floud discusses the basic methods employed in this analysis, although only for the bi-variate case. A good introduction to multivariate analysis of time-series data like those employed here is Robert S. Pindyck and Daniel L. Rub-infeld's *Econometric Models and Economic Forecasts* (1976).[2]

There are also several examples of historical work using methods similar to those employed here. Among them are Eric Monkkonen's *Police in Urban America, 1860–1920* (1981) and Maris Vinovskis and Carl Kaestle's *Education and Social Change in Nineteenth Century Massachusetts* (1980). I mention this to place my work in its proper context; there is absolutely nothing extraordinary about these methods or their place in historical analysis.[3]

There is, however, a problem peculiar to time-series regression anal-ysis, and that is serial correlation. What follows is a discussion of that problem and the corrections for it in this analysis. This discussion may be of more interest to those who use regression analysis regularly than to others.

One of the assumptions of multiple regression analysis is that the error terms from different observations are not correlated. When esti-mating parameters on the basis of time-series data, this means that we assume that the correlation between the errors at different (usually adjacent) time periods is zero. Here this implies that higher than ex-pected levels of expenditure will not regularly be followed by high (or low) levels. If this assumption is violated, then the errors are said to be serially correlated or autoregressive. When this correlation is be-tween the errors of adjacent time periods (i.e., those at time t and at time $t - 1$), the condition is called first-order serial correlation.[4]

When this condition exists, the coefficients estimated by the ordinary least squares (OLS) regression equation are unbiased and consistent but inefficient—that is, they are not the coefficients with minimum variance. Moreover, the estimated variances of the OLS coefficients will be biased downward in the case of positive serial correlation and upward in the case of negative, so that the loss of efficiency is either masked or ex-aggerated. The effect is that serial correlation exaggerates or minimizes the success of the equation, as measured by the t-ratios and R^2, making hypothesis testing unreliable. This problem is almost always found to some degree in equations with time-series data, and experimental work has suggested that the bias in the variances can be serious, at times approaching 80 percent. In the case of equations like those in chapter

8 of this book, which contain lagged values of the dependent variables as independent variables, the conjunction of these lagged endogenous variables with the autocorrelation can produce OLS estimates that are not only inefficient but also biased and inconsistent—in other words, they do not converge to the "true" values, even with infinite samplings. Moreover, Douglas Hibbs has pointed out that in this situation the bias normally inflates the causal significance of the lagged endogenous variables and minimizes that of the other variables in the OLS regression.[5]

If the amount and sign of the serial correlation were known, the problem could be solved by differencing the OLS variables by some measure of the correlation. In fact, this is the solution by generalized differencing or generalized least squares (GLS). In the OLS model, as noted, the expected value of this correlation is zero. In the GLS model, the expected value is p (rho), and the model is given as:

$$Y^* = B_1 (1 - p) + B_2 X^*_{2t} + \ldots + B_k X^*_{kt} + v_t$$

Where:

$$Y^*_t = Y_t - pY_{t-1}$$
$$X^*_{2t} = X_{2t} - px_{2t-1}$$
$$X^*_{kt} = X_{kt} - pX_{kt-1}$$

$$v_t = e_t - pe_{t-1}$$

Obviously, because the value of rho cannot be known in advance of analysis, it too must be estimated in order for generalized least squares to be conducted. This is the role of the Cochrane-Orcutt procedure, which is one of several procedures for doing the same thing. Assuming that the serially correlated error at time t can be estimated by multiplying the residual at time $t - 1$ by rho and adding a random disturbance term, the error-generating process can be modeled as below:

$$e_t = pe_{t-1} + v_t$$

The Cochrane-Orcutt procedure uses the residuals from the OLS regression to estimate the value of rho, then differences the variables in the original equation by this value. First the OLS regression is run to obtain the serially correlated residuals, which are then used in the equation just given to estimate the value of rho (p). The original regression is then rerun, with the variables differenced by this estimate of rho. Residuals are again obtained, and the procedure continues in this fashion until the estimates of rho change less than 0.001 in successive iterations. The variables in the original regression equation are then differenced with this value of rho. Because it is a correlation coefficient, rho ranges from -1 to 1, indicating the presence of either negative or positive first-order serial correlation.[6]

But why resort to this relatively cumbersome procedure, which is less widely available in social-science computer packages, when one can turn to the more familiar and universally available technique of first differences? Comparing the parameters of the generalized- and first-difference equations, we can see that first differencing is only a special case of generalized differencing in which the value of rho is assumed to be 1:

GLS parameters

$$Y^*_t = Y_t - pY_{t-1}$$
$$X^*_{2t} = X_{2t} - pX_{2t-1}$$
$$X^*_{kt} = X_{kt} - pX_{kt-1}$$
$$v_t = e_t - pe_{t-1}$$

First-differences parameters

$$Y^*_t = Y_t - Y_{t-1}$$
$$X^*_{2t} = X_{2t} - X_{2t-1}$$
$$X^*_{kt} = X_{kt} - X_{kt-1}$$
$$v_t = e_t - e_{t-1}$$

Contrary to what many believe, then, first differences is not a general treatment for first-order serial correlation. On the contrary, it is appropriate and effective only when one has reason to assume that the first-order serial correlation is positive and that the value of rho is approaching 1. Because one rarely has advance information about the value of rho, however, first differences tends to be a blind treatment for this problem. Generalized differencing, which is conducted with some estimate of rho, is a more accurate procedure for dealing with first-order serial correlation. If there is reason to suspect that the autoregressive process is of an order higher than 1, then other techniques must be employed. Evidence in this analysis indicated that the problem was first-order.

This technique has been employed in every equation in this analysis with a fiscal dependent variable. Thus I have not reported the Durbin-Watson statistic in each equation; it is essentially meaningless after the equations have been transformed. Instead, I have reported the estimate of rho, although I have not commented on it.

Notes

PREFACE

1. E. J. Hobsbawm, "From Social History to the History of Society," *Daedalus* 100 (1971): 20–45; Jacques Le Goff, "Is Politics Still the Backbone of History?" ibid., 1–19.

2. Robert R. Alford with Harry M. Scoble, *Bureaucracy and Participation: Political Cultures in Four Wisconsin Cities* (Chicago, 1969), 2. Alford reviews many of these studies in Alford and Roger Friedland, "Political Participation and Public Policy," *Annual Review of Sociology* 1 (1975):429–479. Richard I. Hofferbert, "State and Community Policy Studies: A Review of the Comparative Input-Output Analyses," *Political Science Annual* 3 (1972):3–72.

3. Joseph A. Schumpeter, "The Crisis of the Tax State," *International Economic Papers* 4 (1954):7. This is the English translation of Schumpeter's pamphlet *Die Krise des Steuerstaats* (Graz and Leipzig, 1918).

4. David M. Potter, "Explicit Data and Implicit Assumptions in Historical Study," in Don E. Fehrenbacher, ed., *History and American Society: Essays of David M. Potter* (New York, 1973), 16.

1. THE PROBLEMS OF POLITICS AND PUBLIC POLICY IN THE HISTORY OF THE AMERICAN CITY

1. Samuel P. Hays, "The Changing Political Structure of the City in Industrial America," *Journal of Urban History* 1 (1974):6.

2. Ibid.

3. Charles N. Glaab and A. Theodore Brown, *A History of Urban America* (New York, 1967), 168, 198.

4. Ibid., 201.

5. Oscar Handlin, *The Uprooted* (New York, 1951), 220; Richard Hofstadter, *The Age of Reform: From Bryan to FDR* (New York, 1955), 184; Samuel P. Hays, "The Politics of Reform in Municipal Government in the Progressive Era," *Pacific Northwest Quarterly* 55 (1964):162.

6. Robert K. Merton, *Social Theory and Social Structure: Toward the Codification of Theory and Research* (Glencoe, Ill., 1949), 21–81; Alvin W. Gouldner, *The Coming Crisis of Western Sociology* (New York, 1971), 347.

7. Hays, "Changing Political Structure," 7; Morton Keller, *Affairs of State* (Cambridge, Mass., 1977), vii.

8. Eric E. Lampard, "A Conversation with Eric E. Lampard," interview in Bruce M. Stave, ed., *The Making of Urban History* (Beverly Hills, Calif., 1977), 275.

9. I have considered some of the themes in this chapter in other essays, including Terrence J. McDonald and Sally K. Ward, "Introduction," in McDonald and Ward, eds., *The Politics of Urban Fiscal Policy* (Beverly Hills, 1984), 13–38; Terrence J. McDonald, "Putting Politics Back into the History of the American City," *American Quarterly* 34 (1982):200–209; and McDonald, "Toward an Interdisciplinary History of the American City: Comment," *Journal of Urban History* 8 (1982):454–462.

10. E. J. Hobsbawm, "From Social History to the History of Society," *Daedalus* 100 (1971):21; Samuel P. Hays, "A Systematic Social History," in George Athan Billias and Gerald Grob, eds., *American History: Retrospect and Prospect* (New York, 1971), 317.

11. See Arthur M. Schlesinger, Sr., *The Rise of the City, 1878–1898* (New York, 1933), and "The City in American History," *Mississippi Valley Historical Review* 27 (1940):43–66. For a useful critique of Schlesinger's work, see William Diamond, "On the Dangers of an Urban Interpretation of History," in Eric F. Goldman, ed., *Historiography and Urbanization: Essays in American History in Honor of W. Stull Holt* (Baltimore, 1941), 67–108. The "activity context" is Hays's term; see his "A Systematic Social History," 319. Trevelyan is quoted in Hobsbawm, "From Social History to the History of Society," 21.

12. Every major city and many minor cities have their biographies. They range from the encyclopedic, like Bessie L. Pierce's *A History of Chicago,* 3 vols. (New York, 1937–1957), to single-volume works like Bayrd Still's *Milwaukee: The History of a City* (Madison, Wis., 1948). Works of urban local color are too numerous to mention. This type of work might include local variations on such books as Herbert Asbury's *The Barbary Coast* (Garden City, N.Y., 1933), or Lloyd Wendt and Herman Kogan's *Bosses in Lusty Chicago* (Bloomington, Ind., 1943). My "debonair scoundrel" category is borrowed from the title of a biography of San Francisco's "Boss" Abraham Ruef by Lately Thomas, entitled *A Debonair Scoundrel* (New York, 1962).

13. Handlin, *Uprooted,* 210–213, 221.

14. Hofstadter, *Age,* 182–185.

15. For criticism of Handlin, see Rudolph J. Vecoli, "*Contadini* in Chicago: A Critique of *The Uprooted,*" *Journal of American History* 60 (1964):404–417. J. Joseph Huthmacher, "Urban Liberalism and the Age of Reform," *Mississippi Valley Historical Review* 49 (1962):231–241.

16. Eric Lampard, "American Historians and the Study of Urbanization," *American Historical Review* 66 (1961):49–61.

17. Stephen Thernstrom, "Reflections on the New Urban History," *Daedalus* 100 (1971):359–375.

18. Theodore Hershberg, "The New Urban History: Toward an Interdisciplinary History of the City," in Theodore Hershberg, ed., *Philadelphia: Work, Space, Family, and Group Experience in the Nineteenth Century. Essays Toward an Interdisciplinary History of the City* (New York, 1981), 28.

19. David M. Potter, "Roy F. Nichols and the Rehabilitation of American Political History," in Don E. Fehrenbacher, ed., *History and American Society: Essays of David M. Potter* (New York, 1973), 216.

20. This theme runs throughout Hays's works, which have been collected in Samuel P. Hays, *American Political History as Social Analysis* (Knoxville, Tenn., 1980). For the originals, see, for example, Samuel P. Hays, "History as Human Behavior," *Iowa Journal of History* 58 (1960):193–206; Hays, "The Politics of Reform in Municipal Government in the Progressive Era," *Pacific Northwest Quarterly* 55 (1964):157–169; Hays, "The Social Analysis of American Political History, 1880–1920," *Political Science Quarterly* 80 (1965):373–394; Hays, "Archival Sources for American Political History," *American Archivist* 38 (1965):17–30; Hays, "Political Parties and the Community-Society Continuum," in William Nisbet Chambers and Walter Dean Burnham, eds., *The American Party Systems: Stages of Political Development* (New York, 1967), 152–181; Hays, "New Possibilities for American Political History: The Social Analysis of Political Life," in Seymour Martin Lipset and Richard Hofstadter, eds., *Sociology and History: Methods* (New York, 1968), 181–227; and Hays, "A Systematic Social History," in George Athan Billias and Gerald Grob, eds., *American History: Retrospect and Prospect* (New York, 1971), 315–366.

21. Hays, "Social Analysis," 374; "Political Parties," 152; "Politics," 169; Robert P. Swierenga, ed., *Quantification in American History* (New York, 1970), 189.

22. Hays, "Politics," 165; Hays, "Changing Political Structure," 6.

23. Hays, "Politics," 161, 166, 169.

24. Ibid., 166, 161, 162.

25. Michael H. Ebner and Eugene M. Tobin, eds., *The Age of Urban Reform: New Perspectives on the Progressive Era* (Port Washington, N.Y., 1977).

26. Charles N. Glaab and A. Theodore Brown, *A History of Urban America* (New York, 1967), 174; Alan D. Anderson, *The Origin and Resolution of an Urban Crisis: Baltimore, 1890–1930* (Baltimore, 1977), 27, 8.

27. Hays, "Changing Political Structure," 16.

28. Ballard C. Campbell, "American Governmental History Versus the College Textbooks," paper read at the 1983 meeting of the Organization of American Historians, 11. Campbell has made the same point in his book, *Representative Democracy: Public Policy and Midwestern Legislatures in the Late Nineteenth Century* (Cambridge, Mass., 1980). Anderson, *Urban Crisis,* 9–12.

29. Roy W. Bahl, "Studies on Determinants of Public Expenditure: A Review," in Selma J. Mushkin and John F. Cotton, eds., *Sharing Federal Funds for State and Local Needs* (New York, 1969), 185. For other considerations of these studies, see Richard I. Hofferbert, "State and Community Policy Studies: A Review of Comparative Input-Output Analyses," *Political Science Annual* 3 (1972):3–72; Robert R. Alford and Roger Friedland, "Political Participation and Public Policy," *Annual Review of Sociology* 1 (1975):429–479.

30. Harvey E. Brazer, *City Expenditures in the United States* (New York, 1959). Brazer's study compared data collected in 1951 on 462 cities with populations of over 25,000 people.

31. Robert L. Lineberry and Robert E. Welch, Jr., "Who Gets What: Measuring the Distribution of Urban Public Services," *Social Science Quarterly* 54 (1974):700–712; Alford and Friedland, "Political Participation," 440–441; Lineberry and Welch, "Who Gets What," 700.

32. J. Rogers Hollingsworth and Ellen Jane Hollingsworth, *Dimensions in*

Urban History: Historical and Social Science Perspectives on Middle-Size American Cities (Madison, Wis., 1979), 139, 141. Anderson, *Origin & Resolution* 26. I have considered the arguments of these books in some detail in a review essay, "From Economics to Political Economy in the History of Urban Public Policy," *Journal of Urban History* 8 (1982):355–363.

33. Anderson, *Origin and Resolution,* 1; Hollingsworth and Hollingsworth, *Dimensions in Urban History,* 38, 125.

2. THE INSTITUTIONAL CONTEXT AND OVERALL TRENDS

1. *An Act to Repeal the Several Charters of the City of San Francisco, to Establish the Boundaries of the City and County of San Francisco, and to Consolidate the Government thereof* (San Francisco, 1856). Hereafter I refer to this as the "Consolidation Act" (1856). See also *Statutes of California, 1856* (Sacramento, 1856), 145. The act was introduced in the State Senate by Horace Hawes of San Francisco in January 1856 and passed on April 19, 1856, to take effect on July 1 of that year. For more information on the legislative history of the act, see Susan M. Kingsbury, "Municipal History of San Francisco to 1879" (master's thesis, Stanford University, 1899), 204–209.

2. Earthquake and fire damage to city property is assessed in Doris Muscatine, *Old San Francisco: The Biography of a City* (New York, 1975), 431. A more formal report is contained in a special section of the San Francisco *Municipal Reports* for the fiscal year 1905/06.

3. "Consolidation Act" (1856), 23. The reform charter was narrowly approved by the San Francisco electorate on May 26, 1898, approved by the state legislature on January 26, 1899, and in effect in San Francisco on January 8, 1900. See *Charter of the City and County of San Francisco* (San Francisco, 1900).

4. "Consolidation Act" (1856), 26–27.

5. Ibid., 23. For the change in the maximum tax rate, see Kingsbury, "Municipal History," 242, and also *The Consolidation Act or Charter of the City and County of San Francisco* (San Francisco, 1866), 30. Hereafter I refer to this edition of the 1856 act as the "Consolidation Act" (1866). It contains amendments to the original passed in its first decade.

6. "Consolidation Act" (1856), 3. For more on the duties of these officers, see Kingsbury, "Municipal History," 222–224.

7. "Consolidation Act" (1856).

8. Ibid., 26. A third fund, the Police Fund, which was a supplement to the main expense of policing covered in the General Fund, received no tax monies.

9. The rate for the fiscal year 1859/60 was published in the *Daily Alta California,* September 19, 1859, 1. The 1890/91 rate is given in "An Order Providing Revenue for Municipal Purposes for the Fiscal Year Ending June 30, 1891," printed in the appendix to the *Municipal Reports* for 1889/90, 261.

10. "Consolidation Act" (1856), 30.

11. *Statutes of California, 1877/78,* 111–113, 333–334. The effect of the act is explained in John P. Young, *San Francisco: A History of the Pacific Coast Metropolis* (San Francisco, 1912), II:530.

12. For details on the duties and organization of the supervisors see Kingsbury, "Municipal History," 223 ff. San Francisco *Examiner,* August 3, 1870.

13. William A. Bullough, *The Blind Boss and His City: Christopher Augustine Buckley and Nineteenth Century San Francisco* (Berkeley, Los Angeles, London, 1979), 57.

14. Examples of such headlines can be found in San Francisco newspapers for January 27, 1899, the day after the charter was approved by the legislature.

15. For background on these charter campaigns, see Mildred P. Martin, "City Government in San Francisco: A Half Century of Charter Development" (master's thesis, University of California, Berkeley, 1911), 50–55; Young, *San Francisco,* II:555–556, 702; Stephen P. Erie, "The Development of Class and Ethnic Politics in San Francisco, 1870–1910: A Critique of the Pluralist Interpretation" (Ph.D. diss., University of California, Los Angeles, 1975), 309–312.

16. Martin, "City Government," 44–45; Young, *San Francisco,* I:406, II:546.

17. R. Hal Williams, *The Democratic Party and California Politics, 1880–1896* (Stanford, Calif., 1973), 4; San Francisco *Bulletin,* August 3, 1873.

18. Jon C. Teaford, "Special Legislation and the Cities, 1865–1900," *The American Journal of Legal History* 23 (1979):189–212; Teaford, *The Unheralded Triumph: City Government in America, 1870–1900* (Baltimore, 1984), 83–102. Quotations are from *Unheralded Triumph,* 91–92, and "Special Legislation," 194.

19. On the anti-debt provisions in the state constitution, see William C. Fankhauser, "A Financial History of California: Public Revenues, Debts, and Expenditures," in Adolph C. Miller, ed., *University of California Publications in Economics* 3 (1913):118. Roger Lotchin, *San Francisco, 1846–1856: From Hamlet to City* (New York, 1974), 137. It is worth noting that in his history of Los Angeles, Robert M. Fogelson has noted similarly that "Los Angeles' government was fettered less by its legal inferiority [to the state legislature] than by its citizens' political attitudes." Fogelson, *The Fragmented Metropolis: Los Angeles, 1850–1930* (Cambridge, Mass., 1967), 28. On the legislative history of the Consolidation Act, see Kingsbury, "Municipal History," 204–209.

20. "Consolidation Act" (1856), 22. Teaford, *Unheralded Triumph,* 84.

21. The procedure for conducting this survey was straightforward. The supplemental acts were located in a volume entitled *The Consolidation Act and Other Acts* (San Francisco, 1876) and were traced by title into the annual volumes of *Statutes* published by the legislature. All supplements passed from 1856 through the compilation in 1876 were checked in these volumes in order to find their bill numbers and house of origination. With this information, all but four of the ninety bills could be located in the indexes to the *Journal* of the house of origination, and from there it was possible to locate in the proceedings of the respective house the information just summarized.

22. State of California, *The Journal of the Assembly During the Twenty-first Session of the Legislature of the State of California,* 1875/76 (Sacramento, 1876), 479, 483.

23. For this situation in the case of the police department, see "Consolidation Act" (1856), 9, which sets the maximum number of police at thirty, and also the "Consolidation Act" (1866), which sets the maximum at 100.

24. McCoppin's report was given in the *Daily Alta California,* May 3, 1864.

25. For histories of the city-state relationship in the professionalization and expansion of the police and fire departments and the settlement of the "outside

lands," which led to the founding of Golden Gate Park, see Kingsbury, "Municipal History," 269–273, 280–283, 301–304. Leontina Murphy has analyzed the origins of the hospital and almshouse in "Public Care of the Dependent Sick in San Francisco, 1847–1936" (master's thesis, University of California, Berkeley, 1936), 29–63. In each of these cases, the pattern just described was repeated: the board of supervisors initiated the action, the legislature confirmed or enacted it, and the board was given fiscal control of the project within certain boundaries set by the legislature. This sequence of events is discussed in more detail in chap. 5 for the case of the police department.

26. These remarks are quoted in Young, *San Francisco*, II:515.

27. "Consolidation Act" (1856), 24. The act or ordinance that began the actual series of volumes has been lost.

28. Ernest S. Griffith, *The Modern Development of City Government in the United Kingdom and the United States* (London, 1927), I:86.

29. Unless otherwise specified, all revenue and expenditure data referred to in the rest of chap 2 are taken from the San Francisco *Municipal Reports* for fiscal years 1859/60 through 1905/06. Unless otherwise specified, all dollar amounts have been converted to real (as opposed to current) values on the basis of the price index discussed in appendix A. A series of values for annual population has been developed by means of linear interpolation on the basis of the real values discovered in the censuses of 1860, 1870, 1880, 1890, 1900, and 1910. Within each decade, then, population is assumed to have increased at a constant amount, determined by the beginning and ending values of the census reports. While this is obviously a less than perfect measure—and one that surely understates the volatility of population growth in the nineteenth-century city—it is the way that the San Francisco city government itself figured population growth. For example, the population series developed by the school and health departments were calculated on this basis. Moreover, this is becoming standard practice among historians using time-series data. For examples of the use of linear interpolation of population series in other works, see Eric H. Monkkonen, *Police in Urban America, 1860–1920* (New York, 1981), and Maris Vinovskis and Carl Kaestle, *Education and Social Change in Nineteenth-Century Massachusetts* (New York, 1980). Rates of growth of all variables referred to in chap. 2 were calculated by means of log linear equations of the form log $y_t = \log A + bX$, where X = time. In this form, the rate is the coefficient on X. For an explanation of this procedure, see Robert S. Pindyck and Daniel L. Rubinfeld, *Econometric Models and Economic Forecasts* (New York, 1976), 422–428.

30. The best overviews of the system of taxation in California during these years are Carl C. Plehn, "The General Property Tax in California," in American Economic Association *Economic Studies* 2 (1897):119–198, and Fankhauser, "Financial," 180–321. For these definitions in 1860 and 1872, see Fankhauser, "Financial History," 131, 232. The differences are not significant. For the value of San Francisco's assessment, see Plehn, "General Property Tax," 167, 173–175. The new political codes were collected in *Political Code of the State of California* (Sacramento, 1872).

31. Plehn, "General Property Tax," 130–131 discusses the evasion. C. K. Yearley, *The Money Machines: The Breakdown and Reform of Governmental and Party Finance in the North, 1860–1920* (Albany, N.Y., 1970), 71.

32. The assessment form is reproduced in Plehn, "General Property Tax,"

188–194, who declared that the escape of personal property from taxation was the principal inequality in the property tax law of this period. Ibid., 152.

33. Ibid., 133. *Eleventh Census,* "Wealth, Debt, and Taxation" (Washington, 1890), II:377.

34. Fankhauser, "Financial," 234–235; Plehn, "The Taxation of Mortgages in California," *Yale Review* (May 1899):39–44. I have excluded these temporary increases in the valuation from the statistical analysis in the chapters that follow.

35. Fankhauser, "Financial History," 276–299 reviews these changes.

36. Fankhauser describes the powers of the board and the changes demanded in the San Francisco levy in ibid., 284–289. The loophole in the revenue provisions of the political code of 1872 was provided by "An Act in Relation to the Assessment and Collection of Taxes upon Personal Property in the City and County of San Francisco," which exempted the city's revenue procedure from the provisions of the political code and thus from changes in that code. For the act, see *Statutes of California, 1874* (Sacramento, 1874), 477–479. The differences in state and city procedures are explained in the "Revenue Orders" of the *Municipal Reports* for the fiscal year 1882/83, appendix, 210. For an example of a successful attempt of city officials to dissuade the state board from raising the assessment, see "Financial Exhibit and Revenue Orders," *Municipal Reports,"* 1896/97, appendix, 398–406.

37. Plehn describes this change in "General Property Tax," 134; on the techniques of evasion, see ibid., 154.

38. From 1860 to 1872, the state revenue laws required the setting of the tax rate before the assessment roll was completed, and thus before local and state officials had any idea of the revenue available. This resulted in both high and fluctuating tax rates—high to protect against uncertainty, low when a previous year's caution produced a large surplus of revenue that was carried over into the next year.

39. I have followed the history of these funds through the *Municipal Reports.* For additional information on the School Fund, see also Kingsbury, "Municipal History," 289–290; Young, *San Francisco,* I:454–456; and Lee A. Dolson, Jr., "The Administration of the San Francisco Public Schools, 1847–1947" (Ph.D. diss., University of California, Berkeley, 1965). Although the board of supervisors set the school tax rate—that is, the portion of the total tax rate which was to go for school expenses—and thus controlled the overall level of expenditure on the School and School Building Funds, a separately elected board of education allocated these funds.

40. For details on the Street Fund, see *Daily Alta California,* August 23, 1871; for a history of the financing of street work to that point and for overall accounts, see Kingsbury, "Municipal History," 273–276; Young, *San Francisco,* I:91, 408, II:518, 568–569, 753; and Lotchin, *San Francisco,* 166. For the Park Fund, see Young, *San Francisco,* II:637.

41. I have followed the history of the city's indebtedness through the *Municipal Reports.* For the history of bond issues before 1880, see Kingsbury, "Municipal History," 245–246. After 1880, no new bonds were issued until 1899. On the history of the Corporate Debt Fund, see "An Act to Authorize the Funding of the Floating Debt of the City of San Francisco and to Provide for the Payment of Same," *Law of 1851* (Sacramento, 1851), 387; "Consolidation Act" 1856, 5; and Young, *San Francisco,* I:193. Fankhauser, "Financial History," 208, lists the railroad indebtedness of all localities in California. Young chron-

icles San Francisco's experience with railroad bonds in *San Francisco,* I:359–362. The state legislation authorizing the bonded indebtedness in all of these cases also specified the amount that was to be placed in the sinking funds for each year. Successive city administrations had no choice about the amount of expenditure for indebtedness; rather, they were honoring the commitments of previous administrations.

42. I have analyzed the details of salary and nonsalary expenditures on the subcategories of the General Fund (e.g., police department, fire department, almshouse, etc.) in McDonald, "Urban Development, Political Power, and Municipal Expenditure in San Francisco, 1860–1910: A Quantitative Investigation of Historical Theory" (Ph.D. diss., Stanford University, 1979), 27–79. For further information on the police, see Kingsbury, "Municipal History," 269–272, and Young, *San Francisco,* I:447, II:541. On the history of the fire department, see Kingsbury, "Municipal History," 106, 277–280, and Young, *San Francisco,* I:106. The category "social welfare" is my invention and represents the total of expenditures for the purposes listed. These are also analyzed in McDonald, "Urban Development." For further discussions of these services, see Kingsbury, "Municipal History," 283–297, and Young, *San Francisco,* II:784. The city did not control or finance its harbor for most of this period, and gas and water supplies were privately owned.

3. TESTING THE SOCIOECONOMIC STRUCTURAL THEORY

1. In calling these developments structural, I am loosely following the definition of political sociologist Robert Alford, who considers structural factors to include "relatively unchanging elements of the society and polity," such as "the economic base of the community, its social and economic composition, . . . the distribution of population in a community by class, age, and other characteristics, and the amount of land reserve." These factors, he adds, may be regarded as "those which are at least potentially quantifiable." Robert R. Alford with Harry M. Scoble, *Bureaucracy and Participation: Political Cultures in Four Wisconsin Cities* (Chicago, 1969), 2. The specific contents of the socioeconomic structural hypothesis discussed in chap. 3 are taken from the historical literature, of course. In addition, since this is a work of history, it is probably useful to consider structural factors not as "relatively unchanging" over time, but as unchangeable at a certain historical moment—the social and economic "givens," as it were, of particular historical situations. Charles N. Glaab and A. Theodore Brown, *A History of Urban America* (New York, 1967), 174.

2. Alan D. Anderson, *The Origin and Resolution of an Urban Crisis: Baltimore, 1890–1930* (Baltimore, 1977), 8.

3. Ernest S. Griffith, *The Modern Development of City Government in the United Kingdom and the United States* (London, 1927); Bayrd Still, *Milwaukee: The History of a City* (Madison, Wis., 1948); Glaab and Brown, *History;* Zane Miller, *The Urbanization of Modern America: A Brief History* (New York, 1973); Howard P. Chudacoff, *The Evolution of American Urban Society* (Englewood Cliffs, N.J., 1975); Anderson, *Origin and Resolution.*

4. Anderson, *Origin and Resolution,* 9–13, 47.

5. Griffith, *Modern Development of City Government,* I: 82–83; Still, *Mil-*

waukee, 230; Glaab and Brown, *History*, 168, 198, 201; Miller, *Urbanization*, 51; Chudacoff, *Evolution of American Urban Society*, 126.

6. C. K. Yearley, *The Money Machines: The Breakdown and Reform of Governmental and Party Finances in the North, 1880–1920* (Albany, N.Y., 1970), 3; Michael H. Ebner and Eugene M. Tobin, eds., *The Age of Urban Reform: New Perspectives on the Progressive Era* (Port Washington, N.Y., 1977); Maury Klein and Harvey Kantor, *Prisoners of Progress: American Industrial Cities 1850–1920* (New York, 1976); Alexander B. Callow, ed., *The City Boss in America* (New York, 1976), 5; Samuel P. Hays, "The Changing Political Structure of the City in Industrial America," *Journal of Urban History* 1 (1974):16.

7. The Mexican governor is quoted in John P. Young, *San Francisco: A History of the Pacific Coast Metropolis* (San Francisco, 1912), I:229. Martyn J. Bowden discusses the history of the city's population in "The Dynamics of City Growth: An Historical Geography of the San Francisco Central District, 1850–1931" (Ph.D. diss., University of California, Berkeley, 1968), I:174.

8. For an analysis of the ethnicity of the population, see Stephen P. Erie, "The Development of Class and Ethnic Politics in San Francisco, 1870–1910: A Critique of the Pluralist Interpretation" (Ph.D. diss., University of California, Los Angeles, 1975), 261.

9. Jules E. Tygiel discusses the dominant ethnic groups in "Workingmen in San Francisco, 1880–1901" (Ph.D. diss., University of California, Los Angeles, 1975), 24–29. Robert A. Burchell, *The San Francisco Irish, 1848–1880* (Manchester, 1979), 34. Peter R. Decker has also pointed out that at least until 1880, most migration from within the United States to San Francisco was from eastern cities. See Decker, *Fortunes and Failures: White-Collar Mobility in Nineteenth Century San Francisco* (Cambridge, Mass., 1978), 24, 171.

10. Young discusses the settlement of these claims in *San Francisco*, I:152, 409, and the spread of the city's population during the 1860s in ibid., I:412–414.

11. Young describes the surveying of the city into the 50 and 100 vara lots in *San Francisco*, I:119. The boundaries of the districts were detailed in the San Francisco *Municipal Reports* for the fiscal year 1886/87, 306–311. Decker discusses the development of the street railway system in *Fortunes*, 212, and Young outlines the effects of transportation facilities in the 1870s, 1880s, and 1890s in *San Francisco*, II:573, 753. Other accounts of the spread of the population through the city's boundaries include Margaret King, "The Growth of San Francisco, Illustrated by Shifts in the Density of Population" (master's thesis, University of California, Berkeley, 1928), and Lilian G. Hughes, "Housing in San Francisco, 1835–1938" (master's thesis, University of California, Berkeley, 1940).

12. The annual number of real estate sales in the city as a whole and in the districts within the city was published in the San Francisco *Real Estate Circular*, which was published in the city from 1867 until 1920. By means of these figures I was able to calculate the average share of citywide sales in each district and determine the years in which the shares in each district were higher than average.

13. Decker, *Fortunes*, 31. Decker's book is now the standard secondary account of the city's commercial development in the years from 1852 to 1880.

14. Young stresses the city's commercial predominance in these years in *San Francisco*, II:488, and outlines the development of the city's trade in ibid.,

I:390–397. Mansell G. Blackford has argued that it was not until the close of the 1890s that San Francisco had real commercial rivals in Seattle and Portland. See Blackford, *The Politics of Business in California* (Columbus, Ohio, 1977), 9.

15. On the history of banking in the city, see Young, *San Francisco*, I:282, 349, 411, and, in general, Ira B. Cross, *Financing an Empire: A History of Banking in California* (Chicago, 1927).

16. Data in table 11 were compiled from the census reports for 1870 through 1900.

17. Annual statistics of business at the port were collected from the *Annual Statistical Report* of the San Francisco Chamber of Commerce for 1916. For more detail on the business at the port, see Benjamin C. Wright, *San Francisco's Ocean Trade, 1848–1911* (San Francisco, 1911).

18. Young, *San Francisco*, II:581; San Francisco *Real Estate Circular.*

19. For the history of the clearinghouse, see Young, *San Francisco*, II:525–526 and Blackford, *Politics*, 98–100. Young argues that the clearings underestimate the amount of business in ibid., II:667. Statistics on clearings were taken from the *Annual Statistical Reports* of the San Francisco Chamber of Commerce for 1903 and 1916.

20. Decker discusses this mismeasurement in *Fortunes*, 163–164, as does Neil Larry Shumsky in "Tar Flat and Nob Hill: A Social History of Industrial San Francisco During the 1870s" (Ph.D. diss., University of California, Berkeley, 1972), 22.

21. The best secondary sources on the city's early industrialization are the Decker and Shumsky works mentioned in note 20 and Robert A. Elgie, "The Development of San Francisco Manufacturing, 1848–1880: An Analysis of Regional Locational Factors and Urban Spatial Structures" (master's thesis, University of California, Berkeley, 1966).

22. Elgie, "Development of San Francisco," 25. Elgie has analyzed the factors inhibiting the development of manufacturing in the city in ibid., 8–24. For other analyses of these problems, see Decker, *Fortunes*, 65, 164, 179; Shumsky, "Tar Flat," 20; and Young, *San Francisco*, I:387; II:491, 738.

23. Elgie has traced these developments carefully in "Development of San Francisco," 25–48. See also Decker, *Fortunes*, 163–167; Shumsky, "Tar Flat," 20–23; Tygiel, "Workingmen," 18–21.

24. Data in table 12 are from census reports for 1860 through 1900.

25. Elgie, "Development of San Francisco," 28; Decker, *Fortunes*, 167; Tygiel, "Workingmen," 21; Young, *San Francisco*, I:398–400.

26. Statistics were taken from the "Report to the Surveyor General" in the *Municipal Reports* from 1866 through 1906. The origins of these reports are discussed in William C. Fankhauser, "A Financial History of California: Public Revenues, Debts, and Expenditures," in Adolph C. Miller, ed., *University of California Publications in Economics* 3 (1913):186. Even these figures suggest that the average size of manufacturing plant in the city was small, however. Among others, Tygiel has noted that the basic trend in the city's economy was toward diversification in the nineteenth century, and therefore "the majority of productive units in the city remained relatively small." Tygiel, "Workingmen," 85.

27. Decker, *Fortunes*, 166; Burchell, *San Francisco Irish*, 67; Tygiel, "Workingmen," 89.

28. Data in table 13 are taken from census reports for 1860 through 1900.

29. Decker, *Fortunes,* 171.

30. The studies of Decker and Tygiel are individual-level mobility studies. Erie, "Development of Class and Ethnic Politics," considers overall changes in the city's occupational structure from 1870 through 1910. All three of these studies categorize occupations and thus mobility according to the ranking of occupations first developed by Alba Edwards in the 1930s and popularized by Stephan Thernstrom in the 1970s. For the original see Alba M. Edwards, "A Social Economic Grouping of the Gainful Workers of the United States," *Journal of the American Statistical Association* 27 (1933):377–387. Thernstrom presents his version of the scale in appendix B in Thernstrom, *The Other Bostonians: Poverty and Progress in the American Metropolis, 1880–1970* (Cambridge, Mass., 1973), 289–302. The quotations in this paragraph are from Decker, *Fortunes,* 253; Tygiel, "Workingmen," 34–35.

31. Decker, *Fortunes,* 86; Tygiel, "Workingmen," 24; Erie, "Development of Class and Ethnic Politics," 192–193.

32. Tygiel, "Workingmen," 30–32.

33. Ibid., 31, 32.

34. Ibid., 85–86 discusses similar trends on the basis of census statistics.

35. Wilbur Thompson, *A Preface to Urban Economics* (Baltimore, Md., 1968), 148.

36. Erie, "Development of Class and Ethnic Politics," 416; Anderson, *Origin and Resolution,* 18–19.

37. We test this hypothesis by means of multiple regression analysis, a statistical technique explained in more detail in appendix B.

38. Elgie has located the major industrial concentrations in the city in these areas in "Development of San Francisco," 74–100. To determine the size of the industrial area, I simply added the acreage of these four districts, using the sizes for each given in the *Municipal Reports* for 1886/87. The boundaries of the districts did not change over time after 1870.

39. Young, *San Francisco,* I:413.

40. Again, I used the acreages of the city's districts as given in the *Municipal Reports* for 1886/87.

41. For a useful introduction to the use of dummy variables, see Robert S. Pindyck and Daniel L. Rubinfeld, *Econometric Models and Economic Forecasts* (New York, 1976), 77–84. A more advanced and more detailed analysis is available in Jan Kmenta, *Elements of Econometrics* (New York, 1971), 409–430.

42. Multiple regression analysis is based on several assumptions, one of which is that no exact linear relationship exists among the independent variables. If such a relationship does exist and two or more of the independent variables are collinear, then the equation cannot calculate accurately the independent effect of each independent variable. Because the sum of the three dummy variables we have created is exactly 1 for each of the cases under analysis, including all of them would introduce perfect collinearity in the equation and make it impossible for the equation to be calculated. The inclusion of population as an independent variable causes high multicollinearity because it is closely related to several of the other variables in the equation. In the case of high multicollinearity, the results of the equation will be calculated, but they will be unreliable because it will be difficult to determine the separate effects of the variables highly related to population. By dropping one of the dummy variables,

we avoid perfect collinearity; by controlling for the population as indicated, we reduce the problem of high multicollinearity. These are standard approaches to these problems discussed in the econometrics textbooks already noted.

4. TESTING THE POLITICAL CULTURAL THEORY

1. Ira Katznelson, "The Crisis of the Capitalist City: Urban Politics and Social Control," in Willis D. Hawley and Michael Lipsky, eds., *Theoretical Perspectives on Urban Politics* (Englewood Cliffs, N.J., 1976), 215.

2. Charles N. Glaab and A. Theodore Brown, *A History of Urban America* (New York, 1967), 158; Zane Miller, *The Urbanization of Modern America: A Brief History* (New York, 1973); John M. Allswang, *Bosses, Machines, and Urban Voters: An American Symbiosis* (Port Washington, N.Y., 1977), 24; Richard Hofstadter, *The Age of Reform: From Bryan to FDR* (New York, 1955), 185.

3. Ernest S. Griffith, *The Modern Development of City Government in the United Kingdom and the United States* (London, 1927), I:151; Martin Schiesl, *The Politics of Efficiency: Municipal Administration and Reform in America, 1880–1920* (Berkeley, Los Angeles, London, 1977), 2–3.

4. The most systematic analyses of these differences in leadership, constituency, and incentive have been written by political scientists. See, for example, Raymond Wolfinger, "Why Political Machines Have Not Withered Away and Other Revisionist Thoughts," *Journal of Politics* 34 (1972):365–398, and Martin Shefter, "The Emergence of the Political Machine: An Alternative View," in Willis D. Hawley and Michael Lipsky, eds., *Theoretical Perspectives on Urban Politics* (Englewood Cliffs, N.J., 1976), 14–44.

5. Allswang, *Bosses,* 15; Oscar Handlin, *The Uprooted* (New York, 1951), 201–226.

6. Hofstadter, *Age,* 185, 316, 319; Allswang, *Bosses,* 32; Samuel P. Hays, "The Changing Political Structure of the City in Industrial America," *Journal of Urban History* 1 (1974):16.

7. Alvin W. Gouldner, *The Coming Crisis of Western Sociology* (New York, 1971), 124.

8. Shefter, "Emergence," 19.

9. General histories of San Francisco adopting this characterization of politics include Oscar Lewis, *San Francisco: Mission to Metropolis* (Berkeley, Calif., 1966); Doris Muscatine, *Old San Francisco: The Biography of a City* (New York, 1975); and John P. Young, *San Francisco: A History of the Pacific Coast Metropolis,* 2 vols. (San Francisco, 1912).

10. Stephen P. Erie, "The Development of Class and Ethnic Politics in San Francisco, 1870–1910: A Critique of the Pluralist Interpretation" (Ph.D. diss., University of California, Los Angeles, 1975), 108.

11. Election data were taken from newspaper reports of local election results.

12. From 1856 through 1871, supervisors were elected in and by the districts they represented. In 1872 the state legislature changed the method of election so that the entire board was elected biennially in the district the members represented by citywide vote. For an explanation and lamentation of this change, see *Daily Alta California,* Monday, December 3, 1872. This system remained in effect from 1873 until 1898. In 1899, the new charter required

the at-large election of eighteen supervisors. See *Charter of the City and County of San Francisco* (San Francisco, 1900), 4.

13. John S. Hittell, *A History of the City of San Francisco and Incidentally of the State of California* (San Francisco, 1878), 257. Hittell was a contemporary and admirer of the People's party, and his account portrays the party's legitimation of itself. For other accounts, see Robert M. Senkewicz, "Business and Politics in Gold Rush San Francisco, 1851–1856" (Ph.D. diss., Stanford University, 1974); Roger Lotchin, *San Francisco 1846–1856: From Hamlet to City* (New York, 1974), 213–275; Erie, "Development of Class and Ethnic Politics," 109–114; and Hittell, *History of the City*, 263, 264.

14. Accounts of San Francisco municipal politics in this period include Alexander Saxton, *The Indispensable Enemy: Labor and the Anti-Chinese Movement in California* (Berkeley, Los Angeles, London, 1971), 67–156; Neil L. Shumsky, "Tar Flat and Nob Hill: A Social History of Industrial San Francisco During the 1870s" (Ph.D. diss., University of California, Berkeley, 1972), 250–338; Helen H. Ingels, "The History of the Workingmen's Party of California" (master's thesis, University of California, Berkeley, 1919), 104–123; Mary Frances McKinney, "Denis Kearney, Organizer of the Workingmen's Party of California" (master's thesis, University of California, Berkeley, 1939); Erie, "Development of Class and Ethnic Politics," 128–184; ibid., 147; Shumsky, "Tar Flat," 277, 267.

15. Accounts of Buckley's rise to power and the general character of municipal politics in the 1880s include Alexander B. Callow, "San Francisco's Blind Boss," *Pacific Historical Review* 25 (1956):261–279, and William Bullough, *The Blind Boss and His City: Christopher Augustine Buckley and Nineteenth-Century San Francisco* (Berkeley, Los Angeles, London, 1979). See also Bullough, "Chris Buckley and San Francisco: The Man and the City," in James P. Walsh, ed., *The San Francisco Irish 1856–1976* (San Francisco, 1978), 27–41; Bullough, "Hannibal vs. the Blind Boss: 'The Junta,' Chris Buckley and Democratic Reform Politics in San Francisco," *Pacific Historical Review* 46 (1977):181–206; and Bullough, "The Steam Beer Handicap: Chris Buckley and the San Francisco Municipal Election of 1896," *California Historical Quarterly* 54 (1975), 245–262. Callow, "Boss," 264; Bullough, "Chris Buckley and San Francisco," 27; ibid., 34.

16. Bullough, "Chris Buckley and San Francisco," 35. Buckley said that he "placed a stiff value on my services and always regarded myself as a high priced man."

17. Bullough, "Hannibal," 190–206; Callow, "Boss," 277–278.

18. Bullough, "Chris Buckley and San Francisco," 35.

19. Erie, "Development of Class and Ethnic Politics," 115–119. The reform efforts of these mayors were noted in a contemporary account: Julian Ralph, "Reform in San Francisco," *Harper's Weekly* 39 (1895):230–231. The election of 1892 was the first held after the state legislature passed the Reform Ballot Act of 1891, which introduced the Australian ballot and made it easier to get parties on the ballot and vote a split ticket. This law was at least partially responsible for the increase in the number of parties on the ballot in the 1890s. The effects of this law are discussed more carefully in chap. 6. For a copy of the law, see *The Election Laws Governing Primary, City, County, and Presidential Elections*, E. G. Waite, comp. (Sacramento, 1892).

20. Phelan's life and municipal career are chronicled by an admirer in Roy Swanstrom, "Reform Administration of James D. Phelan, Mayor of San Francisco,

1897–1902" (master's thesis, University of California, Berkeley, 1949). Jud Kahn has outlined Phelan's conception of the "city beautiful" in "Imperial San Francisco: History of a Vision" (Ph.D. diss., University of California, Berkeley, 1971).

21. William Issel, "Class and Ethnic Conflict in San Francisco Political History: The Reform Charter of 1898," *Labor History* 18 (1977):341–359; ibid., 357. According to Swanstrom, "Reform Administration," 45, charter advocates were "convinced that a new charter would fare better at a special charter election, depending on the advocates of reform to turn out at the polls in greater proportion than those who were opposed or indifferent." Issel, "Class and Ethnic Conflict" reports the voting statistics.

22. *Charter of the City and County of San Francisco* (San Francisco, 1900).

23. The best account of these developments and their political implications is Edward J. Rowell, "The Union Labor Party of San Francisco, 1901–1911" (Ph.D. diss., University of California, Berkeley, 1938), 1–35.

24. Rowell, "Union Labor Party," 10–13. Police officers were assigned to convoy nonunion wagons through the streets, to break up picket lines, and to clear waterfront streets of strikers. In the process, 110 strikers were arrested, although only 15 were eventually convicted of an offense.

25. Walton Bean, *Boss Ruef's San Francisco* (Berkeley, Los Angeles, London, 1972); James Walsh has argued that "Boss" Ruef had no machine in "Abe Ruef Was No Boss: Machine Politics, Reform and San Francisco," *California Historical Quarterly* 51 (1972):3–16. Rowell has noted the party's nonelite leadership in "Union Labor Party," 22–24.

26. Rowell, "Union Labor Party," 22–24; Erie, "Development of Class and Ethnic Politics," 196–230. Rowell, "Union Labor Party," 125–131, 132–135, 229.

27. McCoppin was quoted regarding the control of the independent parties in the San Francisco *Bulletin,* August 23, 1869. Bryant is quoted in William Heintz, *San Francisco's Mayors: From the Gold Rush to the Silver Bonanza* (Woodside, Calif., 1975), 98. Both Buckley and his Republican opponent, Martin Kelly, published serialized memoirs in the San Francisco *Bulletin* after the turn of the century. Each noted the decline of the "old" style politics after 1892. See James H. Wilkins, ed., "The Reminiscences of Christopher A. Buckley," San Francisco *Bulletin,* August 31–October 9, 1918, December 23, 1918–February 5, 1919, and Wilkins, ed., "Martin Kelly's Story," ibid., September 1–November 26, 1917. Swanstrom, "Phelan" and Bean, *Boss* discuss the contrasts between the reform period from 1892–1901 and the Union Labor party period that followed (see table 19).

28. Hittell, *History of the City,* 263–264; Bullough, "Chris Buckley and San Francisco," 34 suggests that Buckley found jobs for his supporters "not infrequently on the public payroll." San Francisco *Chronicle,* January 5, 1897. Rowell, "Union Labor Party," 36–106 analyzes the party's need for patronage in its various campaigns.

29. The name, office, and term of each official were collected from the *Municipal Reports.* Year of election and party were collected from newspaper reports of election returns. Occupation and address at the time of the election were taken from city directories, and the latter were mapped against the city's ward boundaries to determine ward of residence. Place of birth was available in the *Great Registers* of voter registration for 1866, 1867, 1869, 1871, 1875, 1876, 1877, 1880, 1882, 1886, 1888–1892, and 1894–1904.

30. The scale according to which occupations have been categorized is actually the Edwards-Thernstrom scale, as modified for San Francisco by Jules Tygiel. For the originals, see Alba M. Edwards, "A Social Economic Grouping of the Gainful Workers of the United States," *Journal of the American Statistical Association* 27 (1933):377–387, and appendix B in Stephan Thernstrom, *The Other Bostonians: Poverty and Progress in the American Metropolis, 1880–1970* (Cambridge, Mass., 1973), 289–302. Tygiel's categories are found in the appendix to "Workingmen in San Francisco, 1880–1901" (Ph.D. diss., University of California, Los Angeles, 1975), 417–422. Although there has been some debate over the validity of these categories, they are the basis of all existing studies of San Francisco's occupational structure. By adopting these categories I was able to tie my collective biography to the rest of the city's social structure. To date, no one has proved the costs or benefits of the use of alternate occupational categorization schemes. What is needed is an experimental test that applies all of the various schemes to the same place to determine how the use of one or another changes our view of history there. Lacking such a test, the proponents of the various schemes are simply talking past one another, and others are justified in choosing the scheme that allows them to build most effectively on the work of others.

31. Information on the ethnicity of the population was taken from census reports. Ward boundaries were taken from the *Municipal Reports.*

32. Richard Wade, "Urbanization," in C. Vann Woodward, ed., *The Comparative Approach to American History* (New York, 1968), 187–205; Zane L. Miller, *Boss Cox's Cincinnati: Urban Politics in the Progressive Era* (New York, 1968).

33. Tygiel, "Workingmen," 22.

34. Ibid.

35. Statistics on ethnicity of the population are from census reports.

36. The observant reader will note that the number of years under analysis and the definition of the political eras in the equations analyzing the officials are different from those in the equations analyzing fiscal policy. This is intentional but requires explanation nonetheless. Chap. 4 attempts to accomplish three analytical tasks with different types and amounts of data for each. First, it tests for statistically significant differences in the backgrounds of officials elected in the five periods of the city's political history already established. For this purpose there are data on the background of officials elected at every election from 1859 through 1905 inclusive, and we properly bound the political eras with the first and last election of each era. Thus the PTP era (period of local reform parties) is bounded by the first election of the era for which we have data, which was 1860, and the last, which was 1873. All of the eras displayed in table 19 are defined in this way. The number of observations in these equations is thirty-one—the number of elections held between 1860 and 1905 (annually from 1860 through 1871, biennially thereafter). The second analytical task is to determine whether these political eras have statistically significant effects on the fiscal variables. The data available for this are influenced by the third task, which is to compare the effects on the fiscal variables of the political cultural eras and the socioeconomic structural variables in combination. As we saw in chap. 3, because of missing data in some of the independent socioeconomic variables, the analysis of the fiscal variables there could be conducted only on the years 1870 through 1905. Because regression analysis can be con-

ducted only on complete cases, when the political cultural and socioeconomic variables are combined in the same equation, we can include only the years 1870 through 1905. To compare the effects of these variables separately, the analysis must also be conducted on the same number of years (i.e., 1870 through 1905). Therefore, every analysis of fiscal variables in this book has been conducted only on those years. The political eras in the fiscal equations are defined differently from those in the analyses of officials, both because of this different number of observations and because of the difference between election years and fiscal years. Because we are analyzing fiscal data only from 1870 through 1905, only the last five years of the PTP era can be included in the analysis. This would be unfortunate if the officials elected in those five years were markedly different from those elected in the rest of the era. Luckily, they are not. The socioeconomic backgrounds of the officials during the last five years of this era were quite similar to those of the officials during the first ten years. Whatever effect background has on fiscal policy is safely captured within this portion of the whole era. The political eras defined in table 25 also differ from those in table 19 because officials did not control their own fiscal policy until the year after they were first elected. The era of irregularity is an example that demonstrates this. Officials elected in September 1875 took office in January 1876 and were bound by the budget of their predecessors until June 30, 1876, which was the end of fiscal year 1875/76. The budget prepared by the new officials was for fiscal year 1876/77, and the level of expenditure and so forth was recorded in the *Municipal Reports* released in 1877. For this reason, although the electoral political beginning of this era was 1875 and end was 1881, the fiscal political era extended from 1877 through 1883.

5. ESTABLISHING THE BOUNDARIES: POLITICAL INSTITUTIONS AND FISCAL IDEOLOGIES, 1856–1882

1. James H. Wilkins, ed., "The Reminiscences of Christopher A. Buckley," San Francisco *Bulletin,* December 23, 1918.
2. The analysis of fiscal political ideas in chaps. 5, 6, and 7 is based on three sources: (1) the published and unpublished secondary sources on the history of San Francisco; (2) the published and unpublished papers and memoirs of San Francisco politicians; and, most important, (3) an informal content analysis of newspaper accounts of all municipal election campaigns during the years 1860–1905. This analysis was informal because it did not involve the search for and counting of certain phrases, statements, and viewpoints. It was systematic, however, in two respects. First, it included all stories and editorials relating to the campaign for a period beginning two months before the date of every election. This allowed the analysis to encompass both the local nominating conventions and meetings of platform committees, and the actual elections themselves. Second, to avoid partisan political bias, the analysis of each election was conducted in four newspapers: the *Alta* and the *Chronicle,* which were nominally Republican; the *Examiner,* which was steadfastly Democratic; and the *Bulletin,* which was frequently independent. In each case I looked for ideas about the relationship between economics and politics, the role of the local public sector, and

the fiscal issues in each campaign. The investigation of the actual mechanics of fiscal policymaking is based on the information developed in chap. 2, along with the annual newspaper and official reports of the setting of the tax rate and the allocation of expenditure. Prior to 1881, the meetings at which these acts of fiscal policymaking were performed were covered only in the newspapers. Thereafter, a report of the proceedings was published annually in the *Municipal Reports*. I again followed these proceedings through time in several newspapers for the first period, and through newspapers and the official reports during the second.

3. I traced registration and other voting requirements through five compilations of the state's election laws: (1) *The Election Laws of the State of California*, J. F. Bowman, ed. (San Francisco, 1872); (2) *The Election Laws Governing Primary, City, County, State, Congressional, and Presidential Elections*, W. C. Hendricks, comp. (Sacramento, 1890); (3) *The Election Laws Governing Primary, City, County, State and Presidential Elections*, E. G. Waite, comp. (Sacramento, 1892); (4) *The Election Laws Governing Primary, City, County, State, and Presidential Elections*, E. G. Waite, comp. (Sacramento, 1893); and (5) *The Election Laws of California*, C. F. Curry, comp. (Sacramento, 1903). The editor of the first of these was a San Francisco attorney; the other compilers were all California secretaries of state.

4. I collected registration statistics from local newspaper accounts of election returns and from the *Municipal Reports* for 1908/09, which contained a historical table of all registration and election statistics from 1878 to that date on page 1118. The number of males aged twenty-one and older was estimated by means of linear interpolation between census observations at 1870 and every ten years thereafter. Both Peter R. Decker, *Fortunes and Failures: White Collar Mobility in Nineteenth Century San Francisco* (Cambridge, Mass., 1978) and Jules E. Tygiel, "Workingmen in San Francisco, 1880–1901" (Ph.D. diss., University of California, Los Angeles, 1975) have discussed differences in mobility dependent on occupation, property holdings, age, and marital status. Robert G. Barrows has written of similar findings in "Hurryin Hoosiers and the American 'Pattern': Geographic Mobility in Urban North America," *Social Science History* 5 (1981):192–222. Richard Alcorn has discussed the political implications of mobility in "Leadership and Stability in Mid-Nineteenth Century America: A Case Study of an Illinois Town," *Journal of American History* 61 (1974):685–702. Eric Monkkonen has discussed these and other implications of the mobility literature in "The Fluid World of Late Nineteenth Century British and American Cities," in Richard Bessel, ed., *Themes in British and American History: A Comparative Approach, c. 1760–1970* (Milton Keynes, England, 1985), 77–83.

5. Susan M. Kingsbury considers changes in the schedule of elections between 1856 and 1879 in "Municipal History of San Francisco to 1879" (master's thesis, Stanford University, 1899), 247–251.

6. Election returns were collected from local newspaper reports. To avoid partisan bias and check for error, each of the results was checked in two different newspapers.

7. Party-printed, straight-ticket ballots were the rule in the state until the election of 1892, when the so-called Reform Ballot Act passed in 1891 took effect. The content and effects of this act are considered in more detail in chap. 6. Systematic analysis of the social bases of political action within the city is impossible because of the destruction of official precinct-level election returns

in the earthquake and fire, shifts in the size and definition of election districts, and inconsistent reporting of election returns below the level of the ward in local newspapers.

8. Study data.

9. This is a composite of several descriptions of these years published in San Francisco newspapers, including San Francisco *Bulletin,* October 15, 1861; ibid., October 13, 1860; San Francisco *Daily Alta California,* September 19, 1859; ibid., May 17, 1863; *Bulletin,* August 4, 1871; and San Francisco *Examiner,* October 15, 1892. These are just a few examples of the literally hundreds of similar references throughout the nineteenth century. All but the last were editorials; the last was a speech made at the ratification meeting for the Non-Partisan ticket in 1892. The use of this theme in that campaign, and again in 1898, is testimony to the longevity of this description of the city's early political history.

10. For secondary accounts of these events, see Robert M. Senkewicz, "Business and Politics in Gold Rush San Francisco, 1851–1856" (Ph.D. diss., Stanford University, 1974); Roger Lotchin, *San Francisco 1846–1856: From Hamlet to City* (New York, 1974); and Decker, *Fortunes.*

11. Coon, "Bancroft Dictation," in H. P. Coon Papers, Bancroft Library, University of California, Berkeley, 6. For details on the emergence of the party out of the vigilante movement, see John P. Young, *San Francisco: A History of the Pacific Coast Metropolis* (San Francisco, 1912), I:211–213; Mildred P. Martin, "City Government in San Francisco: A Half Century of Charter Development" (master's thesis, University of California, Berkeley, 1911), 41; Lotchin, *San Francisco 1846–1856,* 245–275; and Decker, *Fortunes,* 138.

12. Decker, *Fortunes,* 139–149.

13. Ibid., 130, 140.

14. Roger Lotchin discusses the motives of the vigilantes in *San Francisco 1846–1856,* 245–250. Although a variety of ex post facto rationales—some of which were undoubtedly true—explained the formation of the People's Reform party on the grounds of highest principles, Lotchin has argued that the most pressing immediate reason was to protect the vigilantes from political or judicial retribution from their opponents. As he has put it, "the desire for reform and the fear of retribution finally bore tangible results" in "an independent vehicle for [political] regeneration."

15. On the fiscal policy and effects of the People's party, see Martin, "City Government," 41; Young, *San Francisco,* I:216; Decker, *Fortunes,* 139, and Lotchin, *San Francisco 1846–1856,* 245–246. Lotchin convincingly attributes most of the savings to the Consolidation Act of 1856.

16. Lotchin calls these claims the "deterioration interpretation" of the origins of the vigilantism and the People's party in 1856 in *San Francisco 1846–1856,* 250. For his analysis of the claim of extravagance, see ibid., 160–163. Lotchin's is the most balanced and thoughtful account of this very controversial period of the city's history.

17. During the election of 1866, the *Alta* declared that the "People's Party is now the Republican Party" (September 3, 1866), and the *Bulletin* reported that the local candidates on the Union ticket had been nominated by the People's nominating convention (August 6, 1866). In 1869, incumbent Democratic Mayor Frank McCoppin declared that his Taxpayer party opponent was linked

with the People's party, which he called "the most cowardly [party] that ever held sway in a great city." For his statement, see the San Francisco *Examiner,* August 23, 1869. In 1871, both the *Alta* and the *Bulletin* linked the People's and Taxpayer's parties: *Alta,* August 30 and 31, and September 8, 1871; *Bulletin,* August 6, 1871. In 1873, the *Alta* called the Taxpayer's candidate for mayor the "People's and Republican" candidate (September 1, 1873).

18. Again, there are scores of citations presenting this view of municipal politics. Two editorials entitled "The People vs. The Politicians" will suffice: see the *Alta,* May 15, 1861, and the *Bulletin,* August 27, 1869.

19. *Alta,* May 15, 1861; *Bulletin,* May 13, 1863; *Bulletin,* August 25, 1871.

20. *Bulletin,* May 2, 1863. Young has noted that the secret nominating procedures of the first People's ticket continued among the independent parties for eighteen years after 1856 and were conducted by a "self-perpetuating body." See Young, *San Francisco,* I:311, 406. Martin, "City Government," 42 gives the same number of years.

21. *Bulletin,* October 13, 1866; *Alta,* May 18, 1863. According to the *Alta,* the People's party had "made, of one of the most disorderly communities, a model city," and, against the accomplishments of the independents, there were only "the indecent clamorings of a few place hunters." Ibid.

22. Coon, "Dictation," H. P. Coon Papers, Bancroft Library; Thomas H. Selby, "Bancroft Dictation," 10, Selby Papers, Bancroft Library. In spite of his pose as a political innocent, Coon was very active in politics. He had been an elected police judge for two terms before his nomination for mayor, and he served two terms in the latter office as well.

23. The chi-square of the relationship between occupation and party is 62.858 at a significance level of 0.0882, indicating that we can reject with confidence the null hypothesis that there is no relationship between party and occupations in this period. Data for this analysis are taken from the same sources as those reported in chap. 4.

24. The chi-square measuring the relationship between party and place of birth is 25.21 at the 0.0003 level of significance, indicating that we can confidently reject the null hypothesis that there is no relationship between party and place of birth in this period.

25. *Alta,* October 19, 1860; ibid., May 13, 1863.

26. Ibid., August 22, 1869. For similar uses of the "Legend," see ibid., May 27, 1860, May 15, 1862, May 18, 1863, September 3, 1866, August 31, 1871; *Bulletin,* October 15, 1861, August 4, 1871.

27. Young, *San Francisco,* I:214, and Decker, *Fortunes,* 127 reflect this perception regarding Broderick. For a different perspective see Lotchin, *San Francisco 1846–1856,* 213–244.

28. Alexander Saxton, *The Indispensable Enemy: Labor and the Anti-Chinese Movement in California* (Berkeley, Los Angeles, London, 1971), 67. Saxton's book is the best analysis of San Francisco politics during the 1870s.

29. Coon describes his decision in "Bancroft Dictation," 26.

30. *Examiner,* August 2, 1860. Study data.

31. Saxton, *Indispensable Enemy,* 67–91.

32. *Examiner,* September 4, 1867, August 29, 1870.

33. Canavan's speech was reported in the *Examiner,* October 27, 1868. For McCoppin's speech, see ibid., August 23, 1869.

34. Stephen P. Erie, "The Development of Class and Ethnic Politics in San Francisco, 1870–1910: A Critique of the Pluralist Interpretation" (Ph.D. diss., University of California, Los Angeles, 1975), 143.

35. *Examiner,* August 20, 29, 1869.

36. *Examiner,* October 1, 1868, August 24, 1869, October 21, 1869. Following up on this theme in 1873, the newspaper waxed eloquent on party spirit: "There is nothing so true, so devoted, so self-sacrificing as party spirit. It is nothing less than pure, unqualified, devotion to principle" (August 11, 1873).

37. *Examiner,* August 26, 1870, August 26, 1875, August 27, 1870. For similar themes, see also ibid., October 21, 1867, August 24, 1869, among many others.

38. *Examiner,* August 15, 1867. For an interesting analysis of the ideological roots of this position, see Saxton, *Enemy,* 21–30, 92–104. R. Hal Williams has also pointed out that during the last three decades of the nineteenth century, a similar position was characteristic of the dominant "Bourbon" or conservative wing of the Democratic party, which supported "rigid restrictions on government activity." See Williams, *The Democratic Party and California Politics* (Stanford, Calif., 1973), 60–61.

39. Young, *San Francisco,* II:561, 566; I:404.

40. *Alta,* April 27, 1864, ibid., May 15, 1862.

41. Ibid., April 27, 1864; *Bulletin,* May 8, 1863.

42. *Bulletin,* May 15, 1861, August 6, 1873.

43. Selby, "Dictation," 11; William Alvord, "Bancroft Dictation," Bancroft Library.

44. *Alta,* May 6, 1865; *Examiner,* August 5, 1875. I considered the development of these institutions in chap. 2.

45. See, for example, *Alta,* May 4, 1864, April 20, 1869; *Examiner,* June 9, 1874.

46. *Alta,* April 28, 1863. The school directors sought increases in their allocations in 1869 and and 1871; the tax collector requested two new deputies in 1869. See *Examiner,* April 20, 1869, April 18, 1871.

47. Study data. The chi-square measuring the relationship between occupation and type of office held in these years is 23.453 at the 0.1022 level of significance, indicating that we can reject the null hypothesis of no relationship between office held and occupation. As indicated by the percentages presented earlier in this chapter, an important part of this overall relationship is accounted for by the underrepresentation of these occupations among the supervisors.

48. Democratic Mayor Frank McCoppin claimed that the People's party officials deliberately lowered the rate and increased the valuation between 1860 and 1869, so that "while taxes appeared to be low, they in reality were never so high." He is quoted in the *Examiner,* August 23, 1869.

49. Among others, Young has noted the complaint of "newspaper critics" who claimed that "much money was being spent, but there was little or nothing in the way of improvement to show for the expenditure." Young, *San Francisco,* II:517. By 1875 the *Examiner* was lamenting that reform administrations had "annually increased the cost of government to alarming proportions" (August 31, 1875).

50. Bryant is quoted in William F. Heintz, *San Francisco's Mayors: From the Gold Rush to the Silver Bonanza* (Woodside, Calif., 1975), 98.

51. In 1866 and 1867, both the *Alta* and the *Bulletin* lamented the combination of local and state elections. The former proposed switching support

from the People's to the Union ticket on September 3, 1866, while the latter claimed that the change in the election schedule had been engineered by "professional politicians" who would thus "have a better opportunity to get possession of the city government" (August 24, 1867). Saxton has pointed out that the Union party was, in fact, "Republican sponsored" in *Indispensable Enemy*, 80–91. The *Alta*'s advice to independents was given on August 18, 1873. Already in 1870, the *Examiner* had declared that the Taxpayer's party was simply a "radical dodge" made up mostly of Republicans, and that it was the People's party under a new name. *Examiner*, August 25 and September 6, 1870.

52. *Alta*, August 22 and 26, 1875. The first editorial said that "we are making a fight this year which will tell on the presidential campaign." This would have been independent party heresy only a few years before.

53. Study data. The chi-square measuring the relationship between occupation and party, including only Democrats and Republicans, is 5.9 at the 0.3302 level of significance, indicating that we cannot confidently reject the hypothesis of no relationship between these variables.

54. The chi-square of the relationship between party and nativity in this period was 6.85 at the 0.1439 level of significance, indicating that there are 15 chances in 100 of a chi-square of this magnitude if there is no relationship between these variables. As we saw, during the first period the chi-square of this relationship was 25.21 at the 0.0003 level of significance, indicating that there were only 3 chances in 10,000 that these variables were, in fact, independent. The point is that the strength of this relationship is deteriorating over time.

55. Just as important as the ticket itself in causing the high level of participation in the election of 1879 was the passage by the state legislature of "An Act to regulate the registration of voters, and to secure the purity of elections in the City and County of San Francisco" on March 18, 1878. Among other things, this act changed the locus of voter registration from city hall to the election precincts, thus facilitating registration and participation. For a copy of the act, see *The Election Laws Governing Primary, City, County, State, Congressional, and Presidential Elections*, W. C. Hendricks, comp. (Sacramento, 1890), 31–40.

56. These changes in economic activities are discussed in chap. 3.

57. Bryant's speech was reported in the *Examiner*, August 27, 1877. He had also denounced indebtedness in his first campaign; cf. the *Examiner*, August 19, 1875, and the *Bulletin*, August 4, 1877. Both the county and the municipal Democratic platforms favored taxation to pay for park improvements. See *Examiner*, August 3, 1875 and July 24, 1875. The same theme was reiterated in the 1877 platform in the *Examiner*, July 24, 1877.

58. *Examiner*, June 15, 1878 covers the discussion and lists the cuts. Even then, the mayor said he signed the order after "considerable hesitation" and despite his belief that "the estimates could have been further reduced." *Examiner*, June 25, 1878.

59. *Examiner*, June 17, June 24, July 2, 1879.

60. *Examiner*, June 22, July 7, 1880; ibid., June 17, 1881.

61. Ibid., June 17, June 24, June 28, 1881.

62. David Tyack, *The One Best System: A History of American Urban Education* (Cambridge, Mass., 1974), 71. Tyack points out that nearly universal attendance was achieved in American urban public schools without the neces-

sity of compulsion because of a "broad consensus on the value of schooling." The problem was not enough places for all the children who wished to attend. This was true in San Francisco, where the school directors continually begged the supervisors for more money, only to be turned down, as we have seen and will see in more detail in chap. 6.

63. The charter basis of this relationship is discussed in chap. 2.

64. *Examiner,* July 25, 1881. Study data.

65. I am not aware of a single secondary work that does not take this position. See, for example, Saxton, *Indispensble Enemy,* 118–119; Erie, "Development of Class and Ethnic Politics," 147–148; Neil Larry Shumsky, "Tar Flat and Nob Hill: A Social History of Industrial San Francisco During the 1870s" (Ph.D. diss., University of California, Berkeley, 1972), 267; Decker, *Fortunes,* 248; and Young, *San Francisco,* II:540.

66. The works cited in note 65 also contain accounts of the "July Days" and their aftermath. Decker has demonstrated that this Committee of Public Safety, like the Vigilance Committee of 1856, was "controlled, organized, and financed by the city's elite," in *Fortunes,* 247.

67. The controversy over the police extended from August 1, 1877 through May 14, 1878. To reconstruct the issue, I read the accounts of every meeting of the board of supervisors and the police commission during those months. To avoid partisan bias, I read the accounts in the *Bulletin,* the *Alta,* and the *Examiner.* For the original plan of the Committee of Public Safety, see the *Examiner,* August 1, 1877. The *Examiner* denounced the idea of the committee appointing the police in an editorial on August 7, 1877.

68. *Examiner,* August 14, 1877; *Alta,* September 4, 1877; *Examiner,* September 13, 1877.

69. *Alta,* January 15, January 18, 1878. The *Examiner* discussed the passage and implications of the bill in an editorial on April 11, 1878.

70. Because it allowed the city to establish the size of the police, the bill was in the tradition of legislative interference discussed in chap. 2. *Alta,* April 9, 1878 discusses the authorization of 100 new police; *Examiner,* April 13, 1878 discusses the request of the Police Commission for the entire 400. *Bulletin,* May 7, 1878; *Alta,* May 9, 1878. The police commission also declared that "protection demands the immediate service of the whole force," *Examiner,* May 7, 1878.

71. For the May 6 debates, see the *Examiner, Alta,* and *Bulletin* for May 7, 1878. I added the party, place of birth, and occupation of the speakers from the collective biography data collected for this study. This information helps to demonstrate that opposition to the additional expansion cut across party, ethnicity, and occupation.

72. These debates are reported in detail in the May 14, 1878 issues of the *Alta* and the *Examiner.* Again, I supplied the biographical data on the supervisors.

73. Beginning in fiscal year 1872/73, persons assessed for more than $5,000 in personal property were listed in the *Municipal Reports.* Beginning in fiscal 1882/83, the minimum was decreased to $2,500. I had hoped to find many city officials on this list, and therefore to include personal property holdings as an important item in their collective biography. But between 1872/73, when lists began, and 1898/99, when they ended, only thirty-four of the hundreds of of-

ficials elected in these years appeared on the list, whatever its minimum. Mangels was listed in the volume of the reports for 1876/77.

74. The police committee of the board of supervisors belatedly warned the board of the fiscal implications of the police increase on June 4, 1878. See *Examiner,* June 4, 1878.

75. For accounts of the requests for aid to the unemployed, see Young, *San Francisco,* II:540, and Shumsky, "Tar Flat," 277. Although some have used this refusal as evidence of the callousness of the city government toward the unemployed, in fact, Mayor Bryant's response that he had no authority to comply with the demand was correct. Given the restrictions of the Consolidation Act and the strictures of the budgetary process, both institutional and political, there could be no money for such work until the next fiscal year, assuming that city officials were willing to take up the demand then in any case. The confusion of the WPC (Workingmen's Party of California) on this issue is reflected in its abandonment of such a demand in its own 1879 campaign. This is just one of the many contradictions in this remarkably confused—and confusing—political movement. The *Bulletin* first discussed the 1879 WPC platform on July 24, 1879. See also August 6 and August 19.

76. *Bulletin,* August 7, 1879.

77. Ibid., August 13, August 19, 1879. The Republican platform containing the pledge was printed in the *Alta,* August 13, 1879. The Republican mayoral candidate, B. P. Flint, also spoke in favor of the Dollar Limit during the campaign. See *Alta,* September 2, 1879.

78. *Bulletin,* August 19, 1879.

79. For the platforms, see the *Examiner,* July 28, August 2, August 18, 1881; *Alta,* August 21, 1881. For the *Examiner's* praise of the limits, see August 17, 1881.

80. See "Revenue Orders" in *Municipal Reports* for 1881/82, appendix, 182–185, for the official report of these deliberations. Molineaux was quoted in the *Examiner,* June 18, 1882.

81. *Examiner,* August 17, 1881.

6. ENFORCING THE BOUNDARIES: POLITICAL INSTITUTIONS AND FISCAL IDEOLOGIES, 1882–1896

1. As was the case in chap. 5, the analysis in chaps. 6 and 7 is based on newspaper accounts of municipal election campaigns and newspaper and official reports of the budget process. Among the items collected from the newspaper reports were the platforms of every political party from 1882 through 1905. Reports of the finance committee were published annually between 1883 and 1899 in the "Revenue Order" section of the *Municipal Reports.* These meetings were also covered in the newspapers.

2. James H. Wilkins, ed., "The Reminiscences of Christopher A. Buckley," San Francisco *Bulletin,* January 2, 1918. Schmitz was quoted in a pre-election interview in the *Examiner* for November 3, 1901, during his first campaign for the mayoralty. For good overviews of the political history of the 1880s, see R.

Hal Williams, *The Democratic Party and California Politics, 1880–1896* (Stanford, Calif., 1973), and William A. Bullough, *The Blind Boss and His City: Christopher Augustine Buckley and Nineteenth Century San Francisco* (Berkeley, Los Angeles, London, 1979). Williams provides a sensitive analysis of state politics, Bullough an exhaustive analysis of the intraparty struggles of "Boss" Buckley and his allies and antagonists. Neither of these works considers quantitative data, and neither focuses on fiscal policy.

3. The shift of municipal elections in 1882 was in line with a shift of state general elections to even years, which took effect on April 16, 1880. See *The Election Laws Governing Primary, City, County, State, Congressional, and Presidential Elections*, W. C. Hendricks, comp. (Sacramento, 1890), 2. The shift of municipal elections back to odd years, separate from other elections, was accomplished by the reform charter passed in 1898. See *Charter of the City and County of San Francisco* (San Francisco, 1900).

4. For the text of the Reform Ballot Act, see *The Election Laws...*, E. G. Waite, comp. (Sacramento, 1892), 15–32. For the change in the share of votes needed to qualify automatically for the ballot, see *The Election Laws...*, E. G. Waite, comp. (Sacramento, 1893), 15–32. These acts specifically did not affect the procedures for voting registration in the city of San Francisco.

5. Study data.

6. Registration procedures are outlined in "An Act to regulate the registration of voters, and to secure the purity of elections in the City and County of San Francisco," in *The Election Laws...*, W. C. Hendricks, comp. (Sacramento, 1890), 31–40. The act was in effect from March 18, 1878 until March 4, 1899. Precinct registration was maintained in San Francisco thereafter, however, by the reform charter of 1898.

7. To be counted as a ticket in the analysis of the number of tickets on the ballot, the party or committee had to nominate candidates for at least half of the offices at the electoral level at which it competed. At the local level, for example, this meant at least half of all city executive offices or half of all city legislative (i.e., supervisorial) tickets. This eliminated one-man candidacies or write-ins, and is therefore a conservative estimate of candidates but a good estimate of the number of parties, factions, and so on which took the trouble to make up a ticket. The sheer number of names on the ballot was enormous. On the municipal ballot for all offices in 1892, there were 357 names; in 1894, 350.

8. For complaints about the complexity of the new voting procedures, see the *Examiner,* October 5, 1892, and the *Chronicle,* November 10, 1892. It is worth confronting briefly here the issue of vote fraud and the reliability of vote totals, especially during the period of the political machine (1882 through 1890). Among others, Stephen P. Erie has argued that because Buckley "perfected an organization well versed in the techniques of electoral fraud," the meaning of election returns for these years is "open to doubt." See Erie," "The Development of Class and Ethnic Politics in San Francisco, 1870–1910: A Critique of the Pluralist Interpretation" (Ph.D. diss., University of California, Los Angeles, 1975), 87. At the outset of the present analysis, I assumed that election fraud on the scale imagined by some authors would require a conspiracy so immense as to defy definition. Moreover, most of the assumptions among urban historians are just that—assumptions blissfully uninfluenced by time-series of

election returns. As I hope the evidence in this chapter has made clear, changes in voter registration and participation were more the result of institutional change than of change in political culture. The participation level during the 1880s was high because of the conjunction of municipal elections with state or federal elections and straight-ticket voting. The similarity of participation at the various levels within this period, and among this period and the earlier ones, provides no evidence of wide-scale fraud.

9. *Bulletin,* October 2, 1882.

10. Wilkins, ed., "Reminiscences of C. A. Buckley," *Bulletin,* February 4, 1919; January 1, 1919. Contemporary testimony is unanimous on Buckley's withdrawal from real power after 1891. See, for example, James H. Wilkins, ed., "Martin Kelly's Story," *Bulletin,* October 1, 3, 1917; *Examiner,* September 6, 1894. Bullough, *Buckley,* argues the same.

11. Wilkins, ed., "Reminiscences of C. A. Buckley," *Bulletin,* January 1, 1919.

12. For the Republican platform, see *Examiner,* September 23, 1884. The pledge is discussed in the *Chronicle,* October 10, 1884.

13. In 1894, for example, the *Chronicle* identified the "most important patronage offices" as those of the sheriff, county clerk, assessor, auditor, tax collector, and superintendent of streets. See *Chronicle,* October 28, 1894.

14. For the Democratic platform of 1884, see *Examiner,* October 2, 1884.

15. *Bulletin,* October 4, October 22, 1884.

16. For the Democratic platforms in these years, see *Examiner,* October 5, 1886, October 11, 1888, October 14, 1890; for the Republican, see *Examiner,* September 14, 1886, *Chronicle,* October 12, 1888, *Chronicle,* October 8, 1890.

17. "Revenue Orders," *Municipal Reports,* 1882/83, appendix, 211.

18. Ibid., 1883/84, appendix, 163; ibid., 1888/89, appendix, 329, 335.

19. Ibid., 1884/85, appendix, 273–274; ibid., 1885/86, appendix, 115, 121.

20. *Examiner,* October 24, 1882; September 12, 1886.

21. Ibid., October 24, 1886.

22. "Revenue Orders," *Municipal Reports,* 1884/85, appendix, 272.

23. Ibid., 1889/90, appendix, 252.

24. Ibid., 1884/85, appendix, 274.

25. For the original platform, see *Examiner,* September 14, 1886, and the amendments in the same newspaper on September 15, 1886. The 1888 platform was published in the *Chronicle,* October 2, 1888.

26. For these Democratic platforms, see *Examiner,* October 6, 1886 and October 11, 1888.

27. *Chronicle,* October 12, 1888; *Examiner,* October 11, 1888.

28. Mitchell is quoted in the *Chronicle,* October 8, 1890. So-called mass meetings for municipal improvements were also held in these years. According to John P. Young, *San Francisco: A History of the Pacific Coast Metropolis* (San Francisco, 1912), II:715, one was held at the Mechanics Institute in 1887, and another was reported on in the *Chronicle* on October 7, 1890.

29. *Examiner,* September 11, October 23, 1886.

30. Ibid., June 25, 1889, June 6, 1890. Young, *San Francisco,* II:699, describes the dilemma of the politicians and newspapers somewhat more unsympathetically: "about election time . . . even the warmest advocates of better streets, boulevards, and other civic improvements yielded to the slogan of the dollar limit."

31. *Examiner,* June 11, 1891. It was not a coincidence, of course, that the board had a Republican majority.

32. *Chronicle,* October 8, 1892.

33. *Examiner,* June 2, 1889; Young, *San Francisco,* II:715.

34. *Examiner,* June 2, 1889.

35. Ibid., June 7, 1889.

36. Ibid., June 7, June 14, 1891.

37. Ibid., June 16, 1892.

38. Ibid. For Ellert's report, see "Revenue Orders," *Municipal Reports,* 1891/92, appendix, 361–365.

39. "Revenue Orders," *Municipal Reports,* 1891/92, appendix, 361, 365.

40. Study data.

41. The chi-square measuring the relationship between nativity and party in this era is 3.76 at the 0.0524 level of significance, indicating that we can reject with confidence the hypothesis of no relationship between these variables.

42. The chi-square measuring the relationship between occupation and party is 10.720 at the 0.2181 level of significance. At this level of significance, we cannot confidently reject the hypothesis of no relationship between these variables. In contrast, the chi-square measuring the relationship between occupation and type of office held is 24.48 at the 0.04 level of significance, allowing us to reject with confidence the hypothesis of no relationship between these variables during this era.

43. "Revenue Orders," *Municipal Reports,* 1884/85, appendix, 273–274.

44. *Examiner,* October 6, 1888, June 30, 1891. Buckley was stung by the charge of "silurianism" and defended himself in his memoirs, declaring that he was always for improvement, as long as it was within the Dollar Limit. See Wilkins, "Reminiscences of C. A. Buckley," *Bulletin,* January 16, 1919.

45. For a definition of the geological use of the term, see *Encyclopedia Britannica* (Chicago, 1968), 20:528–535. Despite my best efforts to do so, I have been unable to determine how this came to be so popular a fiscal political term in San Francisco. For the *Examiner's* explanation, see May 25, 1892. The *Chronicle* defined "silurian economy" as "threatening and bull-dozing Boards of Supervisors into doing nothing" (October 24, 1892).

46. Secondary works on the city's political history in the 1890s are scarce. In particular, the period from the decline of Buckley until the rise of Phelan is poorly understood.

47. This difference in incumbency is the only distinctive characteristic of the officials elected in these years. On other measures they were quite similar to those elected in other eras, as we saw in chap. 4.

48. Both Young and Erie take this position. See Young, *San Francisco,* II:750–752; Erie, "Development of Class and Ethnic Politics," 114.

49. Study data.

50. *Examiner,* November 11, 1892 carried Ellert's post-election interview. For Sutro's pre-election reference to the vigilantes, see ibid., September 24, 1894.

51. Ibid., June 18, 1893.

52. Coverage of the report was in ibid., for September 22, 1894.

53. For details on the history of the Merchants' Association, see Young, *San*

Francisco, II:713–715. The *Examiner* covered the first public meeting on October 18, 1894.

54. *Chronicle,* October 5, 13, 1894; *Examiner,* August 16, 1895, June 16, 1896.

55. *Examiner,* June 16, July 10, 1896.

56. For these complaints, see "Revenue Orders," *Municipal Reports,* 1892/93, appendix, 182–184; ibid., 1893/94, appendix, 115–116; 242. For the supreme court decision and its implications, see ibid., 1892/93, appendix, 193.

57. For the finance committee report, see ibid., 1894/95, appendix, 238–244.

58. Ibid., 242.

59. Ibid.

60. *Examiner,* September 8, September 20, September 24, 1895.

61. The exemption was contained in "An Act in Relation to the Assessment and Collection of Taxes upon Personal Property in the City and County of San Francisco," *Statutes of California, 1874* (Sacramento, 1874), 477–479.

62. Carl Plehn discusses the law of 1895 in "The General Property Tax in California," American Economic Association *Economic Studies* 2 (1897):119–198. For the decision of the supreme court, see "Revenue Orders," *Municipal Reports,* 1895/96, appendix, 218. The restoration of the veto was reported in the *Examiner,* March 20, 1897.

63. For an example of how the city defended itself when threatened with an increase by the state board, see the testimony presented in Sacramento on September 4, 1897, which is presented in the "Revenue Orders," *Municipal Reports,* 1896/97, appendix, 398–406.

64. *Examiner,* September 18, 1895.

65. For details of Phelan's life, see Roy Swanstrom, "Reform Administration of James D. Phelan, Mayor of San Francisco, 1897–1902" (master's thesis, University of California, Berkeley, 1949). In the Phelan papers at the Bancroft Library, there is also a four-volume unpublished manuscript attributed to George J. Duraind, entitled "James Duval Phelan Statesman An Epic of Public Service" and dated 1927. The tone of the manuscript suggests that it is a thinly veiled autobiography. It is useful, however, for details of Phelan's early life and political career. The *Examiner* also reviewed his life and record when he was nominated for mayor for the first time in 1896. See *Examiner,* September 19, 1896. Bullough reviews Phelan's anti-Buckley activities in *Buckley,* 208–256.

66. *Examiner,* September 19, 1896.

67. I have used a published copy of the "New San Francisco" speech taken from the James D. Phelan Papers, Bancroft Library, University of California. It is not clear from the copy where or how it was published, although the pages are numbered from 1–16, suggesting it may have been a pamphlet. Duraind claims that after this speech "Phelan became overnight the man of the hour." Duraind, "James Duval Phelan," Chap. XIII, 34. (The pages in the Duraind manuscript are numbered consecutively only within chapters.) For Phelan's relationship with the Merchants' Association in the charter reform effort, see William Issel, "Class and Ethnic Conflict in San Francisco Political History: The Reform Charter of 1898," *Labor History* 18 (1977):341–359.

68. "The New San Francisco," An Address by James D. Phelan at the Opening of the Mechanic's Institute Fair, September 1, 1896, Phelan Papers, Bancroft Library.

69. Ibid., 5, 6, 7.

70. Ibid., 8, 14.

71. Ibid., 11, 15, 13.

72. For the 1896 Democratic platform, see *Examiner,* September 19, 1896.

73. Phelan made literally hundreds of speeches in each of his campaigns, and was probably the most vigorous campaigner in the city's history to that point. He or someone on his staff kept newspaper clippings of his every speech and other activity. Fifteen volumes of these scrapbooks, containing upward of 12,000 clippings, deal with his mayoral years. References to his campaign speeches in this chapter have been chosen because of their representativeness, but the citations include only a fraction of the total number of speeches. For the themes in this paragraph, see *Examiner,* October 20, 24, 18, 28, 16, 1896.

74. For Bartlett's speech, see *Examiner,* September 12, 1886, for Phelan's, *Examiner,* October 16, 1896.

75. For details on this charter reform campaign, see Issel, "Class and Ethnic Conflict," 342–350. Issel has analyzed the backgrounds of the freeholders.

76. Ibid.

77. *Chronicle,* October 1, 1896; *Examiner,* September 16, 1896; *Examiner,* October 16, 1896, October 30, 1896.

78. Study data.

79. *Examiner,* November 4, November 7, 1896. Yorke was interviewed in the *Examiner* on November 6, 1896.

80. Other than a mention here and there, O'Donnell has been completely ignored by historians, and no one has considered his disruptive role in local politics in these years. His electoral record is from study data. His candidacies were noticed by the *Chronicle* and *Examiner* only a few times in these years, and always with denunciation. During the 1890 campaign, the *Examiner* called for O'Donnell's defeat while raising questions about his medical training (October 31, 1890). Even the *Chronicle,* which supported the Republicans and thus would have profited from Democratic votes going to O'Donnell, declared that he was a "shame" on November 1, 1892. The *Examiner* had already attacked him on October 29 of the same year.

81. The best account of O'Donnell's participation in the Workingmen's party, along with this thumbnail biography, is found in Ira B. Cross, *A History of the Labor Movement in California* (Berkeley and Los Angeles, 1935), 101–105, and 321 n. 23. His role in the constitutional convention is considered in Carl B. Swisher, *Motivation and Political Technique in the California Constitutional Convention, 1878–79* (Claremont, Calif., 1930), 35. There he was reviled for his definition of a corporation during the debates as "a corrupt combination of individuals, formed together for the purpose of escaping individual responsibility for their acts." Quoted in Swisher, ibid., 121 n. 87.

82. I have traced O'Donnell's electoral career through the election data collected for this study.

83. For an example of O'Donnell's advertisements, see *Examiner,* June 12, 1885. He was interviewed in the *Examiner* on October 1, 1894, during his last campaign before meeting Phelan.

84. Stephen Erie, in "Development of Class and Ethnic Politics," 164, 177, has made this argument about the social basis of the Workingmen's party.

85. Study data.

86. Study data. The *Examiner* simply ignored O'Donnell during the election of 1896.

7. REDEFINING THE BOUNDARIES:
POLITICAL INSTITUTIONS AND FISCAL IDEOLOGIES, 1897–1906

1. William Issel, "Class and Ethnic Conflict in San Francisco Political History: The Reform Charter of 1898," *Labor History,* 18 (1977):341–359, has detailed the campaign for a reformed charter in 1897 and 1898.

2. I have used the original typescript of Phelan's inaugural in the Phelan Papers, Bancroft Library. It is entitled "To the Honorable, The Board of Supervisors." For coverage of the speech, see *Chronicle,* January 6, 1897. Phelan, "To the Honorable," 2, 8, 10, 11–12, 16–17.

3. Phelan, "To the Honorable," 3–4. Study data.

4. Ibid., 10.

5. The data necessary for these calculations are included in a historical table in the report of the superintendent of schools in the *Municipal Reports* for 1910/11, 444–445.

6. For the official report of these deliberations, see "Revenue Orders," *Municipal Reports,* 1896/97, appendix, 393–397. For coverage of the proposed rate and the list of additional improvements, see *Examiner,* August 2, 1897. Devany is quoted in *Examiner,* August 4, 1897. The observant reader will note that these discussions are being held in August, rather than in June, as was the case before. The changes in the revenue system in 1895 required that the city set its tax rate by September 30 rather than June 30.

7. This meeting was covered in the *Examiner* for August 5, 1897.

8. Ibid.

9. *Examiner,* August 4, August 6, 1897. For Dohrman's figures, see *Examiner,* August 3, 1897; Phelan commented in the *Examiner* on August 6 and August 8, 1897.

10. Roy Swanstrom, "Reform Administration of James D. Phelan, Mayor of San Francisco, 1897–1902" (master's thesis, University of California, Berkeley, 1949), 59–65 covers the details of this struggle. Although Swanstrom's bias is strongly pro-reform, even he notes the technical basis for the suit.

11. For a copy of Wallace's decision, see "Revenue Orders," *Municipal Reports,* 1896/97, appendix, 406 ff. The decision was covered in the *Examiner* on September 16, 1897. Swanstrom, "Reform Administration," 62 identifies the new board; I have checked their backgrounds. For the legal outcome of the conflict, see Swanstrom, "Reform Administration," 63.

12. The *Examiner* compared the rates on September 21, 1897. For changes in the rates, see Swanstrom, "Reform Administration," 63–64.

13. Issel, "Class and Ethnic Conflict," 351–353.

14. Ibid. Freeholders were elected in 1880, 1882, 1886, 1894, and finally in 1897. I collected biographical information on all of them for the collective biography of officials, but did not include them in the statistical analyses of officeholders because they are not municipal policymakers in the ordinary sense. Moreover, their inclusion would bias the analysis in an upward direction because the freeholders were—with the exception of McCarthy—from remarkably high occupational backgrounds. In both background and function, they were not ordinary officials.

15. San Francisco Merchants' Association *Review,* December 1897, 3. The appeal noted that renters, too, paid property taxes through their rent, and added

that "an average of one quarter of a workingman's wages goes to pay rent. This is a far larger proportion than from the income of any other class in the community."

16. Issel, "Class and Ethnic Conflict," 353–356. See also Swanstrom, "Phelan," 43–58.

17. Issel, "Class and Ethnic Conflict," 355–356.

18. Ibid., 357–358. Jules Tygiel, "Workingmen in San Francisco, 1880–1901" (Ph.D. diss., University of California, Los Angeles, 1975), 274, 276–277. According to Tygiel, the national average level of homeownership among cities with a population of 25,000 or more was 25.7 percent. Among 15 cities with populations of more than 250,000, San Francisco ranked ninth in homeownership in 1900, "ahead of cities like New York, Boston, and Philadelphia, but trailing Chicago, Baltimore, and Detroit."

19. For the Republican platform in 1898, see *Chronicle*, September 30, 1898; for the Democratic, *Examiner*, September 21, 1898. For Phelan's remarks, see *Examiner*, October 16, 1898. In this campaign, too, Phelan made much of his commitment to labor. In a speech to residents of the 32nd Assembly District, for example, Phelan endorsed organized labor as "one of the many ways by which the laboring men can protect themselves"; claimed that the election was between "the men who are working in your interest" and those allied to the corporations, who are "not interested in eight hours for labor or decent wages for your labor"; and took full credit for the maximum-hour and minimum-wage provisions in the reform charter. The district included the most industrial areas of the Potrero and inner Mission districts and had been one of the six that had voted against the reform charter in May. For a report of this speech, see *Examiner*, October 20, 1898.

20. *Chronicle*, October 8, 1898.

21. *Examiner*, November 11, 1898.

22. San Francisco *Call*, January 29, 1899.

23. For this request, see "Revenue Orders," *Municipal Reports*, 1898/99, appendix, 287–291. The same correspondence was printed in the Merchants' Association *Review*, April 1899, 3. The Revenue Orders contain the plans for the organization of the evaluation and the final report delivered by the merchants. Essentially the same information is printed in the *Review* for August, 1899, 2.

24. Merchants' Association *Review*, August, 1899, 2.

25. Ibid.

26. Ibid.

27. For the 1899 Republican platform, see the *Chronicle*, October 4, 1899; for the Democratic, *Examiner*, October 3, 1899. The merchants presented their plan in the Merchants' Association *Review* for October, 1899, 1.

28. For biographical information on Davis, see Hubert H. Bancroft, *History of California* (San Francisco, 1890), VII:407–409; Peter Decker, *Fortunes and Failures: White Collar Mobility in Nineteenth Century San Francisco* (Cambridge, Mass., 1978), 233–235.

29. For these themes in his speeches, see *Examiner*, October 26, 1899; *Chronicle*, October 29, 1899; *Examiner*, October 22, 1899; and *Chronicle*, October 22, 1899. Davis's allies, too, stressed these themes when they campaigned for him. For example, Irving M. Scott, owner of the Union Iron Works, one of the largest employers in the city, said the following in a pro-Davis speech: "Now, fellow citizens, don't go back upon the industrial interests, but cast your vote

for a man who is in touch with all of these people . . . and who has made his mark for your city in his efforts." *Examiner,* October 15, 1899. The *Chronicle,* too, although an ally of the charter reform movement and the campaign for improvements, identified the issue in the election as "municipal thrift." The question, it said, was whether "San Francisco is to pass into the hands of men who will crush it with an unnecessary burden of debt or into the hands of others who will enter upon expenditure not only with an eye to the best results, but with both eyes fixed upon economy." *Chronicle,* October 8, 1899.

30. *Examiner,* October 7, 1899.

31. Ibid., October 15, 1899. Phelan called this new attitude the "Spirit of 1899."

32. *Bulletin,* November 1, 1899; *Examiner,* October 28, November 5, 1899.

33. *Chronicle,* November 1, 1899; *Examiner,* November 4, November 5, 1899.

34. *Examiner,* November 5, 1899.

35. *Examiner,* November 5, 1899; November 8, 1899; *Chronicle,* November 8, 1899.

36. *Call,* December 28, 1899. For the story of the bond campaign, see Swanstrom, "Phelan," 74–86; Young, *San Francisco,* II:712. The proposals are described in *Examiner,* November 24, 1899. For results of the bond election, see *Examiner,* December 28, December 30, 1899. Again in this campaign, Phelan and his allies made much of the benefits to workers to come from the bonds. Phelan said that "if the bonds were voted the workingmen would at once derive the benefits, as the contracts could be made immediately for the erection of new schoolhouses, a new hospital, and the sewers." See *Examiner,* December 22, 1899. In a pamphlet entitled "The New San Francisco," issued by the Public Improvements Central Club, it was argued that "never in the history of San Francisco has a grander opportunity presented itself to the wage workers of this city than the proposed bond issues. . . . The large part of the expenditures must necessarily go for labor. How, therefore, any workingman or artisan could possibly object to these . . . improvements . . . passes the bounds of reasonable credulity." Phelan Papers, Bancroft Library.

37. *Examiner,* April 21, 23, 1900.

38. Study data.

39. *Examiner,* June 5, 1900.

40. *Examiner,* April 20, May 25, 1900; Merchants' Association *Review,* May, 1899, 3.

41. Merchants' Association *Review,* July, 1901, 2; study data.

42. *Examiner,* June 6, 1900.

43. Phelan made this statement in his inaugural; see Phelan, "To the Honorable," 1, Phelan Papers, Bancroft Library. This estimate of the additional expense of the charter was published in the *Voice of Labor,* organ of the San Francisco Labor Council, on May 14, 1898.

44. The best secondary account of this period is Edward J. Rowell, "The Union Labor Party of San Francisco, 1901–1911" (Ph.D. diss., University of California, Berkeley, 1938). Walton Bean's *Boss Ruef's San Francisco* (Berkeley, Los Angeles, London, 1972) covers the same period, but comes out of the political cultural tradition of analysis and thus spends too much energy defining Ruef's political machine, rather than explaining the political context of the Union Labor party. For a report of the position of the merchants, see Merchants' Asso-

ciation *Review,* October, 1901, 8. I have used a published copy of Phelan's valedictory address in his papers. See "Valedictory Address," 77, Phelan Papers, Bancroft Library.

45. For Furuseth's comments, see *Examiner,* November 1, 1901. This was a campaign speech for Schmitz.

46. Stephen P. Erie, "The Development of Class and Ethnic Politics in San Francisco, 1870–1910: A Critique of the Pluralist Interpretation" (Ph.D. diss., University of California, Los Angeles, 1975), 238 has argued that "fiscal orthodoxy sharply curtailed the ability of the Union Labor Party to minister to the welfare needs of the city's poor." What is more important to note is that the ULP never claimed it would "minister to the welfare needs of the city's poor."

47. *Examiner,* October 22, October 13, October 24, 1901.

48. Tygiel, "Workingmen," 377. Tygiel actually argues this point differently, contending that the question in 1901 was "who should control government, labor or capital." I do not think that this is how the issue was posed by Schmitz or how it was understood at the time. Given the background of the reform campaign, which Tygiel has not considered in detail, labor and capital were partners in reform until the 1901 strike. It was the violation of this apparent compact of equality—as Schmitz understood—which was the foundation upon which the Union Labor party was built. This explains, too, the party's longevity. It was not just a protest or a class party, because its argument was a pluralist one—namely, an equal position in local decisionmaking for business and labor. In the context of 1901, this was a radical position. Schmitz and the ULP continued to be elected because they had, in fact, restored the balance between labor and capital.

49. *Examiner,* October 12, 24, 1905. Schmitz quoted a story from the *Wall Street Journal* revealing that, controlling for prices, workingmen's wages had declined by about 10 percent since 1900. For this reason, he was the first candidate to use a price index on the stump, too. In this, as in his reference to real estate sales as an indicator of commercial prosperity, Schmitz may have been the first quantitative historian of San Francisco.

50. *Examiner,* October 13, November 3, 1901.

51. *Examiner,* June 19, 22, 1902; June 21, 9, 28, 1903; June 7, 15, 25, 1904.

52. In 1903, in fact, the supervisors noted this, rejecting Schmitz's veto with the argument that "his comments were vague and his cuts irrelevant." *Examiner,* June 28, 1903.

53. Study data.

54. Study data.

55. Study data.

56. Study data.

57. The election of 1899 was the last in which party platforms contained limits on either taxation or assessment.

58. *Examiner,* June 9, 1903. *Examiner,* May 27, 1904.

59. For the background to this decision and copies of the ordinances suspending the limit, see "Revenue Orders," *Municipal Reports,* 1901/02, appendix, 908–911.

60. *Examiner,* April 4, April 16, May 6, 1902.

61. Ibid., May 6, May 16, May 17, 1902.

62. Ibid., May 27, 28, 1902.

63. Ibid.

Sugar
~~PAM~~
Aunt
~~Soda~~
B'Cue Sauce

Spaghetti
Sauce
(Meat?)
Pang P. Cook
Toilet B. Chan

CHS3

64. For voting results on these propositions, see *Examiner,* September 30, October 9, 1903. For details on the ordinance creating the permanent improvement fund, see *Examiner,* April 19, 1905; for the budget containing the proposals for improvements and the downpayment on the Geary Street line, see *Examiner,* May 23, 1905. The newspaper claimed that "no municipal budget that has been offered for years has met with so little criticism as [this one]." *Examiner,* May 24, 1905.

65. James H. Wilkins, ed., "The Reminiscences of Christopher A. Buckley," San Francisco *Bulletin,* February 6, 1919.

66. The phrase "internalizing the externalities" comes from Alan D. Anderson, *The Origin and Resolution of an Urban Crisis: Baltimore, 1890–1930* (Baltimore, Md., 1977), 13.

8. RECONCILING THEORY AND PRACTICE IN SAN FRANCISCO

1. This model of the policymaking process differs from that outlined and tested in my essay, "San Francisco: Socioeconomic Change, Political Culture, and Fiscal Politics, 1870–1906," in Terrence J. McDonald and Sally K. Ward, eds., *The Politics of Urban Fiscal Policy* (Beverly Hills, Calif., 1984), 39–69. In that essay, I assumed that all the independent variables affected all the dependent fiscal variables similarly, because at that point in my research I had not yet grasped the way in which the relationships among the fiscal variables structured the influence of other variables upon them. The reader with an advanced statistical background will also note that this model is presented as if it were entirely recursive, when the relationship between revenue and expenditure is very likely simultaneous. The estimation of simultaneous equation models containing lagged endogenous variables on the right side is extraordinarily complicated when serial correlation is a problem, as in these equations. I am willing to live with the simultaneity bias present as the lesser of two evils.

2. The coefficient on TAX(-1) in the tax equation measures the effect of a $1 increase in the lagged value of the rate at $0.28. A $0.01 increase would therefore be $(0.28)(0.01) = 0.0028$. The coefficient on the valuation in that equation can be interpreted similarly, but in the opposite direction. An increase of $1 per capita in the valuation would cause a decrease of $0.0007 in the rate; an increase of $10 per capita, a $0.007 decrease; and an increase of $100 per capita, a $0.07 decrease.

3. The effect of the reform era on the tax rate is the total of the era coefficient and the coefficient on the Dollar Limit, because of the overlap of the two periods. Thus the tax rate was only $0.14 higher during the reform era than under the new charter $(0.5127 + (-0.3770))$. The rate was also higher during the PTP era than under the new charter.

4. John P. Crecine, *Government Problem Solving: A Computer Simulation of Municipal Budgeting* (Chicago, 1969); Aaron Wildavsky, *The Politics of the Budgetary Process* (Boston, 1979), 13; J. Rogers Hollingsworth and Ellen Jane Hollingsworth, *Dimensions in Urban History: Historical and Social Science Perspectives on Middle-Size American Cities* (Madison, Wis., 1979), 157–158.

5. For this analysis of incrementalism, see John E. Jackson, "Politics and the Budgetary Process," *Social Science Research* 1 (1972):35–60.

6. Robert A. Burchell, *The San Francisco Irish, 1848–1880* (Manchester, 1979).

7. The mobility studies to which I refer are: Peter Decker, *Fortunes and Failures: White Collar Mobility in Nineteenth Century San Francisco* (Cambridge, Mass., 1978); Jules E. Tygiel, "Workingmen in San Francisco, 1880–1901" (Ph.D. diss., University of California, Los Angeles, 1975); Stephen P. Erie, "The Development of Class and Ethnic Politics in San Francisco, 1870–1910: A Critique of the Pluralist Interpretation" (Ph.D. diss., University of California, Los Angeles, 1975). Stephan Thernstrom, *Poverty and Progress: Social Mobility in a Nineteenth Century City* (New York, 1971), 136.

8. William A. Bullough, *The Blind Boss and His City: Christopher Augustine Buckley and Nineteenth Century San Francisco* (Berkeley, Los Angeles, London, 1979), 265–266.

9. James H. Wilkins, ed., "The Reminiscences of Christopher A. Buckley," San Francisco *Bulletin*, February 4, 1919, and passim; Wilkins, ed., "Martin Kelly's Story," ibid., September 1–November 26, 1917.

10. Wilkins, ed., "Kelly's Story," November 9, 1917.

11. For Phelan's comments and the description of his campaign style, see *Examiner*, September 19, October 6, 1896.

9. RECONCILING THEORY AND PRACTICE IN GENERAL

1. Clifford Geertz, *The Interpretation of Cultures* (New York, 1973), 21.

2. Ibid., 23.

3. Eric Monkkonen has considered the value of these volumes in "Municipal Reports as an Indicator Source: The Nineteenth Century Police," *Historical Methods* 12 (1979):57–65.

4. Bureau of the Census, *Bulletin No. 82, Receipts and Expenditures of One Hundred Principal or Representative Cities of the United States* (Washington, D.C., 1891).

5. Ibid., 3. As Kenneth Fox has pointed out, after 1903, city governments themselves began using categories suggested by the census bureau, and this made the bureau's compilations more reliable. See Kenneth Fox, *Better City Government: Innovation in American Urban Politics, 1850–1937* (Philadelphia, 1977), 92–93.

6. Bureau of the Census, *Bulletin No. 82*, 3.

7. Ibid., 1.

8. Jon Teaford, *"Finis* for Tweed and Steffens: Rewriting the History of Urban Rule," *Reviews in American History* 10 (1982):143.

9. Jon Teaford, *The Unheralded Triumph: City Government in America, 1870–1900* (Baltimore, Md., 1984), 7.

10. Ibid., 8, 293, 186.

11. M. Craig Brown and Charles N. Halaby, "Bosses, Reform, and the Socioeconomic Bases of Urban Expenditure, 1890–1940," in Terrence J. McDonald and Sally K. Ward, eds., *The Politics of Urban Fiscal Policy* (Beverly Hills, Calif., 1984), 69–100. Kenneth Fox has noted a similar decline in average per capita municipal expenditure in both real and current dollars between 1880 and 1904. He argues that this is evidence of the "failure" of municipal government because

"in the absence of major improvements in the efficiency of service production, lower per capita expenditure meant less benefit per resident from the activities of the city government." His analysis is flawed, however, because it is based on census reports that do not include the same cities over time and do not control for varying levels of service responsibility. More important, the decline in expenditure simply cannot be interpreted without evidence, such as that presented here, regarding the preferences of municipal electorates for services. See Fox, *Better City Government,* 93–97.

12. Brown and Halaby, "Bosses," 91.

13. Teaford, *Unheralded Triumph,* 283.

14. David C. Hammack, "Problems in the Historical Study of Power in the Cities and Towns of the United States, 1800–1960," *American Historical Review* 83 (1978):323–349. Hammack quotes Schlesinger on page 330.

15. Michael Paul Rogin, *The Intellectuals and McCarthy: The Radical Specter* (Cambridge, Mass., 1967), 9.

16. Rogin's analysis of pluralism is conducted in the first chapter of *Intellectuals,* pages 9–31, and my discussion here and in the next few paragraphs summarizes that chapter.

17. Robert A. Dahl, *Who Governs? Democracy and Power in an American City* (New Haven, Conn., 1961), 85–86. Rogin specifically excludes the pluralists of community power studies fame (e.g., Dahl, Nelson Polsby, etc.) from his analysis. In fact, these studies essentially "operationalized" on a local level the society-wide theories proposed by the pluralists that Rogin does analyze.

18. Rogin, *Intellectuals,* 15–17.

19. For examples of this analysis of the enemies of a pluralist society in the 1950s, see Daniel Bell, ed., *The New American Right* (New York, 1955).

20. Richard Hofstadter, *The Age of Reform: From Bryan to FDR* (New York, 1955), 14.

21. Ibid., 4, 5–22.

22. Ibid., 9. Rogin focuses a good portion of his book on the analysis of Hofstadter and the reinterpretation of the movements Hofstadter analyzed. See Rogin, *Intellectuals,* 26–28, 168–215.

23. Oscar Handlin, *The Uprooted* (New York, 1951), 201–226.

24. Ibid., 221; Hofstadter, *Age,* 182–185. Hofstadter noted that he had drawn on the "perceptive discussion of the immigrant in politics by Oscar Handlin," in *Age,* 182 n. 1.

25. Hofstadter, *Age,* 185, 316, 319; Handlin, *Uprooted,* 226.

26. Robert K. Merton, *Social Theory and Social Structure: Toward the Codification of Theory and Research* (Glencoe, Ill., 1949). A revised and expanded edition of this book was published in 1957, but no significant changes were made in the passages relevant to this discussion. For an interesting parallel look at Merton's definition of the scientific ethos as "a revealing artifact of the effort made by a generation of intellectuals to vindicate a set of social values identified with the liberal political tradition," see David A. Hollinger, "The Defense of Democracy and Robert K. Merton's Formulation of the Scientific Ethos," in *Knowledge and Society: Studies in the Sociology of Culture Past and Present* 4 (1983):1–15.

27. Merton, *Social Theory,* 61–81, 221.

28. Ibid., 72–73.

29. Ibid., 73.

30. Ibid., 74, 372 n. 97.
31. Ibid.
32. Ibid., 372 n. 98, 74; Handlin, *Uprooted,* 212–213; Hofstadter, *Age,* 182 n. 1, 184 n. 4. Lincoln Steffens, *The Autobiography of Lincoln Steffens* (New York, 1931). William L. Riordan, *Plunkitt of Tammany Hall* (New York, 1963). *Plunkitt* was first published in 1905, then reissued in 1948. It was the latter edition that Hofstadter cited.
33. Christopher Lasch, *The New Radicalism in America, 1889–1963: The Intellectual as a Social Type* (New York, 1965), 251–287.
34. John M. Allswang, *Bosses, Machines, and Urban Voters: An American Symbiosis* (Port Washington, N.Y., 1977), 150.
35. Hammack has drawn the research agenda from the patrician elitist work in "Problems," 320–333.
36. Hays, "The Social Analysis of American Political History, 1880–1920," *Political Science Quarterly* 80 (1965):388–389. Hays, too, has acknowledged his debt to Merton in his conversation with Bruce Stave in Stave, ed., *The Making of Urban History: Historiography Through Oral History* (Beverly Hills, Calif., 1977), 291–326. I have discussed the influence of Merton on American urban history in more detail elsewhere. See McDonald, "The Problem of the Political in Recent American Urban History: Liberal Pluralism and the Rise of Functionalism," *Social History* 10 (1985):323–345.
37. I am by no means the first one to suggest jettisoning the "boss-reformer" functionalist framework. Others who have raised serious questions about it include, in chronological order: Lyle W. Dorsett, "The City and the Reformer: A Reappraisal," *Pacific Northwest Quarterly* 63 (1972):150–154; David P. Thelen, "Urban Politics: Beyond Bosses and Reformers," *Reviews in American History* 7 (1979):406–412; Zane Miller, "Bosses, Machines and the Urban Political Process," and Roger Lotchin, "Power and Policy: American City Politics Between the Two World Wars," both in Scott Greer, ed., *Ethnics, Machines, and the American Urban Future* (Cambridge, Mass., 1981), 1–84; and Jon C. Teaford, *"Finis."* None of these essays considers the ideological aspects of the development of the framework, however.
38. I am not the first to suggest such a framework for the study of urban politics. Ira Katznelson argues similarly in "The Crisis of the Capitalist City: Urban Politics and Social Control," in Willis D. Hawley and Michael Lipsky, eds., *Theoretical Perspectives on Urban Politics* (Englewood Cliffs, N.J., 1976), 214–229 and *City Trenches: Urban Politics and the Patterning of Class in the United States* (Chicago, 1981). Katznelson simply appropriates the functionalist framework, however.
39. Classic examples of such work outside of political history might include Stephan Thernstrom, *Poverty and Progress: Social Mobility in a Nineteenth Century City* (New York, 1971); Alan Dawley, *Class and Community* (Cambridge, Mass., 1976); and Michael Katz, *The Irony of Early School Reform* (Boston, 1968). All three authors have tried to combine these fields, but their success has been limited. Here again, the theoretical framework is important, for just as some urban history is indebted to Merton, the political theory of the community study seems to be indebted to Robert Dahl. See Dahl, *Who Governs?* (New Haven, Conn., 1961).
40. Stephen Skowronek, *Building a New American State: The Expansion of National Administrative Capacities, 1877–1920* (New York, 1982), 5.

41. Morton Keller, *Affairs of State: Public Life in Late Nineteenth Century America* (Cambridge, Mass., 1977); Skowronek, *Building,* 10.

42. Michael Katz, "Origins of the Institutional State," *Marxist Perspectives* 1 (1978):7.

43. J. Morgan Kousser, "Voters, Absent and Present," *Social Science History* 9 (1985):226; Richard L. McCormick, "The Party Period and Public Policy: An Exploratory Hypothesis," *Journal of American History* 66 (1979):279–298.

APPENDIX A. THE "GREENBACK" ERA IN SAN FRANCISCO AND ITS EFFECT ON PRICES

1. Wesley C. Mitchell, *Gold Prices and Wages Under the Greenback Standard* (New York, 1966), 1–4.

2. Walton Bean, *California: An Interpretive History* (New York, 1973), 199–200; John P. Young, *San Francisco: A History of the Pacific Coast Metropolis* (San Francisco, 1912), I:389, 346.

3. The best account of these events is in William C. Fankhauser, "A Financial History of California: Public Revenues, Debts, and Expenditures," in Adolph C. Miller, ed., *University of California Publications in Economics* 3 (1913):214–222. For an earlier account, see Bernard Moses, "Legal Tender Notes in California," *Quarterly Journal of Economics* 7 (1892–93):1–25.

4. Peter R. Decker, *Fortunes and Failures: White Collar Mobility in Nineteenth Century San Francisco* (Cambridge, Mass., 1978), 147–151, 164 gives an account of these actions. For the Specific Contract Act itself, see *Statutes of California, 1863/64,* 687.

5. San Francisco *Bulletin,* September 3, 1875; Bean, *California,* 200; Young, *San Francisco,* II:527–528.

6. *Statutes of California, 1863/64,* 365; Fankhauser, "Financial History," 222; *Political Code of the State of California* (Sacramento, 1872), 52; *Statutes of California, 1880,* 8.

7. Paul A. David and Peter Solar, "A Bicentenary Contribution to the History of the Cost of Living in America," *Research in Economic History* 2 (1977):1–80.

8. Mitchell, *Greenback Standard,* 4. I am grateful to Gavin Wright for this suggestion.

APPENDIX B. SOME ASPECTS OF REGRESSION ANALYSIS

1. Hubert M. Blalock, Jr., *Theory Construction* (Englewood Cliffs, N.J., 1969), 35–40.

2. Roderick Floud, *An Introduction to Quantitative Methods for Historians* (London, 1979); Robert S. Pindyck and Daniel L. Rubinfeld, *Econometric Models and Economic Forecasts* (New York, 1976).

3. Erik Monkkonen, *Police in Urban America, 1860–1920* (New York, 1981);

Maris Vinovskis and Carl Kaestle, *Education and Social Change in Nineteenth Century Massachusetts* (New York, 1980).

4. For good introductions to the problem of and corrections for serial correlation, see Pindyck and Rubinfeld, *Econometric Models,* 106–126, 148–152; G. S. Maddala, *Econometrics* (New York, 1977), 274–291; Jan Kmenta, *Elements of Econometrics* (New York, 1971), 269–297; and Douglas A. Hibbs, Jr., "Problems of Statistical Estimation and Causal Inference in Time-Series Regression Models," in Herbert L. Costner, ed., *Sociological Methodology 1973–1974* (San Francisco, 1974), 252–308.

5. Hibbs, "Problems," 294.

6. D. Cochrane and G. H. Orcutt, "Application of Least Squares Regression to Relationships Containing Autocorrelated Error Terms," *Journal of the American Statistical Association* 44 (1949):32–61. I conducted this analysis by means of the SHAZAM Econometrics Computer Program. See Kenneth J. White, "A General Computer Program for Econometric Methods—SHAZAM," *Econometrica* (January 1978):239–240. The reader may be surprised that I have not prefaced this discussion of GLS with a parallel discussion of tests for serial correlation, but the omission is deliberate. Having already conducted the diagnosis of the problem by means of the usual statistics and analysis of the residuals, it is more important here to discuss the correction of the problem. In this sense, I agree with Maddala that "greater emphasis should be not on testing per se but on when one should proceed and estimate the regression parameters by generalized-least-squares." Maddala, *Econometrics,* 291.

Bibliography

I. SOURCES OF QUANTITATIVE DATA

A. *NEWSPAPERS*

Daily Alta California, 1860–1875. San Francisco.
Bulletin, 1860–1905. San Francisco.
Chronicle, 1877–1909. San Francisco.
Examiner, 1865–1905. San Francisco.
Real Estate Circular, 1867–1920. San Francisco.

B. *GOVERNMENT DOCUMENTS*

City and County of San Francisco. Board of Supervisors. *Municipal Reports.* San Francisco, 1859–1917.
———. *Great Register of the City and County of San Francisco,* 1866–1904.
State of California. *Annual Report of the Board of Bank Commissioners.* Sacramento, 1879–1909.
———. *Annual Report of the Superintendent of Banks.* Sacramento, 1909–1915.
United States Bureau of the Census. *Eighth Census.* Washington, D.C., 1864–1866.
———. *Ninth Census.* Washington, D.C., 1872.
———. *Tenth Census.* Washington, D.C., 1883–1887.
———. *Eleventh Census.* Washington, D.C., 1892–1897.
———. *Twelfth Census.* Washington, D.C., 1901–1902.

————. *Thirteenth Census.* Washington, D.C., 1913–1914.

————. *Fourteenth Census.* Washington, D.C., 1923–1924.

————. *Bulletin No. 82, Receipts and Expenditures of One Hundred Principal or Representative Cities of the United States.* Washington, D.C., 1891.

c. *OTHER*

Langley, Henry G. *Langley's San Francisco Directory* (title varies). San Francisco, 1860–1910.

San Francisco Chamber of Commerce. *Annual Report.* San Francisco, 1870–1920.

————. *Annual Statistical Report.* San Francisco, 1910–1920.

II. SOURCES OF SAN FRANCISCO HISTORY

A. *UNPUBLISHED MANUSCRIPTS*

Alvord, William. Bancroft Dictation. Bancroft Library. University of California, Berkeley.

Bartlett, Washington. Bancroft Dictation. Bancroft Library. University of California, Berkeley.

Bryant, A. J. Bancroft Dictation. Bancroft Library. University of California, Berkeley.

William T. Coleman Papers. Bancroft Library. University of California, Berkeley.

Coon, H. P. Bancroft Dictation. Bancroft Library. University of California, Berkeley.

Duraind, George J. "James Duval Phelan Statesman An Epic of Public Service." 1927. 4 vols. n.p. Bancroft Library. University of California, Berkeley.

James D. Phelan Papers. Bancroft Library. University of California, Berkeley.

Selby, Thomas H. Bancroft Dictation. Bancroft Library. University of California, Berkeley.

Adolf Sutro Papers. Bancroft Library. University of California, Berkeley.

B. *NEWSPAPERS AND PERIODICALS*

Daily Alta California, 1860–1875. San Francisco.
Bulletin, 1860–1905. San Francisco.
Chronicle, 1877–1909. San Francisco.
Coast Seamen's Journal, 1897–1902. San Francisco.
Examiner, 1860–1905. San Francisco.
Merchants' Association *Review.* September 1896–May 1906. San Francisco.
Real Estate Circular, 1867–1920. San Francisco.
Voice of Labor, 1895–1899. San Francisco.

C. *GOVERNMENT DOCUMENTS*

City and County of San Francisco. *Consolidation Act of the City and County of San Francisco.* San Francisco, 1856.
———. *An Act to Repeal the Several Charters of the City of San Francisco, to Establish the Boundaries of the City and County of San Francisco, and to Consolidate the Government thereof.* San Francisco, 1856.
———. *The Consolidation Act or Charter of the City and County of San Francisco.* San Francisco, 1866.
———. *Charter of the City and County of San Francisco.* San Francisco, 1900.
City of San Francisco. *Act of Incorporation and Ordinances of the City of San Francisco.* San Francisco, 1850.
———. *New Charter of the City of San Francisco.* San Francisco, 1853.
———. *The Consolidation Act and Other Acts.* San Francisco, 1876.
State of California. *An Act to Incorporate the City of San Francisco.* Sacramento, 1850.
———. *The Election Laws Governing Primary, City, County, State, Congressional, and Presidential Elections* (compiled by W. C. Hendricks). Sacramento, 1890.
———. *The Election Laws Governing Primary, City, County, State, and Presidential Elections* (compiled by E. G. Waite). Sacramento, 1892.
———. *The Election Laws Governing Primary, City, County, State, and Presidential Elections* (compiled by E. G. Waite). Sacramento, 1893.

————. *The Election Laws of California* (compiled by C. F. Curry). Sacramento, 1903.

————. *The Election Laws of the State of California* (edited by J. F. Bowman). San Francisco, 1872.

————. *Index to the Laws of California, 1850–1907.* Sacramento, 1908.

————. *Law of 1851.* Sacramento, 1851.

————. *Law of 1856.* Sacramento, 1856.

————. *Statutes of California,* 1856–1878. Sacramento, 1856–1880.

————. *Political Code of the State of California.* Sacramento, 1872.

————. *The Journal of the Assembly,* 1856–1876. Sacramento, 1856–1876.

————. *The Journal of the Senate,* 1856–1876. Sacramento, 1856–1876.

D. *UNPUBLISHED STUDIES*

Bowden, Martyn J. "The Dynamics of City Growth: An Historical Geography of the San Francisco Central District, 1850–1931." 2 vols. Ph.D. dissertation, University of California, Berkeley, 1968.

Daniels, Douglas H. "Afro-San Franciscans: A Social History of Pioneer Urbanites, 1860–1930." Ph.D. dissertation, University of California, Berkeley, 1974.

Devine, Preston. "The Adoption of the 1932 Charter of San Francisco." Master's thesis, University of California, Berkeley, 1933.

Dolson, Lee A., Jr. "The Administration of the San Francisco Public Schools, 1847–1947." Ph.D. dissertation, University of California, Berkeley, 1965.

Elgie, Robert A. "The Development of San Francisco Manufacturing, 1848–1880: An Analysis of Regional Locational Factors and Urban Spatial Structures." Master's thesis, University of California, Berkeley, 1966.

Erie, Stephen P. "The Development of Class and Ethnic Politics in San Francisco, 1870–1910: A Critique of the Pluralist Interpretation." Ph.D. dissertation, University of California, Los Angeles, 1975.

Huff, Boyd F. "The Maritime History of San Francisco Bay." Ph.D. dissertation, University of California, Berkeley, 1955.

Hughes, Lilian G. "Housing in San Francisco, 1835–1938." Master's thesis, University of California, Berkeley, 1940.

Ingels, Helen H. "The History of the Workingmen's Party of California." Master's thesis, University of California, Berkeley, 1919.

Kahn, Jud. "Imperial San Francisco: History of a Vision." Ph.D. dissertation, University of California, Berkeley, 1971.

Kazin, Michael. "Prelude to Kearneyism: The July Days in San Francisco 1877." Manuscript, Stanford University, 1977.

King, Margaret. "The Growth of San Francisco, Illustrated by Shifts in the Density of Population." Master's thesis, University of California, Berkeley, 1928.

Kingsbury, Susan M. "Municipal History of San Francisco to 1879." Master's thesis, Stanford University, 1899.

McDonald, Terrence J. "Urban Development, Political Power, and Municipal Expenditure in San Francisco, 1860–1910: A Quantitative Investigation of Historical Theory." Ph.D. dissertation, Stanford University, 1979.

McKinney, Mary Frances. "Denis Kearney, Organizer of the Workingmen's Party of California." Master's thesis, University of California, Berkeley, 1939.

Martin, Mildred P. "City Government in San Francisco: A Half Century of Charter Development." Master's thesis, University of California, Berkeley, 1911.

Morgen, Millard R. "The Administration of P. H. McCarthy, Mayor of San Francisco, 1910–1912." Master's thesis, University of California, Berkeley, 1949.

Mortenson, Clara Estelle. "Organized Labor in San Francisco from 1892 to 1902." Master's thesis, University of California, Berkeley, 1916.

Murphy, Leontina. "Public Care of the Dependent Sick in San Francisco, 1847–1936." Master's thesis, University of California, Berkeley, 1936.

Ohlson, Robert V. "The History of the San Francisco Labor Council, 1892–1939." Master's thesis, University of California, Berkeley, 1941.

Rowell, Edward J. "The Union Labor Party of San Francisco, 1901–1911." Ph.D. dissertation, University of California, Berkeley, 1938.

Selig, John M. "The Chief Administrative Officer in San Francisco." Master's thesis, University of California, Berkeley, 1938.

Senkewicz, Robert M. "Business and Politics in Gold Rush San Francisco, 1851–1856." Ph.D. dissertation, Stanford University, 1974.

Shumsky, Neil L. "Tar Flat and Nob Hill: A Social History of Industrial

San Francisco During the 1870s." Ph.D. dissertation, University of California, Berkeley, 1972.

Swanstrom, Roy. "Reform Administration of James D. Phelan, Mayor of San Francisco, 1897–1902." Master's thesis, University of California, Berkeley, 1949.

Tygiel, Jules E. "Workingmen in San Francisco, 1880–1901." Ph.D. dissertation, University of California, Los Angeles, 1975.

Varcardos, Peter. "Labor and Politics in San Francisco, 1880–1892." Ph.D. dissertation, University of California, Berkeley, 1968.

Watchers, Anthony L. "The Development of Civil Service in San Francisco." Master's thesis, University of California, Berkeley, 1937.

E. *PUBLISHED STUDIES*

Asbury, Herbert. *The Barbary Coast.* Garden City, N.Y.: Garden City Publishing Co., 1933.

Bancroft, Hubert H. *History of California.* San Francisco: The History Co., 1890.

Bean, Walton. *Boss Ruef's San Francisco.* Berkeley, Los Angeles, London: University of California Press, 1972.

———. *California: An Interpretive History.* New York: McGraw-Hill, 1973.

Blackford, Mansell G. *The Politics of Business in California, 1890–1920.* Columbus: Ohio State University Press, 1977.

Bullough, William A. *The Blind Boss and His City: Christopher Augustine Buckley and Nineteenth Century San Francisco.* Berkeley, Los Angeles, London: University of California Press, 1979.

———. "Chris Buckley and San Francisco: The Man and the City." In *The San Francisco Irish 1856–1976* (edited by James P. Walsh), 27–41. San Francisco: The Irish Literary and Historical Society, 1978.

———. "Hannibal vs. the Blind Boss: 'The Junta,' Chris Buckley and Democratic Reform Politics in San Francisco." *Pacific Historical Review* 46 (1977):181–206.

———. "The Steam Beer Handicap: Chris Buckley and the San Francisco Municipal Election of 1896." *California Historical Quarterly* 54 (1975):245–262.

Burchell, R. A. *The San Francisco Irish, 1848–1880.* Manchester, England: University Press, 1979.

Callow, Alexander B. "San Francisco's Blind Boss." *Pacific Historical Review* 25 (1956):261–279.

Camp, William M. *San Francisco: Port of Gold.* Garden City, N.Y.: Doubleday, 1947.

Cross, Ira B. *A History of the Labor Movement in California.* Berkeley: University of California Press, 1935.

———. *Financing an Empire: A History of Banking in California.* 3 vols. Chicago: S. J. Clarke Publishing Co., 1927.

Decker, Peter R. *Fortunes and Failures: White Collar Mobility in Nineteenth Century San Francisco.* Cambridge, Mass.: Harvard University Press, 1978.

Fankhauser, William C. "A Financial History of California: Public Revenues, Debts, and Expenditures." In Adolph C. Miller, ed., *University of California Publications in Economics* 3 (1913):101–408.

Gutsch, Gustave. *A Comparison of the Consolidation Act with the New Charter.* San Francisco: San Francisco Charter Association, 1896.

Hackett, Fred H. *The Industries of San Francisco.* San Francisco: Payot and Co., 1884.

Heintz, William. *San Francisco's Mayors: From the Gold Rush to the Silver Bonanza.* Woodside, Calif.: Gilbert Richards, 1975.

Hittell, John S. *A History of the City of San Francisco and Incidentally of the State of California.* San Francisco: A. L. Bancroft and Co., 1878.

Issel, William. "Class and Ethnic Conflict in San Francisco Political History: The Reform Charter of 1898." *Labor History* 18 (1977):341–359.

Lewis, Oscar. *San Francisco: Mission to Metropolis.* Berkeley: Howell-North, 1966.

Lotchin, Roger. *San Francisco 1846–1856: From Hamlet to City.* New York: Oxford University Press, 1974.

McDonald, Terrence J. "San Francisco: Socioeconomic Change, Political Culture, and Fiscal Politics, 1870–1906." In *The Politics of Urban Fiscal Policy* (edited by Terrence J. McDonald and Sally K. Ward), 39–69. Beverly Hills: Sage Publications, 1984.

Moses, Bernard. "The Establishment of Municipal Government in San Francisco." *Johns Hopkins University Studies in Historical and Political Science* 8 (1899):75–153.

———. "Legal Tender Notes in California." *Quarterly Journal of Economics* 7 (1892–93):1–25.

Muscatine, Doris. *Old San Francisco: The Biography of a City.* New York: G. P. Putnam's Sons, 1975.

Plehn, Carl C. "The Taxation of Mortgages in California." *Yale Review* (May 1899):39–44.

———. "The General Property Tax in California." American Economic Association *Economic Studies* 2 (1897):119–198.

Ralph, Julian. "Reform in San Francisco." *Harper's Weekly* 39 (1895):230–231.

Ruef, Abraham. "The Road I Traveled." San Francisco *Bulletin,* April 6, May 21–September 5, 1912.

Saxton, Alexander P. *The Indispensable Enemy: Labor and the Anti-Chinese Movement in California.* Berkeley, Los Angeles, London: University of California Press, 1971.

Swisher, Carl B. *Motivation and Political Technique in the California Constitutional Convention, 1878–79.* Claremont, Calif.: Huntington Library, 1930.

Thomas, Lately. *A Debonair Scoundrel.* New York: Rinehart, Winston, 1962.

Walsh, James P. "Abe Ruef Was No Boss: Machine Politics, Reform, and San Francisco." *California Historical Quarterly* 51 (1972):3–16.

———. *The San Francisco Irish, 1856–1976.* San Francisco: The Irish Literary and Historical Society, 1978.

Wilkins, James H., ed. "The Reminiscences of Christopher A. Buckley." San Francisco *Bulletin,* December 23, 1918–February 5, 1919.

———. "Martin Kelly's Story." San Francisco *Bulletin,* September 1–November 26, 1917.

Williams, R. Hal. *The Democratic Party and California Politics, 1880–1896.* Stanford, Calif.: Stanford University Press, 1973.

Wright, Benjamin C. *San Francisco's Ocean Trade, 1848–1911.* San Francisco, 1911.

Young, John P. *San Francisco: A History of the Pacific Coast Metropolis.* 2 vols. San Francisco: S. J. Clarke, 1912.

III. SOURCES OF METHOD

Afifi, A. A., and R. M. Elashoff. "Missing Observations in Multivariate Statistics I. Review of the Literature." *Journal of the American Statistical Association* 61 (1966):595–604.

———. "Missing Observations in Multivariate Statistics II. Point Estimation in Simple Linear Regression." *Journal of the American Statistical Association* 62 (1967):10–29.

Blalock, Hubert M., Jr. *Social Statistics.* New York: McGraw-Hill, 1972.

———. *Theory Construction.* Englewood Cliffs, N.J.: Prentice-Hall, 1969.

Cochrane, D., and G. H. Orcutt. "Application of Least Squares Regressions to Relationships Containing Autocorrelated Error Terms." *Journal of the American Statistical Association* 44 (1949):32–61.

Dollar, Charles M., and Richard J. Jensen. *Historian's Guide to Statistics.* New York: Holt, Rinehart, and Winston, 1971.

Durbin, J., and G. S. Watson. "Testing for Serial Correlation in Least Squares Regression." *Biometrika* 38 (1951):158–177.

Farrarr, Donald E., and Robert R. Glauber. "Multicollinearity in Regression Analysis: The Problem Revisited." *The Review of Economics and Statistics* 49 (1967):92–107.

Floud, Roderick. *An Introduction to Quantitative Methods for Historians.* London: Methuen, Inc., 1979.

———, ed. *Essays in Quantitative Economic History.* Oxford: Oxford University Press, 1974.

Gordon, Robert A. "Issues in Multiple Regression." *American Journal of Sociology* 73 (1968):592–616.

Hibbs, Douglas, A., Jr. "Problems of Statistical Estimation and Causal Inference in Time-Series Regression Models." In *Sociological Methodology 1973–1974* (edited by Herbert L. Costner), 252–308. San Francisco: Jossey-Bass Publishers, 1974.

Hildreth, G., and J. Y. Lu. "Demand Relations with Autocorrelated Disturbances." Michigan State University Agricultural Experiment Station *Technical Bulletin* 276. East Lansing, 1968.

Kmenta, Jan. *Elements of Econometrics.* New York: Macmillan, 1971.

Maddala, G. S. *Econometrics.* New York: McGraw-Hill, 1977.

Pegenais, M. "The Use of Incomplete Observations in Multiple Regression Analysis." *Journal of Econometrics* 1 (1973):317–328.

Pindyck, Robert S., and Daniel L. Rubinfeld. *Econometric Models and Economic Forecasts.* New York: McGraw-Hill, 1976.

Rao, Potluri, and Roger LeRoy Miller. *Applied Econometrics.* Belmont, Calif.: Wadsworth Publishing Co., 1971.

Swierenga, Robert P., ed. *Quantification in American History.* New York: Atheneum, 1970.

White, Kenneth J. "A General Computer Program for Econometric Methods—SHAZAM." *Econometrica* (January 1978):239–240.

IV. GENERAL WORKS

Adams, Henry Carter. *The Science of Finance.* New York: H. Holt and Co., 1899.

Alcorn, Richard. "Leadership and Stability in Mid-Nineteenth Century America: A Case Study of an Illinois Town." *Journal of American History* 61 (1974):685–702.

Alford, Robert R. "Strategies for Studying Urban Leadership and Policy Outputs." Manuscript, University of California, Santa Cruz, n.d.

Alford, Robert R., with Harry M. Scoble. *Bureaucracy and Participation: Political Cultures in Four Wisconsin Cities.* Chicago: Rand McNally, 1969.

Alford, Robert R., and Roger Friedland. "Political Participation and Public Policy." *Annual Review of Sociology* 1 (1975):429–479.

Allswang, John M. *Bosses, Machines, and Urban Voters: An American Symbiosis.* Port Washington, N.Y.: Kennikat Press, 1977.

Anderson, Alan D. *The Origin and Resolution of an Urban Crisis: Baltimore, 1890–1930.* Baltimore: Johns Hopkins University Press, 1977.

Bahl, Roy W. *Metropolitan City Expenditures: A Comparative Analysis.* Lexington: University of Kentucky Press, 1969.

———. "Studies on Determinants of Public Expenditure: A Review." In *Sharing Federal Funds for State and Local Needs* (edited by Selma J. Mushkin and John F. Cotton), 184–203. New York: Praeger Publishers, 1969.

Banfield, Edward. *City Politics.* New York: Vintage Books, 1963.

Barrows, Robert G. "Hurryin Hoosiers and the American 'Pattern': Geographic Mobility in Urban North America." *Social Science History* 5 (1981):192–222.

Bell, Daniel. *The New American Right.* New York: Criterion Books, 1955.

———. "The Public Household—On 'Fiscal Sociology' and the Liberal Society." *The Public Interest* 37 (1974):29–68.

Blake, Nelson M. *Water for the Cities: A History of the Urban Water Supply Problem in the United States.* Syracuse, N.Y.: Syracuse University Press, 1956.

Brady, Dorothy. "Relative Prices in the Nineteenth Century." *The Journal of Economic History* 24 (1964):145–204.

Brazer, Harvey E. *City Expenditures in the United States,* National Bureau of Economic Research Occasional Paper 66. New York, 1959.

Brown, M. Craig, and Charles N. Halaby. "Bosses, Reform, and the Socioeconomic Bases of Urban Expenditure, 1890–1940." In *The Pol-*

itics of Urban Fiscal Policy (edited by Terrence J. McDonald and Sally K. Ward), 69–100. Beverly Hills: Sage Publications, 1984.

Buenker, John D. *Urban Liberalism and Progressive Reform.* New York: Scribner's, 1973.

Burnham, Walter Dean. "The Changing Shape of the American Political Universe." *American Political Science Review* 59 (1965):7–28.

Callow, Alexander B., ed. *The City Boss in America.* New York: Oxford University Press, 1976.

Campbell, Ballard C. *Representative Democracy: Public Policy and Midwestern Legislatures in the Late Nineteenth Century.* Cambridge, Mass.: Harvard University Press, 1980.

————. "American Governmental History Versus the College Textbooks." Paper read at Organization of American Historians Annual Meeting, 1983.

Chudacoff, Howard P. *The Evolution of American Urban Society.* Englewood Cliffs, N.J.: Prentice-Hall, 1975.

Clubb, Jerome, and William Flanigan. *Partisan Realignment.* Beverly Hills: Sage Publications, 1980.

Crecine, John P. *Governmental Problem Solving: A Computer Simulation of Municipal Budgeting.* Chicago: Rand McNally and Co., 1969.

Dahl, Robert A. "The Behavioral Approach in Political Science: Epitaph for a Monument to a Successful Protest." *American Political Science Review* 55 (1961):763–772.

————. *Who Governs? Democracy and Power in an American City.* New Haven: Yale University Press, 1961.

David, Paul A., and Peter Solar. "A Bicentenary Contribution to the History of the Cost of Living in America." *Research in Economic History* 2 (1977):1–80.

Dawley, Alan. *Class and Community.* Cambridge, Mass.: Harvard University Press, 1976.

Diamond, William. "On the Dangers of an Urban Interpretation of History." In *Historiography and Urbanization: Essays in American History in Honor of W. Stull Holt* (edited by Eric F. Goldman), 67–108. Baltimore: The Johns Hopkins University Press, 1941.

Dobson, John. *Politics in the Gilded Age.* New York: Praeger Publications, 1972.

Dorsett, Lyle W. "The City and the Reformer: A Reappraisal." *Pacific Northwest Quarterly* 63 (1972):150–154.

Ebner, Michael H., and Eugene M. Tobin, eds. *The Age of Urban Reform:*

New Perspectives on the Progressive Era. Port Washington, N.Y.: Kennikat Press, 1977.

Edwards, Alba M. "A Social Economic Grouping of the Gainful Workers of the United States." *Journal of the American Statistical Association* 27 (1933):377–387.

Fehrenbacher, Don E., ed. *History and American Society: Essays of David M. Potter.* New York: Oxford University Press, 1973.

Fogelson, Robert M. *The Fragmented Metropolis: Los Angeles 1850–1930.* Cambridge, Mass.: Harvard University Press, 1967.

Fox, Kenneth. *Better City Government: Innovation in American Urban Politics, 1850–1937.* Philadelphia: Temple University Press, 1977.

Geertz, Clifford. *The Interpretation of Cultures.* New York: Basic Books, 1973.

Glaab, Charles N., and A. Theodore Brown. *A History of Urban America.* New York: Macmillan, 1967.

Goldscheid, Rudolf. "A Sociological Approach to the Problems of Public Finance." In *Classics in the Theory of Public Finance* (edited by Richard Musgrave and Alan T. Peacock), 202–213. New York: Macmillan, 1958.

Gordon, Daniel R. "The Bases of Urban Political Change: A Brief History." In *Social Change and Urban Politics: Readings* (edited by Gordon), 2–18. Englewood Cliffs, N.J.: Prentice-Hall, 1973.

Gouldner, Alvin W. *The Coming Crisis of Western Sociology.* New York: Basic Books, 1971.

Green, Constance McLaughlin. *American Cities in the Growth of the Nation.* New York: J. DeGraff, 1957.

Greer, Scott, ed. *Ethnics, Machines, and the American Urban Future.* Cambridge, Mass.: Schenkman, 1981.

Griffith, Ernest S. *A History of American City Government: The Conspicuous Failure, 1870–1900.* New York: Praeger, 1974.

———. *A History of American City Government: The Progressive Years and their Aftermath, 1900–1920.* New York: Praeger, 1974.

———. *The Modern Development of City Government in the United Kingdom and the United States.* 2 vols. London: Oxford University Press, 1927.

Gusteley, Richard D. *Municipal Public Employment and Public Expenditure.* Lexington, Mass.: Lexington Books, 1974.

Hammack, David C. "Problems in the Historical Study of Power in the

Cities and Towns of the United States, 1800–1960." *American Historical Review* 83 (1978):323–349.

Handlin, Oscar. *The Uprooted.* New York: Grosset and Dunlap, 1951.

Harvey, David. *Social Justice and the City.* London: Edward Arnold, 1973.

Hays, Samuel P. "History as Human Behavior." *Iowa Journal of History* 58 (1960):193–206.

————. "The Politics of Reform in Municipal Government in the Progressive Era." *Pacific Northwest Quarterly* 55 (1964):157–169.

————. "Archival Sources for American Political History." *American Archivist* 38 (1965):17–30.

————. "The Social Analysis of American Political History, 1880–1920." *Political Science Quarterly* 80 (1965):373–394.

————. "Political Parties and the Community-Society Continuum." In *The American Party Systems: Stages of Political Development* (edited by William N. Chambers and Walter D. Burnham), 152–181. New York: Oxford University Press, 1967.

————. "New Possibilities for American Political History: The Social Analysis of Political Life." In *Sociology and History: Methods* (edited by Seymour Martin Lipset and Richard Hofstadter), 181–227. New York: Basic Books, 1968.

————. "A Systematic Social History." In *American History: Retrospect and Prospect* (edited by George Athan Billias and Gerald Grob), 315–366. New York: Free Press, 1971.

————. "The Changing Political Structure of the City in Industrial America." *Journal of Urban History* 1 (1974):6–34.

————. *American Political History as Social Analysis.* Knoxville: University of Tennessee Press, 1980.

Hershberg, Theodore. "The New Urban History: Toward an Interdisciplinary History of the City." In *Philadelphia: Work, Space, Family and Group Experience in the Nineteenth Century. Essays Toward an Interdisciplinary History of the City.* New York: Oxford University Press, 1981.

Hobsbawm, Eric J. "From Social History to the History of Society." *Daedalus* 100 (1971):20–45.

Hofferbert, Richard I. "State and Community Policy Studies: A Review of Comparative Input-Output Analyses." *Political Science Annual* 3 (1972):3–72.

Hofstadter, Richard. *The Age of Reform: From Bryan to FDR.* New York: Vintage Books, 1955.

Hollinger, David. "The Defense of Democracy and Robert K. Merton's Formulation of the Scientific Ethos." *Knowledge and Society: Studies in the Sociology of Culture Past and Present* 4 (1983):1–15.

Hollingsworth, J. Rogers. *The Whirligig of Politics.* Chicago: University of Chicago Press, 1963.

Hollingsworth, J. Rogers, and Ellen Jane Hollingsworth. *Dimensions in Urban History: Historical and Social Science Perspectives on Middle-Size American Cities.* Madison: University of Wisconsin Press, 1979.

Huthmacher, J. Joseph. "Urban Liberalism and the Age of Reform." *Mississippi Valley Historical Review* 49 (1962):231–241.

Jackson, John E. "Politics and the Budgetary Process." *Social Science Research* 1 (1972):35–60.

Katz, Michael. *The Irony of Early School Reform.* Boston: Beacon, 1968.

———. "Origins of the Institutional State." *Marxist Perspectives* 1 (1978):7–22.

Katznelson, Ira. "The Crisis of the Capitalist City: Urban Politics and Social Control." In *Theoretical Perspectives on Urban Politics* (edited by Willis D. Hawley and Michael Lipsky), 214–229. Englewood Cliffs, N.J.: Prentice-Hall, 1976.

———. *City Trenches: Urban Politics and the Patterning of Class in the United States.* Chicago: University of Chicago Press, 1981.

Keller, Morton. *Affairs of State.* Cambridge, Mass.: Harvard University Press, 1977.

Klein, Maury, and Harvey Kantor. *Prisoners of Progress: American Industrial Cities 1850–1920.* New York: Macmillan, 1976.

Kousser, J. Morgan. "Voters, Absent and Present." *Social Science History* 9 (1985):215–227.

Lampard, Eric. "American Historians and the Study of Urbanization." *American Historical Review* 66 (1961):49–61.

———. "A Conversation with Eric E. Lampard." Interview in *The Making of Urban History* (edited by Bruce M. Stave). Beverly Hills: Sage Publications, 1977.

Lasch, Christopher. *The New Radicalism in America, 1889–1963: The Intellectual as a Social Type.* New York: Knopf, 1965.

Lasswell, Harold D. *Politics—Who Gets What, When, How.* New York: McGraw-Hill, 1936.

Le Goff, Jacques. "Is Politics Still the Backbone of History?" *Daedalus* 100 (1971):1–19.

Lewis, Eugene. *The Urban Political System.* Hinsdale, Ill.: Dryden Press, 1973.

Lineberry, Robert, and Ira Sharkansky. *Urban Politics and Public Policy.* New York: Harper and Row, 1974.

Lineberry, Robert L., and Robert E. Welch, Jr. "Who Gets What: Measuring the Distribution of Urban Public Services." *Social Science Quarterly* 54 (1974):700–712.

Lowi, Theodore. *At the Pleasure of the Mayor.* Glencoe, Ill.: Free Press, 1964.

Margolis, Julius. "The Demand for Urban Services." In *Issues in Urban Economics* (edited by Harvey S. Perloff and Lowdon Wingo), 527–565. Baltimore: Johns Hopkins University Press, 1968.

McCormick, Richard L. "The Party Period and Public Policy: An Exploratory Hypothesis." *Journal of American History* 66 (1979):279–298.

McDonald, Terrence, J. "Putting Politics Back into the History of the American City." *American Quarterly* 34 (1982):200–209.

———. "From Economics to Political Economy in the History of Urban Public Policy." *Journal of Urban History* 8 (1982):355–363.

———. "Toward an Interdisciplinary History of the American City: Comment." *Journal of Urban History* 8 (1982):454–462.

———. "The Problem of the Political in Recent American Urban History: Liberal Pluralism and the Rise of Functionalism." *Social History* 10 (1985):323–345.

McDonald, Terrence J., and Sally K. Ward. "Introduction." In *The Politics of Urban Fiscal Policy* (edited by Terrence J. McDonald and Sally K. Ward), 13–38. Beverly Hills: Sage Publications, 1984.

Merton, Robert K. *Social Theory and Social Structure: Toward the Codification of Theory and Research.* Glencoe, Ill.: Free Press, 1949.

Miller, Zane. *Boss Cox's Cincinnati: Urban Politics in the Progressive Era.* New York: Oxford University Press, 1968.

———. *The Urbanization of Modern America: A Brief History.* New York: Harcourt Brace Jovanovich, 1973.

Mitchell, Wesley C. *Gold Prices and Wages Under the Greenback Standard.* New York: A. M. Kelley, 1966.

Monkkonen, Eric H. "Municipal Reports as an Indicator Source: The Nineteenth Century Police." *Historical Methods* 12 (1979):57–65.

———. *Police in Urban America, 1860–1920.* New York: Cambridge University Press, 1981.

———. "The Fluid World of Late Nineteenth Century British and American Cities." In *Themes in British and American History: A Comparative Approach, c. 1760–1970* (edited by Richard Bessel), 77–83. Milton Keynes, England: Open University Press, 1985.

Mowry, George. *The California Progressives.* Berkeley and Los Angeles: University of California Press, 1951.

Musgrave, Richard A. *The Theory of Public Finance.* New York: McGraw-Hill, 1959.

O'Connor, James. *The Fiscal Crisis of the State.* New York: St. Martin's Press, 1973.

Olin, Spencer. *California's Prodigal Sons.* Berkeley and Los Angeles: University of California Press, 1968.

Pierce, Bessie L. *A History of Chicago.* 3 vols. New York: Knopf, 1937–1957.

Plehn, Carl. *Introduction to Public Finance.* New York: Macmillan, 1897.

————. *Revenue Systems of State and Local Governments.* Washington, D.C.: Government Printing Office, 1907.

Ridley, Clarance E., and Herbert A. Simon. *Measuring Municipal Activities.* Chicago: International City Managers Association, 1938.

Riordan, William L. *Plunkitt of Tammany Hall.* New York: Dutton, 1963.

Rogin, Michael Paul. *The Intellectuals and McCarthy: The Radical Specter.* Cambridge, Mass.: MIT Press, 1967.

Ross, Edward. *Sinking Funds.* Baltimore: American Economics Association, 1892.

Schiesl, Martin. *The Politics of Efficiency: Municipal Administration and Reform in America, 1880–1920.* Berkeley, Los Angeles, London: University of California Press, 1977.

Schlessinger, Arthur M., Sr. "The City in American History." *Mississippi Valley Historical Review* 27 (1940):43–66.

————. *The Rise of the City, 1878–1898.* New York: Macmillan, 1933.

Schumpeter, Joseph A. "The Crisis of the Tax State." *International Economic Papers* 4 (1954):5–38.

Secrist, Horace. *An Economic Analysis of the Constitutional Restrictions Upon Public Indebtedness in the United States.* Madison: University of Wisconsin, 1914.

Seligman, E. R., ed. *Essays in Taxation.* New York: Macmillan, 1895.

Shefter, Martin. "The Emergence of the Political Machine: An Alternative View." In *Theoretical Perspectives on Urban Politics* (edited by Willis

D. Hawley and Michael Lipsky), 14–44. Englewood Cliffs, N.J.: Prentice-Hall, 1976.

Silver, Allan. "The Demand for Order in Civil Society." *The Police: Six Sociological Essays* (edited by David J. Bordua), 1–25. New York: Wiley, 1967.

Skowronek, Stephen. *Building a New American State: The Expansion of National Administrative Capacities, 1877–1920.* New York: Cambridge University Press, 1982.

Stave, Bruce, ed. *The Making of Urban History: Historiography Through Oral History.* Beverly Hills: Sage Publications, 1977.

Steffens, Lincoln. *The Autobiography of Lincoln Steffens.* New York: Literary Guild, 1931.

Still, Bayrd. *Milwaukee: The History of a City.* Madison: State Historical Society of Wisconsin, 1948.

Teaford, Jon C. "Special Legislation and the Cities, 1865–1900." *The American Journal of Legal History* 23 (1979):189–212.

———. "Finis for Tweed and Steffens: Rewriting the History of Urban Rule." *Reviews in American History* 10 (1982):143–153.

———. *The Unheralded Triumph: City Government in America, 1870–1900.* Baltimore: Johns Hopkins University Press, 1984.

Thelen, David P. "Urban Politics: Beyond Bosses and Reformers." *Reviews in American History* 7 (1979):406–412.

Thernstrom, Stephan. *Poverty and Progress: Social Mobility in a Nineteenth Century City.* New York: Atheneum, 1971. Originally published in Cambridge, Mass.: Harvard University Press, 1964.

———. "Reflections on the New Urban History." *Daedalus* 100 (1971):359–375.

———. *The Other Bostonians: Poverty and Progress in the American Metropolis, 1880–1970.* Cambridge, Mass.: Harvard University Press, 1973.

Thompson, Wilbur. *A Preface to Urban Economics.* Baltimore: Johns Hopkins University Press, 1968.

Tyack, David. *The One Best System: A History of American Urban Education.* Cambridge, Mass.: Harvard University Press, 1974.

Vecoli, Rudolph J. *"Contadini* in Chicago: A Critique of *The Uprooted." Journal of American History* 60 (1964):404–417.

———. "Ethnicity: A Neglected Dimension of American History." In *The State of American History* (edited by Herbert J. Bass), 70–88. Chicago: Quadrangle Books, 1970.

Vinovskis, Maris, and Carl Kaestle. *Education and Social Change in Nineteenth Century Massachusetts.* New York: Cambridge University Press, 1980.

Wade, Richard. "Urbanization." In *The Comparative Approach to American History* (edited by C. Vann Woodward), 187–205. New York: Basic Books, 1968.

Warner, Sam Bass, Jr. *The Urban Wilderness.* New York: Harper and Row, 1972.

Wendt, Lloyd, and Herman Kogan. *Bosses in Lusty Chicago.* Bloomington: Indiana University Press, 1943.

Wildavsky, Aaron. *The Politics of the Budgetary Process.* Boston: Little, Brown, 1979.

Wolfinger, Raymond. "Why Political Machines Have Not Withered Away and Other Revisionist Thoughts." *Journal of Politics* 34 (1972):365–398.

Woodruff, Clinton. *Municipal Misrule.* Brooklyn, N.Y.: Brooklyn Daily Eagle, 1903.

Yearley, C. K. *The Money Machines: The Breakdown and Reform of Governmental and Party Finances in the North, 1860–1920.* Albany: SUNY Press, 1970.

Index

Designer:	U.C. Press Staff
Compositor:	Auto-Graphics
Text:	10/13 Garamond
Display:	Garamond
Printer:	Thomson-Shore, Inc.
Binder:	John H. Dekker & Sons